DATE DUE

	DE 1 9 '08		
AP 22 '98			
MR 29 '99			
AP 5 '99			
NO 20 '99			
DE 7 '99			
AG 3 '00			
DE 2 0 '00			
OC 9 '02			
NO 21 '02			
NO 13 '02			
SE 2 '03			
MY 12 '04			
DE 1 '04			
DE 2 1 '07			

Southern Voices from the Past
Women's Letters, Diaries, and Writings
Carol Bleser, General Editor

This series makes available to scholars, students, and general readers collections of letters, diaries, and other writings by women in the southern United States from the colonial era into the twentieth century. Documenting the experiences of women from across the region's economic, cultural, and ethnic spectrums, the writings enrich our understanding of such aspects of daily life as courtship and marriage, domestic life and motherhood, social events and travels, and religion and education.

Shadows on My Heart

Shadows on My Heart

∽∽∽∽∽∽∽∽∽∽∽∽∽∽∽∽∽∽∽∽∽∽

The Civil War Diary

of Lucy Rebecca Buck

of Virginia

∽∽∽∽∽∽∽∽∽∽∽∽∽∽∽∽∽∽∽∽∽∽

Edited by Elizabeth R. Baer

The University of Georgia Press

Athens & London

© 1997 by the University of Georgia Press
Athens, Georgia 30602
All rights reserved
Designed by Louise OFarrell
Set in Fournier by G & S Typesetters
Printed and bound by Braun-Brumfield, Inc.

The paper in this book meets the guidelines for
permanence and durability of the Committee on
Production Guidelines for Book Longevity of the
Council on Library Resources.

Printed in the United States of America

01 00 99 98 97   C   5 4 3 2 1

Library of Congress Cataloging in Publication Data

Buck, Lucy Rebecca, 1842–1918.
Shadows on my heart: the Civil War diary of Lucy Rebecca Buck
of Virginia / edited by Elizabeth R. Baer.
p. cm. —(Southern voices from the past)
Includes bibliographical references and index.
ISBN 0-8203-1852-3 (alk. paper)
1. Buck, Lucy Rebecca, 1842–1918—Diaries. 2. Shenandoah
River Valley (Va. and W. Va.)—History—Civil War, 1861–1865.
3. United States—History—Civil War, 1861–1865—Personal
narratives, Confederate. 4. United States—History—Civil War,
1861–1865—Women. 5. Women—Virginia—Diaries. I. Baer,
Elizabeth Roberts. II. Title. III. Series.
E605.B89 1997
973.7'82—dc20
96-766

British Library Cataloging in Publication Data available

To Clint

Editing a journal is, of necessity, creating something new—cleaner and somewhat clearer than the original document. Yet one must be careful to edit the diary without editing the life itself.

—Penelope Franklin, *Private Pages*

Contents

Acknowledgments

I would like to express my deep gratitude to all who provided support for and shared interest in this project during the several years in which I have worked on it. Special thanks go to Carol Bleser, general editor and Kathryn and Calhoun Lemon Professor of Clemson University, who gave unstintingly of her time, despite the demands of her own life; Mary Breazeale, who first introduced me to the Randolph-Macon Woman's College Collection, where I discovered this diary; Ruth Ann Edwards, librarian of Randolph-Macon Woman's College, who cheerfully allowed me to use the collection; Washington College for a grant from the Faculty Enhancement Fund that enabled me to travel and undertake research; the Virginia Foundation for the Humanities, for a generous fellowship that gave me solitude and freedom from interruption at a crucial stage; and Dr. William Pettus Buck of Birmingham, Alabama, for his generosity in granting permission to use Lucy Buck's diary and his warm hospitality in providing access to the diaries and his extensive collection of family memorabilia.

I would also like to thank Mary Morris, archivist at the Warren Heritage Society, for her time and keen insights in assisting my research on Lucy Buck; Larry Lehew, the current owner of "Bel Air," for his kindness in opening to me the home that once belonged to the Buck family; Madeline Howell, for her unfailing help on the production of the manuscript; the staff of Washington College's Miller Library, especially Ruth Shoge and Lois Kuhn, who responded cheerfully to my many requests for assistance, some mundane and some bizarre; Stephanie Meskan, Gustavus Adolphus Class of 1993, whose meticulous help on editing details was much appreciated; and Jean Jacobi, who offered gracious assistance in copying and formatting.

I want to thank my daughter, Hester, whose help was invaluable in the hectic last stages of compilation, and my son, Nathaniel, for his computer expertise, from which I benefited at every stage of the work. Finally, profound gratitude goes to my parents, Emmie and Jim Roberts, for cultivating in their daughters the habits of reading and intellectual curiosity, an appreciation for our country's history, and a belief we could do whatever we set our minds to.

\

Introduction

The Lost World of the Southern Belle

Virginia's scenic Shenandoah Valley is ensconced between the Blue Ridge Mountains on the east and the Appalachian Mountains on the west. For a land made seemingly remote by its location, this valley of Virginia has been the site of a good deal of history. Originally settled by the Shawnee Indians, the valley was explored by Daniel Boone and has boasted such residents as George Washington, Stonewall Jackson, Belle Boyd, Robert E. Lee, Booker T. Washington, and Woodrow Wilson.

During the Civil War, the valley was hotly contested territory. Its well-established farms and orchards led it to be called "the breadbasket of the Confederacy" (Robertson, *Civil War Sites*, 3), and foodstuffs harvested here went a long way toward feeding the Army of Northern Virginia. Perched at the top of the Shenandoah Valley is a strategically located town by the name of Front Royal, originally called Lehewtown when it was chartered in 1788 and nicknamed Hell Town (Hale, *Bicentennial Remembrance*, 32–34). By the time the war began in 1861, Front Royal was a prosperous place, boasting a railroad depot, a postal office, churches, stores, and a school. Because of its strategic location and its prosperity, Front Royal alternated between Yankee and Confederate control literally dozens of times during the four-year war and was the site of a major battle in May 1862, won by Stonewall Jackson.

On a plantation on the perimeter of Front Royal lived an attractive young woman named Lucy Rebecca Buck, eighteen years of age at the outbreak of the war. By all accounts, Lucy could be viewed as a stereotypical southern belle. Her slaveholding father, William Mason Buck, possessed not only a plantation, picturesquely named Bel Air, but also a store in town and interest in a popular resort. Here, in her family home, Lucy was born on September 25, 1842. She was named after her two grandmothers, Lucy Neville Blakemore and Rebecca Buck Ashby. Lucy was the third of thirteen children; the

Lucy (right) and Nellie Buck (c. 1860).
Courtesy of Warren Heritage Society, Front Royal, Virginia.

baby, Frank, was just a month old at Christmas, 1861, yet her two older brothers, Alvin and Irving, had already joined the Confederate army and had gone off to war.

Until that war began, however, little had challenged the Buck family's assumptions about raising either money or children. Lucy and her sister Nell, two years her junior, grew up very close to each other. They attended two schools in Front Royal where, among other things, they learned the social graces expected of women in their station. Reminiscences of these schools were written by a classmate, Kathleen Boone Samuels, often mentioned in

Lucy's diary. "Miss Tensia decided to open a small day school. . . . She agreed to take Lucy and Nellie Buck. . . . It was a most select little school for small girls. We were taught to speak very low and be delicate in our ways" (Spencer, Samuels, and Samuels, 24–25). Kattie Samuels goes on to describe the more advanced education made available to girls in Front Royal, again emphasizing the training in gentility. "When we grew old enough, Miss Tensia Tyler's pupils were sent to the new Front Royal Academy, where old Pressor Smith taught the boys in the right-hand room and Miss Susan Randolph the girls in the left-hand room. Kate Green, Lillie Robinson, Emma Cloud and Lucy and Nellie Buck were among my schoolmates. . . . There was a good deal of trouble in getting a teacher to fill Miss Susan Randolph's place [after she married]. Finally Miss N. Fellows, a regular Yankee woman, was induced to come. . . . She was a splendid teacher and after regular school hours instructed us in manners and calisthenics. We were taught how to greet guests in the parlor, how to draw up chairs for them and how to introduce them" (25–26). Lucy became an avid reader, as her frequent mention of books attests. She and Nellie attended church regularly. At home, the sisters were taught the female arts of music, needlework, and gardening.

The home in which they grew up was their ancestral family home, built by Lucy's grandfather, Thomas Buck, who had served as a minuteman in the Revolutionary War. In 1795, he erected two log cabins on the property high on a hill above Front Royal, and by 1800 he had connected these cabins with a sturdy brick three-story structure in the middle. The cabins, in effect, became wings on the home; these were replaced in the twentieth century.

I have had the good fortune to spend a summer's morning at Bel Air, thanks to the kindness of the current owner, Larry Lehew. One enters an impressive entry hall that features an enormous carved wooden staircase rising to the second floor. On the left is the parlor and on the right a large dining room, which replaced the smaller dining room that was in use during the Civil War. At that time the slaves were housed below the first floor, which is also where much of the cooking was done. Still visible in the cellar are the two cooking fireplaces. In his illuminating study *Back of the Big House: The Architecture of Plantation Slavery*, John Vlach indicates that quartering slaves within the plantation house was common in Virginia in the seventeenth century; field slaves were moved out to separate cabins beginning in the eigh-

Rendering of Bel Air, home of Lucy Buck, done in 1860.
Courtesy of Warren Heritage Society, Front Royal, Virginia.

teenth century, but slaves who worked as house servants sometimes retained living space there as well (154).

The second floor of Bel Air, which has been expanded in the twentieth century, contains several ordinary bedrooms, some with fireplaces. The one at the top of the stairs was Lucy's, and it is the room to which she used to retire to write. A longtime family tradition is still intact on the sloping attic walls and ceiling: the collection of signatures of loved ones and visitors. Because Lucy herself mentions that the family not infrequently sought the roof of the house for a breath of fresh air, or a view of nature or of events in nearby Front Royal, I climbed out on the red tin roof, too. What is in the 1990s a spectacular view stretching to the Blue Ridge Mountains must have been even more so 130 years ago, when the countryside was far less despoiled. Originally Bel Air was surrounded by a hundred acres of open farmland owned by Thomas Buck; today this has shrunk to approximately twelve acres.

Situated as they were at the top of the Shenandoah Valley, Lucy and her family found themselves in the midst of the war: battles were literally waged in her front yard. Lucy frequently speaks of the need for "protection," and it is clear that she felt concern for her personal safety, not so much from bullets but from possible depredations of marauding soldiers.[1] On more than one occasion, troops were quartered in her father's fields; soldiers from both North and South stopped regularly to demand, request, or beg for food and drink. Lucy personally knew the famous Confederate spy Belle Boyd, who used Front Royal as a base of operations. And General Robert E. Lee stopped at Bel Air on his way home from the Battle of Gettysburg: he drank the proffered buttermilk, talked with Lucy and her sister, and kissed baby Frank.

In Search of Lucy Rebecca Buck

On Christmas Day, 1861, eight months into the Civil War, Lucy Rebecca Buck began to keep a diary.[2] From the opening passages, the reader sees made manifest what Lucy will call later in the diary the "shadows on my heart." She takes pains to contrast this Christmas with the one of just a year earlier:

> I cannot but feel a little sad this morning for my thoughts continually revert to those dear absent brothers who were wont to share our Christmas cheer and gladden the hours of this festive season for us. . . . When I think of the unexpected changes that have occurred in the last year I feel as if I could not count upon ever having them with us again as of yore with any degree of certainty. I think of how many hands that wreathed the bowl and twined the holly last year are now mouldering in the dust. The bright locks that were then crowned with roses, now dabbled in gore and covered with the turf of the battlefield . . . I think of it all and sicken.

Lucy's language here is powerful and unsentimental. If one is prone to think of the southern belle as the stereotype that still seems to be summoned by that term—hooped skirts, white gowns, broad hats, leisure, mint juleps, porch swings, tiny waists, sultry manners, flirtation, inanity, affectation, submissiveness, drawls—then this passage and many more throughout Lucy's diary will serve as a long-overdue corrective. She is not coy about her emotions but starkly candid; she confronts mortality in a chilling way. Another passage from Lucy's diary, this one dated March 11, 1862, is also revealing:

> So we had a merry walk to town, Nellie, Nannie, Scott and myself,—first went to pay my bridal call on Kattie Samuels. Found her in her room dressing

for dinner—she was looking well—full of chat and is evidently of the opinion that all the virtues pertaining to manhood are concentrated in one individual—that individual Mr. Samuels. Ah! well-a-day. I hope she may ever
think thus but I feel sad to hear young brides indulging in such bright anticipations as these—I think of the contrast between married life as they imagine it to be and married life as they will find it to be ten years hence.

There is a world-weariness here, a sense of the gap between the ideology of
white southern womanhood and the reality, that one would hardly expect to
find expressed in the diary of such a young woman, a woman apparently heir
to all the privileges her society could bestow. Such ambivalence stands in
sharp contrast to the notion many of us have about elite white southern
women.

Lucy's diary is one of many housed in the archives of the library of
Randolph-Macon Woman's College in Lynchburg, Virginia. The archives
contain an extensive collection of writings by Virginia women; the collection
was begun several decades ago by devoted alumnae and is a rich (and under-
utilized) resource for understanding the world of southern women, white and
black. There I discovered several nineteenth-century white women's diaries,
many of which had been published by families or small journals and presses
and which had fallen into obscurity. The edition of the diary contained
therein is a 1940 transcription, done by Captain Neville Buck.

The original diary is now in the possession of Dr. William Buck of Birmingham, Alabama. A few words about the text of the original diary will be
instructive to contemporary readers. It is actually written in four separate
books. The first, containing entries from Christmas, 1861, to May 23, 1862, is
a brown leather-bound book with tooling in a scroll design and a large vase
embossed in gold. Inscribed on the front were gold letters, "W. M. Buck";
someone, presumably Lucy, has scratched out the "W. M.," leaving only the
"Buck" easily readable. The book was originally a ledger of some kind, with
entries dating from the 1850s. To adapt this book to her purposes, Lucy glued
together pages that already contained written entries. Glued onto the inside
front cover is a poem she clipped from a newspaper, entitled "The Dream
Train." The first of four stanzas begins:

It comes o'er the hills of evening in the beautiful twilight glow
When travelers bound for the land of Nod are dressed in gowns of snow.

It whistles and swings in wonder over the hills and down
To rest at last where the stars sing past on the borders of slumbertown.

Lucy's handwriting is beautiful and easy to read; the ink is brown and not too badly faded until the entry for March 12, where it becomes decidedly lighter. Lucy used the whole of every page, leaving no margins; each page contains twenty-eight to twenty-nine lines. In the pages with entries for March and April, the faded brown shadows of flowers Lucy pressed into the diary are to be found. The book contains several other items—poems copied out in a hand not Lucy's; a page entitled "Noms de Plume" with some forty-five entries, including "Oliver Optic—Boston School Master," "Marion Harland—Virginia Terhune," and "Misses Wetherell—Susan Anna Warner." (Although these are not in Lucy's hand, either, they are further evidence of the reading habits of the family.) Also included is a page of what appear to be translations with such entries as "crul—basket" and "Fechtin—fighting," which may have been lists of words to aid in reading Sir Walter Scott's fiction; the final page of the first book is entitled "Damages," which may be a catalog of damages to Bel Air during the war.

Books 2, 3, and 4 are homemade, with paper appropriated from old ledger books, sewn together and covered with a paper about the color and thickness of a manila folder. In these books, Lucy writes on the pages that already contain ledger entries, suggesting that paper was becoming scarcer; her handwriting is also more cramped, reinforcing the impression of frugality. In book 4, the entries are out of order and the sewing of the pages such that the handwriting is sometimes obscured. This suggests the assembling of the book was done after she made her entries and perhaps not even by Lucy. The entries for May 24–December 31, 1862, and July 29, 1864–April 15, 1865, are missing (see "Editorial Policies").

Read as a whole, Lucy's diary provides readers with a record of her growing restiveness. The act of writing served several purposes for Lucy: a soothing record of her several forms of entertainment—reading, visiting, music; an attempt to gain distance on her many unhappinesses and deprivations during this four-year period; and, persistently, a serious scrutiny of her life as a young woman at a time when she both upheld the ideals of the Confederacy and yet found its prescribed role for white women unattainable, even undesirable. The tension resulting from this disjunction finds expression both in straightforward statements of anger and ambivalence and in the more subtle contours of the journal, including silences that, when studied, reveal her struggle to come to terms with her society's expectations of her. Indeed, it was just such straightforward candor that attracted me to this rich journal, for it provided me, shortly after a move south of the Mason-Dixon line, with answers to my questions about how elite white southern women felt about their society's ideology of womanhood.

The Worlds within Lucy Buck's Diary

Lucy characterizes her opening entry as one of "gloomy retrospective," and indeed, it is a sad note she strikes, longing for her absent brothers, thinking of happier holidays of the past. Yet, until the very last weeks of the war, Lucy's entries are much more typically buoyant and optimistic. She was a fierce patriot, believing in the Southern cause and ready to do her part, whatever that might be. "Your cause is a just one—you are not contending for self-aggrandizement, but repelling the insolent invaders of your sacred rights, fighting for your homes, defending your firesides, protecting brothers, sisters, and mothers! Let these thoughts nerve your arm," she wrote to her cousin, already enlisted in the army, in April 1861.[3] She took a keen interest in the events of the war, recording rumors, headlines, troop movements, Confederate victories and defeats.

Lucy's entries have a rhythm, a pattern that becomes recognizable to the reader after a short while. She almost invariably opens by noting the day's weather conditions. Perhaps this indicates a connection between inner and outer weather for Lucy. Certainly it serves to remind us that in the nineteenth century, people were less shielded from the vagaries of climate than we are today. If it rained, Lucy was confined to the house. Equally significant is the connection that often exists between the weather and the war: troop movements and battles were affected by downpours or snow.

Next Lucy mentions in her diary whatever domestic routines have consumed her time that day: all that went into managing a large home, sewing, harvesting, preparing food, nursing family members with various illnesses (which seem most common in the summer months), birthing, educating her younger siblings, keeping up a voluminous correspondence, entertainments of many kinds, and attendance at religious services. Lucy also greatly appreciated the natural beauty that surrounded her; the modern reader will be struck by how time is taken from her regular round of duties to sit on the stile and enjoy the moonlight, to fish in nearby Happy Creek in the spring, to tend to and name the flowers in the flower garden, to ride horseback into the mountains, to take walks and notice the pleasures of the season, whatever they might be.

Entries usually include mention of visits she makes and visitors to Bel Air as well as any war news that is worthy of note. If she is reading a book, she lists the title. All told, Lucy mentions more than thirty-five titles, including the historical and religious tracts she read to her father and the fiction read for her own pleasure. (To help the reader grasp the diversity of Lucy's reading material, I have included an appendix, identifying most of the more than thirty-five titles she mentions.) Near the end of each journal entry is a notation about mail: whether or not any arrived, who collected it. Lucy usually concludes with a prayer or a note of resignation or a statement of emotions.

The language Lucy uses to write her diary also follows a fairly regular pattern, varying according to the occasion. Most of her entries are written in a straightforward, prosaic style, more intent on getting the events of the day recorded than in impressing future audiences with eloquence. She does, though, have days on which her prose is self-consciously poetic and romantic. The opening entry of the diary, on Christmas Day, 1861, is a good example of this, as are the entries for January 1, 1863, marking the new year, and June 23, 1863, marking the death of her beloved cousin Walter Buck:

> Never shall I forget the sight—there lay the still white figure under the southern window, the attitude one of such perfect, majestic repose as seems to quiet and subdue my grief. The face that lay there among the wreathes and masses of lilies and jessamines was the most beautifully placid one that I have ever seen and so natural, so free from the usual ghastly terrors of death that I could almost have imagined that the dead was breathing as the wind stealing through the window just lifted the hair from the pillow. There was something almost holy in the expression of that loved countenance—the hair was brushed back from the broad smooth brow, the lids just closed as in gentle sleep while about the mouth hovered an expression of high resolve just softened into a peaceful smile.

Such a passage has clearly been influenced by her familiarity with romantic novels, particularly those of Sir Walter Scott, of which she mentions reading four in the course of her four-year journal.

When her voluminous diary deviates from these established patterns, the reader catches glimpses of Lucy's emotions and recognizes that the diary is serving as far more than a prosaic record of quotidian events, or even an effort to impose order. These deviations include outspoken expressions of anger and ambivalence, the use of military metaphors and the language of bondage, silences, and the elision of boundaries between public and private spheres within single entries.

Overt expressions of anger and ambivalence pepper Lucy's diary, emotions not permitted to young white women in the antebellum South, or indeed to any woman aspiring to the "cult of true womanhood" in the nineteenth century. On March 31, 1862, Lucy recounts the following event during one of the Yankee occupations of her plantation: "After dinner I was in Ma's room rocking the baby in my arms and singing 'Maryland' in no suppressed tone and the Yankees came up on the porch step." Lucy describes them as "so insufferably, coolly impudent that I would have like to have shot them. . . . Who could have thought that we could thus receive in our midst our deadliest, bitterest enemies without any sensations other than those of rage and curiosity?" The next month, Lucy describes ascending to the second floor of her home and commencing a letter to her two brothers: "really enjoyed the writing, as it gave a vent to some of my pent up indignation." On June 18, Lucy opens her entry uncharacteristically: "I was angry all the morning, angry with the Yankees for trying to proselyte [*sic*]—angry at them for fibbing and angry with them because they were Yankees. The servants were vexatious too. Rob Roy [one of the free African Americans on the plantation] in whom we had so much confidence even espousing the cause of the Yankee. I never was half so mad in my life. Insinuating wretches!" In her phrase "my pent up indignation," Lucy discloses to the reader both her habit of stifling her anger and her use of writing as a release. Since we can assume that Lucy's anger about the enemy, the topic on which she is focused in these passages, would be more acceptable than anger about the role of women, or, eventually, about the cause itself, we can only imagine what other angers Lucy felt compelled to bottle up.

Her ambivalence about her role as a young woman is best demonstrated by two passages, selected from among many. On her twentieth birthday, Lucy confided in her diary her many self-doubts: "And I'm a woman, repel the unwelcome thought as I will. . . . I *am* a woman in *feelings* as well as in *years*.

Lucy Buck, after the Civil War.
Courtesy of Warren Heritage Society, Front Royal, Virginia.

A woman by this passionate longing and yearning—this hunger of the heart: a woman by this sensitive apprehension of my own unworthiness, of my deficiencies in every respect, in my loneliness, awkwardness and temper. I can't bear to think or write about it." One hears here echoes of Protestant self-examination and regrets about the loss of innocence that any woman on the brink of adulthood might express. But most striking is Lucy's very definition of womanhood as an "apprehension of my own unworthiness." Such a statement of self-abnegation corroborates the finding of Anne Firor Scott that the most often quoted biblical verse in the diaries of southern women is this one from Jeremiah: "The heart is deceitful above all things and desperately wicked: who can know it?" (Scott, 11). Lucy, like many other Confederate women, struggled with what she perceived as a gap of deceit between what her society expected of white southern womanhood and who she knew herself to be.

On another occasion, January 17, 1862, Lucy confided her strongly felt views about women's education to her diary, which run counter to prevailing views in the South, as this passage makes clear: "Messers. B. and H. both came in about seven o'clock and after some desultory conversation we were led to discussing the question of female education. Mr. B and I thought the continuation of the mind to a high degree refined and elevated her character and tastes and softened and beautified her disposition, while Mr. H. on the other hand contended that a female philosopher or metaphysician, or, in other words, a mistress of abstract sciences, was necessarily masculine, bold and ambitious, a perfect monstrosity. The debate at length grew so warm on both sides that I was fain as a prudent hostess to change the subject without either party having departed from his original opinions." Careful reading of this passage demonstrates the felt need Lucy had for submission and silence: although she identifies herself at the outset as being on the side of proper education for females, the closing sentence locates Lucy as an observer of a debate on the topic, and an observer who is compelled by laws of courtesy to stop the debate.

When she departs from her use of either pragmatic or eloquent language, Lucy again signals to the reader the use of her journal to step out of prescribed roles for white southern women. For example, Lucy resorts now and then to the use of military metaphors to describe mundane affairs, almost as if the language that was so much in the newspapers, in the air, encouraged her to use argot from the male sphere to frame her female sphere. To demonstrate her use of this terminology I quote from a passage written on January 9, 1862, in which Lucy recorded her preference for the "society of social elderly gentlemen." She asserts: "They are war scarred veterans on the battle-field of life . . . they understand all the maneuvers, can instruct us how to avoid this and that foe. . . . They can advise much better than the novices in the service."

Although she refers to her slaves as "servants," Lucy often uses the language of bondage to describe the fate that will befall *her* if the North should win. A good example of this exists in the entry for April 13, 1865, when she and her family learn of Lee's surrender: "Our dearest hopes dashed—our fondest dreams dispelled—we and our brave ones who had struggled, bled and suffered—slaves and to such a tyrant."

Other contours of the diary are suggestive, too. The entries for the summer months—June, July, August—are often considerably longer than those for the other nine months of the year. This may be explained in part by the fact that there was more war news in these months as more fighting occurred then. It may also have a simpler explanation: there was far more daylight for writing in the summer than in the winter. That it became increasingly painful for Lucy to keep her diary is evidenced by a five-month break, when she simply stopped writing between September 22, 1864, and February 13, 1865. Some clues may be gathered from the final September 1864 entry and the entry in which she resumes in February 1865. I have spelled this out in more detail in an insertion in the journal, between these September and February entries.

A second significant silence occurs in Lucy's diary: the almost complete silence on the topic of the family slaves. They are simply taken for granted by Lucy as fixtures in her life and home and not granted space in her diary. In this, Lucy Buck reflects the attitude of many white women of the planter class. In an effort to determine what prevailing attitudes might have existed in the Buck household toward the family's eight slaves, I turned to a volume entitled *The Valley Campaigns: Being the Reminiscences of a Non-Combatant While between the Lines in the Shenandoah Valley during the War of the States*, written by Thomas Ashby and published in 1914. Thomas Ashby was Lucy's first cousin, the son of Lucy's mother's brother. He grew up at Oakley, a plantation near Bel Air, where he resided during the war, and later was trained as both a medical doctor and an attorney. The opening chapter of Ashby's book is entitled "The Institution of Slavery"; a subsequent chapter, "The Southern Woman: The Domestic Life of Our People," also contains his views on slavery.

Ashby's views can best be summarized as a mélange of affection and condescension toward African Americans. Though his book was published some fifty years after such infamous defenses of slavery as George Fitzhugh's "Slavery Justified by a Southerner" (1850) and James Henry Hammond's

"Mud Sill Speech" (1858), Ashby's arguments share much in common with theirs. "A civilization of rare culture and refinement represented the high spirit and virtue of the Anglo-Saxon life in the South," he begins. "One of the foundation stones upon which this civilization rested was the institution of slavery. . . . To the people of my generation in the South the ownership of slaves was an inheritance, representing an investment in dollars and cents. . . . The slave owner was, therefore, no more responsible for the character of his property . . . than for any other form of inheritance. . . . The ownership of slaves involved, as a general rule, as little discomfort as the ownership of domestic animals" (11–12). While Ashby concedes that "all human rights were imperiled by a system that regarded human flesh as an article of barter and trade" (13), he also subscribed to the theory that slavery improved those enslaved: "Uncultured and unskilled, ignorant both of human and divine law, a victim of the lowest forms of superstition, vice, and evil passion, the negro had, by the institution of slavery,—despite all its bad features,—been raised to a plane of usefulness, of domestic service, and of happy contentment unknown to him in his natural home" (14). And as Hammond viewed it, African Americans were the "mud sill" of society: "Nature has granted him one pre-eminent gift. He is fitted for domestic service" (15). Ashby also reflects some of the prevailing attitudes of the Reconstruction era, and particularly of D. W. Griffith's film "Birth of a Nation" released in 1915, the year after Ashby's book was published, when he states: "Until the ideals of the race are based upon racial pride and a desire for racial purity and segregation from other races the negro will never arrive at a true status of his own racial value" (108). While one obviously cannot attribute these views in any wholesale way to Lucy Buck, her silence on the topic of slavery does allow speculation that she simply viewed the slaves at Bel Air as the "foundation," the "mud sill" that made her existence comfortable.

This changes dramatically when the family slaves run away in June 1863, causing a shift not only in Lucy's life but also in her prose. "Very, very footsore and weary" is how she describes herself four days later. Yet she takes obvious pride in making her first pot of pea soup and baking her first batch of biscuits. Although the family is initially hopeful of recapturing the runaways, this does not come to pass, and meals, laundry, sewing, and cleaning had to be accomplished for the family of eleven still living at home. Recalcitrant cows had to be milked, farm animals had to be fed, and all the extra

Photograph of Bel Air, taken just after the Civil War.
Note the family members on the lawn.
Courtesy of Warren Heritage Society, Front Royal, Virginia.

demands imposed by the war had to be met. After the departure of the slaves, Lucy often opens her entries by stating who has come to provide help with the housework that day, rather than opening with the weather; it is as if this has become the new determining factor, as if this reports the "domestic" weather.

Finally, it is noteworthy how easily Lucy shifts back and forth in some entries between the private sphere and the public sphere. Lucy's prose reveals the reality of her life: that she was in the midst of public gaze, struggle, and competition, even without leaving her beloved Bel Air. Here is her entry for January 4, 1862:

> Woke very early and found it had been sleeting during the night. Put my shawl over my head and walked the pavement until it was light enough to read; then practiced on the piano and read and wrote till breakfast. Was very busy all day—sewing for Irving. At dusk Nellie and I went into the parlor and amused ourselves singing and playing. Mason and Slidell have really been yielded up to the demands of the British Government. False hearted

cravens! If the Yankee Cabinet did not direct their seizure it endorsed it at the time and now to think of their backing-down in that manner. To think of their once vaunted eagle trailing its plumage in the dust at the very feet of the British lion! We read today the correspondence between Seward and Lord L[yons] in relation to the affair, and I do think for a man with any reputation for ability, Mr. S did make the most paltry attempt at playing the diplomatist and his letter the most juvenile effort at display of legal knowledge that I ever saw. Degraded sycophant! There is, I think reason for believing that Old England has not finished her reckoning with the administration yet. No news of importance tonight.

Note that Lucy does not even insert a transition between her account of activities in the female sphere—sewing and singing—and her account of the activities of Confederate ambassadors Mason and Slidell. Yet her concluding sentence is telling: "No news of importance tonight." Having just recounted what was the big news of the war that day—the Yankee capture of Mason and Slidell from the decks of the British mail ship, the *Trent*—Lucy's estimation of what comprises "important news" is clearly that within the female sphere; specifically, it is likely that she here refers to the lack of mail from her brothers, the lack of casualties of loved ones and friends.

Conclusion

Noted proponent of slavery George Fitzhugh made the following pronouncement regarding the proper behavior of white southern women in his book *Sociology for the South* (1854):

> So long as she is nervous, fickle, capricious, delicate, diffident and dependent, man will worship and adore her. Her *weakness is her strength,* and her true art is to cultivate and improve that weakness. *Woman naturally shrinks from public gaze, and from the struggle and competition of life.* . . . In truth, woman, like children, has but one right and that is *the right to protection.* The right to protection involves the obligation to obey. A husband, lord and master, whom she should love, honor and obey, nature designed for every woman. . . . If she be obedient she stands little danger of maltreatment. (214–15; emphasis mine)

In this prescription for the ideal southern belle, Fitzhugh emphasizes three characteristics: her weakness as a strength, her natural tendency to shrink from public life, and her right to protection.

What I'd like to suggest is that the Civil War, by virtue of its intrusion into the private sphere, created an environment in which white southern women could not feign weakness, could not shrink from the public gaze, and could not assume the presence of protection that was supposedly their right. This radical disjuncture, coming as it did during a period of extreme deprivation and loss, caused so-called southern belles to question the very ideology with which they had been raised. Because their society did not brook such questioning in a public context, white southern women often turned to their private journals to express their ambivalence and anger, both overtly and by virtue of silence. The journal thus became a site for the expression of frustrations, for exploring such topics as education, religion, duty to family, marriage, slavery, and the Confederacy, topics they felt constrained from discussing publicly. Diarists often railed against conforming to the ideals of the southern belle and confided serious doubt about the rewards of complying with such expectations. Thus Lucy's diary does become an expression of the shadows on her heart. Reading these journals today, at both the textual and subtextual level, enables us to reevaluate the unfair stereotypes of white southern women and to gain a more accurate portrayal of the struggles they endured.

Editorial Policies
Creating This Edition

Although Lucy Buck's Civil War diary is rich with information about the battles between the Yankees and the Confederates in the Shenandoah Valley, it is even richer with information about how the war affected the domestic sphere, the life of a plantation daughter from the elite class and her extended family. Readers who come to this diary for minute annotations of all the Civil War skirmishes mentioned herein will be disappointed; my focus, rather, has been on Lucy herself, on her diurnal life, and what she does and does not confide in her diary.

Significant attention is paid in my endnotes to helping the contemporary reader understand the unfamiliar terms Lucy uses to refer to clothing, games, culinary habits, health problems, music, art, mythology, social customs, and reading patterns. When Lucy's references to war news are annotated, it is often with an eye to verifying the accuracy of the information to which Lucy had access, through newspapers, the mails, or general gossip. I am very grateful to Carol Bleser, a historian and the editor of this series, for her support of my somewhat unorthodox approach to Lucy's diary.

Two editions of Lucy Buck's diary are extant, neither of which is easily available. The first, a typewritten edition transcribed by family member Captain L. N. Buck, was privately printed in Baltimore in 1940, and about seventy copies were distributed with a soft cover, bearing a drawing of the Confederate flag, to family members and archives. This is not a complete transcript—certain passages have been deleted. The second edition, entitled *Sad Earth, Sweet Heaven*, was published in a small run by the Cornerstone Publisher in Birmingham, Alabama, in 1973 and recently reissued. Dr. William Pettus Buck, also a family member, edited this version. Since he has most of the original diary in his possession, he was able to include deleted entries; however, he chose to delete other entries, so this is not a complete

Diary
of
Lucy Rebecca Buck

186! – 1865

Cover of the 1940 edition of Lucy Buck's diary,
edited by Captain L. N. Buck, privately printed.
Courtesy of Randolph-Macon Woman's College
Archives, Lynchburg, Virginia.

edition, either. Dr. Buck added extensive annotations to his edition, almost all of which focus on Civil War aspects of the diary. I have worked with both editions, as well as the original diary, in creating this third edition.

Portions of the original diary appear to be irrevocably lost; this is probably because two to three pages of the original diary were tipped into most of the seventy copies distributed to family members and archives. This practice was presumably to demonstrate both the authenticity of the diary and the challenge of doing the transcription. The original transcription, done by Neville Buck, is also missing, and correspondence in Dr. William Buck's possession suggests that it may have been sent to one Thomas Suter in 1945; Major Suter, a stranger, had written to the Buck family and promised to print three hundred copies of the diary privately. This had a powerful appeal to the family, as Wellford Buck had tried unsuccessfully to interest several presses, including the University of North Carolina Press and Wilfred Funk, Inc., Publishers, in publishing the transcription. Wellford Buck had also contacted a literary agent in New York about handling the manuscript. Major Suter never followed through on his promise, and the materials sent to him were never recovered by the family.

To enable the contemporary reader to grasp more readily some of the turning points in Lucy's life during the four-year period in which she wrote, I have divided her diary into eight chapters; these divisions are not found in either earlier edition. I have chosen phrases from the diary itself to serve as chapter titles, phrases that convey the import of that period for Lucy.

After considerable deliberation and because of the excessive length of Lucy's diary, I have omitted portions of the text that I deemed extraneous and repetitious. Following are a set of guidelines that I decided would create a readable text and would at the same time maintain the integrity of Lucy Buck's writing.

I left the first five weeks intact (February 2, 1862, is the first edited entry) to provide the reader with an opportunity to see what Lucy's language, pacing, and topics were like; similarly, I did not edit any entries after Lucy resumes writing in the diary on February 13, 1865, following a hiatus of several months. These final entries are brief and poignant and are written in a different tone than earlier passages.

All deletions are indicated by an ellipsis. Lucy does not use this punctuation mark herself. I have also indicated where, rarely, I have deleted the entire entry for a given day; deletions from the 1940 edition only are indicated.

Most deletions are redundancies, repetitions, descriptions of rounds of visiting, and minor war news. I am acutely aware that in cutting such redundancies, I am cutting some of the tedium, the isolation, the very repetition that Lucy herself experienced and recorded. However, I avoided the practice used by some editors of cutting *all* references to certain topics, thereby providing a focus to the diary but also badly skewing the sense of the diarist's interests.

In fact, one of the things I am interested in preserving in Lucy's diary is her diversity of topics and the ease with which she moves from "private sphere" to "public sphere" and back in her daily entries.

Finally, a comment on spelling in this new edition. Spelling errors and inconsistencies are few in the 1940 typescript edition, indicating Lucy's own good habits. I have not corrected those that occur, wishing to demonstrate to readers Lucy's ability, despite her paucity of formal education. The exceptions to this are silent corrections of proper names, place names, and arcane terms that might otherwise be misunderstood.

Family Members and Other Principals

Father

William Mason Buck
b. Aug. 30, 1809
d. 1878

Mother

Elizabeth A. Ashby
b. Sept. 25, 1820
d. January 1904

Married Apr. 3, 1838

Children

Alvin D. Buck
b. Dec. 18, 1838; d. July 1922

Irving Ashby Buck
b. Nov. 24, 1840; d. September 1912

Lucy Rebecca Buck
b. Sept. 25, 1842; d. Aug. 20, 1918

Ellen Catherine Buck
b. Sept. 6, 1844; d. August 1903 ("Nellie")

Marcus Newton Buck
b. Apr. 30, 1846; died as an infant

Laura Virginia Buck
b. Aug. 20, 1847; d. July 1927

Orville Mauzey Buck
b. Oct. 25, 1849; d. August 1877

Robert Carey Buck
b. May 21, 1851; d. February 1916

Annie Neville Buck
b. July 31, 1853; d. January 1907

William Richardson Buck
b. June 4, 1856; d. June 1947

Cora Blakemore Buck
b. Oct. 31, 1858; d. May 1859

Thomas Evred Buck
b. Jan. 9, 1860; d. January 1911.

Frank Latrobe Buck
b. Nov. 27, 1861; d. April 1909 ("Dixie")

African American Residents of Bel Air

William Richardson Buck wrote a memoir of his family in 1936 in which he said the following about the African American residents at Bel Air:

My father owned about 8 slaves. I remember Martha, the chamber-maid, Mahala, the cook; Eliza Ann, the nurse, and her 3 children, John Henry, Mary, and Allfair (Allfair was named by my sister, Laura Virginia, for her favorite character in a fairy tale); Horace and Alex, field hands, Uncle Gilbert, a freeman, worked the garden, but would never work in the fields except during harvest time, when a keg of liquor was served to the harvest hands. Then Uncle Gilbert would follow along and stack the shocks in order to get a share of the refreshments. He continued to work the garden faithfully until his death long after the war, when he was mourned and wept over like one of the family, and buried in the Negro Cemetery at Happy Creek.

Shadows on My Heart

Chapter One

఼఼఼఼఼఼఼఼఼఼఼఼఼఼఼఼఼఼఼఼఼఼఼఼

I Cannot but Feel a Little Sad

఼఼఼఼఼఼఼఼఼఼఼఼఼఼఼఼఼఼఼఼఼఼఼఼

December 25, 1861–May 13, 1862

Christmas Morning—1861

A sweet day that seems woven of the spirit of the Christmas benediction—
"Peace on earth—good will to men." The anniversary of the birth of the
holy Christ-Child, the anniversary of so many pleasant hours that have vanished never to return, but the memories of which come back to us "as sad as
earth, as sweet as heaven."

I cannot but feel a little sad this morning for my thoughts continually
revert to those dear absent brothers who were wont to share our Christmas
cheer and gladden the hours of this festive season for us. Poor boys! I wonder
if they think of the blazing hearthstone at old Bel Air and wish for a place in
the home-circle. When I think of the unexpected changes that have occurred
in the last year I feel as if I could not count upon ever having them with us
again as of yore with any degree of certainty. I think of how many hands that
wreathed the bowl and twined the holly last year are now mouldering in the
dust. The bright locks that were then crowned with roses, now dabbled in
gore and covered with the turf of the battle-field. I think of the bright eyes

3

that softened neath the love glances of fond friends then, how they look forth now with a yearning, hopeless gaze from the close grating of the gloomy prison window. I think of it all and sicken when I think. Thus far *we* have been peculiarly blest; our friends have been strangely preserved and protected from death and suffering through the war; our homes uninjured or unpolluted and we enjoying comparative tranquility and repose. But ere another revolution of the wheel of time, and who of "Those we love and those who love us" may not have ceased to speak with us on earth. And oh! who can tell how we may be called to pass through the "deep waters" and endure the fiery trials in the interval of another year. And how many of us will sink weakly under the heat and burthen of the day; and how many of us who now "cherish noble longings for the strife" may not—

> "By the wayside fall and perish
> Weary with the march of life."

But Oh God forbid! May He give us "Strength as our day" and be to us the "Great Rock in a Weary Land" when we feel nigh unto fainting. And ere the dawn of another Christmas morning may His "Peace, Be Still!" be spoken to angry billows of political strife—calming and restraining their fury; and may our loved country be restored to tranquility and we the happier and better for this refining process which shall consume the dross of selfishness and leave us the truer and purer.

—Evening—

This has been quite a pleasant day despite its rather gloomy retrospective beginning. Henry Buck came down about eleven o'clock to beg Nellie and me to make up one of a party which was to spend the holidays at Clover Hill—said party consisting of the Misses Tyler—Menie Leach, Nannie Ford, Smith Turner and some others. We had made a prior engagement with Aunt Betty Ashby and so declined Henry's invitation, though I knew they would enjoy themselves so much. We made our toilettes and went over to Oakley about half past eleven. Found Aunt B and Mr. Brerwood awaiting us and very soon Mr. Hoblitzell came in looking as usual satisfied with himself and the world in general. He had invited a young friend, Mr. Wilson of Baltimore, to meet him at dinner and the young fellow when he came proved to be a very great addition to our company. We finished drinking our toasts and then Mr. B. and I had quite a discussion with Mr. Hoblitzell upon the extent to which the command "Children obey your parents" was to be obeyed, particularly where matrimony was concerned. 'Twas all very unprofitable though, for at the close of the debate we all retained precisely the opinions as at the commencement. After dinner we had cards and "consequences" and enjoyed ourselves very much.[1] Heard "My Maryland" today for the first time—'tis a beautiful song.[2] Returned home before six and to our great surprise and delight found Emma Cloud, wife of T. N. Buck there. We were invited to Mrs. Stewart's tonight but did not go.

December 26th, 1861

The early part of the day which was cold and disagreeable, was spent about the fire laughing, talking and eating nuts. In the afternoon Emma and I called at Mrs. Cloud's and there met with Miss Martha Simpson and Mrs. Hamp Miller. Was glad to find the former amicably disposed, for 'tis so unpleasant to meet with one of whose sentiments with regard to yourself you are doubtful. I do not like to feel unkindly to anyone.

I noticed while at Mrs. C.'s that Miss Mary's pictures were all wreathed with Christmas garlands of evergreens and upon examining them I was particularly attracted by one of them—"Evangeline."[3] Although I had previously often seen and examined the picture, yet I had never *felt* it so before. It seemed that with her the artist must have "grieved for one whose image lay too deep for tears" else he could not so faithfully have conceived and depicted the expression of countenance of the crushed world-weary girl. There was such a depth of sorrowing despair in the dark eyes, such a wistful, longing gaze and yet withal such a chastened meek look about the gentle face, that I felt my own heart throb in painful sympathy and tears come into my eyes, just as if she had been a real human being loving and grieving. Tis indeed a wonderful art that which transfers to blank canvas the warm life-hues, the endless variety of passionate expressions that belong to our breathing glowing spirits enshrined in their flesh and blood caskets. What a talismanic power does the artist possess! How he rifles the tombs of the past and bids the forms of beauty, those mighty spirits of old—men of genius, strength and goodness—come forth from the dust of ages and awake to life-likeness—re-enacting their sufferings, their loves and their triumphs upon the cold canvas neath his magic touch! How we reverently bow before them, those heroes and martyrs of old as he brings their image to our gaze. How he revives memories of every age and country! How he leads our fancies with him through distant lands! How we gaze with awe and wonder upon the mighty relics of by-gone eras! How the treasures of every clime, all that is sublime in nature or in art are revealed to us by his potent spell, from the glowing, gorgeous tropics to the sterile, ghostly region of the iceberg! He even leads us into those bright realms of fancy where revels his own poet-soul. Oh 'tis a glorious talent entrusted to man! one which enables him to wield untold influence over the hearts and minds of his fellow beings in every age and condition of life.

We had company this evening Aunt Bettie Ashby, Uncle T. Ashby, Messrs. Brerwood, Hoblitzell, Wilson and C. There were bright lights, warm fire, cheerful faces and merry voices and *blind man's buff,* music and cards combined to render all easy and sociable. We spent a most delightful evening reminding me not a little of last winter. Mr. H. sang "Maryland" again and I learned to play it for Father after he left. I think Mr. Wilson captivated the whole family—he seems such a thorough gentleman, so easy and gentle in his manners, and yet possessing a deal of dignity for one so young. Poor boy! I feel so sorry for him. He has been sick at the hospital and I am sure he does not look like one who could long endure confinement in those loathsome asylumns for the suffering. It is so well that his mother and sisters who have raised him so tenderly do not know that he has been so sick among entire strangers. They would grieve so.

Aunt Bettie and Mr. B. insisted on our spending the ensuing evening at Oakley. I scarcely think we will though. Father went over to the cars hoping to receive some report of the anticipated convivialities at Centreville, but the boys did not write and we were forced to be content with Charley Brown's verbal testimony that they were well and enjoying themselves.

December 27th, 1861

What unimpeachable weather we are having—cold, 'tis true, but bright and fair as midsummer. I rejoice in it for the sake of our poor Southern boys in camp.

Dissipation does not agree with me, that's evident from the feeling of extreme lassitude and weariness I have experienced today. Emma left early and I spent the forenoon reading "Lucretia," practicing and sewing.[4] Charley

Brown came in for a couple of hours this morning and amused us much with his droll account of "life in camp." Received a note from Mr. B soliciting the "pleasure of our company" for the evening and presently the amiable trio—Messrs. H. W. and B. came in person to renew the request, but we were not in tune and declined. Willie Buck came in to play draughts and backgammon with Nellie tonight while I read aloud to Father. Received by cars a note from Irvin—short but welcome bringing an assurance of their well-doing.

I've thought too much of this day, year and drawn the contrast between the present and the past and the two pictures presented are a good representation of sunshine and shadow.

December 28th, 1861

Willie entertained us with his pranks until eleven. Then I spent the remaining hours of the forenoon in watering and dusting my geraniums, and giving myself a thorough drenching besides. Was sitting in Grandma's room when Nellie came in to say that Mr. Wilson had come to say adieu. He had received orders an hour previous to be ready to leave immediately and he goes down tomorrow with some friends: he thinks to return in three weeks, and I hope he will for he does not seem at all like a stranger, and I regret to see him go. Adjourned to Ma's room after dinner and spent the afternoon reading, singing and talking together. Charley Buck came in at 9 o'clock and remained over night. He goes to Centreville tomorrow and departs I am sure with a heavy heart.

December 29th, 1861

No service in any of the churches and we spent a quiet morning at home, Willie and Jacquiline being with us until late. Father spent the day at Mountain View and there was no reading aloud. He came in about sunset and Uncle Newton said he thought he heard heavy cannonading in the distance. Nell and I went in the house and listened to what did indeed closely resemble the bombing of artillery. The evening was lovely and I turned to look on the landscape spread before me. In the foreground the smooth, lawn-like meadows and the little Happy Creek like a silver thread meandering through them. Then the quiet village with the crimson sunset on its windows, and its bright wreaths of curling smoke, and beyond the undulating hills—and in

the distance like a fitting frame to this sweet picture stretched the blue mountains all with a cloudless heaven over-head, painted with the sunset pencils
forming altogether a scene of surpassing loveliness. So tranquil did everything seem that I could scarce persuade myself of the fact that just beyond
those mountains barriers lay the encampments of an invading foe cruel and
relentless, who had come with the avowed purpose of deluging this beautiful
land with the blood of the noblest and best of its sons. They were our enemies
who would fain see the dun-cloud of the battle-field or the sombre smoke
from our pillaged burning homes ascending to the blackened heavens instead
of the sweet Sabbath atmosphere which pervaded the scene now. Those who
would ensanguine that little stream with human gore, those who would mar
and devastate the face of the earth that they might thus blot out from remembrance everything of beauty from our now beautiful Virginia. Then my
thoughts reverted to our own little bands of patriots, and my heart thrilled
gratefully as I remembered how gallantly they had hitherto repelled the ad-
vances of the insolent foe, and I felt an exulting confidence that ere another
winter's frost should have browned the woodlands with the blessing of heaven
we should have been welcomed into the family of nations, an honored and
respected member of the vast fraternity. And now the evening star "lit its
silver lamp" and the sight brought to mind the dear ones who had so often
looked with me upon it and I wondered if we should ever meet together
again, as in the long ago at twilight and sing the happy songs of our childhood. Dear Brothers! 'tis doubtful very, and even if we were permitted another such reunion, and such a long weary time must first intervene I felt as
if I could not wait—as if I could not possess my soul with patience. Ah, well-
a-day!

Father seeing Nellie and me both unusually thoughtful proposed a walk
after tea; we accordingly walked over to Oakley where we spent the evening
pleasantly till eight o'clock and then walked home by star-light. No news.

December 31st, 1861

We had settled ourselves in Ma's room this morning, sewing in hand when
Aunt Bettie came in. So glad to see her, it seemed so natural to have her
spending a quiet, sociable day with us, which is something she has not done
in a long time before. Uncle Tom came in this afternoon and remained till

seven P.M. I concluded to watch the advent of the New Year and Grandma decided to keep vigil with me. I felt as if this year just being ushered in was to form an important period in the annals of our country, and while waiting for the waning moments to sink into the great abyss of the past, while watching for the last grains dropping from the hour-glass of the year, I recalled the last New Year and the stirring scenes and events that had transpired since its first dawn. I saw a great and glorious Government, which had erst been the pride and the boast of a free and happy people, in that brief period become a by-word of hissing and reproach "a thing of scorn and contempt" through the faithlessness of those who administered the laws made for the blessing and protection of the governed. I saw how one portion of the people became rich and prosperous under the government, but cruel and avaricious too and with all its wealth, jealous and envious of the possessions of the weaker part of the nation. And I saw it stretch forth its greedy power to snatch from the few the inheritance, the privileges and birth-rights which that Government had endeavored to secure to them by wise and just laws. I saw this people that had waxed strong grow proud and boastful too. I saw it trample upon the laws, desecrate the symbols and outrage every principle upon which this government was founded. Then I saw the oppressed rise up and assert its rights. I saw it plead with the oppressor for equal privileges as brothers of one house-hold. I saw concessions made and efforts for compromise, but the strong would none of it. *Might* was *right*, and the only compromise to be accepted was entire submission and resignation of self-respect by the weak. Then I saw the oppressed sorrowfully yield to the force of circumstances. I saw it prepare to leave a home when the authority of the ruling powers was not strong enough to prevent the strong from imposing on the weaker of the nation. I saw it strive to quietly go its way alone where it might worship under its own "vine and fig-tree" with "none to vex or make it afraid." But a factorum was not to be given up thus tamely and the oppressor raised a great furor and with threats and chastisements and scourges tried to force the little one into subjection. I saw a young Republic born into the family of nations which like Hercules was in its infancy attacked by a monster-serpent that endeavored to crush the bantling in its crib.[5] But like Hercules it courageously grasped its enemy and held it at bay till its muscles could cope with it in strife. I saw the deadly assailant writhe in the hands of its youthful adversary, and still the contest continued. I thought of this all and vainly questioned the future as to the issue of this conflict. That the unholy designs of the aggressor would be brought to naught I did not doubt, but there was so much of uncertainty in the future that with my utmost penetration I could not fathom. Well 'tis best perhaps that we cannot know what is before us in our onward way—better far trust in the goodness of God and rest assured that He will not give us more trials to bear than strength to bear them.

My fleeting fancy next brought before me a picture of the domestic revolutions and changes that this eventful year had produced in the sweet homes of the "Sunny South." I saw the proud mansions that were wont to be glad with mirth and music as each New Year sped on with fleet wings, now shrouded in gloom and darkness. I thought how the warm light had died out from the hearthstones and from the eyes that had beamed brightly around them. I thought of the sad silences of those ancestral halls that erst rang with the music of foot-falls that would stray on earth never more now. I knew how many happy a mother had been called to yield up her "Cornelian jewel"— her *all* and had sent him forth to the battle field with blessings on his bright young head—knew the hapless anguish of her spirit when they told her the gory grave held now the dear form so often clasped to her bosom. I thought of the gentle sister who resigned the play-fellow of her childhood, the dear protector of her youth to be sacrificed on the altar of his country never again to know the joy of a brother's love. I thought of the young bride who had torn from her brow the nuptial wreath and folded about her the sable weeds of her widowhood. I thought of the babe orphaned ere it could lisp a father's name. Thought of the helpless ones deprived of parents when they most needed a parent's watchful care. Of the maiden who listened and thrilled as she listened to the vows of love from lips stilled in death ere the burning words grew cold upon them. I thought of the hardships endured, the cold and hunger and the harshness to the brave and noble young Southerners whose cradle had been rocked in luxury—who knew of nothing but gentle words and loving smiles in the dear home far away. I thought of the delicate forms of the boys tenderly nurtured now rent with anguish resting on the loathsome hospital couches, no gentle hands to minister to their wants, no dear voice to whisper comfort and cheer when the dark shadows from the Valley of Death closed about them, none to smooth the pillow, none to drop a tear when that wasted form was borne off to the stranger's rude grave. There was none to hear the last whispered message breathed by the dying for those who waited his coming in the home he had left and who might never know where the loved one slept. I thought of the lonely pinings in the gloomy, deadly prison. I thought of the friendships formed, of the loves that had blossomed, of the ties that had been rudely sundered. I thought of the fire and the sword of the rapine and pillage that had devastated the land. And I thought of the profound depths of wickedness and deceit that had been revealed, of the hypocrisy and falsehood of the human heart that had been unveiled to the gaze, the most artless, the purest and most innocent. Oh, the deeds for good or evil that may be concentrated within the period of one little year! How the heart may grow old and cold, how the sympathies, the sensibilities may become dulled and deadened in that little time!

Then I remembered all these things and knew that we could judge of the future but by the past, I felt how perfectly impotent we were in the hands of the Almighty Ruler, how entirely dependent upon Him we were for happiness, and I realized how that we could not do better than say, "Now as the old Year with all its deeds is slowly waning—the last sands dropping from the glass, help Thou me! Oh God, to make this resolve, as Thou hast genuinely protected, blessed and preserved me in this year that has just passed, and has shown me that I know not what is good for me, so do Thou be with me in the coming New Year, help me to resign myself to Thy will, to commit to Thee issues of coming events and to only be careful that I discharge my duties to Thee and to my fellow-beings to the extent of my ability."

Commenced writing a letter but laid it by unfinished at one o'clock and retired.

January 1st, 1862

All hail to thee, New Year! Year destined as thou art to be fraught with events of vast import—events that leave an ineffaceable impression on the world—events that shall re-shape influences through the destinies of nations to remote ages. What deeds of high-souled daring, what sacrifices of life and fortunes and affections will not thy sun shine upon. What examples of chivalrous devotion to country will not be set to the nations of the earth.

Surely season never dawned more beautifully. Summer's sunshine, Autumn's soft sky and Spring's balmy breath with the bracing influences of a Winter's morning—a combination of all the seasons to welcome the advent of '62. Nellie, Laura and myself could not sufficiently enjoy it indoors, so we went on the house top and watched the lifting of the mist from the valley. How beautiful it looked, soft and white as a snow-wreath and braided with the gold and crimson of the sunshine. It rose slowly from the earth and the higher it ascended the more graceful and beautiful it seemed—just like our thoughts and desires that become ever more pure the nearer they lead to heaven.

The morning I spent in writing, in the afternoon Nellie and I concluded to make some calls. Just as we were setting out Cousin Mary Cloud came in, but she excused us and we went over—mailed my letter and went over to Mrs. Stewart's. Saw Alice, Fannie and Miss Boyd[6] and was introduced to one of the young disciples of Esculapius.[7] Tho not at all favorably impressed with the two latter individuals, one seemed all surface, vain and hollow; the other rude and evasive. It was my first acquaintance with Alice, and I was much pleased with her. Chatted awhile and had some music, and we then went down to Dr. Brown's where we spent a most pleasant hour. I never knew the Misses B. so agreeable and friendly.

Felt very much dissatisfied with myself tonight when reviewing the events of the day—there was a consciousness of having compromised my dignity in mingling upon terms of equality and apparent friendship with persons whom in my heart I despise—persons whom I felt to be false and heartless. I never am brought in contact with such persons without feeling a conviction that if forced to confine myself to their society I shall become as frivolous apparently as they. Received a petite epistle from dear Irvie after retiring.

January 2nd, 1862

Another bright day spent very quietly in the house. Cousin Mary C and Mr. and Mrs. Glasscock dined with us. In the afternoon Fannie Stewart called with two soldiers, acquaintances of hers. They were by no means prepossessing and I was duly glad when, after singing the song they came to hear I had the pleasure of receiving their adieux. Fannie however left assuring us that she intended next accompanying the young Dr. over to see us. I sincerely trust though she will not. Would be glad to see her but could not conscientiously extend a warm welcome to her proposed "Appendages." Read, wrote and sewed until bedtime.

January 4th, 1862

Woke very early and found it had been sleeting during the night. Put my shawl over my head and walked the pavement until it was light enough to read; then practiced on the piano and read and wrote till breakfast. Was very busy all day—sewing for Irving. At dusk Nellie and I went into the parlor and amused ourselves singing and playing. Mason and Slidell have really been yielded up to the demands of the British Government.[8] False hearted cravens! If the Yankee Cabinet did not direct their seizure it endorsed it at the time and now to think of their backing-down in that manner. To think of their once vaunted eagle trailing its plumage in the dust at the very feet of the British lion! We read today the correspondence between Seward and Lord L[yons] in relation to the affair, and I do think for a man with any reputation for ability, Mr. S. did make the most paltry attempt at playing the diplomatist and his letter the most juvenile effort at display of legal knowledge that I ever saw. Degraded sycophant! There is, I think reason for believing that Old England has not finished her reckoning with the administration yet. No news of importance tonight.

January 5th, 1862

Too cold and disagreeable to go to church today, so concluded to remain at home and read in lieu of the service. Cousin Mary left with the promise of returning tomorrow. Uncle Tom spent a couple of hours with us in the morning. While reading aloud to Father in the afternoon Uncle Mack came in and soon after Messrs. Wilson and Brerwood. So glad to see Mr. W. had returned last night very unexpectedly on a long furlough and seems delighted to be back. He's a nice fellow. Mr. Brerwood seemed unusually cheerful. While they were yet here, Mack Richardson, Willie Buck, Jacquie and "Allie" came in and we had quite a levee until dusk.[9] Read aloud to Father after they left. Oh! this bitter weather, what trials and sufferings does it not bring the poor soldier. May God "temper the wind to the poor fellows."

January 6th, 1862

Found a slight fall of snow on the ground this morning and the sky looking very wintery, though it did not snow as we expected. Cousin Mary came over at 9 o'clock and spent the day. Busied myself in reading, sketching and nursing little Dixie.

'Tis seldom that I experience a feeling of such perfect equanimity as I have today. It is generally the case that my spirits are too buoyant and untrammelled, or else in the reaction they are depressed to that degree that I take a painful pleasure in my gloom and glower. But today I have been quietly happy and cheerfully content with everything around me—'tis so delightful. I do wish I could control and direct this wayward disposition of mine.

Cousin Mary and I read aloud to Father tonight. No news tonight by cars.

January 7th, 1862

Occupied all the morning washing and cleaning the silver. Was taken quite sick about noon and felt too unwell to do anything all the evening and retired quite early. Oh! how low-spirited I felt all day and how vexed that I could not conquer my weakness and teach my spirits to rise superior to mere physical indisposition! But thus it is, I must be either beyond the bounds of all sobriety or else depressed as today. Poor mortality!

January 8th, 1862

Clear and cold this morning—health and spirits much renovated by a night's rest. Assisted Ma in her sewing and read a little during the day. Uncle Tom and Cousin Sam dined with us, and in the afternoon Cousin Mary went home with them, but speaks of returning tomorrow. Heard that the "Warren Rifles" were ordered to Evansport—hope the report is groundless—suppose we will hear the truth tomorrow.[10]

How well I remember this day year, or rather this night. We were at Dr. Turner's—a small company of as merry young people as ever assembled. Cousin Sam, Emma, Jule, Nellie and Miss Tensia every one of us. Irvie and Will Richardson too. Wonder where we will all be this time next year.

January 9th, 1862

Worked hard till ten o'clock this morning cleaning the parlor, putting up curtains, etc. Expected company to dinner but indisposition prevented them from complying with their engagement. Was taken in the forenoon with one of my nervous headaches, which incapacitated me for further employment. Felt better later in the evening and wrapping a shawl about my head went on the porch to enjoy the sunset. It was very beautiful, the air soft and balmy and the sky so blue—mellowed into a rich orange and then burning a bright gold in the West where floated a few glowing clouds like sentinels guarding the sunset chamber. Then a gentle breeze stole out and drew a curtain of mist over the brightness and set in its fleecy folds a single watch star. While sitting intensely enjoying the tranquil scene I heard footsteps on the pavement and turning saw Mr. Cook and Mr. Berry approaching. Invited them in the parlor, where I entertained them until Father appeared and then Nellie sang a little. I do so enjoy the society of social elderly gentlemen sometime—there is so much benefit to be gleaned from their individual experiences. They are war scarred veterans on the battle-field of life—they know all the trials and privations to be endured in that long campaign—understand all the maneuvers, can instruct us how to avoid this and that foe, what is necessary in emergencies arising. They can advise much better than the novices in the service, and hence are often preferable companions to the unsophisticated. I fear though that the lessons thus conned are often too soon forgotten to be productive of as good results with me as they should.

I have been sitting here tonight thinking of the last 9th of January. I remember it so well. Irvie was with us and there was a company of mirthful friends in the evening collected about the parlor fire at old Bel Air, and the gleeful games in the dining room. I recollect the philopena gift, the wish and the songs and music.[11] All those pleasant scenes are traced in golden characters on my memory pages. I wonder if the record will ever again be as bright.

January 11th, 1862

Felt "gay and happy" this morning and after going through my usual routine sat down to do a good day's sewing. Ma and Grandma went Saturday preaching to church and left Nellie and myself in charge of the house and "infantry." Had just brushed my hair and settled myself down when Messrs. Brerwood and Wilson were announced. Mr. W. told us he had come to leave his adieux as he was to take his departure in the morning for O———. We spent a couple of pleasant hours chatting and singing and then they left. Ma came home

about noon and brought me a letter from Dick, Saucy fellow! Made a cravat
for Mr. Wilson and sent it to him with the cap which Nellie finished for him
tonight. And in return she received a very nice note of thanks and assurances
of remembrances. I feel very much interested in the boy and hope he may do
well whether he returns to military service or receives an appointment in the
Civil Departments—Nothing from Irvie—no war news.

January 12th, 1862

Nellie, Father and I walked over to Oakley this morning—found Aunt Bettie
all alone and she seemed glad to see us, very. We went out on the front
portico and sat for some time finding it most delightful. The air was balmy
and almost sultry—indeed we might have thought a July day had gotten a
furlough and come to visit the New Year. Mr. Brerwood came in some time
after Father left and we gathered in the sitting room chatting till dinner time.
After dinner listened to Mr. B.'s amusing account of his visit to L., and ate
apples and nuts. We all walked up to "Soldiers' Rest" late in the afternoon.
It was the first time I had ever been there and it saddened me to see already
the number of graves there—mere heaps of earth with rough head and foot
boards upon which were inscribed the names and dates of the deceased with
the companies to which they had belonged. And there under my very feet
they rested so still, so silent, those men who had for the love of country and
freedom risked their lives and lost them in battling the usurper of their sacred
rights—lost them, not gloriously fallen on the field bathed in their own
heart's blood, but stricken with disease they had languished in agony upon
friendless couches and at last died no less martyrs to their cause. I could
scarce realize that those whose arms had been strong in the conflict, whose
feet had been so swift in the battle, were now lying all so powerless, that I,
weak girl that I was, might boast of a giant's strength in comparison. I
thought so much of the distant homes from which their never returning footsteps had departed and longed to send some word of comfort to the bereaved
hearts there—to say to each mourner "Weep not, he rests well and though
he slumbers on, apparently unknown and unnoted, yet in far after years the
children he assisted in freeing from bondage shall lean over the grave of the
sleeping patriot and drop the tribute of a sigh or tear and call him "blest"
who died in defense of such a cause."

It was quite late when we returned to Oakley and the soldiers in camp were singing their evening hymns, and very sweet it sounded as it came mellowed by the distance to our ears. We sat on the portico and Nellie and I sang for Uncle Tom—went to tea and while we were at table Father walked in to accompany us home. We had spent a delightful day and had a pleasant walk home in the moonlight. Found George Williams here, he had come to tell us "good-bye" as he was to start on the morrow for the seat of war— had obtained a situation in Beauregard's Headquarters.[12] He will doubtless have a merry time of it with old friends there. Saw Henry and Jule from a distance today. No news.

January 13th, 1862

Nellie and Laura started to school again today, much to my sorrow, for I do miss them so much when they are away and fear I shall get to moping. Busied myself recording, writing and nursing the little Dixie in the forenoon. In the afternoon sewed and practiced some little. Kattie Boone has sent me a special invitation to visit her tomorrow, and I mean to go if the weather is favorable. Read aloud to Father until he went to the cars tonight; when he returned bringing a nice letter from Irvie containing a number of our Generals' autographs for me.[13] Dear fellow, how pleased I am to hear from him and know that he and Alvin are well and comfortable. Am afraid though he does not write as cheerfully as usual.

January 17th, 1862

Had most troublesome lessons to hear, and did not get through with them till dinner—then had the baby to care for as he was very restless. Sewed and read till about four o'clock when Nellie and Laura came in with bright faces accompanied by Eliza Hope and Mr. Brerwood. They sat only for a short time, but Mr. B., made an engagement to return after tea to play a game of Cassino.[14]

Messrs. B. and H. both came in about seven o'clock and after some desultory conversation we were led to discussing the question of female education. Mr. B. and I thought the continuation of the mind to a high degree refined and elevated her character and tastes and softened and beautified her disposition, while Mr. H. on the other hand contended that a female philosopher or metaphysician, or, in other words, a mistress of abstract sciences, was necessarily masculine, bold and ambitious, a perfect monstrosity. The debate at length grew so warm on both sides that I was fain as a prudent hostess to change the subject without either party having departed from his original opinions. We taught Mr. B. Cassino and then closed with music and a serenade from the gentlemen as they departed. Henry Buck stopped in after nine—just from Centreville—boys all well but had not time to write. Irvie sent Nellie a little sketch with a promise of a letter very soon. No news of interest.

January 18th, 1862

Raining this morning and as a matter-of-course visiting was for the present postponed. Henry was with us till eleven. In the afternoon the sun scattered the clouds and the air was so warm and pleasant that it moved us to a walk. Nellie and I called to see Kattie where we remained till sunset, the walking was disagreeably muddy, but I felt fully rewarded for having ventured out when upon passing the post office I saw in our box a letter directed to me in Charles Richardson's handwriting. He wrote that Dick had been appointed Orderly Sergeant and was quite an efficient officer. He also promised to preserve for me Genl. Longstreet's autograph. Read aloud to Father until bed time.

January 21st, 1862

Raining harder this morning than on yesterday and Nellie was for once weather bound and unable to get to school. So glad! We heard that Allie and Mr. Brerwood were both sick and Father went over to ascertain if it were true. Soon returned saying that Allie was quite unwell and Mr. Brerwood somewhat indisposed too. Received a long letter from dear Irvie telling me how much engaged they all were in the office. I am so glad he is going to remain there instead of going West next spring. Practiced some time this evening and after tea read aloud to Father a dissertation upon "Law." I have heretofore imagined that the study of law must be the most unmitigatedly, dull, uninteresting thing in the world, but in this my first glimpse into its mysteries I was agreeably surprised to find the subject a most interesting one treated in this way.

January 22nd, 1862

Oh such a time as I had this morning with my pupils![15] I'm convinced my forte is not the management of juvenile masculinity and my patience waxes weaker and weaker at every trial. The fact is I would like to know what my sphere here is—Sometimes I'm afraid my "Leaf by some o'er hasty angel is misplaced in Fate's eternal volume." I am sure that I am not fitted for any vocation to which I have yet turned attention.

Wrote Uncle John this evening. How quiet everything seems in the military line—they do not seem to have the excitement of an occasional skirmish.

January 27th, 1862

Allie was placed on the list of convalescents this morning. We were all sitting in Ma's room this morning before breakfast and Father came in and had a pacquet of letters brought from Centreville the night before by Benton Roy. Upon breaking the seal, we found letters from Alvin and Irving to Father and myself, and from George Williams to Cousin Sue announcing that Genl. Beauregard was ordered to Kentucky and they as Clerks would accompany Col. Jordan, and requesting that their clothes might be put in a state of perfect repair so that everything might be ready for their departure at a moment's warning. The intelligence was unexpected and sudden as a thunder bolt, and I was so stunned as for a time to lose the power of speech and volition—but soon I realized the whole force of the unwelcome news. My darling brothers were going to a distant State with no prospect of our seeing them for a long, long time and no chance of ever hearing from them except at long weary intervals. They were to go where they must be surrounded by hostile armies liable to be cut off from communication with us; going among entire strangers who knew nothing and cared nothing for them, going where they could not be gently and tenderly nursed in sickness as we ever had nursed them. It was so hard. I knew that many, very many in the Southern Army who were much less pleasantly situated than they would probably be, but I never before realized so fully what it was for the poor fellows to be separated from home and friends until thus brought home to me. As soon as we recovered from the shock occasioned by the tidings we fell straightway to work renovating the cast off undergarments of the boys as requested. Cousin Sue had some sewing to do for Cousin George and, therefore, went down to Rose Hill that she might have the benefit of the sewing machine there.

Benton Roy came over between 11 and 12 and sat a short time—looked badly. He told us the boys would be up to see us before they take their departure. Thank goodness! We will have the pleasure of once more having them together with us under the old homestead roof for a short time though it be.

Uncle Tom came over about five o'clock and I went home with him. Found Messrs. Lionberger and Almond there having just arrived. Mr. Brerwood and I sat with Allie until after tea and then Aunt B came and sat with me until twelve o'clock. After that she lay down and I had the quiet and the light and fire all to myself. My vigils were not lonely though for I had reading and writing to occupy me and besides I could not have slept anyway, so sad, so anxious and distressed I felt. Received a letter from Fannie Stewart today long looked for and welcome.

January 28th, 1862

Woke this morning with a dull pain at the heart which I could not at first account for, but soon the recollection of yesterday's events flashed to my mind and I comprehended it all. Remained ministering to Allie until near ten when I started forth braving the inclemency of the weather in my walk home. It was raining and sleeting dreadfully and I found it required all my little strength to maintain my equilibrium and not having an appetite for paying my respects to Aunt Bettie's nice buckwheat cakes and sausages at breakfast, I had very little of the above mentioned "commodity" to depend upon. Met Benton on the corner of the street and learned from him that the train the night before had brought no intelligence from the boys and no orders for himself. Arrived at home safely contrary to Aunt B.'s predictions and immediately addressed myself to the task of repairing the boys' clothes. Mrs. Morehead and her brother Dr. Rixey came in about four o'clock and after tea

Benton came also and remained till after the cars went out when he went over to get the news. Found upon closer acquaintance that he was really much more sociable than I had fancied him in the morning yesterday, then I thought, like most of the boys who had been in the army, that he had become so pugnacious that he could talk, think, or breathe nothing but war and military. It's so stupid when that's the case.

We went to the office but heard nothing from the boys. Neither was there any news by paper.

January 30th, 1862

A very disagreeable winter day, snowing and sleeting. Resumed my teaching this morning with Nellie as Assistant. She has not been to school this week and consequently I have not been so lonely as usual, though I did feel right blue today attributable to the snowy weather and physical indisposition. Nellie and I had a nice long practice on the piano before tea and after tea prepared ourselves for a game of backgammon when Benton was announced. He had come over to say "good bye" preparatory to leaving in the morning—looked sad, seems to be grieved to see his Mother's distress at his going away from her. We had a long old fashioned talk and quarreled a little, and I played and sang a little, then about nine o'clock he left to go to the cars. Nellie and I played our game of backgammon until the cars came in when we went out to watch for the boys who did not come, neither did they write. I do feel so anxious about them. Irvie promised he would write before he came up and I hoped he would. Tomorrow, and certainly they will come unless something unusual has occurred to prevent them. Patience!

January 31st, 1862

We none of us heard the cars come in at the regular hour this morning and so concluded they were detained by some accident. Sure enough about nine o'clock we saw a crowd assembled at the depot and heard the whistle of the cars. Saw Benton on the train as it passed by and he waved to us. The engine had gotten off the track, which caused the detention. Had a fatiguing time with my scholars this morning and felt quite unwell, but in good spirits anticipating the arrival of the dear ones, thinking of them all day. After tea

wrote a letter to Mr. C. for Father and then had everything in readiness to welcome the travelers. Father went over to the cars at about ten o'clock. We saw him coming up the yard with the lantern, though we could not distinguish any of his companions. Out we rushed and found ourselves in the midst of them—Alvin and Irving and Cousin George W. Oh it was a happy reunion! and we sat up until after twelve listening to their accounts of "adventures by fire and flood" by their companions. They met Benton en route for Centreville and when he learned the Genl. and his staff had left there he concluded to return home with them. I think the poor boys all look pale and haggard, but I hope a few days at home and recreation will restore them. They have all, excepting Irvie, a furlough until Monday—he is to spend a day in Richmond and will therefore have to leave here a day earlier. Oh dear!

February 1st, 1862

It snowed this morning, but we were all too happy indoors to heed the wild play of the elements without. I was up early and had a fire in the parlor. After breakfast we adjourned to Ma's room and we had a thorough review and renovation of the boys' trunks and respective ward robes—a mighty task it proved occupying us 'til dinner time. Meanwhile Uncle Tom came in and carried Irvie home with him—Cousin George leaving at the same time. Cousin Bettie came in to dinner, Irvie also returning, we had a merry meal of it. After dinner we all went into the parlor and sang and played for the boys and then Ma, Nellie, Laura and myself sat down and had a nice cozy chat with them all to ourselves. Had not enjoyed it long though when the door opened and Messrs. Roy and Williams were announced and very soon after, Cousin Will Cloud was ushered in and Cousin Bettie came from downstairs, so the room was pretty well filled and such chattering as they kept up. It reminded me so much of last winter when the same pleasant circle gathered about the blazing hearth in light hearted enjoyment, and then when they all gathered about the piano while we played it seemed so natural I could almost imagine the wheel of time had been reversed and we were re-enacting the pleasures of that memorable winter of '61. I was so provoked because too hoarse to sing as I wished. What a queer piece of humanity Scott Roy is—I like him, but can't exactly understand his varied and variable moods—this evening he was sarcastic and humorous, gave a very graphic description of camp life before he left and seemed very sociable, and then took his departure with the others at five o'clock without so much as a bow or a "good eve-ning."[16] I do believe I like him for his eccentricities for they afford consid-erable variety in the study of his character and constantly lend piquancy to that study. If I could only get some clue to his disposition.

Cousin Will remained over night and Uncle Mack came in and remained till nine o'clock and we did have a merry time of it. A very amusing incident occurred just as Irvie was projecting a sky rocket, the first ever seen instead of going up, it went around the corner of the west end and frightened all the colored folks looking on—which kept us all in convulsions of laughter until Uncle M. left. But notwithstanding our lively enjoyment of the fun, I cannot help but wish we could have had the boys more to ourselves and have had more unrestrained intercourse with them. Dear fellows! It's the last time they may be together with us for a long, long time and I do not feel as if I had had any of their society at all. Poor Irvie looks unusually sad tonight, more so than the fact even of his departure tomorrow would account for, but he will not acknowledge that anything troubles him or that he's unwell. He went over to the cars tonight and returned after tea saying he and Benton would cer-tainly leave in the morning. So we have been sitting up with him till after eleven, making some final preparations and having some farewell talk with him, bless him!

February 2nd, 1862

Was up at three o'clock to see Dear Irvie off and when the cars passed by went out on the pavement to wave the light to him. It was hard to see him go away from us looking so depressed and unhappy—I know I shall think of it enough after he's gone—perhaps he is more unwell than he would have us believe. Oh me! tomorrow Alvin goes too.

Have taken a very deep cold and was too unwell to accompany Ma, Father, Nellie, Alvin and Cousin Will. Remained at home and tried in vain to sleep away my cold. . . .

February 3rd, 1862

Alvin went over to the cars at four o'clock this morning and soon returned stamping the snow from his feet and shivering with the cold. He had seen Col. Jordan who told him that he would go on to Richmond and remain there two days which time Alvin might, if he liked, spend at home! Benton went on with the Col. and George went to the Junction where he would procure tickets for Alvin and himself and return tonight. I am so glad George is coming back. He has already improved so much on nearer acquaintance that I am glad to have an opportunity of knowing him better. We hovered about the fire all day listening to Alvin's merry account of the sayings and doings of the mess at Centreville, and reading, laughing and singing. It was altogether a very pleasant day. In the afternoon A. walked over to town with Cousin Will. We all sat in Ma's room Father and I listening to Alvin's interesting conversation and Nellie and Cousin Will playing draughts and backgammon until late.

February 4th, 1862

Went into the parlor with Nellie this morning and commenced playing and singing when the door opened and entered Cousin Will, Alvin and George who had arrived last night after we retired and unknown to us. He reported Irvie well, but very much vexed at having missed connection with the Richmond train. After breakfast Cousin Will left, Alvin went to resting and George and I played backgammon and draughts until eleven o'clock, and then I commenced making him a cap, which I finished by the time he came over after tea and for which I received his gracefully expressed thanks. How I have enjoyed this last day of Alvin's stay at home, we were all well and with nothing to mar our happiness but the thoughts of tomorrow's separation. Mr. Brerwood came in at twilight to tell him good-bye and wish a pleasant journey. George came in about nine o'clock while we were sitting about the fire and thereupon he and Alvin commenced a running fire of retort and repartee which lasted until they unwillingly took leave for the night. Poor Alvin! He does all he can to conceal his reluctance at leaving.

February 5th, 1862

Was up at 3 o'clock this morning to see our travellers off. They came in and sat with us a few moments and then with warm farewells and hearty good wishes they left us in the house very lonely.

I had the recitations to hear and then spent the remaining part of the forenoon in reducing my writing drawer to some appearance of order. . . .

I have thought so much of the dear absentees today and each hour I have wondered where they were, what they were doing and missing them so much all the time and longing for another season of happy communion with them. O! when will that be ever again. When! When!

February 8th, 1862

Alice Morehead, Nellie and I spent the day in Ma's room laughing, talking and singing until my school hour when I left them to attend my customary duties which occupied me until dinner. After dinner Alice and I played backgammon for an hour or so and jested and joked each other generally. . . .

We fully expected to hear from the boys tonight and what a disappointment it was when our eager inquiries were answered with the "No letters." We sat up late—twelve o'clock laughing and talking. The news by the papers was very discouraging. The enemy had free access to the Tenn. River and there is no knowing when their ravages will cease. I trust that their occupation of Fort Henry may not enable them to interfere with the sailing of boats between Kentucky and the Southern States.

February 9th—Sunday, 1862

Lovely morning but although there was a company in the house could not enjoy the day. I do not know the time when I felt so low-spirited. Was so uneasy at not hearing from the boys—will not probably hear from them now until they reach Columbus. By eleven o'clock my feelings were wrought up to such a pitch that I stole upstairs to indulge in a good cry. Felt better after that and went down stairs to try and make myself agreeable. Uncles Tom and Mack were there discussing the perils of the times. Took a walk all by myself about sunset. Went down to the creek and stood upon the bare rocks looking down into the water where were reflected the dull grey of the sky, the dry rustling grass and leafless trees among the branches of which the wind sighed so mournfully in low fitful gusts. It was a dreary scene and harmonized well with my own sad spirit, but I really enjoyed it as though I had been holding communion with a congenial friend—and felt better on returning to the house. Had a little chat with Father before tea and read aloud to him until bed time. . . .

February 10th, 1862

. . . I was sitting by the fire reading to Father when the door opened and Scott Roy and Charley Richardson came in. Such a time as we had laughing and talking, singing and playing until ten o'clock. Scott seemed so much the boy of other days and I felt so easy and unrestrained with him—he's a clever good boy despite his mischievous propensities. Whilst turning my rings about on my finger, I fractured the little black one placed on my finger with a wish a year ago. Was so sorry for it.

Heard such dreadful news by papers. The Yankees have possession of the Tenn. River and are carrying everything with a high hand in Alabama. They have taken possession of Roanoke Island and threatening Norfolk. It is distressing to hear of such disasters and the worst of it is that they are probably but the forerunners of other and greater evils, but we can only trust in God for the issue.

February 11th, 1862

Was late at breakfast this morning. Alice and I concluded to spend the day at Rose Hill and commenced preparations for an early walk when Walter came in very unexpectedly. Dear boy how glad I was to see him! Said he was at home on two weeks' furlough and intended making his holiday one of pleasure. While chatting with him there was a knock at the door and very soon Scott was ushered in. Came to bring us a letter from Irvie, which was brought the night before by private hand from Richmond. Upon reading it, we found his impressions of Richmond anything but pleasant. Said they would leave the next Sunday for Lynchburg, to re-join the other boys. S. also brought me the miniature which B. told me he would send from Rd. We had a game of draughts and backgammon and then he undertook to mend my ring and we had quite a romp over it. I am so sorry he is going away tomorrow, and wish he could have been over more frequently during his stay at home. He and W. left together about eleven and then Alice and I started for Rose Hill. Found the family indisposed, but nevertheless spent a very pleasant day—particularly so as we found Emma there on our arrival. About five o'clock we concluded to walk up to Oakley, where Nellie had engaged to meet us and stay all night. Emma went with us. Had a late walk—indeed the moon was shining quite brightly as we passed up the street and we felt a little badly being entirely unprotected. Nellie and Uncle Tom met us at the door and we were soon discussing a cup of nice coffee and some of Aunt B's famous biscuits and then we played cards with Mr. B. until ten and then we adjourned to our chamber chatting together until twelve o'clock. No news or papers tonight.

February 12th, 1862

We opened our eyes on a bright morning and were a light hearted party that met in the breakfast room. . . . Found the family rather blue on reaching home. They had gotten the papers the night before giving an account of the extended ravages of the Hessians, their progress South-ward, etc., all of which depressed them very much. Indeed, the clouds seemed to be lowering very darkly over our country now and a prospect of settlement more distant than ever before. Yet I do not fear for the ultimate success of our cause. I but fear me for the fiery ordeal through which we must pass first. We can only trust in "One Who can give us strength as our day." . . .

February 16th, 1862

Read aloud to Father a dissertation upon language until he left for church. The walking was so disagreeable as not to admit of our accompanying him. Aunt Letitia Blakemore came in about eleven o'clock and concluded to remain several days. Allie and Mr. Hoblitzell came in while we were at dinner and stayed until about four in the afternoon. Then Dr. Dorsey came in and sat some time. Went upstairs and had a nice long dreaming spell for myself. Heard Emma repeat the "Raven" for the first time this evening.

. . . Latest advices from the seat of war announced a glorious victory at Fort Donelson—the enemy repulsed upon every side. We were on the qui vive for another attack at the latest despatches.

February 17th, 1862

Oh such a time with my pupils! Completed my task of instruction and felt so utterly wearied out that I had to restore my equilibrium by a practice on the piano. Read with Emma during the day and at twilight we assembled in Ma's room where Emma recited the "Raven" while each contributed a ghost story for the edification of the company and some of the party were, I think, more affected by them than they were willing to admit. Uncle Fayette dined with us today.

Papers bring a full account of the victory at Donelson, but the conflict has been renewed. We have evacuated Bowling Green and the enemy shelled and burned the place.

February 18th, 1862

Sewing, reading and teaching all day. No letters by mail, but there were the sad tidings of the fall of Donelson—learned nothing of the particulars of the unexpected calamity, but 'tis enough to know its capture gives the foe command of the Cumberland River and access to the heart of Tennessee.[17] Another item this, in the "geng debt" we are "piling" for the brutal foe.

'Tis strange we hear nothing from the boys and can learn naught of the whereabouts of Beauregard. Trust he was not at Fort Donelson.

February 20th, 1862

Was arranging the contents of my "treasury" this morning when Nellie came bounding in bidding Emma and me "Guess who was married last night" at the same time answering her own question—"Kattie Boone and Mr. Samuels." What a surprise! The ceremony strictly private, no invitations, no attendants, no kind of demonstration. Well, it *does* seem strange when I think of my old school mates making for themselves homes thus when I cannot learn to regard them or myself as anything but children. Heigh-ho—so wags the world—marrying and giving in marriage unto the end.

Nellie seemed well and in fine spirits until night when she retired with a violent sore throat and we retired to bed feeling quite uneasy about her. Soon after we went to bed, Walter knocked at the door—just arrived from Centreville and reported all things well. No letters but most dreadful news by papers. Our loss at Fort Donelson incredibly great, Beauregard sick at Nashville and that city itself menaced by the enemy—and our prospects in Kentucky altogether very dark. Heaven help us!

February 22nd, 1862

The glorious twenty-second! rendered doubly dear to every Southern heart witnessing as it will the inauguration of our first Confederate President—the establishment of a new and independent government.[18] May the God of Nations smile approval upon this our country's natal day, may He bless and consecrate it and make of us a great and happy people, and may wisdom from on high descend upon the ruler this day chosen to minister over us and may his administration be a happy and a prosperous one!

Mrs. Morehead left early and I was left alone to entertain Messrs. B. and H. until they left at ten o'clock. Nellie then rose, dressed herself and announced herself decidedly convalescent—in support of which she proceeded to shingle my hair closely. Spent the day sewing and reading. Walter and Henry came in—the latter left early, the former remained all night. We had such a nice confab together in the twilight, just like those we have so often enjoyed together long ago, talked about my darling Alvin and about himself. I told him how I had thought him so changed and how glad I was to find my mistake. He explained the apparent inconsistency of his behavior to my entire satisfaction. . . .

February 23rd, 1862

Raining and dreary. Had a most stupid two hours entertaining the "Guard" stationed at the parlor fireplace. They left as soon as it cleared off,—Mr. Hoblitzell bidding us a final adieux as he expects to rejoin his regiment tomorrow. Walter left before breakfast with the promise of returning to say good bye after a while. Accordingly about noon in he came with a saucy speech, a kiss and a caress for each of us and then was gone away in a twinkling. He's a dear fellow to be sure!

Dick B. came for Aunt Letitia in the afternoon and took her home with him so we are all alone again. Ma, Grandma and myself were quite sick tonight. Must stop as I am not able to sit up later. Read over some old letters this evening. Pleasant occupation.

February 25th, 1862

After Cousin E. and W. left this morning attended to my pupils. Father again left for Capon at noon.[19] He has gone to remove what he can of bed linen as it is unsafe where it is—will pack the articles in bales and keep them here until he can send them off. In the afternoon I had commenced a quite long letter to the dear boys when Mr. Brerwood came in to protect us in Father's absence tonight. Soon after Cousin Ellen Richardson and her little girls came in, and after the cars were come and gone, Cousins Edwin and Will. They are to leave in the morning for Arkansas, so we determined to enjoy this our last night together and what with music, laughing and jesting we did not retire until after 12 o'clock. Papers brought news of the burning of the Lynchburg bridge.

February 27th, 1862

Had a disagreeable time with my scholars this morning. Mr. Brerwood came in at noon and said there was current in town a rumor that Winchester would be evacuated by our forces,—we did not believe it—'twas too startling for credence. In the afternoon Cousin Mary came in and after tea while we were sitting about the candle discussing recent events the door opened and Father walked in—had just returned from Capon—much earlier than he had expected on account of hearing there was sickness in the family. And alas! he confirmed the report of the evacuation of W. Oh how shocking! What a calamity it will prove to us. The enemy will then have possession of the railroad as far as Manassas Junction which affords them great facilities for transporting to flank our army or Centreville. Then they could with some justice cry "On to Richmond"! Surely, surely, our condition must be a desperate one to hazard such a movement! and then the individual inconvenience if they take Winchester our mails will be interrupted and then adieux to letters or papers. Dear brothers, they are so far from us that we shall be unable to hear anything at all from them, and how terrible must be our anxiety for them! Then our homes will be rifled and pillaged and—oh I can't bear to think of it all.

February 28th, 1862

Our President has appointed this day for one of humiliation and prayer and our spirits were very much in consonance with such a decree. Intended going to church, but though I had my bonnet on ready for attending the summons of the bell, Grandma and Father vetoed the resolution in consideration of the inclement weather. Uncles Tom and Mack came in the afternoon, but as I was spending the day on the bed I did not see them. We were all sick in consequence of the prolonged fast and retired to bed quite early. The cars did not get in until eleven o'clock and we did not therefore hear from the office.

March 1st, 1862

Felt better this morning and was dressing for breakfast when Laura rushed in exclaiming "Come into Ma's room all of you and hear Irvie's letter read." In we went and there sure enough was a letter from the dear fellow. He wrote from Columbus where they all with the exception of Alvin had arrived safely after many "hair breadth 'scapes." A. had left them at a way-side station en route for Hopkinsville and they had not heard from him since. I very much fear he will have serious difficulty in getting to his place of destination. But we were so rejoiced at getting a letter from them that I would not long harbor the thought of danger to them. . . .

[March 2, 1862, entry omitted]

March 4th, 1862

Anniversary of the inauguration of the arch-fiend Lincoln and the anniversary of the inauguration of a despotism as atrocious as ever the fair sun shone upon. Truly will it be a day memorable in the annals of our nation's woes.

Was very unwell in the forenoon, but felt better later in the day when Cousin B. and Dick came in. They remained with us until late in the afternoon. Cousin Bettie is in deep distress and not without cause. They have heard through a letter received from a friend that Cousin Marcus and Dick Blakemore were certainly at Donelson during the battle there, and as nothing has been heard from them since the probability is that they are either killed, wounded or prisoners. Heaven forbid that either should be the fact, poor fellows! . . .

[March 6, 1862, entry omitted]

March 8th, 1862

Went into the dining room immediately after breakfast and heard the boys' recitations—had a sorry time of it too. Mr. L. and Cousin M. left this morning. Had settled myself to my sewing when Cary came in to tell me that "Cousin Jule" was "in the other room." In I went and was delighted to see her really there. We were chatting away at a great rate when Father came in bringing a letter from Benton to his Mother dated from *Jackson, Tenn.* They had been ordered down from Columbus to rejoin Beauregard, who was sick in J. He describes the town as a perfect little paradise—says the party is in good plight and that they enjoy themselves much. It was so thoughtless in him not to have mentioned whether or not Alvin had rejoined them—if he has not done so ere this the probability is that he is a prisoner and that's too dreadful to think of. Oh if Irvie would but write!

. . . Saw a large number of horses and wagons coming from Winchester today. What *does* it all mean I wonder?

March 9th, 1862

Such a day of tumultuous excitement as we have endured! This morning whilst putting on my bonnet for church I heard a knock at the door which I soon discovered proceeded from Mr. Brerwood—he stood there perfectly white and trembling with excitement. Upon inquiring the cause of his perturbation, he said that advices had been received to the effect that both Winchester and Manassas were being evacuated by our troops, who were falling back towards Staunton on the one hand and Richmond on the other. When we went to church everyone seemed stupified by the intelligence and discussed it in suppressed whispers even in church. Mr. Berry preached a beautiful sermon from the text "Faint, yet pursuing."

. . . The "tyrant's heel" will be upon us, but although he may restrain speech and action he cannot shackle the thoughts and feelings that glow within us, and which, like all suppressed flames will burn all the more fiercely when they blaze into actions.

March 10th, 1862

Rather a pleasant day—went through my usual routine of teaching and reading. . . . Late in the evening Scott came in and sat an hour, said he was going in a day or two to rejoin his regiment although not yet fit for service—feared to remain lest the Yankees should dash in and capture him. We went into the parlor and had music—singing some of our old songs that served to remind us pleasantly of "by-gone hours." Scott was so like himself and so like the nice fellow he really is we enjoyed his society very much. Left promising to call and say "good bye" tomorrow. Mr. Brerwood and Wythe Cook were with us tonight.

March 11th, 1862

A day as beautiful as ever blessed the eye of man. Mr. B. and Wythe left about nine o'clock and Ma, Nellie and myself concluded to pay our farewell visit to town. While preparing to start Scott came in and remained a couple of hours. Then Charley and Nannie Buck came in, the former to say "good bye" previous to leaving for the Army. Poor fellows! 'tis so hard for them to be forced to flee their homes for fear of imprisonment, to be forced by such a *villainous* crew of cowardly Yankees.

After Charley went away Cousin Mary and Emma Cloud came in and they seeing us equipped for the walk insisted on our going and leaving them here to "make themselves at home." So we had a merry walk to town, Nellie, Nannie, Scott and myself,—first went to pay my bridal call on Kattie Samuels. Found her in her room dressing for dinner—she was looking well—full of chat and is evidently of the opinion that all the virtues pertaining to manhood are concentrated in one individual—that individual Mr. Samuels. Ah! well-a-day. I hope she may ever think thus but I feel sad to hear young brides indulging in such bright anticipations as these—I think of the contrast between married life as they imagine it to be and married life as they will find it to be ten years hence.

From Mrs. Boone's went to the hotel to see Miss Pollie Haynie—was seized on my way by Alice S and Belle Boyd who insisted on carrying us captive into the parlor—made our escape but were re-captured in Miss Pollie's room and forced in self defense to comply with their request to sing and play. Our audience consisted of Dr. Dorsey, the young physicians and some of the ladies—made Dr. Blackford's acquaintance—not at all favorably im-

pressed. Fannie Stewart and her Father leaving tomorrow for the South flee-
ing the enemy. Will write to the boys by them to be mailed at some inter-
mediate point. The cars have ceased running to town and we have no other
way of sending letters now than by private hand.

Found the family and Mr. Brerwood at dinner on my return home. My
visit to town saddened me so—there was so much excitement—each one has
a different tale to tell, a different opinion to advance, but all agreeing in one
particular viz—in being as wild and as insane as possible. Among other rumors they had it that General Beauregard was dead—don't believe it though
just because Dr. Kennedy told me.[20]

Cousin Mary left after dinner and Emma and I had to entertain Mr. Brerwood until Father came home about four o'clock P.M. He was directly from
Strausburg and stated that the wires had been cut between that place and
Winchester, but seemed to think the citizens unnecessarily alarmed as Jackson was still in W.

Scott came in about five o'clock. Emma repeated the "Raven" for us and
Scott sang some of his most amusing songs. He expects to leave for the army
tomorrow, poor fellow! so sorry—don't know when we shall ever see him
again. (Later) Giles has been over to bid us "good bye"—he goes to the army
tomorrow—was with us till quite late but as I was writing to the boys saw but
little of him. He brings a rumor of a victory achieved by Price in Missouri. Also
a successful brush by Magruder at Newport News. Hope it is true.

March 12th, 1862

Bright morning. Emma, Ma, Laura and Willie went down to Rose Hill and
soon after they left Mr. Richards called by to say that Jackson had fallen back
from Winchester and the enemy were in possession of the place—one of the
river bridges had been burned. So we might look for our guests expectant
any day. Eliza Hope came in to sit with us in the morning, but was very soon
summoned home. In the afternoon Nellie and I made some preparations looking to the advent of the Yankees. We opened our writing drawers and had a
general review of old letters and notes—burning some and putting others in
a place of security.[21] Such a time as we had with these pleasant mementoes of
a happy past;—with the souvenirs of absent friends, miniatures, locks of hair,
faded flowers, little poems, etc. While surrounded with this heterogeneous

mass, a rap at the door was followed by the entrance of Scott—his face flushed and eyes dancing with excitement as he exclaimed: "Good News!" "Guess what it is!" Not being Yankee enough to accomplish this, he told us that the "Warren Rifles" were at Gaines' X roads and that Willie R. had come across from thence home where he would remain a whole day and two nights. Johnston's army was moving across country thru Page—it was supposed towards Staunton. Scott thought as the Rifles would probably go in that direction, he would join them in Luray. While discussing the matter, the little children came running in to say that the "Yankees were coming." Upon looking in the direction indicated, we really did see a Cavalry company entering town, but it proved to be portions of Ashby's regiment, and Ma coming home from Rose Hill soon after told us Walter was among them and would be over in the morning to see us. Jackson had retired from Winchester and the Seventh Regiment, being the rear guard, were very near being cut off by the enemy, who had already possession of W. Oh dear, what commotion!

Scott sat until sunset singing and playing with us and then took his final leave—poor fellow. I wonder shall we ever see him again. . . .

March 13th, 1862

Walter came in with such a cheerful face this morning. Gave us a hearty injunction not to be discouraged by present unpromising appearances—assured us "all was well," we would "soon be free" and with a kiss and embrace had vanished like a ray of sunlight. His company is stationed as advance picquet at Nineveh—poor fellow, he deserves a nobler foe than these hound Yankees.

Scotty, Giles, and Charley left for C. this morning as it proved a mistake about the Rifles going to L., they were at C.

Grandma and Aunt B. were away today and we had a quiet time of it. In the afternoon Nellie and I went down to see poor old Aunt Betty—found the old woman very sick indeed—ministered to her wants and then came back to Ma, who I knew would be lonely. Read and worked on my knitting until late. Mrs. M., Julie and Eliza with us after tea. Father learned from the paper smuggled in today that Beauregard had evacuated Columbus bag and baggage, and was fortifying Island #10 in the Mississippi—*Can* it be true? The reported victory at Norfolk is confirmed—our vessel, The Merrimac, sunk two of the Federal craft. Glorious![22]

March 16th, 1862

Though cold and muddy this morning, we concluded to go to church. Found Eltie, Cousins Mary and Emma there almost alone, it being quite early. Eltie leaned over pew and told that our bogus Military Governor appointed by U.S. "Pierpont" had issued an edict to the effect that every man within the Yankee lines who refused to bear arms for the North should be arrested and imprisoned—perhaps executed. This intelligence proved one drop too many in my cup of sorrow, and when they just then commenced singing "How firm a foundation," that old soul-stirring hymn, which even in childhood had the power to melt and subdue my heart as nothing did, my heart overflowed with the fulness of conflicting feelings. I cried as if my heart would break. The first tears shed since our army deserted us. It was not fear that affected me so much as pain at the contrast between our present situation and the times when we were wont to hear and sing that old familiar hymn. It used to be my favorite "lullaby" and then it was the strain we brothers and sisters always were wont to sing with united voices when together assembled those Sabbath evenings at dear old Bel Air—an unbroken home circle and so happy. Later, I remembered it as it used to ascend from the congregation collected together in the old church where we all went, still an unbroken bond—still happy. And now—Oh, the change! Separated from those dear members of our household by more than mere distance of miles—by circumstances that might well preclude our ever hearing from them again. Our country over-run by our remorseless foes—there we sat, completely in the power of our implacable enemies whom we were hourly expecting—enemies who would pillage and destroy our homes, imprison or exile all our natural protectors and leave us poor females and children defenseless, without the means of subsistence and at the mercy of these St. Bartholomew assassins.[23] Oh it was all so terrible and everything seemed so much darker than ever before. Cried until relieved by giving vent to long pent up feelings and then composed myself to listen to the most impressive and comforting sermon from the text "Let not him that girdeth on his armor boast as him that putteth it off." So appropriate to the occasion and so applicable to the state of our country that it was a whole sermon within itself, and then Mr. Berry made it the source of so much comfort to us. Felt quite calm by the time church was dismissed and after exchanging greetings with our friends came home. Father laughed at the idea of our distressing ourselves so needlessly about the retrograde motion and quite reassured us by saying he was convinced it was a false alarm. After dinner Ma proposed walking over to see Mrs. Hope. Found them very blue, but they cheered up very much before we left. Remained until after tea and then walked home across the fields. This is certainly the most terrible day I've spent this year.

March 17th, 1862

Ma, Nellie and I concluded to do some visiting before the Yankees came. Ma went shopping and Nellie and I called at Mrs. Cloud's—found all quiet there notwithstanding the excitement prevailing elsewhere. . . .

. . . Found Aunt Bettie and Mr. Brerwood on the look out for us, spent a pleasant day laughing and talking. Commenced reading "Grace Truman," which Nellie had borrowed from Mrs. R.—not much struck with the commencement of the book. We left at five o'clock and called at Capt. Roy's for Cousin May, who had promised to go home with us. She told us, however, that Mrs. R. was alone, the Captain having left during the day for the farm and she had promised not to leave her. She and Cousin E. begged Nellie and I so earnestly to remain with them that we at last consented. Spent a pleasant evening and just before tea Gibson Roy came in to give us the items of news from the court held during the day. After tea we spent an hour in the parlor singing and playing and looking over daguerreotypes—Nellie's favorite past-time. Had quite a discussion of the times seen in a spiritual point of view. G. deducing arguments from events now transpiring to support his opinion that we were fast tending to the millennial period and making some very original and striking observations. Retired after ten but Cousin M. and I were awake chatting nonsense until after twelve o'clock.

March 18th, 1862

Awoke about four o'clock this morning and lay ruminating until dawn when the sweet little spring-birds poured forth their glad matins. A bright, beautiful morning—dressed and went down stairs to enjoy the envigorating air, but was soon glad to take refuge in Mrs. R.'s room from the cold. Remained until ten o'clock when giving a parting benefit to our music we coaxed Cousin Mary off and came home. . . . Father soon entered and told us that heavy cannonading had all day been heard in the direction of Strasburg. We

all flocked to the old trysting tree and could distinctly hear each heavy booming report, rolling and reverberating through the mountains—sounding
perhaps the death knell of many brave young spirits—aye even those near
and dear to us for Father said that Ashby's Cavalry was undoubtedly engaged
in the contest and Walter and other cousins were there. I felt as I stood there
that I would give anything on earth to know they were safe, and that our
cause was victorious. Mrs. M. and E. Hope came running over from home
attracted by the firing and wishing to learn from us something of the cause of
it. We, of course, could tell them nothing. While standing there talking who
should ride up but Dick Bayley. He had "run the blockade" through the
Federal line—escaped from Winchester, where he was living comfortably
and in comparative safety and come to join the Southern Army at this most
unpropitious time. How I admire his spirit—and he so young, too. He represents the Yankees as very jubilant over their late successes, but behaving with
more moderation than could be expected of them. Had seen Northern papers
in which it was confidently asserted that Beauregard was fortifying Island #10
and denying the formal report of his death. That's good news at least. . . .

March 19th, 1862

Commenced sewing for Dick quite early—Cousin Mary assisting us—but
a message from her mother soon hastened her home. After a short time
Aunt Bettie came in to spend the day and then Dick and Mr. Brerwood and
Mr. Berry and Uncles Tom and Mack—quite a levee we had. The cannonading still continues and everyone believes a sharp conflict is going on—
though nothing definite can be learned. Worked steadily until five o'clock
when we completed our task and gave it to Dick to carry home with him. He
took a final leave of us—expects to join his regiment tomorrow. Poor fellow—how little he realizes the trials and dangers of the service into which
he has entered. He seemed so gleeful when he left. Father came in late saying
Ashby had received orders to engage the enemy near Woodstock and continue falling back until he decoyed them into the narrow pass in the mountains where Jackson would wait to give them the warmest of receptions.
There has been much firing, but "nobody hurt."

[March 20, 1862, entry omitted]

March 23rd, 1862

Muddy and disagreeable, but Father, Nellie and I went to hear Mr. Berry. Ma was with Aunt L. Buck. Immediately upon taking my seat by Emma she inquired what I thought of the "news from Winchester"—was much surprised at my ignorance of any news and proceeded to enlighten me. It seems a soldier had just arrived from Strasburg and he stated that our troops were advancing to that place en route for Winchester which place the Yankees had evacuated—the reason ascribed for their movement was that they were ordered back for the protection of Maryland, where the inhabitants had risen in rebellion against the vandal crew in power there. I laughed incredulously at the rumor—but oh what a feeling of thanksgiving I experienced when, after church was dismissed, I found that those who were competent to judge credited and corroborated the tale. O, if it be but true! . . . Mr. Berry's sermon was such a good one—the subject, the contest between David and Goliath, in which he so plainly proved the superiority of the physically weak, who rely upon a Higher power, to the might of the strong, who confide entirely in their own strength. It was so comforting.

March 24th, 1862

Nellie absent and I had the prospect of a lonesome day before me—but reading, teaching and sewing prevented ennui. Ma was quite sick in the afternoon and as she took refuge from the noise of the children in Aunt B's room, I followed her thither and sat reading the "Richmond Despatch," which however, contained no items of interest save a very pithy editorial about the bogus neutrality of England. . . .

After night I was sitting alone by the fire thinking of our absentees when Father came in and said that Jackson had been worsted in the conflict yesterday. It seemed that he received forged despatches from Johnston ordering him into Winchester upon the plea that the enemy was evacuating that place to go for the protection of Washington and Maryland. 'Twas a miserable Yankee trick, a trap which they had laid for him, for when our little army of 3000 advanced, it was immediately surrounded by 20,000 of the enemy lying in wait for them. Jackson stood his ground manfully and only retired after killing ten to one of the enemy and losing three pieces of the artillery.

Oh, it is too mean, too contemptible, the petty stratagems to which they must needs have recourse! They cannot meet us in open honorable warfare, cannot subjugate us by force, and so depend upon their Yankee craft and cunning.

March 25th, 1862

Had seated myself to teach the children this morning when Cousin Mary and Elizabeth Cloud were announced. Went in to see them and Cousin M. had just commenced telling us the contents of B's letter when Uncle Newton and Aunt Jane entered, and soon after came Emma, Cousin Newt and Cousin Tom, the latter the same genial affectionate relatives that they ever were. Cousin N. told us he had seen the young Blakemores, not one of whom had fallen at Donelson. Oh, so glad to hear it! After dinner we played and sang a little until Cousins N. and T. took their departure and then Cousin Mary, Emma, Laura and myself went upstairs and had a great time concocting a scheme of mischief and revenge. While thus engaged, Ma hastened in pale and breathless with excitement to say that Uncle Newton had just come in bringing intelligence that the Yankees were over the river at Mr. Richards'. Our company instantly dispersed like a flock of frightened pigeons. Father went up to Strasburg today and Nellie was at Mr. Richards', both in the midst of the Yankees, and we were so anxious to have them safe at home again. I felt utterly astonished at the nonchalance with which I heard of the miscreants being so near us—did not experience the least symptoms of fear. I suppose we have so long been expecting them that their advent has become a matter of course. Father came in about five o'clock under considerable excitement— said he was on the pinnacle of Fort Mountain and witnessed the progress of the Yankees down the Valley from that point—was once very near meeting them face to face in a narrow defile of the mountain. Just about sunset when patience had waxed thread-bare, we were startled by a loud shout and presently in bounded Nellie and Dick waving scarfs and cheering "Jeff Davis." Forthwith they launched into an animated description of the descent of the Yankees—told how they were very near capturing Dick in his Confederate uniform and how they *did* take poor Mr. Kendrick away from his little sick children and poor delicate wife, leaving them almost heartbroken. They described them as being "men" but anything else than *gentle* men. They have returned to Winchester—am so delighted that they did not cross the "Rubicon" this time. . . .

March 26th, 1862

The morning was so bright and beautiful that we could not resist the temptation of spending it in the open air. Emma, Nellie, Laura and myself with Dick, Orville, Allie, Carey, Woodville Moore, Willie J. and Eddie Myers all boarded a nice little truck on the railroad and were soon flying along as if by steam. We spent a most delightful morning—went down to the old "Tank" and found some beautiful little white flowers, the first of the season. It reminded me so much of the excursion which we took about this time last year, and the remainder of the pleasures of the morning were much marred by thinking of the difference, the carelessness of our enjoyment then, and the fitful gleams of clouded sunlight that were cast upon our lives now. But our happiness or misery in this world are so often all comparative, for had I not known the brighter, sweeter joys of the past would I not now feel my usual delight in the present—in the dawning spring, for the sunshine is as golden, the birds and brooks sing as musically, the sky is as blue, the air as invigorating as ever it was when such sweet influences used to thrill my soul with exquisite pleasure. I sometimes wonder if there comes to the denizens of this world one single hour of perfect happiness and content. One hour in which the soul does not yearn for something which it has not and cannot have. If there is, I have never known that hour—at least not since childhood. . . .

Commenced reading the "Pilgrims of the Rhine," am delighted with it! There seems to be so little real happiness that I would like to make for myself an imaginary life in the mimic world created by the author's pen. I like to merge my individuality into that of the imaginary characters, enter into all their joys, share their trials and forget the ugly realities of real life around me. 'Tis wrong I know, enervating to the mind and unfitting one for the part which, however reluctant, we must play in the world and in the end creates for us a deal of unhappiness, but, for the present, it diverts one from sad reflections, and I feel that anything is preferable to thinking and fretting over disappointments entirely unavoidable and irremediable.

March 27th, 1862

Had a bad headache this morning—taught the children though and then tried a nap without success. Poor Dick came in late in the forenoon to kiss us goodbye, for he's going in reality this time. I could but look at him so young and small going to engage in such arduous duties and endure hardships such as were never dreamed of in his philosophy—Poor fellow! I thought it was a hard school for him to learn in. He told us Mrs. R. had a letter announcing the welfare of the boys, that was all.

Had the headache terribly until Cousin Mary came in about three o'clock, when I had to arouse myself to entertain her. She brought B.'s letter to Ma, but gave no news. She says Henry Buck is at Clover Hill and Cousin Mount at Cousin Sam's sick. Fear the Feds. will get him. While we were chatting before the fire, about five o'clock Laura ran in and announced that "The Yankees were coming" and verily there were about forty Cavalrymen gallantly cavorting along into town with as much assurance as if they had a right to do it. I do not think we any of us felt the least sensation of fear—every tremor of timidity seemed swallowed up in one great feeling of anger and indignation. We expected though that they would certainly immediately commence a series of depredations, but they did not remain in town over fifteen minutes. Rode up to the hotel and made some inquiries respecting the political sentiments of the people and received the comforting assurance that they were "Sesech" to a man. One, who proved to be the veritable renegade "Porte Crayon" inquired if the Rev. R. T. Berry were in town.[24] Being answered in the affirmative, he and the rest of the company raised their caps and hoping that we might "never have a more unfriendly visit from them" said "Good-bye" and decamped. Cousin Mary went home after the exodus. Must go to bed and try to sleep my headache off.

March 31st, 1862

This morning was bright and beautiful as yesterday was gloomy. Was hearing the children recite when someone came in and said that the Yankees were down at the mill. We immediately looked out and saw three of the wretches coming over the hill by the ice house, crossed the meadow, went down to the little foot bridge over the creek and stood there taking a leisurely survey of the premises. On our bridge they stood where we have so often spent such delightful hours sitting on it in the twilight looking at the creek shimmering in the moonlight and gemmed with the stars—stood there with as much assurance and composure as if the place belonged to them. We were so provoked at their coolness. They went on up the mill road to town. After dinner I was in Ma's room rocking the baby in my arms and singing "Maryland" in no suppressed tone and the Yankees came up on the porch step. We were determined not to let them *see us*—so peeped out of the window and saw two of them sitting on the porch and one leaning against the pillar, looking so insufferably, coolly impudent that I would have liked to have shot them. To think that they should dare come here and pollute with their foot steps the dear old familiar home spots sacred to the memory of so many dear associations! They requested something to eat, and though we would have rather given them a "stone or a serpent" than the "bread" they asked—yet we were in their power and dare not refuse them—spread for them a very frugal meal for which they had the hypocrisy to thank Father. Doubtless they were overpowered by their debt of gratitude. Mr. Brerwood came in and he and Father subjected them to a regular cross-examination which they endured with commendable fortitude. Certainly their faces do bear most ineffacably the impress of their characters. I never yet saw the traces of low cunning and beastly ferocity so plainly written on human countenances. They soon departed with many promises of good behavior—*of course*, they'll *keep* them (?). After they left, Aunt Bettie came in and Mrs. Moffatt, Julia and Eliza and we had quite a hive of buzzing Sesessionists. All left about sunset. Who could have thought that we could thus receive in our midst our deadliest, bitterest enemies without any sensations other than those of rage and curiosity?

April 1st, 1862

This month one year ago witnessed the commencement of our horrid war— witnessed the inauguration of all the sorrows we suffer—witnessed our separation from our soldier friends. Will the anniversary of it dawn upon the conclusion of all our troubles—will it restore to us those dear ones in health and safety? Heaven only knows. I had almost said I would wish to lift the pale that shrouds the future and read the record of the coming year, but I would not. "Sufficient unto the day is the evil thereof."

Ma, Laura and I went to town—Nellie preferred remaining to superintend the spring cleaning in the parlor. We went first to Mrs. Roy's—found her still in bed, but full of mischief—she taught me the only prayer I can ever offer for Abraham Lincoln. Cousins M. and E. tried to tease us about our "Yankee guests" as they termed them. . . .

In the afternoon Aunt L. Buck and Miss B. came up apparently for the single purpose of talking "War," a theme of which I have grown weary enough. Sitting by the window we saw five soldiers ride towards us and at first thought they were Yankees—but so soon as they saw us they raised a shout for "Front Royal and the ladies" and called out "No Yankees here." We sprang to our feet as if electrified and moved to and cheered them most heartily. They seemed like dear friends, those brave Confederates and we watched them with straining eyes and beating hearts as long as they remained in sight. They were perhaps the last of *our* soldiers we should see and seemed to be a tie between us and our army and absent friends, and when they were gone that tie was severed and we felt more than ever forlorn and abandoned.

When we returned home in the evening after tea, they told us the Yankees had all left the River and were gone to Winchester. Glorious! Found on my arrival at home a card bearing "Porte Crayon's" name—an April fool from Cousin Mary Cloud—will retaliate. Read aloud to Father the speech made by Henry L. Benning in the Charleston Convention, a most able and lucid argument. Heard cannonading again today.

April 2nd, 1862

Was engaged with my pupils this morning when Eltie R. came in—was most agreeably surprised to see her—surprised because the day was so damp and disagreeable. Had the neuralgia terribly all day and was too stupid to make myself at all agreeable, but the family did the talking and I listened. "Cuffee" came in the afternoon bringing Eltie a "Dispatch" and a letter from Willie. The latter wrote that *our* boys were well. When Father came in to tea he explained the cannonading heard yesterday. It seems Ashby's Cavalry had been hovering about the advancing columns of the enemy until he—Ashby—reached Woodstock when he rode through the place—planted several pieces in the further end of the street opposite to where the enemy would enter, piled bales of straw and rubbish about him and stood waiting their entrance, the inhabitants having been previously warned to remain indoors. As soon as the advance guard of the Yankee cavalry crowded into the streets, he gave the order to "Fire!" and the shrieking, hissing messengers of death dropped into their very midst, killing and maiming numbers of them. In this confusion Ashby ordered the straw to be ignited and under cover of the thick smoke retired, and by the time they commenced returning his fire, he was, unknown to them, standing on an adjacent hill coolly surveying their operations. Noble and gallant spirit! May he live to reap and enjoy a rich fruitage of success and ample reward for his untiring devotion to our glorious cause.

Wrote a note to "Porte Crayon" and one to Cousin Mary tonight.

April 5th, 1862

Mr. Brerwood came in this morning through the rain to say that he intended going to Maryland as soon as he could—would return in September. After dismissing my scholars went upstairs to read, and thus employed about an hour when Willie came up to say that there were "Two Baltimore soldiers downstairs, one exactly like brother Irvie." Went down and was introduced to two young gentlemen—a Mr. Barrett and Mr. McCormick of *Clarke County* not Baltimore as Willie imagined. They had been at the Virginia Military Institute until within the last week—when reflecting upon the great need the State had for *all* her soldiers, they took French leave "and came off to join their comrades in the ranks." They had walked all the way from Lexington—spent several days with Jackson's Army and were now en route for home where they would remain but a short time before returning to the Army. How I glory in such spirits! So young as they are and yet so resolute in discharging what they conceive to be their duty to their country. Mr. McCormick was the prototype of dear Irvie so that I felt that he was like a familiar friend instead of a perfect stranger. The sight of him has troubled the depths of my spirit and created within my heart such a yearning to look again upon the dear absent brother's face. After dinner Nellie and I played and sang for them and they made ready to resume their march promising to call on their return next week. Orville and Cary acted as their guides a short distance. They are apparently nice young fellows and I dislike to see them venture into danger as they are doing in returning to Clarke now.

April 9th, 1862

Did not wake until late and had quite a scuffle to be ready in time for breakfast. Found the snow eight or ten inches deep on the ground and travelling on foot out of the question. Everything looked lovely—the peach trees were just ready to bloom and each little pink bud was encased in dazzling crystal armor, which produced a beautiful effect where the rays of the sun fell upon them, and the violets, too, looked royally through their gem-like covering. It snowed steadily until in the afternoon. Jule and I went upstairs and had a cozy little chat all to ourselves—a philosophic dialogue—very edifying. After dinner I tried to continue my reading but the girls were leagued against me for a general romp and tried to force me to join them. I was disinclined. They tried to vex me into it, and at last I had to take refuge from them in my room. Threw myself on the lounge and tried to get a nap, but could not succeed. On going down into the parlor again, I found the girls looking very sober. In explanation they said Uncle Mack just returned from town where he heard that Jos. E. Johnston had been ordered to Fredericksburg, where an attack was expected. Uncle Mack was very much distressed and we were all very sad to hear it, but tried to be hopeful and had our usual singing in the evening and sat up until quite late laughing and talking about "old times" with Aunt L. And after going upstairs the girls played a number of pranks that kept us laughing until long after we were in our beds.

April 10th, 1862

The sunbeams were abroad early, thus gladdening us all by their enlivening presence. I think I never saw a more beautiful snow scene in my life—the dark pines and evergreens borne down by their fleecy burdens making the woods look like a gigantic encampment with its white tents. And these were mingled with the more delicate and graceful of the sisterhood of trees that looked liked cascades of diamonds. 'Twas so beautiful! Some of the girls proposed walking home, but Cousin Mary and I vetoed the wild resolution. Alice and I read steadily all the morning and until three o'clock in the afternoon and finished our book despite the efforts of Nellie and Jule to prevent us. I do not think the work a very profitable one, it's well written and interesting as giving a very vivid picture of the manners and customs of the people and age and well serves to beguile a weary hour—yet one could be better employed than in reading it. In the afternoon Nellie appeared in the parlor in masquerade and amused us very much by her representation of the invalid North Carolinian just from the "horsepital." This reminded Jule and me that we might have a deal of fun by coming out at night in full fancy costume and we made preparations accordingly, but while sitting at the tea table a servant came in and announced that Rob Roy had brought an open wagon to carry us home in, and said they had sent us word there were two young Baltimoreans at our house. I did not know who to believe they were, but concluded they were some acquaintances. We were a merry party that drove off from the house cheering for "Jeff Davis" and so waving adieux to Aunt L., who stood in the door to see us off. On our way down the mountain we met Uncle Mac who insisted upon our returning to Bellemonte with him and wait until daylight for our trip, but we concluded moonlight was preferable and go we *would*. He told us that news had reached town of a very important victory achieved by Beauregard at Corinth in which he had taken vast numbers of the enemy prisoners and captured eight batteries. Magnificent, if true! How we shouted and blessed Beauregard! The moon was shining brightly by the time we reached the foot of the first hill and we all commenced singing our traitorous songs, which were ever and anon interrupted by some wild sally or gleeful burst of laughter from one of the party. Everyone seemed intoxicated with the beauty of the night and the pleasure of the ride. We were singing "Maryland" when driving around the hill at Bel Air, and all the family were on the stile to greet us, seemingly as much excited as ourselves. Each one had something to tell, or some question to ask, and such a chatter as we kept up for the ensuing half hour. There was a saucy letter from Scott to Nellie, enclosing her an excellent parody upon "Maryland." They had heard in camp of the victory at Corinth and were, of course, jubilant. We learned that our Baltimore guests were a young Reed and Coffield—new acquaintances but rebels, who had run the blockade and come over from Maryland to join the celebrated Ashby Regiment. Though very youthful in appearance, the young gentlemen were evidently no novices in the service, having been living a sort of bandit life on the banks of the Potomac for seven months past, and it was most amusing to hear them recount their various escapades while in this guerrilla service—they are shrewd boys, both of them. We gave them "My Maryland" in full chorus and very soon after they departed not daring to remain where they would be so convenient to the Yankees should the latter take a fancy to cross the river at the invitation of some of the traitors in our midst. As they would go to the army early in the morning and offered to mail any letters we wished to send to the Confederate lines, Jule, Nellie and I put on our dressing gowns, drew up a table before the fire, trimmed our "tapers" and commenced writing, although it was near twelve o'clock. Nellie wrote to Scott, Jule to Henry and I to the two "boys." Nellie concluded her incubations half past twelve, Jule at one o'clock and now, weary and utterly exhausted after writing a long, long letter, I retire at three A.M. 'Tis very doubtful as to our having another opportunity to send letters out.

April 12th, 1862

Were all very sober this morning with our reading and sewing. At noon someone came in saying they had seen a gentleman from Jackson's army— he brought news that a dispatch had reached that General from General Johnston, stating that Beauregard had not only achieved a victory, but a *great* victory, having taken from 6,000 to 9,000 prisoners, 50,000 stand of small arms with eight batteries. We were perfectly enchanted with the glorious news, which, if true, must prove a great thing for us.

I ran out in the garden this afternoon to gather some violets for the girls, who had a great romp over them when I came in. Alice and I were flying through the back-yard when suddenly while circumambulating a mud-puddle I lost my footing and was most unceremoniously precipitated upon my face. Such a graceful sight as I presented upon regaining my equilibrium? Muddy from the waist to the hem of my dress, hands, face, sleeves and all. The girls enjoyed the spectacle wickedly. . . .

April 13th, 1862

Cool and cloudy, but pleasant withal. Very stupid but the walk somewhat refreshed me. The sermon was as usual most excellent. After church was dismissed noticed groups of gentlemen in earnest debate in the church yard, and upon inquiring learned that Dr. Dorsey had seen a newspaper containing an account of the victory achieved at Corinth on the Sunday preceding—but it seems this advantage was counteracted by the defeat which we experienced the next day when the Federals, being reinforced, attacked and captured a large number of our forces. The news cast a gloom over many a countenance that had before been comparatively bright—but I for one do not believe it all. Jule went to Dr. Turner's—Ma to Uncle Tom's to dinner. Alice, Nellie, Laura and I came home. Found Cousin S. Buck there, had a message for Alice. After dinner Alice and I amused ourselves reviewing old letters until three o'clock, then she left—much to my regret. Read and wrote all the evening—then Orville and Cary came home from Bellemonte and announced that Walter was at home—had just come on a scouting expedition with no very agreeable companion—viz,—the "Mumps." Ma and Father came home at eight o'clock. Ma had seen a "Dispatch" in which the late battle of Corinth alias Shiloh was discussed—'twas no defeat on our part.[25] Beauregard *did* gain a victory and only retired from the battle-field at Shiloh to his entrenchments at Corinth. Good—he may still be victorious!

Walter came in early this morning and told us an Irishman had taken prisoner a Yankee courier down at the "Y" and sent him on to Genl. Jackson. It does me so much good to see Walter. He is so cheerful, so sanguine of success that his very presence inspires me with renewed confidence. He confirmed the news of the victory at Shiloh, which was a very important one though not so great in results as was at first represented. He was busily talking when Jule and Neville entered. They said they must start home immediately as the Yankees were reported only six miles distant and expected in town every hour. Walter laughed very much at the idea of our feeling so anxious about him, saying he defied them to take him if they would only give him a mile's start of them. Walter and Jule both left about eleven o'clock and then, the weather being so tempting, Ma went to town to spend the day. Amused (?) myself renovating my summer ward-robe, as I see no prospect of having it replenished this season. Mr. Berry dined with us and I had to preside at the table. Went in the parlor to practice after finishing my sewing when little black Mary came in with a note from Aunt Bettie begging us to spend the night with her, and as an inducement said that Cousin Sue was there. Found upon reaching there, not only Cousin Sue, but two young soldiers members of Ashby's cavalry who had been on very dangerous service and very daring in scouting in the enemy's lines. . . .

April 17th, 1862

This morning while dressing heard that a cavalry company had been quartered in town during the night and could see their horses picketed in the depot lot. After breakfast they rode by the house en route for Harrellsville. 'Twas such pleasure to wave to and cheer brave Southern boys! Walter soon came in to say that Bowen's were in town—presently a sick soldier came in to rest and recuperate. After the company which passed this morning (Capt. Gilmore's of Clarke) returned and quartered in town for the remainder of the day. Two of them came over to get their dinners and I did enjoy waiting on them at table—for ragged and unpolished though they might be, they were yet our defenders and protectors and perhaps the last Confederate soldiers we should see. The day was one of great excitement—running to the door every few minutes to wave to the scattered detachments of scouts constantly passing to and fro—each time thinking that the next soldier we should see might be a foeman—'twas no wonder that we looked wistfully and sorrowfully for our own men. Walter was over three times during the day, and then about twilight when we were all in the garden twining the roses over their frames when he came in, took a hasty supper, spun us some camp yarns and was off again on some *mysterious* and I *knew* dangerous expedition. Went in the parlor after he left and played and sung—recalling the anniversary of the night when we first were startled with the intimation that the Virginia troops would be the next day called to gird on their swords for the contest. The sick soldier returned to stay over night and he amused us much by his account of the Battles of Manassas and Kernstown.

April 18th, 1862

Were out early this morning to see the return of our picquets when Walter dashed up to the stile and begged for a bit of breakfast—had been out all night with Gilmore's company—walked six or seven miles through the "Forks" seeking a detachment of Yankees who had been the day before pillaging there—but the birds had flown and their toil and trouble were of no avail. Walter seemed worn out with the fatiguing walk and loss of rest and went to bed and slept until ten o'clock. Uncle Mack came in at noon and said that Jackson was falling back from Mount Jackson because of the insufficiency of his force. Oh, it seems every day that our desertion by our army seems more and more inevitable, but we must trust to Providence and under Him to our Generals. Could hear no confirmation of the reported victory gained by Johnston and Magruder at Yorktown.[26] Oh, for a Richmond paper! Was very unwell all day—got cold working in the garden yesterday evening. Sat up as long as I could and crept up into Laura's sanctum where I lay down thinking so much of this day a year and of the changes since then, a sad, sad year it has been to many hearts. This was the day year that so many dearly loved relatives and friends left us in the bloom and glow of high-hearted, fresh-feeling youth and who might never be with us again, or if they do return can never be as they have been to us. Our merry-hearted play-mates will be all gone, and in their stead we shall welcome home stern, war-worn soldiers. We shall never *any* of us be the same as we *have* been. Do I not know how gradual and yet how sure a change this comparatively short season has wrought in me—because not *physical,* the alteration may be imperceptible to others—but none the less sure and marked. And alas! 'tis not for the better—for I grieve for the loss of a freshness and buoyancy of feeling which the progress of the year has swept from my heart as a rough step brushes the dew off the flowers. The blossoms are apparently unimpaired in their loveliness, but, deprived of the refreshing, cooling drops, that lent them such a charm, they soon wither and fade. I wonder if the boys remember this day. . . .

This, too, is an anniversary memorable for the great riot in Baltimore.[27] Tried to be well enough to pursue my usual routine of duties, but was soon forced to go to bed where I remained until the afternoon, when feeling better, I went downstairs. Walter rode up in all the hard rain to bid us good bye, as he intended returning to camp with Gilmore's company when they came back from their picquet duty. He laughed and told us an adventure which he and Lieut. O'Farral had just had. They heard, it seems, that the Yankees were crossing the river at the mill and they concluded to try and bag a prisoner and started off together. Upon reaching the hill overlooking the ford, they saw four of them on this side of the river, two on horse-back and two in the boat just pulled up to the shore. Walter flung his reins into O'Farral's hands and leaping to the ground ran nearer the river and fired—but as he had nothing of longer range than army revolvers the ball fell short of its designation. The Yankees, startled by the report and thinking there were, of course, more than two men among their assailants, made for the river throwing their very guns in the water, so frightened were they and one even left his overcoat on the bank. Walter ran down to the bank and fired again, and this time, although the boat was near the middle of the stream, the ball just whistled by the ear of one of the voyagers. He shouted to them assuring them that they were only rebels, two of them, and entreating them for an opportunity of making a horse by the encounter. They replied by a shower of minnie balls from their long range rifles—five more Yankees having joined the fugitives who had reached the opposite shore. They fired volley after volley, but their balls whizzed harmlessly by our brave boys. By the time five or six Confederates, who had heard of the skirmish, came up, the Yankees were gone. Those who from a distance witnessed the firing said they were firmly convinced that Walter bore a charmed life else he could not have escaped being shot. *He* did not tell us all this, but we heard from those who saw the whole affair—he *did* tell us though how mortified and disappointed he was that he did not capture one at least of the miscreants. We were anxious to have him leave immediately before the Yankees (who were daily expected) should come in, but he resisted all our entreaties—said that he could not leave Gilmore in such a predicament as he was in—cut off from every avenue of egress to our lines and a perfect stranger to the mountain by-paths. 'Twould be discourteous and cowardly in him—he must wait for Gilmore at any rate. When he said this, we said never a word more, and I was secretly glad of his decision. Brave, generous fellow! We may well be proud of him.

April 21st, 1862

Still raining. Played for Emma and Walter after breakfast until the latter said he would go to the river and make enquiries for "that overcoat the Yankee left" him and be back in a little while. Soon after he left Gilmore and his whole company passed the house, bringing with them some half dozen captured horses and a brace of the Yankee captives themselves. The Capt. was mounted upon the most superb charger I ever saw—paused at the gate to enquire if we had any commands to be executed in the Confederate lines—then bowing, turned the head of his noble steed and rode on in front of his braves. How enthusiastically we cheered them and waved our Secession Scarfs and how they shouted and cheered in return! They had been 'in *eight miles of Winchester* and escaped to a *man*. I suppose Walter has gone with them and we won't see him anymore—it is sad enough to think of indeed. . . .

April 22nd, 1862

Ceased raining and cleared off this morning and Emma persisted in "going home," despite my assurances that she would freeze, mire and get drowned. . . . Jackson is moving towards Richmond and the Valley is fairly evacuated. Well it *is* hard, but I suppose we might as well submit with a good grace to the varying fortunes of war. Mr. Berry came over in the afternoon and told us he had seen a paper giving an account of the "brush" at Yorktown, which seems to have been a small affair. We repulsed the enemy though. Walter went yesterday.

April 23rd, 1862

Mrs. Cook came in about nine and sat till near noon—says our latest advices treat of another and more decisive victory on our part at Yorktown. But we did not believe it. Dr. Dorsey dined with us and croaked like a very bird of ill-omen—said Island No. 10 was certainly taken and that we had lost very heavily in the engagement; that the enemy had possession of Fredericksburg, where they had burnt our manufactories. Confusion! Ma and Grandma were already very low-spirited and hearing this they were literally submerged in the "Slough of Despond." [28] As the day was so fine, Nellie and I concluded to go to Mountain View. We took Cary with us and had a delightful walk through the woods, gathering wild flowers and mosses. Found all well and received a hearty welcome. Aunt Bettie came in from Mrs. Wheatley's and took tea with us. Uncle Newton came in from town and told us a great deal about the depredations committed by the Yankees in Fauquier. After tea they were discussing a bill before the Federal Congress for the confiscation of all

Secession property in the hands of their troops. If it be passed there's no telling the awful consequences that will flow from it. The ruin and exile of hundreds of families and our own large family of little children. Oh! it has depressed and troubled me more than anything I have yet heard—my heart feels so sore and heavy with the thought of it.

Mr. Friston will run the blockade and go to Richmond tomorrow, so Nellie and Aunt Jane wrote to Charley and sent the letter by him.

April 24th, 1862

Found it very cloudy and threatening this morning. Cary left after breakfast and then Cousin Sue took us up to her book-case and gave us a carte blanche invitation to its contents. Nellie laid violent hands on some periodicals and I took down "Shakespeare" and Tennyson's "Idyls of the King" to read, while Cousin Sue was engaged with the children's lessons. Had been long wishing to read these "Idyls" and never had the opportunity before. How I enjoyed the poems so peculiar in style, so quaint in expression, so much freshness and beauty of thought—altogether so unique and charming. Finished before dinner. Willie went to town this morning and returned with the news that the Yankees had been in town and taken Mr. Fristoe prisoner. So! the villains will have the pleasure of reading Charley's letters—if they do, they will not be the first who have made good the old adage "Eavesdroppers never hear any good of themselves." They did not tarry long, but went away carrying with them Mr. F. and two horses, which they somehow managed to get from Uncle Fayette. We read nearly all the afternoon, and Nellie and I played and sang a little for Aunt Jane and Cousin Sue. . . .

Sat up till late tonight reading. I've thought so much of this day one year ago when we went over to Dr. Turner's and sewed for the first time for Confederate Soldiers. We spent such a pleasant day and Willie R. and Walter were there and how Walter laughed when I could not understand his ruse to conceal the reception of my letter. Poor boys, I wonder where they are now.

April 26th, 1862

Warm this morning and a prospect of a clear day. Dressed quite early and went out into the porch and sat a long time listening to the birds just beginning their matins as the sun drew aside its cloudy curtains and beamed forth on the world. Everything was very peaceful and lovely—the mountains just beginning to wear that soft, hazy vernal appearance they always present when the forest trees are in blossom and the fields and meadows spread with their first emerald velvety turf. But 'twas not of the present so much as of the past that I thought. The 26th of last April witnessed the departure of our dear boys and the presentation of the Warren Rifles Flag to the little band, leaving home and loved ones to battle in their defense. What a thrilling address made by Mr. Cook as he placed the standard in their hands—what tears responded to it—what farewell embraces and kisses, what warm, firm grasping of kind, true hands that were clasped perhaps for the last time—the piteous wail that went up from the sorrowing hearts of the multitude, who witnessed the departure of their dearest and best on earth. The tears that coursed down rugged, furrowed cheeks, all unused to such baptismal. The bright drops that bedewed the faces of the young soldiers themselves—drops that were an honor to their manhoods—not weakening their resolve, not unnerving them for duty, but attesting their heart-felt appreciation of the love of kindred and country—the priceless value of the things they were to contend for. All this I thought of all this day and felt thankful that I could review the campaign upon which they entered with pleasure and pride, for not one of those we loved had proved recreant, not one fallen by the hand of the foeman. It was more than we could have thought or hoped for. Just then the soft notes of a flute floated out on the morning air and mingled with the bird songs so plaintive and sweet the melody that I could not repress a gush of tears. Cousin Sue came out and proposed a promenade down the walk and by the time we had taken a few turns the breakfast bell rang.

April 27th, 1862

Fine bright morning. Uncle Mack, Mr. R. and Kattie M. here early. Had our bonnets on to start to church when they said the Yankees were coming—went out on the stile and saw them march in—a file of infantry with their bayonets glistening and arms flashing in the morning sun. But for all their fine accoutrements they were a hard looking party to judge from the specimens we saw straggling up the railroad. We went to church wearing thick brown veils. Passed one of the vermin on the street with his arms about the neck of a strapping "colored gemmun," and his lips in loving proximity to the lips of ebony.[29] In comparing the two together, I confess I thought the Yankee lost by the contrast. Was too angry and excited to profit much by Mr. Berry's sermon. We had vowed not to let a Yankee see our faces, but just after church, while standing in the yard with my veil up, speaking to a friend, a most Satanic looking Yankee passed and looked me right full in the eye. It was too provoking, and we very quickly dropped our veils and turned our backs on him.

We could see them all day straggling about so brutally intoxicated that they could scarcely circumambulate. Picquets were stationed at the entrances to town and relief guards sent regularly out, to prove to us, I suppose, that we were regularly invested—rather *infested*. Uncle Tom came over in the afternoon and told us about three who had been at his house. They asked for "dinner" immediately after their arrival and alleged as a reason for going there that they wished to see the residence of so noted a "Secesh" as "Col. T. Ashby" (of course this was all a romance—they knew Col. Ashby did not live there). They then paid a flattering tribute to his prowess, and hoped that he might never be shot as they wished to capture and keep him for a "show." Then they wanted to know if Uncle Tom justified Ashby's course? He replied in the affirmative and added that he also endorsed his son's. At table they behaved like Goths as they are. After dinner one of them sought more congenial society in the kitchen. Uncle Tom proposed that he should return to the house, as in Virginia gentlemen were not accustomed to occupy the kitchen. He and his comrades soon after that departed, remarking as they left that "They liked this part of Virginia so much they intended locating here." At Uncle Tom's suggestion that they should select farms they replied "they had already done so." They announced that the Virginians "were really nice people," not near so "stuck up" as they had imagined.

Ma and I walked up to Mrs. Hope's this evening. Found them all very "wrathy," but withal amused at the uncivilized conduct of the interlopers. Well, one comfort, they've not been near the house today. Some of them said in town today that the Union could never be reconstructed, and they were tired of fighting. I believe the servants despise their deliverers from the bottom of their hearts. Bah! They're greatly their superiors in good breeding.

Accidently broke the philipena ring which was put on my finger with a wish last year. So sorry! Can it be ominous? I could never bear the idea of breaking a ring. Now the wish will never be realized.

April 28th, 1862

Had a very restless night—suffered from neuralgia in my face.[30] Felt better after breakfast and went bravely to sewing. There were several visitors this morning; Mrs. Marshall and her daughters and Mrs. Moore. Was miserable— whiled away the time reading the Northern papers. It is exasperating to read their "canards" and their poor attempts at wit at the expense of the Confederacy and Secessionists. I wonder if they suppose we are crushed and discouraged because of a few reverses in the tide of fortune. If they *do* I hope they'll ere long have optical demonstration of the fallacy of their opinions. Father heard that there had been a complete and decisive victory by our army at Yorktown.[31] Oh, for truth! . . . Heard that forty-two of these creatures dined at Clover Hill on Friday and behaved very rudely. Should like to have seen Jule and Aunt Lizzie—know they were the personification of unmitigated dignity.

April 29th, 1862

Raining. Heard a low sullen whistle from a locomotive in the direction of the "Y" this morning, and presently a rumbling sound announced the approach of a train of cars. One might have guessed they were Yankee cars by the slow manner in which they came in. Nellie says the whistle was "under breath"— "suppressed and fearful." Suppose they were afraid some rebel guerrilla would hear them, discover that the railroad was repaired and being used and would take the pains to come and destroy the track again. They were evidently very cautious, for it took them one-half hour to run from the "Y" to town where *our* cars used to accomplish the distance in five minutes. It was so provoking to watch the old green Pennsylvania passenger car as it passed the house crowded with the "azure imps." Don't know anything that has provoked me more than their using for their own wicked purposes the road which cost our State so much time, trouble and money. They were very quiet though—did not make any kind of demonstration over their grand entry as we expected they would, but we shall have more of this anon, I suppose.

It cleared off beautifully toward evening, and after teaching the children and finishing my sewing, went up to my own cozy little room and hoisted my window. A perfect shower of bird songs and bright sunbeams floated in on the evening breeze—I drew out my portfolio and commenced a letter to the boys, which will be a kind of diary, continued from day to day, until I have an opportunity of sending it out to them—really enjoyed the writing, as it gave a vent to some of my pent up indignation. After tea, Ma, Nellie, Laura and myself went up on the house top, thinking to get a sight of the Yankee camp over on the river hill—but found we could not, and it was no great disappointment. Had a glimpse of a most lovely landscape instead—valley, hill, meadows and mountains all looked so charmingly fresh and verdant in their soft spring vestments, and the little "Happy Creek" was murmuring a vesper in unison with the birds, lending interest to the scene, which would else have been all too still and lifeless. After coming down, Nellie and I were in our room revising a song—a parody on "My Maryland," when we heard strange footsteps on the porch below, and presently Ma came up to say there was a Yankee Q. M., down in the dining room drinking milk. It seems that Father heard in town of his having made considerable exertion to protect Mr. Armstead's property the other day when the cowardly rogues were depredating there, so as the young fellow passed through the yard just now, having missed his way to church, Father and Ma, who were sitting on the porch, saw him, and the former thanked him for his courtesy to a fellow citizen and invited him to partake of a glass of milk, which invitation he gladly accepted. Am half sorry that Father should voluntarily offer one of our enemies refreshment, but I suppose it is well to encourage honesty and humanity whenever it is found among them. The Yankee behaved like a civilized being and departed leaving his card, "Daniel B. Hildt," the name inscribed thereon. He professes to be acquainted with Cousin T. H. Blakemore and avers that he is himself a merchant of Philadelphia. Declared himself as very tired of the war, but did not refer to politics at all.

Have rocked the baby to sleep, practiced on the piano and now "welcome Somnus."

April 30th, 1862

Ma and I walked over to town this morning with our *thick veils* on. Stopped at the store at first, then while Ma went up to Mrs. Roy's, I called at Mrs. Cloud's. . . . Kattie Samuels has a letter from her husband and he writes from Conrad's store near Harrisonburg. So Jackson has not left the Valley as we thought—and oh! who knows but he may come to release us from bondage soon? God grant it.

Found Mr. Myers and little Laura Gallister at home upon our return. Mr. Myers says he heard McClellan was shipping his men from Yorktown— what means it I wonder! We were sitting in the chamber this afternoon, laughing and talking when a slight tap at the door was followed by the entrance of three great uncouth Yankees. Nellie and I kept our eyes upon our work, and did not vouchsafe so much as a glance at the intruders. Ma was afraid our manner might exasperate them and quickly directed them to the sitting room. They wanted their dinners and Father coming in just then carried them to the dining room, where they devoured the food spread before them, for which they offered to pay—just as if they thought we kept "private entertainment." Father declined their pay and told them that there were hotels in town where persons usually went when they wished to contract a bill for boarding—this was customary in Virginia. He did not know *how* it might be where *they* came from. That Southern gentlemen never refused a meal *gratis* to those who could not afford to pay for it. They had scarcely left the house before two or three more of the roughest looking creatures came to "get" their "suppers." Ma had not even given orders for that meal and so they said they would wait until it was prepared. I was angry enough to have given them battle—they, Ma and Grandma, would not let Nellie or I put our heads out the door while the Yankees were here, would not let us leave the room and here we were in "durance vile" until that supper was given out, cooked and dispatched. While waiting for it, they told Father that a movement on McClellan's part had disarranged Genl. Johnston's plans at Yorktown, thereby compelling him to fall back towards Richmond and the final struggle would take place between the two places. They also said New Orleans was in their hands and there's only too much reason to believe their tale. Oh me! the cords seem drawing closer and closer about us. Tomorrow a detachment of Geary's men are expected in town, and then martial law will be proclaimed.[32] And oh what next no one can guess. Have just been reading aloud to Father.

May 1st, 1862

A disagreeable, rainy, misty morning—congratulated myself upon what I thought would afford us one day's exemption from the troublesome vampires.

Vain hope! Was sitting in Grandma's room when we saw a Yankee wagon drive up to Father's barn, and the soldiers accompanying it commenced appropriating the hay therein. We watched them from the window—presently Father appeared upon the scene, and then the wagon drove off and he with a half dozen of the creatures came towards the house. Among them was Hildt, our quondam visitor.[33] Guards were placed around the house and they went to work examining first the granary and then the smoke house. This time, however, they took nothing there being as Hildt averred "nothing to spare" in the way of meat or corn. They will doubtless be back again and re-consider the matter. Oh it was so provoking to see the sentinels pacing the yard as though they really considered Bel Air a prison and we their lawful captives. Father went to town and when he returned told us 3000 of Geary's men would be in about three o'clock and Front Royal would probably suffer. He had just seen one of their Lieuts., who told him that he had always heard this was a "*fast* place" and that "if the people did not behave themselves very nicely it would be *slower* before sundown." The wretch! We have heard the fall of New Orleans confirmed. Ah, woeful day for the South! I don't despair of our final success, but there seems to be such a vast fathomless gulf of misery through which we must wade to attain to it. Oh my heart shrinks with dread at the prospect! If I were only prepared for death how gladly would I yield this troublous existence for one of that "Peace that passeth all understanding."

. . . Geary did not come, neither did his men. One night more of grace allowed us. I am utterly worn down—this existence of passion and excitement is wearing away my strength like a consuming fever. When the day closes, I feel as if it had been lived in a perfect delusion. I agree with Nellie that if this state of things continue, I shall burn up with wrath. Heaven forgive me if I sin in it!

May 2nd, 1862

. . . Sally came in very soon and told us they were going to administer the oath to every gentleman in the place—unmitigated wretches! About five o'clock a hundred infantrymen marched into town, bearing with them their poor disgraced old "Star Spangled Banner." Made no demonstration upon taking possession of the place. Hildt called in to "buy some eggs" in the evening and told that there had been a skirmish between the Yankees and

Ashby's men, and also that there was a battle going on at Yorktown, but did not state the results as thus far developed. Ah me! truly we have fallen upon evil days.

May 3rd, 1862

Looked out of the window very early this morning expecting to see the "Stars and Stripes" floating over the Court House, but was most agreeably surprised to find it "non est." Martial law was proclaimed in poor little Front Royal and sentinels stationed at every avenue from the place. Three of Father's servant men who went into town on business were arrested and detained in town until late. When Father attempted to go over to have them released, he was halted by the sentinel and told that he would not be permitted to return home again if he should go within their lines—so he was forced to beat a retreat. I had not been able to get Ma to confess she was angry until from an upper window she saw Father compelled to submit to dictation and restriction thus upon his own premises. She *was* exasperated then truly. It was a lovely day and we spent the greater portion of it upstairs at the windows from which with the aid of our spy glass we could witness a great deal of what transpired in town during the day. Could see the citizens as they were every now and then arrested by the patrol and marched off to "Headquarters." Could see the tents pitched in the Court House yard and all the bustle and confusion consequent upon the first forming an encampment. Oh but 'tis galling to see them taking such cool possession of *our* town and our property and *figuratively* shaking their fingers at us and threateningly telling us—"Now behave yourselves—we're your masters and if you but so much as *breathe* rebellion against our authority we will consign you to a corner of 'Davy Jones' lockers." And we dare not resist so much as by a glance of defiance! When we know too that if one of Ashby's companies should dash in they could bind every Yankee villain of them hand and foot and carry them away over the mountains—for they have neither their artillery nor gunboats here now, and everyone knows a Yankee can accomplish nothing without *these*.

All day the creatures were calling in or passing by the house, keeping us in a state of continual ebullition, but the climax of our indignation was not capped until about five o'clock when a cavalry company passed and among them we recognized a mulatto in uniform. This boy a short time since had fled from the best of masters and joined these miserable hypocrites. Yes, there he rode at the head of the detachment as grandly as the first officer among them, and he looked as if he felt a savage satisfaction in thus coming back to his old home and lord where he had once served. Yet I should not blame him near as much as I do his instigators. I am so weary and exhausted with rage that I could scarcely drag myself up to my room tonight. Ma tells me it is so wicked to allow my passions to get such an ascendancy over my better feelings, but I cannot help it—it seems as if I am *possessed* of an evil spirit as well as *surrounded* by them.

May 4th, 1862

To think that although it was so pleasant this morning we could not go to church because of our Christian-like garrison! Saw from the upper porch their Sunday morning dress parade, which took place in *Uncle Tom's front yard at Oakley*. Poor Aunt Bettie! How lonely she looked standing out on her portico, for all the world like the prisoner she is! There she stood looking through her spy glass at *us* and *we* regarding her so wistfully in the same way. Was sitting in Ma's room about 9 o'clock reading when I was attracted to the window by the sound of coarse, rude tones addressing Father—and saw three ragged old "Teutons" gesticulating violently and heard one of them say— "But we've a *right* to know and we *will* know." This frightened me, but I at once concluded that they suspected Father of harboring some designs against them. Laura just then ran in saying—"Come Lucie, give your testimony." Stepped into the passage and saw Ma there with Father and she told me these men had been on guard last night and fancied they saw us displaying signal lights to the "Secesh Cavalry" in the mountains. Father told them that the baby had been sick during the night, and that Ma had to have a light in her chamber (which was the case) and then taking them into the front yard explained how it was they had seen the light shining through her windows. They professed themselves perfectly satisfied with the solution of the mystery and begged for a draft of milk—this they disposed of with remarkable gusto. They then warned us against permitting any lights to be seen after nine o'clock, as they had been ordered to fire into them wherever seen—advised us to either extinguish them or have very thick curtains over the windows. They had been ordered to fire at the house last night and would have done so but for the kindly interposition of Mr. Seymour, who told them that what they saw was probably a sick lamp, as our family was a large one and doubtless some member indisposed. Now was ever there such cowardice! Soldiers frightened because of a sick taper in an infant's chamber! Veteran Warriors. I presume we are to have a revival of the old Curfew system, but surely such a state of affairs cannot last always.

After the Dutchmen left, I got "Butler's Analogy" and read aloud to Father. Had just become interested in the book when poor Father was called to see another Yankee. This one, however, a young Corporal from Philadelphia seemed to be rather better than the generality of his class, and I was very much amused at his conversation, which I heard without making myself visible. He had come to ascertain whether or not there had been any of the previous night's guard over to see about *that* light—then explained that the sentinels were intoxicated and they imagined they saw such a pyrotechnic display. He remarked that the matter was a subject of entire indifference to him anyway, as he had not come here to fight or for love of the Union—he had been very desirous of travelling and seeing more of the Southern country and thinking a soldier's life would best permit the indulgence of his fancy he joined the army. Professed to have no sympathy or patience with the Abolitionists and said that if they with the turbulent spirits of the South had been hanged long ago, it would have averted all these troubles. He prophesied that Lincoln was the last Republican President who would ever occupy the executive chair. Father was much pleased with these sentiments expressed with such naivete and upon the strength of it offered him some tracts, which he took saying he would reciprocate favors the next day by bringing him some papers—gave Father his card "Charles McGetigen" of Philadelphia. Well, he does seem more like what a human being *ought* to be than anyone of his tribe that I have yet seen.

Much to our surprise and delight Aunt Letitia Buck came in while we were at dinner—she had "run the blockade" to church and then succeeded in getting over here. We were so glad to see her as she was the first of our friends we had been able to see since our imprisonment—then she could give us items from town. Uncle Mack she said had attempted to come to church, but they even *threatened to shoot him* if they ever saw him on horseback again, because "some Secesh" cavalry in citizen's garb had shot some of their men sometime since. Poor Uncle Mack! What is to become of such an active restless spirit limited and confined thus? 'Twill be terrible to him. Poor Father is writhing in spirit under this galling restraint. I can see though he speaks but little he grows perceptibly older day by day—looks already so bowed. Aunt L. also told us that the "Rangers" were reorganized under Cousin Horace Buck as Capt., Mr. Simpson, 1st Lieut., Mark Wells, Second and dear Walter Junior Second. So delighted to hear it! Soon after Aunt L. left, Julia Hope and Mrs. Moffatt came up and told us Mr. Fristoe had been released and returned home and his captors did not take either his money or his papers from him. Mirabile dictu!

How delighted we were this evening when we saw the tents struck and the whole of Company E marched out of town. We at once concluded that the whole garrison had been summoned away to reinforce Banks up the valley. But alas! we were doomed to disappointment for the other two companies remain. Oh dear! what an unsabbath like Sabbath we have spent! and yet how could it be otherwise in such excitement.

May 6th, 1862

Another morning we've risen in safety to welcome the bright May sunshine! The boys were engaged with father, so I did not keep school. Ma and I concluded to sit a couple of hours with Mrs. Hope but nothing would satisfy her until we promised to stay and dine with her, as she wanted us to share her peaches and cream with her, and also a cup of *real genuine* coffee, something of a novelty to me now, as I left off drinking the *rye* coffee the first of May, thinking our present supply should be reserved in case of sickness and knowing we shall in future be dependent on the Yankees for our groceries— of course, I do not wish to patronize them. . . .

Read aloud to Father tonight.

May 7th, 1862

Felt very sick and low spirited this morning—even Aunt Bettie and Uncle Tom who came in during the forenoon and sat a couple of hours, were not a remedy, although we were so glad to see them. After dinner, I took myself off upstairs where I sat writing and ruminating until Ma came up to sit with me. Just then Mr. Richards rode up, and . . . told us that Jackson had engaged Banks at McDowel and defeated him, driving him back 12 miles. That was all very well, but alas! he tells us our prospects are very gloomy in every other respect and we cannot but credit what he says from everything we hear. Thus the horrors that have hovered over me all day have begun to assume a tangible form. Never before have I allowed myself to dream of subjugation, but now when even Father is despairing, I begin for the first time to realize all the perils and dangers of the stormy sea upon which we are launched—for the first time opened my eyes to the awful consequences of subjugation. God knows what is to become of us all—our bark seems fast hurrying against the breakers—if "he does not interpose a strong arm to arrest our destruction we are indeed lost!" Lost! My own dear brothers!

May 8th, 1862

This morning Mrs. Moffatt and Eliza came bounding in whispering—"We've such good news for you." They then repeated the news we heard yesterday with regard to Jackson's victory over Banks and added that General Johnston had surrounded McClellan in such a manner as to completely cut him off from receiving reinforcements or supplies—that the Yankees in town were looking very dispirited and a number of little incidents she related which served to revive our courage no little. Spent the greater part of the day up at the window, reading, sewing and spying. In the evening after tea we walked with Father down to the old mill where I had not been for an age. It really looked like an old half forgotten friend with its discolored mossy wheel dripping with the cool bright drops that fell into the water below with the same musical unobtrusive tinkle so like I have heard them hundreds of times long ago. Then the weeping willow—how it had grown! and how like a cascade of verdure it looked in the soft May twilight with its graceful flow of verdant branches. We stopped to exchange the compliments of the Season with old Uncle Ben and Aunt Bettie. On our return found May in the garden with the flowers and we stood there a long time watching the mountain which was burning—it looked beautifully, reminding me of a volcano so liquid seemed the flame and smoke that shot up and hovered about the peak. We admired the scene until the damp evening air admonished us to return to the house.

Laura read to Father and I commenced reading "Queechy" aloud to Ma— have so often heard it highly spoken of that I have been anxious to read it for a long time—have not gone far enough to get into the merits of the book if it has any—so cannot judge how I shall like it yet. What lovely moonlight evenings we have now, but alas cannot venture out to enjoy them for fear of lurking Yankees.

May 9th, 1862

The day promised to be so beautiful that Ma and I concluded it would be a moral impossibility to stay at home any longer, so we agreed to spend the day with Aunt Bettie. Tried to persuade Nellie to accompany me, but she would "none of it" and we were obliged to content ourselves with Carey as her substitute. Had not the slightest difficulty in getting to town—called at Capt. Roy's where all were apparently delighted to see us and such chattering as was kept up the hour we remained.—So much to hear, so much to tell. Cousin Mary took me up to her room and pointed out the encampment just back of the house and I saw how all hours of the day they were annoyed by having the Yankees passing through the yard for water. They're ruining the lot and have actually torn the lining out of Capt. R.'s carriage to use instead of curry combs for their horses. . . .

Did not encounter a single Yankee on our way home. As we reached the foot of the hill I thought I had never seen anything looking more beautifully about the dear old home. The lilacs in the front yard were literally over-whelmed—bowed down beneath their sweet burdens of rich plume-like blos-soms, while the soft evening air was redolent with their perfume. Nellie was sitting on the stile waiting to tell us the good news; she had heard the victory at Corinth confirmed and flattering news from the Peninsula. Am afraid to believe it all though. Played some on the piano this evening for the first time in an age. Have been reading aloud to Ma tonight.

May 12th, 1862

We were much amused this morning by the arrival of two couriers and a messenger besides from Major Tyndall, the Provost, requesting Father to form one of a committee of citizens who were to convene at his Headquarters in the afternoon. Good! Instead of Father having to go and solicit of his "Majesty" he is cordially *invited* to see him. . . .

Father came home before tea and told us all about the furious meeting at Headquarters. All the principal citizens were present, the object of the convention being (as Major Tyndall said) to "consider how best to arrange for the mutual benefit and convenience of citizens and soldiers." He presented them with a paper which they were to sign—by this paper they were to pledge themselves not to do anything which would induce a collision between our men and theirs, whereupon all the Yankees were to be withdrawn from the immediate vicinity of town and not permitted in any way to interfere with the peaceful occupation of the citizens. This, upon consideration they concluded to do particularly as they knew how utterly powerless they were to give aid or information to our Army, no matter how much they might wish it. Yet, I am sorry for it—hate to think of my Father binding himself in any way to the old Yankee's conditions. . . .

May 13th, 1862

Very bright and beautiful. Grandma and Aunt B. in town. Have a very sore finger and could not sew, so spent the day reading aloud in "Queechy." I like it much better than I at first imagined I should. We were all sitting on the front steps in the afternoon when Father came up and said he had just heard that seven thousand of Shields' men were on their way through here from Luray en route for Fredericksburg and that the long expected Geary was coming too from the opposite direction. No more reading for us. As I felt very dull and unwell, Ma proposed a walk to the creek thinking it would do me good. . . .

Chapter Two

꙳꙳꙳꙳꙳꙳꙳꙳꙳꙳꙳꙳꙳꙳꙳꙳꙳꙳꙳꙳꙳꙳꙳꙳꙳

"Headquarters" Was Duly
Established at Bel Air

꙳꙳꙳꙳꙳꙳꙳꙳꙳꙳꙳꙳꙳꙳꙳꙳꙳꙳꙳꙳꙳꙳꙳꙳꙳

May 14, 1862–June 20, 1862

May 14th, 1862

An ever memorable day to the inhabitants of Bel Air. Found it raining very hard upon awakening this morning, felt quite unwell and went up to my room to lie down immediately after breakfast. Presently Nellie came bounding up the steps laughing, yet vexed, to tell me about three Yankee Dutchmen who had just come in to demand their breakfast—one proved to be a connoisseur of flowers and had been discoursing eloquently upon my poor little geraniums set out on the pavement for the benefit of the rain. Went downstairs with her and observing an unusual stir at the door, I stepped on the porch to learn the cause. Father came forward with a very grave face to say that General Kimball's brigade would be in immediately to quarter in the meadows in front of the house.[1] We were all perfectly thunderstruck and had not time to recover our scattered ideas before we heard the notes of the band and looking over toward the depot, saw the head of the column advancing into the field. On they came, a dark mass of human beings winding through the meadows like a great black serpent until the whole four thousand were in the two fields. They were a sorry looking sight, wet and muddy, with their dripping banner clinging dismally to the staff. Next came the wagon trains and the artillery—eleven pieces besides their caissons, and the horses and wheels cutting up the beautiful green fields terribly. Father's beautiful stone fence, too, had to be levelled to afford them ingress. Then came a regiment of cavalry to the barn where they unceremoniously proceeded to turn their horses upon a fine field of clover, which Father and I had been admiring so much just two days ago. One of Genl. K.'s staff now rode up and announced that Genl. K. would pitch his tent near the house to prevent the troops from molesting us—He remarked moreover that the General being much indisposed, would much prefer being under roof if he could. Knowing that they were to be such close neighbors at any rate, we concluded that it would be best for them to be in the house where their presence would be some protection to us. Father, therefore, told the officer that there was a vacant room in the west wing, which they might occupy if they wished. The proposal was gladly accepted and the other members of the staff having arrived, "Headquarters" was duly established at Bel Air. By this time the troops had gone through with their evolutions and the signal given to break ranks when ensued such a scene of destruction as I hope never to see repeated. All Father's beautiful fencing disappeared—melted. I could not tell how. It seemed as if the rails were endowed with a strange vitality so rapidly were they spirited away. They commenced upon the plank-fencing along the railroad and I could compare the quick regular blows of their demolishing hammers and axes to nothing but the gnawing of a monster worm in the wood. It was all endurable until the fence enclosing the field of luxuriant, heavy wheat began to disappear, then when I remembered that our dependence for bread next year was in this very wheat, I could only wring my hands and cry. To the credit of the General (Yankee though he be) I believe he did all he could to prevent unnecessary destruction; sent couriers to all the officers of his regiment expressly forbidding them to permit the demolition of outside enclosures threatening to hold them responsible for the disobedience of his order. The work of desolation was thus gradually arrested, and there were sentinels placed about the house and yard to prevent annoyance from intruders. The meadows soon wore a most stirring military appearance—dotted with white tents and miniature huts of rails and boards from which ascended curls of smoke looking quite comfortable. There were three tents pitched in the back yard ten feet from the door—one for the Adjutant and Capt. of the Staff, one for the clerks and orderlies and one for the servants of the Staff. If I live a century, I do not think I can ever forget this day—it was all the time dark and cloudy and the rain descending in torrents. All the while they were bringing in news of increased losses—now they had captured the pigs, now the cows had gotten loose and deserted to the thirsty Yankees, and now the mill was broken into and pillaged—comparatively speaking, little things—yet, in our nervous, excited state of minds, most vexatious. Poor Father! he could only walk the pavement with folded arms and drooping head looking helplessly on the scene of desolation, trying to bear up philosophically under all his troubles and losses for our sakes, but we could see what a mighty effort it required for him to appear unconcerned, how he struggled, how the day was doing the work of years bowing his form and furrowing his brow. This distressed us more than anything else. One incident of the morning impressed us very favorably—standing on the porch noting the arrival of the Staff, Charley McGetigen made his way up the hill, but as he passed headquarters was halted by the Genl., who demanded "Why he was there"? Saluting his officer respectfully, he replied "I have business with Mr. Buck" and hurried to where we stood and grasping Father's hand told him how sorry he felt for him and begged to know how he might serve him—if he should not detail a safety guard.—Upon our informing him that the Genl. had appointed one for duty here, he politely bowed and retired. He lingered near however, and a little while after—seeing Father at the back door, out of the sight of the officers—he tried to come to him through the back gate. But the sentinel stationed there refused him admittance, was deaf to all entreaties and the little Corporal with a farewell wave of the hand and a gesture of impatience cried out—"They won't let me see you" and walked slowly off. We *did* appreciate his evident sympathy and desire to serve us so much, he could have had no sinister motives in this I'm sure—if he *is* a Yankee I must believe him sincere.

It seemed so strange to have the sentinels pacing the pavement all the day, to see dozens of couriers dashing to and from the doors, to hear the tramp of dragoon boots, the rattle of spurs and clanking of sabres. And then such a busy scene as the camp presented, such washing and cooking, such housekeeping on a small scale! We had dinner for five—Genl. Kimball, a tall, spare, yet muscular man of about forty-five, a grave, firm looking face, acquiline nose, projecting chin, grey eyes, heavy brow and dark brown moustache and hair slightly grizzled: Captain Mason, a small, dapper specimen of masculinity, sharp nose and chin, florid complexion, pale blue eyes, vermillion hair, eyebrows and mustache—a disagreeable, sinister expression of countenance; Capt. Bunting, a Falstaffian looking mortal—bullet-head, full, chubby face, florid complexion, red hair and blue eyes—a perfect personification of the good-natured, well-fed, well-to-do Quarter Master; Adjutant Schweiger decidedly the finest looking of the party, tall and straight as a young pine, well proportioned, frank and modest countenance, fresh, healthy, boyish complexion, beautiful brown hair and whiskers and dark blue eyes and withal a very pleasant, quiet demeanor; *last* but not *least* Mr. Crippen, the reporter for the brigade—a foreign looking personage—a very frog-eating "Monsieur." [2] Nellie and I concluded not to eat salt with these Yankees and to wait until the second table to avoid an encounter—what was our surprise then upon stepping into the dining room to see the colossal Q.M., sitting tranquilly at the foot of the table—retreat was impossible, for he had observed us immediately and greeted us most politely whereupon we were reluctantly compelled to take our seats at the same board with his Yankeeship. In the afternoon I happened to be looking some hard things at a Yankee out of the window, when I saw a singular, cleric-military figure in regimentals crossing the yard. It proved to be one Freeman, the Chaplain of the 8th Ohio Regiment. He established himself in Ma's room, where he "proceeded to dry his feet" and I having occasion to go through there for a restorative to apply to Cary's head was introduced to him and compelled to show some seeming of good breeding. He drew me into conversation and made me so angry that Ma, fearing I should say something to exasperate him, came in and interrupted us. I got up and slammed the door. Old Hypocrite! his very countenance proclaims his insincerity. I was provoked enough with myself for condescending to exchange words with the old "wolf in sheep's clothing." He told me three consecutive falsehoods without any apparent violence to his feelings—seemed determined to convince me that the South was nearly subjugated and I was actually so excited as to indulge in a hearty cry when I went upstairs, thus losing the benefit of two bands performing in the meadows below the house.

There are some queer specimens of humanity quartered in the back yard. One whom Nellie (from seeing him perform some extraordinary feats) denominates "Breakfast"—another exactly realizes my ideal of that famous nursery bug-bear "Raw-head and bloody bones." Then there were "Wasp," "Freckles," "Red-head," "Mouth," "Nose" and "Mutton"—all characters in their way.

Took tea at second table with a red-headed Yankee much to my disgust, though truth to say he did behave very discreetly and I had the opportunity I had all day been looking for of saying something of all I have been thinking about them. After tea, Ma, Laura and I went on the house to see the camp fires, which looked beautifully despite the rain. Besides the brigade stationed here, there are two more quartered near Dr. Turner's. There were large fires on every hill surrounding town, and just where the principal encampments lay we could see the twinkling lights like thousands of stars clustered together in every variety of constellation. The camps immediately below the house looked like distant cities, but with rows of gas burners. The sight altogether was beautiful and novel.

Have been reading aloud to Ma until now at bedtime. It seems so strange to be sitting here in Grandma's cozy quiet room and hear the tramp of the sentinel on his beat just under the window—anon rings out on the night air the sound of hoofs as a courier dashes by, or the tattoo's beaten by some distant drum. I shall lay my head on my pillow tonight with a sense of perfect security, for I know the two sentinels before my door are responsible under pain of death for any intrusion or disturbance. Shields is really in town. . . .

May 15th, 1862

Was awakened by reveille and found to my chagrin that it was cloudy and rainy, which rendered a departure of the troops today very improbable. Eight Yankees to breakfast. We had *real coffee* and, not feeling well, I could have enjoyed a cup of it very much if it had not been *Yankee* coffee. As it *was*, we did not drink it at all. After breakfast they said *some* of them were going away and we went up to the dormer window to witness their departure. 'Twas only the artillery corps left with some few stragglers—still we accepted their removal as a favorable augury of a general exodus tomorrow. The children, although freely declaring their rebellious inclinations, have apparently made themselves great favorites with their new acquaintances. One of them gave Willie the benefit of the Butler's establishment today and being introduced to its delights, they have ever since been revelling in the unwonted luxury of oranges, candies, etc. The officers are all men with families and seem glad to be in the midst of little children again. The General in particular generally manages to have some intercourse with them as they pass him in his promenades on the pavement, sometimes catching them in his arms and kissing them. He met Willie yesterday and taking him into his arms inquired his name—upon being answered he clasped him to him and said "God bless you! I've got a little Willie at home too!" at the same time giving him a piece of silver. If he loves his "little Willie" so well he should have remained at home to take care of him.

Not so many couriers today, but a great clangor of drums, horses and fifes. When I went down to dinner today, Ma leaned over the table and told me the officers said it was rumored in camp that Ashby had been captured and carried off in an "ox-cart." I knew then how to account for the shouts that went up from camp a little while before. It was too provoking, and although Burwell, the red-headed Yankee, was at table I could not help expressing my aversion and contempt for people who were never better pleased than when they were circulating and crediting all sorts of palpable falsehoods, and wanted to know why it was that Beauregard, whom they had reported dead *eight* times had yet survived long enough to give them so much hard work at Shiloh. Ma remarked that the officers only gave the news as a camp rumor, and would not and could not vouch for the truth of it, one and all agreeing that there was not a man in the brigade who would *shoot* Ashby if they *could* so highly was he respected by them—Of course not, that's what they *all say* and yet, I never have heard of their neglecting a single opportunity of having a shot at him. Genl. Kimball said at table that the band would be ordered up in the afternoon to "play for the ladies." Uncles Tom and Mack came in after dinner. We were *so* glad to see them. Uncle T. says he has four or five very gentlemanly officers, one was Gen. Carroll quartered with him, and thus far had suffered no damage—expected an officer *with his wife* there tonight. Grandma and Aunt Betsy were still there, apparently very well contented. Mr. Berry also came over and contradicted the report of Ashby's capture. He says Shields had called a meeting of the citizens and told them that they should be reinstated in their losses. Am afraid the promise is too good to be true. While talking in Ma's room the band, a very fine brass one—had come up on the pavement and struck up an inspiring air, attracting a number of outsiders to the yard. The music was very fine and had the performers been any other than they were, I should have enjoyed it unspeakably. As it was, I liked it until they struck up "Yankee Doodle" and "Dixie"—*that* would not do *any way* as Nellie, Laura and I gave them to understand by turning our backs to the window and dropping the curtains. They were requested to play the "Mocking Bird" in memory of Irvie and some other popular airs. They did not know them, but offered to go down to camp, practice the pieces and come back and perform them. They just played their old "Yankee Doodle" with so much gusto because they knew how obnoxious it had become to good Southerners. And as for "Dixie" 'tis the height of impudence in them to appropriate one of *our* National airs. We were a good deal provoked and I had just gone into Grandma's room to try and regain my temper by reading when another band more magnificent than the first commenced discoursing sweet music under the windows. Dear absent brothers! when they played the "Mocking Bird," "Annie Laurie," "The Dearest Spot on Earth" and "Be Kind to the Loved Ones at Home," songs so often sung together in our home in so many happier hours—I could not restrain my tears. Just then that hound old crocodile Freeman stepped forward on the porch and called out in an insulting tone—"Boys! boys! you're no true Yankee soldiers if you could think of omitting to play "Yankee Doodle." Whereupon they commenced vigorously playing the odious Yankee air a second time. Down went the curtains and down they remained until the musicians departed. I do not know when I have been so provoked as at this piece of effrontery—for such it evidently was. Old Freeman has noticed how little pains we some of us— have taken to conceal our disgust for him. How we have tried to avoid him, and this was a species of mean petty revenge for personal contempt. The officers have conducted themselves with as much courtesy and delicate consideration as I ever saw in my life, but this miserable old Chaplain carries his character in the hypocritical expression of his face. Suffered all evening from a severe headache in consequence of "Yankee Doodle" and begged Father and Ma to let me go into the parlor and play "Johnston's March to Manassas" as a restorative. They consented provided I would not announce the name, as they thought it unnecessary to aggravate the Yankees, but, of course, I did not care to do so on these terms. They say there's a Virginia regiment in this brigade. For shame! I hope they'll keep out of sight.

Father and General Kimball while promenading the pavement this afternoon seemed engaged in an earnest conversation—the subject of which I guessed—the result I felt curious to learn. Presently Father came to the steps where Ma and I were seated and remarked that it was very strange what a horror all these officers seemed to entertain of abolitionists—all with whom he had conversed upon the subject denouncing them and General K. just having gone so far as to say if any man wanted to raise a fight all he had to do was to go down to camp and tax one of his men with being an emancipator. It is remarkable though that they still permit contrabands to go with them and harbor all who flee their masters, but I must say although I have endeavored to detect them in some way trying to influence our slaves, that thus far the effort has been vain. Their own servants were perfectly respectful to the family and seemed to have little to do with the others. Our servants conducted themselves even better, or at least more cheerfully than before. I have not discovered the least trace of abolition's cloven hoof unless it be in the black attendants they have with them and these are less numerous than I had supposed. When I went down to tea tonight, I heard Ma and Capt. Mason (the other officers had left the table) talking. Capt. M. was just saying— "When a minister of the gospel gets up into the pulpit and loses sight of religion in discussing political questions I feel perfectly disgusted with him and am well assured he has no right there." And he proceeded to give his experiences in that line. I liked his views so much and immediately conjectured that the conversation had reference to the Chaplain—so I enquired what he had been doing and was perfectly delighted to hear that the old sinner's free expression of opinion at the table had called forth a justly merited rebuke from the General who told him he thought "If Ministers of the Gospel would content themselves with expounding the scriptures and teaching morality and virtue" that "politics would come right of themselves." The Capt. seemed to enjoy the old nuisance's discomfiture most hugely, said he knew the General would not let slip so good an opportunity of giving him a hint— never *did*—and he had been expecting it all the evening. After he left the table, Ma told me how shamefully Freeman had talked—he's a black-hearted villain—an Abolitionist. Said he had formerly resided in Louisiana, but had left there with the full determination to do all in his power to "crush the

miserable rebellion." Poor old soul! if it depends upon your exertions—
either praying, preaching or fighting I think the South may rest perfectly
easy,—secure of achieving her independence.

We went up on the house to see the camp-fires and as the atmosphere was
clear they were seen to a greater advantage than on last night. Just as we
stepped out on the roof a band in the meadow below commenced playing—
not "Yankee Doodle," but a sweet, plaintive air, one of dear Irvie's favorites—immediately everything was forgotten, my surroundings, the Yankees
and everything, and the tide of thought and feeling flowed far away toward
the dear brothers whose sympathies I felt would be so surely ours now could
they but know our trials. Poor boys! how unconscious they are that their
home shelters, their hearthstone warms, and their fondest friends are compelled to contribute to the comfort of their bitter deadly enemies—enemies
hungering and thirsting for their heart's blood, and the life blood of every
true Southerner in the field. What though these foes wear the guise of gentlemen—the hilt of the dagger may be jeweled and velvet-cased, and yet the
blade none the less cruel and keen. What *would* Alvin and Irving think could
they know that their mother and sisters and little brothers were in the centre
of a hostile camp dependent upon their oppressors for protection from insult
and injury; to know that their father had to stand impotently by and see the
toil of years brought to naught in as many hours—had to stand tamely by
and have the names he honored, the sentiments he revered cast into his teeth
as terms of reproach. Oh! how long I sat there and "revolved the sad vicis-
situdes of things" until we were forced down from our retreat by the inclemency of the weather. Passing through Ma's room where sat Capt. Bunting and the old Chaplain telling anecdotes of their early life, I paused at the
window to listen until growing weary of the relation I came into Grandma's
room to prepare for bed.

May 16th, 1862

The reveille was the signal for my uprising this morning. The camp early
gave evidences of contemplated removal by the incessant hum and stir of the
assembled multitude. I was so glad when the first tent fell that I actually took
the trouble of going upstairs to witness preparation for the exodus—'twas
so very amusing to watch their "packing up." There was one little Yankee,

apparently an attache of the staff—Frank Crippen, who has quite won the hearts of the children by his telling stories and treating them—he did seem so very kind and fond of them and is such a lively, bright looking young fellow that I am reluctantly half inclined to think he's a good-hearted fellow. But no doubt he is an accomplished hypocrite and his suavity assumed to subserve some selfish purpose. We were on the porch when the General and staff took their departure—their adieux were very politely made, the General even promising to do all in his power to have Father reinstated—but, of course, we know the value of their promises. When the troops commenced their march we went up on the roof to see them defile past the house and were there all the morning for not only the three brigades, the one stationed here and the two at Dr. Turner's, but one at the river, making in all some twelve or fourteen thousand troops were on the move. I never had seen so many soldiers together before, and I marvelled at the mighty multitude, but thought how the number would sink into insignificance in comparison with the vast hordes now before Richmond.

Looking down on the deserted encampment just as the last column left the field, we saw Father (who had gone down to try to reclaim some of his "confiscated" plank and timber) joined by the little Corporal who grasped him most cordially by the hand. Presently they came to the house and as the young fellow congratulated us upon the removal of the troops, he seemed to feel almost as glad as we were. While they were all talking, Uncle Tom came in and said that Company McGetigen's had just been ordered from town on account of their having just heard that a part of Jackson's command was in pursuit of Shields. Do hope 'tis true. The Corporal left very hurriedly upon receipt of this information.[3]

Spent the day cleaning up the house and writing a little. Oh Me! what an intense relief this is! to be without a houseful of Yankees once more.

May 17th, 1862

A company of Yankees came in about four o'clock the band playing "Johnston's March to Manassas." Thieves! they come to steal our liberty, steal our property, our slaves, and, not satisfied with this robbery, actually steal our *National music*, which I should think would be the very last thing they would desire to do.

May 18th, 1862

'Tis said martial law is more rigidly enforced in town than ever. So much for trusting to Yankee promises! All Major Tyndall has to say in excuse of his perfidy is—"Tis a military necessity" and we have to succumb quietly. Dear, dear, dear! Such petty tyranny! . . .

Made several ineffectual attempts to read to Father, being always interrupted by the entrance of someone. . . . Nellie and I after tea went out to our old seat under the locust tree—it was a strange, gloomy twilight, the moon was shining, but in fitful, straggling gleams that cast a weird, pallid light over everything, the very faint shadows of the trees on the ground had a ghostly appearance. As we sat there and thought of the future before us so dark, so hopeless, as we thought of the separation from friends by greater barriers than distance, as we turned upon every side for light and comfort and saw nothing but grim, black despair, our hearts sank within us and we felt the still gloom of the night but a fitting type of the still horror of our souls. There is such an oppression on my heart tonight that I can scarcely breathe—such a suffocating sensation in my throat. If I could only cry! but it seems as if even my tears have been frozen up. There is surely some great evil impending over us—some awful "coming event" that "casts" this dreary "shadow before." God help me now! I feel how "vain must be the help of man."

May 19th, 1862

Was busily engaged bonnet making this morning and trying to inspire Ma with hopes that I could not cherish myself. Mrs. M. and E. Hope came in looking very mysterious and told us they "wanted to see the flowers in the garden." Upon going into the garden, however, they made the *real* purpose of their visit known by telling us they had news for us—it must be a profound secret though. A Southern paper had been smuggled in confirming out victories at Staunton and Corinth, and also stating that we had hurt the enemy severely at Williamsburg.

But alas! poor Willie Richardson, Giles Cook and Willie Rust were all slightly wounded—the 17th suffered heavily, but none of our immediate friends had fallen thank Heaven! Poor dear wounded boys! What would I not give for the privilege of nursing them carefully, tenderly now?

Cousin Mary Cloud, Mrs. Kiger and Kattie Samuels spent the afternoon with us—a pleasant afternoon it was. Kattie says Belle Boyd is in town en route from Richmond and will carry letters through to be mailed for our friends within our lines—will write the boys by her. Poor boys!

May 20th, 1862

Aunt Letitia Blakemore came up from Rose Hill quite early this morning and said they were all very much distressed about poor Willie. But alas! we *know* what they do *not*—having heard today that his left arm has been amputated and he a prisoner in the enemy lines. Poor fellow! what a mortification, what a misfortune to him! Giles Cook made a very narrow escape, but was only slightly wounded. Willie Rust had two fingers shot off. How thankful I am that they all escaped with their lives though.

I spent the day alone in my room writing a long, long letter to my dear brothers—it was a very dreary morning, but the clouds without were not as dark as the shadows on my heart. For weeks these shadows have been gathering thick and fast and I have struggled hard enough to dispel them with borrowed sunshine, until today when they lowered stiflingly around me I could restrain my feelings no longer and the long pent-up agony burst forth with resistless strength, and I wept passionately, wildly, wept as I had never done before in my life. At last relief came from sheer exhaustion—, relief from the *passionate excitement* of sorrow, but *not* from *distress itself*, for I felt completely crushed and heart-broken, yearning for the dear brothers whom I might never see more—for the cousins—one sick unto death in the hands of strange friends, one wounded and suffering in the hands of the enemy and others perhaps even now cold and still on the bloody field of death—victims to this horrid war. I felt how hopeless were our prospects for success in this life and death contest, where every advantage save the justice of the cause seemed to weigh in favor of our adversaries. Even Father has given up now.

In the afternoon Dr. Dorsey came in to vaccinate the children for the smallpox, two cases of which were reported in town—they sent for me, not knowing how hopelessly all day I had been sunk in the "Slough of Despond" to come down to hear him talk. He was in a perfect flow of spirits; had seen a paper containing an account of another victorious skirmish at Corinth, confirmation of the news from Jackson and Milroy and the battle at Williamsburg, though claimed as a victory by all the Yankees—was nevertheless a victory so dearly bought as to be equivalent to defeat. The news was altogether very favorable and the doctor conversed so encouragingly that I felt so much cheered and comforted and am calmer and more hopeful tonight than for several days past.

May 21st, 1862

Early finished my letter and Nellie and I took it over to Mrs. Boone's and asked Kattie to go with us to the hotel that we might deliver it in person to Miss Belle. Found a carriage at the door in which was seated the young lady with a Yankee officer—concluded not to intrust my letter with one who appeared upon such familiar terms with those whom we most dreaded, so crossing the street we went on up to see Cousin Mary and spent the day very pleasantly with her. Brought home some Baltimore papers giving an account of a repulse the enemy's gun boats had received at Drury's Bluff. Some of our scouts were said to have been seen in town last night. Wonder what *that* means?

The flowers are beginning to bloom beautifully and at any other time I should enjoy the season beyond measure.

May 22nd, 1862

Warm and bright—made a bonnet for Laura—had the blues badly. Poor Willie is really a prisoner and his arm *has* been amputated too—his family is so distressed about him. The Yankees went down to Rose Hill yesterday and stole all Cousin Elizabeth's bacon, salt and canned fruit. Miserable wretches! and they had actually the villainy to taunt her with her wounded boy's misfortune—such ruthless savages as they are! . . .

May 23rd, 1862 [4]

Was all the morning busily engaged sewing for Father. He came in about twelve o'clock saying he had made a very narrow escape from town—martial law having been so rigidly enforced in town that none of the citizens were allowed to leave the place, and he not being aware of this had gone over and narrowly escaped detention there. He said he feared the citizens would suffer for the necessities of life, for they were not permitted to go out to get either fuel or provisions. I told him I thought this extreme caution rather a favorable augury than otherwise, for I felt convinced that they had good reason to believe that the garrison here was menaced in some way, that I was willing to endure this oppression calmly for a short time if, as I believed, it presaged some change in the existing state of things here. He brought Ma a letter from Mrs. Millar giving an account of the death of her husband.

Although the afternoon was oppressively warm, so anxious and restless were we that Ma and I concluded to go up to Mrs. Hope's to see if they had heard any news. Found them very desponding—had heard no news save that Banks was reported to be moving his stores from Winchester, which proceeding on his part would seem to indicate a threatened attack upon that place, though we could not think what reason he had for fearing such a thing. While sitting there talking, a Yankee obtruded his head in the door and asked if he could "buy some pies and pigs" and scarce had his foot steps grown cold on the threshold when there was heard the quick, sharp report of a rifle and another and another in rapid succession. Going to the door we saw the Yankees scampering over the meadow below our house and were at a loss how to account for such evident excitement on their part until presently Miss B. White rushed in with purple face and dishevelled hair crying—"Oh my God! The Southern Army is upon them—the hill above town is black with our boys! Julia Ann, give me water or I shall die!" Of course, Ma and I did not wait to see the result of her case, but started for home in double quick time, all the time hearing the firing exchanged more and more rapidly. Found all excitement upon reaching the house—all the family upstairs at the windows. Nellie, spy-glass in hand clapping her hands exclaiming—"Oh! there they are! I see our dear brave fellows just in the edge of the woods on the hill over the town! There they are, bless them!" I looked in the same direction and saw surely enough some of our cavalry emerge from the little skirt of woods above the Court House. As long as I live, I think I cannot forget that sight, the first glimpse caught of a grey figure upon horseback seemingly in command, until then I could not believe our deliverers had really come, but *seeing* was *believing* and I could only sink on my knees with my face in my hands and sob for joy. Presently someone called out "Only see! The

Yankees run!" Leaning out the back window we saw them, contrabands and Yankees together, tearing wildly by. One obese Dutchman as he ran through the yard sans arms heard cheering from the window likening his speed to the Bull Run race—he looked most malignantly at us over his shoulder, but had not time to give vent to his feelings in words. There had been quick random firing all this time, and now, those of the Yankees who did not run at the first alarm, rallied and formed into line, some climbing into the dome of the Court House, some into the upper hospital windows, firing from these and making some feint of resistance.

By this time some scattered parties of Confederate infantry came up and charged their ranks, when firing one volley they wheeled about—every man for himself they scampered out of town like a flock of sheep—such an undignified exodus was never witnessed before. John Gilpin's race wasn't a circumstance to it. However, when they reached the hill north of town— opposite to where our men were entering the place, they halted and drew up in line in support of a battery that had been planted there. We all stood on the upper porch and waved and cheered our dear rebels, who were by this time pouring in eagerly from every direction. The larger body came down the Manor Grade, others down the Chester's Gap road, and others on the F. R. and Luray Turnpike, while there were yet others who eschewed all the regular roads and flocked through the fields and across the hills without re- gard to order or uniformity. Capt. Alexander's company now dashed by the house, returning our salutations and cheering manfully. Two of them, who proved to be dear Walter and the Capt. himself, cantered up to the door to inquire which way the Yankees had gone. We had been all the afternoon vainly trying to obtain a glimpse of Walter and now that he was really among us, his own cheerful, confident self, we were almost beside ourselves with joy. The children caught and kissed his hand as if he had been a host of deliverers in himself. He turned to Nellie, who stood sobbing near him and exclaimed in his joyous way—"Why Nellie, child! Crying? Cheer up! now is the time to be laughing. Jackson's army is coming and we're going to drive the Yankees away from you!" We could not speak for joy at his words and just then the enemy opened fire from a battery stationed on a hill north of town and Walter thinking there was work for him elsewhere ordered us all to the basement for protection and then rode calmly away regarding the bul- lets falling around him less than I should a heavy dew. We descended all of us to the basement where we found some frightened contrabands assembled.

The house was exposed to a cross-fire and we were all in really much more danger than we were at the time aware of—at any rate I could not bear the idea of being entombed ingloriously in the cellar while our deliverers were gallantly endangering their lives in our defense—it was not to be thought of for an instant—I must witness if not assist in the struggle. So Nellie and I went on the porch with a pitcher of water with the contents of which we refreshed our soldiers as they would ever and anon stop in their chase weary and thirsty. And all the time the cannon on both sides were carrying on a most animated dialogue—one shell whistling over the house and cutting the twigs off the aspen in front of the porch where we stood, another exploding in the barn—a third striking the mill—another falling in the meadow below. I did not feel the least fear as the missiles of death screamed and shrieked around—the sound was rather pleasantly exhilarating and I watched the discharges with positive enjoyment—did not one instant doubt our success in driving the varlets out. Our men soon succeeded in silencing the enemy battery on the hill and drove them across the river, having to encounter however a very heavy fire from a well disposed battery on Guard Hill. After some trouble we dislodged and pursued after them as far as Nineveh killing numbers of them.———here a most disgraceful circumstance occurred.[5] Two of our cavalry in a reckless charge fell into the hands of the enemy who called upon them to surrender, whereupon, seeing no possibility of escape, they grounded arms. Their inhuman captors no sooner saw them unarmed than they fired at them piercing them through the breast with rifle balls and killing them immediately. Such is the method taken by our invaders for cementing our affections to the Union. Now the death song of the Union has too long since and too often been sounded in the gasps of mortal agony bursting from the lips of the thousands of murdered brethren—the wail of bereavement going up from our thousands of desolated Southern homes and hearth. Union forsooth.

The skirmishing lasted until about sunset—a good deal of the fighting was done on the Rose Hill farm near the house and knowing how delicate the family was we were anxious to know how they stood it. Presently we saw Uncle Tom coming from there into town and we concluded to go across the street and intercept him to make inquiries. While standing there the main body of the army came in and we had an opportunity of cheering and welcoming in our gallant boys—regiment after regiment filed past all looking so pale and haggard, dusty and ragged and yet when we saluted the battle flag when they were going by, their countenances brightened, their step grew

elastic and cheer after cheer rent the air as they seemed to forget suffering
and danger in their enthusiasm. Cousin———to where we stood and chatted with us a few moments telling where and how the boys were and adding
that some of our friends had a letter from Irving—dated the 3d saying all
were well and in good spirits. Then he went on to rejoin his company and
we returned home to tea. Found Mr. Morris———and our afternoon acquaintances there—indeed he remained all night. After tea went out on
the pavement to listen to our bands playing as the regiment celebrated and
while there we heard the car whistle and in a little while a train of several
cars came in. Major Wheat of the New Orleans Battalion had captured
the———————————telegraph wires had been cut at 11:00 A.M. so
that all communication between the two divisions of the enemy was entirely
at an end for the present. Almost———————o'clock two officers came
in to tea—Colonel Johnson and Adjutant Ward of————————old regiment.———two of the most agreeable gentlemen I have seen in an
age———. While presiding at the supper table Ward made some———
———————and then told me that he was the "Cousin Frank" about
whom Nannie wrote so much—he had known her in Germantown and although no relation were like brother and sister. Spoke in high terms of them
all and begged me to write Nannie and tell her he had thus far passed through
the ordeal safely and was on his way to his dear Maryland. With this theme
of mutual interest for conversation we soon were quite well acquainted—he
gave me some trophies taken only this day—photographs of General "Peerless Beauregard," of the Yankee Commander———McClellan, Burnside
and Corcoran. He had also a couple of daguerreotypes of some ladies in
Baltimore—Dulcineas of some of the Yankee lovers who had thus ingloriously deserted their miniatures. In return Nellie and I sang "Maryland" and
the "Bonnie Blue Flag" for them with a great deal of pleasure. They left at
about eleven o'clock, but so excited and happy did I feel that I did not close
my eyes until one A.M.

This then is the reason why they thought our cavalry hovering near—
they have been very near, some of them every night for a week and I can't
for my life imagine why it is they were not taken by the Yankees. I never
heard of such boldness as they have been displaying of which we had not a
suspicion until now. Speaking of boldness reminds me of an exploit attributed
to Miss Belle Boyd Wednesday. Tis said that she wished some information

conveyed to the army about the time of the keenest firing and not being able to get anyone to go for her, she went herself to a most exposed point, where the bullets fell like hail stones about her riddling her dress. I know not what truth there is in the rumor.

Of one thing I am particularly glad—our First Maryland Regiment was the first to charge the Yankee First "Maryland"—drove them out of town, captured and then marched back to town singing "Maryland." They have always wanted to meet and have been justified with a vengeance, on one side at least. Old Colonel Kenley's prisoner too. What a memorable day this and how often have I thought of my darling brothers wishing they knew all and could rejoice with us. Little did they think when they left old Front Royal, that ere they returned she should have won herself a name in future history. I must write them now, bless them.

A contraband and Yankee who were about—applying the torch to the depot was this evening arrested by our men. The servants are disappointed and furious beyond mere words at the treatment their Yankee friends have received at the hands of "rebels" who they have been taught to believe were a race entirely extinct with the exception of a few outlaws in the mountains who would be easily taken. They don't say anything but are so sullen. The surprise was evidently very great and very disagreeable.

May 24th, 1862

Up bright and early this morning and went downstairs. Ma met me and told me that they had just heard that Colonel Sheets had been killed in yesterday's engagement. I was so shocked and grieved to hear this for truly the South had no truer, braver son than he—and to lose him now, just in the full tide of honorable success. Just as he had been promoted to distinction. It was sad, sad. When General Kimble was here his men spoke of Colonel Sheets and in terms of highest praise for his valor and bearing. Well the hearts of a grateful country should ever hold sacred the memory of this brave spirit who thus wasted his life in his country's care. We had some thirty soldiers to breakfast among whom were some Tigers, Louisiana troops under Dick Taylor. Just before breakfast who should come in but Mr. Hoblitzell and a young friend of his Mr. Russel a very pleasant little fellow too. Mr. H told us that Mr. Laird and Dr. Reeves and a number of those who spent last winter here were in town—also told of Mr. Wilson having joined the Navy. Was jubilant over the capture of the Yankee First. He begged for "Maryland" and "A Home by the Sea" and we had them both in full chorus. While singing I noticed the arrival of a very nice looking personage, to whom I was afterward introduced as Mr. Moreton, the most polished, refined little fellow I ever met—one of the F F V's[6]—conversed very pleasantly and was singing duets with Nellie and me to my very great satisfaction when Grandma came in and interrupted us by saying that Henry Heater was here wounded in the hand. We went out immediately to see him but found his wrist was only sprained. After dressing his wrist repaired Mr. Moreton's belt for him with a great deal of pleasure. Presently Captain Gardner of the N. O. Bn. came in. He wore the badge of the bn. one of the prettiest imaginable designs—a little silver crescent in the concavity of which revolved a silver star upon a pivot on which was enscribed on one side "The Star Bn. from the Crescent City" in a revolution,—on the reverse side "Wheat's New Orleans Bn." It was a cunning little ornament and I really coveted it. Nellie and I were busy playing the agreeable until eleven o'clock when———————————and went down to read some amusing letters captured yesterday. Cousin Mack Bayley, Mr. Merriwether and others came in to dinner—the first mentioned gave an account of a severe skirmish which took place at Buckton yesterday in which his horse and that of little Sandie were shot from under them—I can't conceive how any of them escaped with their lives. Here the gallant and lamented Sheets died just as he had waved his sword above his head in the act of giving the word of command, fell pierced through the heart, expiring instantly. They think they secured the varlet who committed the act—I sincerely hope they did. Mack was looking very well and seemed in excellent spirits and unusually affectionate. He and Cousin———both left at evening promising to call again. We shall not see the other boys for they pressed on with their company in expectation of engaging with the enemy.

The N. O. Tigers played a most amusing prank on the Yankees today. It seems that in their hasty flight yesterday they left arms, ammunition and clothing, tents, wagons and a large amount of commissary stores in our possession. The Tigers doffed their uniforms and donned the Yankee blue—then they got on the cars and steamed off to Markham where the news of the fall of Front Royal had not arrived and the Federal troops of course took them to be some of their own men, and coming out of quarters at the invitation of the Tigers a number of them concluded to "take a ride up the road a little ways."

The hospitable rebels not only extended the ride to Front Royal but also gave them lodging and board there au gratis. Prisoners have been pouring into town all day—ship Mitchell going by with five (armed with two revolvers a piece), all of whom tis said he took on his own responsibility and alone. Heavy cannonading in the direction of Winchester—hot work going on in that region I expect. Alec came in this evening saying Jackson was just carrying everything before him like a reaper in the grain.

It had been raining but cleared off in the evening cold and as there was every prospect of frost we all went into the garden and covered the young plants. Felt very tired so went to bed early.

They tell us that we did give the Yankees a prodigious whipping at Williamsburg notwithstanding all their boasts and Jackson also got the better of Milroy at McDowell notwithstanding old Fremont's "Freemans" romancing.

May 25th, 1862

Clear and cloudless. Mr. Berry preached today—so Father, Aunt B, Nellie and myself concluded to go first to hear Colonel Sheets' funeral sermon and then to the Presbyterian Church. We were too late—the brave fellow was consigned to the earth at an early hour with only a short service and no military display whatever owing to the inability of a few poor soldiers left for duty. He sleeps in the cemetery on the hill "Soldiers Rest" in an obscure spot—but if I'm permitted to follow the bent of my inclination it shall be no neglected grave.

We had an excellent sermon from Mr. Berry—which to tell the truth I listened to with very divided attention so much confusion was there with the thunder of wagons and artillery as they rolled through the street. Heard from Charlie B. He was almost entirely well and on his way home. So glad. There were some of our wounded men at private houses as well as wounded prisoners—Cousin E. B. has several with her one of whom had his leg amputated and died soon after. So far as I know we lost but four men in the skirmishes of Friday, though I suppose some others must have fallen that we know nothing of. I am uneasy about my friends—they have been fighting desperately and it seems too much to hope that they are all safe. We have taken Winchester, captured a very great number of prisoners and commissary's stores to the amount of one million dollars and best of all driven old Banks with the remnant of his army to the Potomac and the last heard from him Ashby was in hot pursuit of the fugitives declaring no pains to be spared in arresting their progress. Hope he'll get them. . . .

May 26th, 1862

A bright day. Finished sewing for Father quite early. Little Wilbur Trout and Edgar Jones came in this morning to get milk for the sick soldiers in town, of whom, including all, there were some eighty. I was so glad to think that the ladies were caring for them and resolved to do what I could to assist them. Saw a very large number of prisoners going out of town toward Winchester this morning—it is well they're being sent away—for I believe nothing but the ignorance of our members here, has prevented them from doing much mischief here.

Went into the garden where I received a fragrant greeting from innumerable floral pets. The roses were looking so lovely—I had not been able to enjoy the flowers as much all the summer before. Indeed there is an atmosphere of beauty pervading everywhere—making all nature "gladsome as the face of joy"—so different from what it was a week since. Then our spirit was so little reminiscent of brightness that light, fragrance and beauty would have been a sad discord surely—now all is harmless. Oh we have so much for which to be thankful in this episode. I feel that we cannot enough appreciate the blessing of liberty—know not its worth until deprived of it. I have enjoyed the accomplishment of its possession hugely today, though to tell the truth it certainly requires freedom, seems a blessing at times too great to be a reality. After one has a limb tightly bound—for a length of time— he becomes so accustomed to the confinement—that after the ligature is removed—he cannot for a long time realize his freedom from restraint. He still feels the impress of the bonds—still for a time imagines that they are about him and suffers from imagination that which he before endured in reality. At such time he is awakening to a reality that is delightful. So it is with what I now experience. Often when sitting at the door I hear a strange footfall on the pavement and spring up to leave the room as I always did when the Yankees came but I instantly recollect that there are none in the immediate vicinity to "vex or make us afraid" now—often I see figures move to and fro hurriedly and a huge anathema hangs pendant on my lips, and a big wave of indignation rolls over me as I think—"there they go—our tormentors—on demoniacal thoughts intent." Then I bethink me "Oh no—our dear blessed rebels—our protectors" and then at night upon taking my candle to my room and observing the curtains were not low how I would involuntarily throw my hands up in dismay at my carelessness at allowing lights to shine through the window—the Yankees would see it and think it a signal to the "secesh" out there—but I recollected then that such an act might be performed with impunity now for the eyes of no other than those we loved and those who loved us were on us now. Oh! this consciousness of freedom is a glorious thing to have. But it will not last—the Yankees will return when they rally their panic, they will return and we shall suffer much more from them, but surely we can bear a little tyranny now after having enjoyed the privilege of seeing and talking to our precious soldier boys again. Bless them. Commenced a letter to my brother as I thought I might soon have an opportunity of sending it to Dixie.

Ma was in town this evening and when she came back told us that the evening our troops came Captain Roy was at an upper window waving to them when the Yankees discovered him and fired at him—the balls taking effect in the parlor window—shattering three of the glasses and sinking in the frame. It looks something like war.

May 27th, 1862

Jacquie brought this morning a pacquet of letters among which we hoped to find the one written by Irvie to Ma, but no, there was one from him to Walter and another to Cousin Horace and one from Benton to Mrs. Roy which we immediately forwarded by Carey. Irvie wrote in fine script—was still with Beauregard and all was well. He said in regards to the battle of Pittsburg Landing that we had whipped them very badly notwithstanding the fibs they have told about it, and if they attack them again we were ready to repeat the dose. He also said that he had written to Ma and forwarded it to Winchester from which place he hopes she will get it. The letters had been sent by private conveyance—Mr. Marshall—from Corinth. We were so delighted to hear from the dear fellow again. Carey soon came in with a letter for me enclosed in Mrs. Roy's. Benton wrote very encouragingly and hopefully—had separated from the other boys so, and instead of being with Beauregard was on Hardee's staff—"Captain Roy"—how queer that would look as the direction on his letters. There was also an enclosure from Dick Blakemore to Dick Bayley—the former is at Corinth too and his brother and cousin Willie and Alex how delightful for them all to be there together. I sat right down and finished the boys letter and then commenced one to Benton that I might send them all out together by Tom Petty who goes to Richmond tomorrow. . . .

May 28th, 1862

We all woke "bright and early" this morning and Nellie and I concluded, even before rising, to go up for breakfast at Uncle Tom's. Cousins tried to dissuade us and even commenced a long confidential conversation after we had completed our toilette. But I presently espied Father coming in at the gate with a package to be sent off by Cousin W. So we met him at the door bonnets in hand. Leaving the package with a bundle and adieux in Cousin E's hand for Cousin Willie we started and walked as far as the corner with him found them just dressed for breakfast. Sat in the parlor talking with Uncle Tom until the meal was ready and then amused ourselves looking at the prints until Aunt Bettie was at leisure to take us through her flower bed and point out the improvements therein—after a little chat with her we set out for home. It looked so natural as we passed the hospital to see the invalid Confederate soldiers lounging about the halls—seemed so much like it did last winter and fall that I almost could have imagined that they had never left us. Met an old acquaintance Mr. Bayley on the street—was enroute to Winchester to get news. He promised to call on his return and meantime gave us some very amusing incidents from Lou J's experiences with the Yankees— told how they stole her pony and how she went to the captain in person demanding its restoration and enforcing her claims until he was compelled in self defense to comply with them. Busily engaged in sewing on a bonnet all day. . . .

There was today a rumor to the effect that Shields is returning to circumvent Jackson's plans.

May 29th, 1862

. . . Nellie and I were left guardians of the house as Ma, Grandma, Laura and some of the children spent the day at Oakley. We had Captain Marshall and a brother-in-law of his to dinner today—the latter proved to be the bearer of our dispatches from Corinth, a very clever, agreeable gentleman. He had been with the boys at Corinth and brought cheering news of their condition there. We had our bread baked and sent to the hospital before Ma returned in the afternoon. They say that there is some excitement in town in consequence of the reported advance of Shields. Wonder if it's true—if comes he has been very heavily reinforced, but still I trust we may administer a quietus to him.

May 30th, 1862

A baneful day—one to which I shall hereafter refer as one of dark forebodings and uncertainties. It dawned brightly—but still from the beginning it seemed sad. First a house containing the dead bodies of the smallpox patients was burned. Charlie Buck came in very unexpectedly about nine o'clock and was looking thin but remarkably well. Alice Morehead and Dr. Rixie next dropped in, each one bringing in some fresh rumors about the advance of the Federals; it seems there must be great alarm in town. Presently a courier came by today saying the enemy was this side *Salem* and on the march—so Charlie concluded he had better ascertain the truth and be off in time to escape them, knowing that the few invalids here would not be able to offer any resistance to the expected army, but promising to return to see us in case there was no foundation for the report. He had not left many minutes ere Dr. R. who has been in town returned telling Alice they must hasten away as the place would certainly in a little time be occupied by the Feds. It commenced sprinkling rain about the time they mounted their horses but the firing had commenced but they dashed fearlessly and even cheerfully away. All the morning the government wagons had been going toward Winchester, and a little while before Dr. R. came over our troops marched out—they did not go "hurry-scurry" like the Yankees but marched out with becoming dignity. We watched them as if they had been well known and much loved friends each one of them, and it was with a feeling of horror that I reflected upon the probability that our poor sick would fall into their hands. Cruel hands they would prove. The depot containing stores was fired and Father went over to protect the store. Our cavalrymen in squads were dashing out of town just as the Yankees appeared on the hill. There was some pretty brisk firing for a time, and suddenly a horrid shell came shrieking and whizzing over the house. They had planted a piece on the hill next to the orchard, and as they had threatened to shell the place we concluded that they were fulfilling their threat. All took refuge in the basement, the little children screaming and all confusion and uncertainty. Worse than all Father was still in town and we did not know whether they would permit him to come out or not any more. However, there were only a few shells sent on their errand of death, when the hills seemed to be overcast with dark clouds of the enemy's columns. They poured in from every direction, infantry, artillery and cavalry, through the waving wheat trampling it under foot, over the blooming clover crushing out fragrance and beauty there as remorsely as they would have crushed out life and hope in our bosoms. The horrible beings poured in from all sides looking all the more so since our eyes had grown accustomed to seeing our dear Southerners. When Jackson entered town although the cannonading was of much longer duration and far heavier I rather enjoyed it, but during the firing today I was really sick of heart—every report was an insult—a demoniacal roar of triumph, each boom probably the death knell to many a brave spirit. Until Father came in about two o'clock we felt very unprotected with the ruffianly fellows careening through the yard, but he appeared at that time much to our joy and told us the storehouse and all other buildings save the depot were uninjured—that was of course consumed.

But a little while ago and I boasted of my willingness to abide a little tyranny for a while—now after having had the pleasure of again seeing our own army—but I find the prospect of slavery more revolting than ever before—probably because I know they will strive to render it more abject. General Kimball was among the first to enter and sent a message at three o'clock to the effect that he would wish to occupy his former quarters here and have dinner by the time of his arrival. They came the Gen., the adjutant—Captains Mason and Bunting—Frank Crippen, Kent, Skin, Bob Burwell,—Rawhead and Bloodybones to all of them. I was too angry and outraged to witness their arrival but shut my door and sewed away as fast as I could until it was time to attend to arranging the dinner table—or supper table it was in reality. Nothing could exceed my horror on going down to tea, after the officers were supposed to have retired from the table, to see the horrid old hypocrite Freeman there. A haughty inclination of the head was all I could possibly vouchsafe the old sinner. There was another hoary headed old traitor just leaving the table—one in civilian garb—doubtless acting the officer's pilot to his Yankee friends—him, we did not condescend to notice at all. The climax was capped though when in walked that horrid coarse raw-head and bloodybones and took his seat. No more supper for me—so hastily finishing my glass of milk I retreated upstairs. By this time the whole brigade had marched into the former camp below the house and taken quiet posses-sion there—of quiet did I say? Oh no, for as it was raining they had an excellent excuse for a repetition of their previous destruction and fences were prostrated with as much rapidity as on the former occasions. . . .

Nellie and I were standing in the door when they made a rush for the wheat field fence and Rob Roy, standing by sick and weak looked on with dismay saying "Oh look yonder! Mass William just put the last rail to that fence yesterday; just fixed what they tore down before and they are taking every bit again." Nellie darted off to tell Father and General Kimball imme-diately appeared pistols in hand and marched down to the point of attack and quelled the assailants by the time the panels had all been thrown down the distance of a hundred yards. Martha who was standing at the kitchen window evidently did not have much faith in the General's threat that—"somebody should be shot" for the sake of saving a "secesh's" rails—for she remarked as he passed her "Law Miss Lucie! that man ain't going to do anything to his men to save that fence—he knew they were going to take it, so why did not he *stop* them *before they commenced?"*—an echo repeated the query— "why"? The creatures were coming to the house till ten o'clock at night begging suppers. Nellie and I had to abdicate our room in favor of Captain Bunting tonight.

I was so sorry when Eliza H and Mrs. M came up this evening to say Mrs. H was thought to be dying and they wanted a little ice for her. Poor thing! Tis no wonder she should sink under such a pressure of calamity— those less delicately constituted than herself can scarce bear up under it.

May 31st, 1862

Was awakened quite early this morning by Eliza Ann telling me that Ma had been summoned to Mrs. Hope who was thought to be dying and Grandma wanted me downstairs to assist her. Went down and dressed the children, helped to tidy the room, and saw about breakfast. Found it was still raining and disagreeable without and yet there on the cold wet pavement lay stretched at full length the guard of the night sleeping soundly on their hard bed despite muddy blankets and a deal of noise and looking for all the world like a trio of resigned and happy pigs.

I'm so sorry I treated that poor old man rudely last night—for Grandma tells me he is a good secessionist who was kidnapped by the wretches who destroyed his enclosures, despoiled his little lot, left his family unprotected and forced him on pain of destruction to act as guide promising at the same time however, to send him home after the accomplishment of his mission. She tells me she had just heard him out on the porch talking to some of the Yankees—old Freeman for one—and telling them just what he thought of their meanness and how little sympathy he had with them anyway. Well, never mind, I'm determined to show you some marked courtesy in presence of your tormentors if I possibly can, poor old man!

After breakfast I did![7] While sitting at the breakfast table in marched Frank, Skin, Burrell, Kent and the poor old rebel. I did not see any but the latter to whom I bowed a pleasant "Good morning" and as there were but few seats prepared at table I motioned him to the most desirable and busied myself assiduously in helping him. The others noticed it I know, though they did not let on. That Frank! he is apparently a clever sort of fellow and if he only just was not a Yankee I should like him so much: he has the faculty of winning the confidence and affection of children which speaks certainly very well for him. I was a good deal amused, when they all came down to breakfast and found the table was not ready for them, instead of standing with staring eyes and gaping with stupid embarrassment like the others he threw himself into a chair standing near the window and remarked pleasantly that he was "sorry they had intruded so soon but he understood from Mr. Buck that breakfast was waiting for them" and addressed some remarks to Grandma until the seats were arranged for them. That's just the way he does—always seems perfectly respectful, never staring at us when we go to the door and conducts himself like a gentleman if he were not a Yankee! but he is, and that is enough.

Ma came in from Mr. Hope's—Mrs. H is better and all as well as could be expected. She heard while there that Longstreet was expected to reinforce Jackson and if so I hope they'll give General Shields something to do. Such a horrible noise as they are making all this morning in camp. I try to read but can't hear myself think for the confusion. They are making a slaughter pen of the lot before the house and the sharp reports of firearms, the agonizing shrieks of the poor butchered animals mingled with the savage yells and laughter of the inhuman soldiery—all combined to make the morning hideous. There is some movement on foot—a long train of artillery has just passed, couriers are constantly arriving and departing and a general stir in camp. Perhaps they think Jackson will attack them here. There! that caps the climax, they have just hoisted a flag on the house—not the hateful "Stars and Stripes" tis true, but a flag to denote Kimball's quarters—a Yankee flag and I do not feel as if I could get my breath. What would Alvin and Irving say to see the enemy's flag waving over the time honored roof of old Bel Air? Poor dear boys! It is no less disagreeable than dangerous, for if our men should come in, they would in all probability mistake this for a traitor's house and shell it or at all events shoot at the flag. Too bad! The brigade has orders to move I know by the motions in camp. The tents droop and now they begin to discharge the old loads from their guns. Oh mercy! That volley must have been fired by a whole regiment at once, and they've got their guns pointed toward the house—actually firing into the hill. No wonder the poor children run screaming to our sides and hide their heads in our dresses. There it goes again! Well this is too much for human endurance. I'll go out and see if there are none of the officers about who can stop this—went out on the porch and seeing Frank sitting composedly under the aspen reading "Sparegrass—Papers" I commenced abusing the Yankees to Ma for their inhumanity in shooting toward a house full of women and little children. He instantly sprung up and came forward—they would soon stop now as they were only discharging in order to reload preparatory to marching—that they would not fire so high as to strike the house. Presently they moved off—all gone with the exception of the general and his staff. The air is bright with sunshine again and we feel free to go in the garden to see the flowers. Such flowers! The rose bushes every one seem deluged with beauty, great clusters of lovely half-blown buds, great glowing red hearted full flowers, heliotrope, honeysuckle, fleur-de-lis, carnations and syringas. We gather handfuls and make bouquets, not for the Yankees but for the house.

It is raining again this evening, and there is something going on which we can't account for: Kimball's brigade has returned *bringing in with it some ambulances* and the officers speak of a little skirmishing going on over the river this evening. I wonder if "somebody" has not been hurt. They are evidently apprehensive of an attack—have placed cannon on the hill immediately in range with the house with the mouth pointing the opposite direction. But that does not make any difference, for our men would have of course tried to silence the enemy's battery and so we should be in danger from our *own cannon*. We are just in a cross fire between three of them—or should be if attacked. Father speaks of sending us off to Belmont till after it is all over, but I think twould be very wrong for us to desert Father and the house now. Our flight would leave everything much exposed to pilferers and Father, poor fellow, has his hands and head full now of business. Besides we could take refuge in the basement from the shells and balls. Grandma insists on it—she is nervous and sick, and indeed I believe we're all well nigh worn out with this constant excitement—I tremble and feel so weak that I can scarcely stand up. Even the little children are as nervous as they can be and I was right much amused at poor little Willie a little while ago. He was lying half asleep when a thunder clap burst overhead sounding precisely like the report of artillery; he did not utter a word but with one bound sprang from the bed into my arms and then he shrieked, quivered as if he were frightened almost to death.

Well, Father has told us to make all preparations for an early start in the morning. Nellie and I want to stay with Father but Ma thinks it would be imprudent, and won't go without us. Oh dear! this is a glowering night and I'm heartsick. It has been raining and lightning and thundering every night since they came to it, and now it is storming furiously. The guard has not been detailed for the house and Father is afraid to go to bed leaving the house unprotected and surrounded by four thousand desperadoes. He is looking so haggard and worn it makes me sad to see him.

We finished all preparations and as it was almost one o'clock a.m. I must woo "tired nature's sweet restorer." Oh! the myriad sad hearts that throb tonight!

June 1st, 1862

Awoke quite early feeling very little refreshed. Father at first thought it doubtful as to whether we would go to B today owing to want of convey- ance, the horses having strayed off in the night. It had ceased raining, and the first sound I heard on going downstairs was a band playing to an advancing regiment—playing "Gay and Happy" in the most unsabbath manner. It was Ord's division going by and while standing there looking they commenced discharging their guns again and the balls actually struck the front of the house a few inches below the window of Father's room. Horrid wretches! As they pass by for sheer amusement they kick the water gate to atoms. While they were passing Frank came out and stood near the door—he remarked to Grandma that General Kimball had detailed him to act as escort should we wish to leave today and now for the first time in my life I entered into conversation with a Yankee soldier. I enquired if it were not dangerous to leave the house for fear it should be plundered—I knew that deserted houses generally suffered from such a proceeding. "Oh no, not at all!" He would promise "it should not be so" and from this we entered into a regular discussion which I really enjoyed for I made him acknowledge the superior generalship displayed by our "Stonewall," made him own up to the "Banks panic" etc. After breakfast we went to work packing and locking up bed clothes and after all were prepared went out on the porch to witness the departure of the officers. All of them looked extremely sad although they spoke confidently of success. When Gen K. came to make his adieux the little baby was in Laura's arms on the porch and walking up to it he put his arm about it and kissed it several times—thinking probably of his own little ones who might that day be made fatherless. He very cordially shook hands with all save Nellie and myself and in reply to our bow he said—"Farewell *daughters*." Nellie was so much amused at the idea of being called daughter by a Yankee officer. After they left Frank mounted his horse and taking Rob Roy with him went off in search of our horses. And now such a time as we had, we had no officer on guard (though Gen K. told Father that Gen. Tyler would be over during the day to quarter here if twould not inconvenience him). The stragglers in the wake of every army now poured in from all sides and annoyed poor Father almost to death. Then the shooting recommenced and was kept up for an hour straight ahead: it seems sometimes as if a whole regiment would sometime discharge their pieces simultaneously until the very heavens seemed to be torn asunder by the reverberation. The bullets whistled and sang a tune among the trees around the house, and the little children crying and sobbing with fright crept to our sides burying their heads in our dresses and begging Father to go out and make them quit. Poor children! Little they knew how limited was Father's power over them and what he was suffering for them. Frank came back after awhile with the horses which after some difficulty he had succeeded in securing, and he made the soldiers point their guns another way and in a little while they stopped all together and marched out. I had a most refreshing argument with Frank while the wagon was being harnessed. He told me that Stanton had certainly received an official dispatch announcing the fall of Richmond a week before—that the South would soon accept terms of peace etc. etc. All of which I laughed to scorn. In debating the justice of this, on their side, aggressive war—he made a very feeble attempt to vindicate their justice, but he had so little faith in what he was saying that he ended in a hearty burst of laughter and gave it up, saying he wished it were well over. He told me they expected an attack from Jackson at the river, two miles from here, but that there was no possibility of his escaping being made prisoner—he and his whole army, for he was completely surrounded by Gen. Fremont, Rozencranz, all McDowell's division, Ords, Shields, and the hero Banks himself was advancing from Harper's Ferry on him—making altogether eighty thousand men. My heart thrilled almost to suffocation at the thought of the danger in which our poor little army was—but I did not allow him to see that. I was the least bit discomposed and laughingly assured him that I should never believe they had Jackson till I saw him. Even when Frank went over to town to get Father a guard and came back again a dispatch had been received to the effect that Fremont had taken him in Strasburg, even though Father told us to be prepared for the worst, even though I heard the heavy cannonading, I did not and would not believe Jackson would fall into such hands. I never felt such a pain in my heart as when we told Father goodbye and the wagons filled with every member of the family—we drove from the yard, refugees from our dear home which we might return to and find a heap of smouldering ashes. And Father looked so heartsick and almost wept outright. Frank and Bob both accompanied us as escorts and I never in my life saw more delicate attention from anyone than from the former—we went through an entire brigade and Frank would ride on ahead and clear the path for us even getting down to pull the fence away to give us passage. And when the rude soldiers stared and grinned at the fugitives, he would ride between us and them and apologize for them. It was a most intensely hot day and what with a heavy heart and————blood seething through my veins I felt well nigh crazed—though I cooled myself sufficiently to give Frank some retorts. When we got to the mountains we found they had a guard—among them a young Bostonian Clapp, a very polite but saucy fellow, when Frank went away I could not forbear giving him my hand and well wishes for his *individual* safety. After giving him my hand I vented my spleen on little Clapp and talked him quiet—tis so refreshing to abuse someone when you've a heart full of bitterness.

Did not hear anything definite from our army except that Jackson was utterly powerless in their hands. Oh no!

[June 6th, 1862, entry omitted]

June 7th, 1862

Well we are at home again, almost worn out.[8] Walked down from Belmont through a scathing sunshine and reached home to find everything about the house safe but in awful disorder which we immediately set about to rectify and have been hard at work ever since. Poor Father! They've ruined him—have taken all his corn, have broken his mill, stolen his implements, burnt his fencing and destroyed his crop and cut the farm to pieces. Gen. Tyler did not come over as he expected, but one Captain Sanderson of Phil. and Mr. Berry quartered here—the former protecting him as far as he could, but he had a hard time of it indeed. The little boys returned home on Monday. We have spent the week I scarcely know how only that we were so spent with nervous excitement that we slept a great deal of the time. Monday I slept and read all day. Commenced raining Sunday evening and rained all day Monday. Heard Jackson and his whole army were on the point of grounding arms. Never saw anything like the number of baggage trains and troops—was glad to see the troops had pretty much cleared out from around Bel Air. The Yankees were up at Belmont before breakfast; took Uncle Mac's spyglass away from him. However, he went down to camp and recovered it. Tuesday————raining: amused ourselves watching the arrival and departure of troops from Front Royal. Today they have Jackson prisoner and his *son dead*—never knew he had one before. Some bitter cannonading on Monday and some Tuesday but no battle as was expected. Jackson we concluded had retired up the valley—the enemy pursuing. A number of Yankees there for corn—cavalry—very saucy. Read, sewed and slept. Homesick. Wednesday. Thought it was going to clear off but it did not—gathered some beautiful roses, Ashby is dead, today. More Yankees and more impudence but the guard kept them at bay till late when some of them stole Uncle Mac's horses and one of ours, but he went to camp and recovered them with great difficulty. No cannonading. Sleeping, reading and a little sewing. Thursday: Raining, still. Jackson and five hundred of his *men have escaped.* Should not be surprised if his whole army did after a while. Had a paper announcing the evacuation of Corinth and villifying Beauregard to such an extent that I felt like throttling the editor. It also took complimentary (?) notice of Miss Belle Boyd's heroism on the 23d. There were accounts of the battle at Richmond— of course they were victors. Clapp was up this evening but did not see him. More Yankees and more impertinence. Sewed a little—homesick very. Had a note from Father encouragingly written. Friday: Nothing from the army in the Valley. It was clear and we had intended going home but it was too muddy for walking and they had taken one of our horses and we had no driver, and Uncle Mac could not send us. Captain Sanderson came up at noon and told us there had been a battle at Richmond in which McClellan's whole army was engaged, and that we had repulsed them with very great loss.[9] G-l-o-r-i-o-u-s ! How much better we all felt for the intelligence. He confirms the evacuation of Corinth and thinks Beauregard has gone with reinforcements to Richmond. Oh! if it be but true that we've whipped them at R! As for Beauregard—whatever he does he has a reason for and we shall soon see if it isn't for the best. . . .

I've noticed for a long time that Friday has been a most unlucky day—to verify my belief yesterday Father had six hundred head of mules turned in upon his little meadows, utterly ruining them. . . .

June 9th, 1862

Whitsuntide. Was quite busy all day sewing and nursing while Martha weeded the garden. Had a guarded appointed. Mr. Berry came in and said there was great commotion in town owing to a report that Jackson and Longstreet were advancing down the Valley. Said they were reported to have had an engagement at Corinth in which we had whipped them. Hope tis so. There is a great running to and fro of cars and the baggage trains are very busy carrying off supplies. There is something on foot, that's evident. Wonder where Fremont, Rosencrans, and company are? McDowell is in Washington under arrest. Wonder if they'll decapitate him?

June 10th, 1862

Raining and disagreeable. Was summoned to the door by double knock where I found two impudent little Yankees who wanted dinner furnished them! They were sent to the kitchen and presently another one a major from "Der Vaterland." He took lodging for the day and night. He did make me so mad telling how one of our men wounded him and how he shot him for it. He was an intelligent man—had been in the German wars and amused Father very much giving an account of his imprisonment and escape from a Prussian fortress and his final exile to America. I had the toothache terribly and Ma went into the room to get something to put in it. As soon as the major saw her at it he sprung up, went to his portmanteau and took out innumerable little flasks of all kinds of brandies—prune, wild cherry, etc.—some of which he presented to her. Dutchman to the last. One of the little Yankees informed us today that Jackson was well nigh surrounded as "Fremont had taken him in hand now." Baah!

June 11th, 1862

Suffered so much from my teeth all night and today it is very painful. Harriet is sick and there is a great deal to be done. I go down and try to help Nellie and Laura but am so unwell as to make a poor "out" of it. Nervie came in to get a little salt for their bread and he told us that they heard from a reliable source that Jackson had given Shields and Fremont a most complete "Dressing." Laura went up to Mrs. Hopes in the evening and returned bringing a confirmation of the account and addenda in the fact that they had been hauling off the dead and wounded all the night before in the cars besides a large number who were said to be in a house some distance up the creek. They also said it was reported that there had been several of our men seen in the mountains—some were even known to have been in town. Wonder what it all means?

June 12th, 1862

Did not dress till ten o'clock—was very unwell all night, suffered so much with my head that I could not sleep and was this morning so nervous and

weak that I could scarcely stand. I heard them say Natala was sick too and
knowing there must be a great deal of work to do, presently roused myself,
made up my bed, cleaned the room and went downstairs. Was too sick all day
to do anything. . . .

June 13th, 1862

Went downstairs this morning before breakfast and made up my first biscuit
and helped to get breakfast. Then we girls washed up the dishes and cups and
set the table for dinner. Ma, Nellie, and Laura milked and strained it and put
it away. Then Nellie and I cleaned up our rooms and went to help Martha
iron. Finished ironing by dinner time and after resting a while went down
and folded the clothes. Brought them up and put them away. Dr. Turner came
in and told us that there had been 240 wagon loads of wounded brought down
from above and that the Yankees themselves acknowledged to the defeat. Oh!
I wish I could see Frank now to ask him where all those men are who were
to have surrounded and eaten Jackson's army up bodily. He said he did not
know how Shields' men would feel in a retreat, but I guess he knows now.
Helped to get supper and my biscuits were a decided success. Dressed myself
and went out to gather some sweet brier roses to put on Father's plate—I
always like to see them on the tea and breakfast tables and they are Father's
favorite flowers. After tea we washed the cups and saucers, set the breakfast
table and felt tired enough to be glad when my day's work was done. But I
feel a great deal better satisfied with myself to know that I am competent to
discharge these duties than I would to know that I was a mere idler useless to
myself and all around me.

June 14th, 1862

Grandma pronounced my biscuits "most excellent" this morning and she is a
good judge! Hadn't much to do after cleaning off the table and righting my
own room, so I devoted the morning to writing. Two young New Yorkers
called to get some milk and making the children's acquaintance he showed
them the photographs of his family and his own on which was written his
name "Fred Alden"—the boys brought them up and showed them to us. The
other one—Johnnie Rokett was a combination of resemblance to Irvie and

Dick. He was a school boy and orphan, very tired of the war and homesick. Father was without a guard and learning that their regiment was near acting in that capacity he engaged them as sentinels to protect the house and yard. They returned in the late evening and took up quarters here. I do think little Rokett reminds me more of Irvie as he sits out there his face buried in a book—and Alden is not unlike Alvin.

Uncle Tom was over this evening and told us that a Yankee major had given him an account of the battle. Jackson had sent all his wagons ahead of him and the prisoners were sent to Lynchburg long before the Feds came into Winchester. He marched to a certain position, took his wagons to a high point, put cannon behind them, unhitched the horses and waited for the Feds who, when they rushed forward to seize the supposed abandoned wagons, were met with a withering fire from the "masked batteries." The slaughter was fearful and the major confessed they were cut to pieces. They fought two days, one in which Shields was used up and the other Fremont. Oh this is more than our most sanguine hopes could have asked. But I very much fear Colonel Ashby is dead—they all bring the same account of his death. Poor fellow—tis said—"Whom the Gods love die young" and it seems so in this case truly, for both friend and foe vie in giving him credit for his gallantry as a soldier and his nobility as a man. May God give thy spirit rest, noble son of a worthy mother—valiantly and well hast thou contended for the freedom of our home and thy people. Well hast thou earned a patriot's monument in the hearts of thy brother and sister Southrons, and mayst thou win a crown of glory in that higher destiny that awaits thee—the crown of the Christian soldier. What an irreparable loss to the South! Woe! Woe!

June 15, 1862

Read aloud all the morning to Father. Received a very welcome note from Jule and answered it by bearer. Mrs. Moffat brought us a paper in which was published a dispatch from Walter to poor Colonel Ashby when the former was scouting in the mountains just before Jackson's army came in. It was captured on the cars at Staunton and had W's full signature to it. Father was afraid it would get Uncle Mack into trouble, but I guess twould be more apt to make captivity an awkward thing for the writer should he ever be taken. Nellie and I played and sang some tonight. Poor Kattie! Mr. S. was carried off prisoner yesterday. He was sick at the time and I can imagine she must be very distressed and anxious about him.

June 16th, 1862

This morning Orville came over from Uncle Tom's and told us that there were two Confederate prisoners there taken in the battle at Port Republic— they were of Louisiana 7th which suffered so much and one of these were wounded. There were also a wounded Yankee there. We had been intending to go over to Oakley all the morning and although we heard Shields was to be in about noon—we concluded to go and return before that time. Father could not go himself so he sent Johnnie Rokett to guard us across the fields but I was very sorry he did so when instead of going back then, he walked on through town and up to Uncle Tom's. I never did have any fancy for perambulating with a Yankee—be he never so civilized a specimen, and besides, I know the Fed all took us to be Unionists and that I hated. Found Aunt Betty sitting on the front porch with the "Secesh" and Union boy very amicably shelling peas together. Arthur Wough, our little Confederate, was a trim nice fellow whom I should have taken to be seventeen, if he had not told me he was twenty—he gave us a cordial grasp of the hand such as only a Southerner could give and seemed very glad to see us. I was so glad to see a grey coat again for my eyes have been aching with monotony of blue cloth. Twas right amusing to see the captor and captive together. Ma, Nellie and myself went out to help them in their task and when little Secesh saw the Yankee fishing in the basket after the pea pods so awkwardly he would say—"Stop Captain, I'll show you how" and he would skillfully shake the basket up for him. Every once in a while our old Yankee would read something from the paper detrimental to our cause, but little Wough always gave back as good as they sent. After such little ebullitions they were soon as sociable as ever and making arrangements with each other relative to going to Washington their destination. The other prisoner was in his room wounded but I met him once in passing through the hall. Aunt B had gotten some dress goods and we were busily engaged measuring off patterns when Uncle Tom came in and said a letter had been received from Bailey Jacobs since the battle at Richmond and he wrote that poor Charlie Richardson was wounded—perhaps mortally. Poor, poor Charlie, how often he has jested about going to Richmond to defend it, and how often has he spoken of his willingness to lay down his life for his country and now—but I do hope still that it may all be a mistake. He mentioned no other friends who were hurt. Nothing has been heard from Willie R since he left Williamsburg and we are so uneasy about him. Oh! me—I do wish this was well over!

We left Uncle Tom's about eleven o'clock—we gave Wough little bouquets of one white and two red rosebuds when we bade him "goodbye." He said his captors were very kind to him and he hoped soon to be exchanged, when he would rejoin his regiment. He said poor Ashby was certainly dead, but he confirmed the most flattering accounts we had from Port Republic and moreover said we had just gained a signal victory at Richmond where McClellan had been repulsed *thirty miles*. Better and better. Carey came home with us. Shields' army did not come in till four o'clock and when they did come such a looking party! Every other one was barefooted, some coatless, some with garments well nigh torn off them, all dirty and harassed almost to death. Ambulances and wagons passed and went by with the sick and wounded passed by and the house and kitchen were besieged until late at night by soldiers begging for food—"just a bit of any kind of bread," for they were "almost starved," or else they wanted "a morsel for a sick friend." I had vowed never to cook anything for a Yankee but when a man walked in and begged for a little thickened milk for a sick friend, my humanity overcame my hate and I made him a nice bowl of the coveted refreshment. I even went so far as to make up the biscuit dough—I could do this when they were in retreat, but had the case been otherwise I would not have done it. Colonel Thorborne—acting brigadier general in Carrol's absence engaged quarters here—the brigade camping in the barn field back of the house. General Kimball had said that in case of a return he would like to stop here, but he did not do so, for reasons I think I can comprehend. Kent, Frank and Skin came in quite early to tea, though, and we invited Frank to the first table. He came in like a man who expected to pass a severe ordeal and was resolved to do it gallantly, so when we demurely asked him for Jackson's address that we might call on him and cheer his imprisonment—he commenced deploring "poor Ashby's death." We soon disposed of that though and he acknowledged their defeat, said he would "not sorrow for it as they would get home the sooner by it" but added that if their brigade and Shields had been there in person, they would have had a different tale to tell. I asked why they were not there?

Well the men wanted shoes, they couldn't march without shoes. Why couldn't they march over the same barefoot as well as Jackson's men had many of them done? Well, he confessed, he was tired of this war and would be glad to be home again. We would not vex him any more after that but Skin and the other boys took their departure soon after expecting to return with the brigade.

After a while some officers came down to the table to supper and while Ma presided, Nellie and I stood at the side table washing cups and saucers. They commenced talking of their defeat, lauding Jackson and praising their own intrepidity and at last spoke of Ashby's death and what a great loss he would be to the Southern Confederacy, seeming to think it a death blow to Jackson's power. I couldn't hold my tongue any longer, but turning to the spokesman remarked that while Colonel Ashby was bitterly deplored by the Southern people, yet Ashby's men, who had done the fighting for him, were still alive and able to do them a deal of mischief. The officer replied that he had some of them in camp now who looked very harmless—spoke it so tauntingly that I could not help reminding him that lately it was thought they *were* considered harmless. Ma came in just now and told me that it was Colonel Shalosse and his staff to whom I was talking. Well I don't care, in fact I'm glad of it for I've been wanting to give vent to my feelings a long time and now that it is done I feel relieved. Oh! dear me! dear me!

Frank told me that in the engagement at Port Republic the parties fought even with *stones* and that in taking a battery a party of Southerners had hold on one end of a cannon and the Northerners tugging at it for dear life.

June 17th, 1862

Well, this *has* been a tiresome day and I believe another such will about finish my little stock of patience. In the first place I discovered that our compulsory guests were Virginians—so called—traitors I consider them and at the second breakfast table Nellie and I had a quarrel with a young lieutenant and clerk—trying to shame them in their treason, but they evidently considered us the heretics and tried to convert us from the error of our way. They succeeded so far as to strengthen yet more our secession opinion. One comfort—the colonel and all his staff at the breakfast table owned that (to use their own expression) they *did* "skedaddle faster than they ever did in their lives before," and one of them laughed and said he had "left Jackson all his nice clothes." They jested each other a great deal and I enjoyed it under *these circumstances*. All day long the horrible Yankees were coming in the yard wanting milk, wanting bread, and I think these men not less than one thousand here for water and notwithstanding the wet season we've had, they pumped the well dry—a thing that has not been done before since it was dug sixty years ago. And then the few cherry trees in the yard and garden had a little half ripe fruit on them and they were a constant source of annoyance— the Yankees through the garden—trampling down the young corn and breaking the palings and ruinously mutilating the trees. They were scared almost to death this morning thinking Jackson was going to attack them; the Colonel told Father they were expecting a battle here and Father prepared us for it. But our brave Stonewall did not come.

Oh I'm very tired of oppression!

June 18th, 1862

I was angry all the morning, angry with the Yankees for trying to proselyte—angry at them for fibbing and angry with them because they were Yankees. The servants were vexatious too. Rob Roy in whom we had so much confidence even espousing the cause of the Yankee. I never was half so mad in my life. Insinuating wretches! to come here and tell Father how kind and good they are going to be to us after our subjugation—how they will soothe the pains of submission—trying to win him over to the opinion that the Lincoln government when once established will be very mild and equitable. Gracious heavens! If I thought it were my fate to submit to them I believe it would craze me! No—

> "Better the fire should o'er me roll
> Better the shot, the blade, the bowl
> Than crucifixion of the soul."

An old traitor came into them from the mountains today and his presence served to increase until by supper time I was in a fine mood for abusing. Ma, Nellie and myself did give Lt. Mesod a good talking tonight and Capt. Stephens too. After supper Father begged us to play and sing, to which move I strenuously objected until they called for Southern music—whereupon I sat down and played "Johnson's March to Manassas," "Bonnie Blue Flag," and "Maryland," in this latter Captain S accompanied me. He then proposed the "Red, White and Blue" which I respectfully declined. Nellie would not even go into the parlor where we were. After playing Captain Stephens dived into politics again and we had quite a quarrel—Lt. Morrel wished to take a part but being told that lawyers would distort anything into an appearance of fact he forebore.

June 19th, 1862

No sign of movement yet, spent the morning in my room upstairs, about eleven o'clock Jacquie brought us a letter from Irvin, bless him! It was dated May 15th and therefore the latest advice we had—sent by flag of truce to the Yankee line where it was mailed to Cousin H. Helen Hieronimouns and forwarded by her to Front Royal through a member of the Signal Corps now at Uncle Mack's. I was so glad to hear that they were all well and in good spirit—he said we must not be uneasy about their welfare as Col. Jordan would take good care of him. He spoke of enclosing a letter to me which I did not receive—I do wish I could have gotten it for no doubt he wrote more at length in that and more unrestrainedly and probably that is the reason they would not let it come through. Poor boy! I wish I knew where they were now.

I noticed the porch looked very untidy and seeing it vacant, went out to sweep it off. While thus employed Capt. Stephens came out from his headquarters and sauntering up asked me if I were acquainted with Miss Hattie Gillespie. When I told him that she *had* been an acquaintance of mine he proceeded to inform me that she and all her family were at the hotel in town, "having been forced to leave their home on account of Dr. S. having accepted a commission in the Federal Army." I wonder how many Southerners have been driven away from their homes by the Yankee forces. The little kid glove captain succeeded in what he had been endeavoring to do for some time—picking a quarrel with me. I tried to retain my equilibrium by reflecting on his insignificance, but his cool assurance was too much for me and by becoming angry and excited gave him decidedly the advantage. The idea of his advocating perfect social equality and affectionate intercourse among parties differing as widely in political opinions as Unionists and Secessionists—

giving parties to each other, and, cherishing feelings of bitter, venomous hatred in their hearts, yet clasp hands in apparent friendship—and concealed under a hypocritical mask of bright smiles the scorn we feel. As an argument he cited the example of his own family which was half Union and half Secession, and yet were perfectly harmonious as ever before. I told him that I had no fancy for hypocrisy and as for feeling any desire of coming in contact with any Union acquaintances I did not, as the intercourse would be productive of nothing but ill feelings on both sides. He then fell to depreciating our generals and it seemed to me did everything he could to incense me—and succeeded beyond his expectations. I should not have cared so much if he had been anything else than a Virginian, as it was, I felt that the old state was disgraced in having such a renegade son—and I presently picked myself up and marched off. He's so different from Capt. Kephart—the latter is so quiet and well behaved, not often speaking except to tease the other officers and administer a wholesome rebuke to their vaunting and boasting—he's not a Virginian though. Uncle Tom came over in the evening and told us that Miss Hattie Gillespie and her sister went up to his house to call on the wounded Federal Officer there. I think it would have been more proper to have sent their mother as proxy.

. . . A poor little drummer boy fell out of the cherry tree today and broke his arm. If it had been one of the "fighting" men who had broken his neck I should not have objected much—but this was a very small child, and as I had my arm fractured I can guess how much he will suffer particularly with no gentle nursing—and care. Poor child.

June 20th, 1862

We thought they were really going this morning—such a stir as there was in camp, such arriving and departing of couriers, but they did not go. Skin came over about eleven and informed us that the first brigade would move in the evening. After he left Frank came over and dined with us, telling us that Longstreet was coming over the mountains and that men had been sent out to capture his train of wagons—however the news was very unreliable. I never saw anyone so haggard and dispirited as Frank, he said he had been sick (to account thus for not having been over before) and I believed him, he certainly was homesick. He and his brother both said they were heartily tired of the war, they had seen enough in Virginia and if they could but get home now would be content to remain and never come back. It seems to be the universal sentiment and I have not heard one yet who did not wish he could leave the ranks and retire. Frank spoke of one of the regiments being almost in a state of mutiny and said that old Captain Bunting spoke of resigning. I hope tis true for I always wanted to like that man, but I felt that I could not, sustaining toward me the relation they did.

Certainly there is some move of importance in contemplation, for the orderlies have been dashing about all day in the most distracting manner with their dispatches. I just wish that I knew what it all means. One of the orderlies told Father that they were trying their best to get away from Jackson who was believed to be approaching. He said for his part he thought it a shame to be playing such a game. "If they intended doing anything, why didn't they push boldly forward instead of killing the men with their marching and countermarching? The men were getting very tired of it he knew." That's the way I like to hear them talk. . . .

Chapter Three

We Learned to Accommodate
Ourselves to Circumstances

୧୨୧୨୧୨୧୨୧୨୧୨୧୨୧୨୧୨୧୨୧୨୧

June 21, 1862–December 31, 1862

June 21st, 1862

Captain Kephart and Lewis Rouse were at breakfast when I went down to
the table. The former, in course of conversation, being asked very demurely
by Nellie if they would "burn the town when they left," assured her, with a
look of astonishment, that they had no idea of such a thing—that such proceedings were positively forbidden—they *might* have to burn some stores,
but certainly not the town. He was told that some of the Federal officers had
censured Jackson very severely for burning stores when *he* left here—they
choosing to denominate it—"wanton destruction." He said it was most singular that an officer should have said any such thing when everyone knew
that it was a standing rule with commanders when they could not remove
stores to destroy them to prevent the enemy enjoying any benefit from them
and that Jackson had as much right to burn them here as Banks had in
Winchester. Rouse then told us that we would very soon see our friends in

Longstreet's division as they would probably enter town a few hours after their departure, he laughed and said they were retreating from him as hard as they could. This fellow is the most complete specimen of Yankeedom that I've yet seen. When he first came, we all treated him as we do all of them, with sublime contempt; very soon however by little attention to our convenience and some remarks to his chums in our presence, he produced the impression that he was a good hearted simple sort of school boy very homesick, and we somewhat relaxed toward him. That he is homesick and very tired of war I surely believe, but as to his simplicity I was never more mistaken in my life. He's as shrewd a Yankee as Yankees generally get to be. I thought we would hurt ourselves laughing at his quizzing one of the soldiers this morning just before they left. The man was quite saucy and inclined to boast, and would speak of the battles he had been in and give a glowing account of Yankee prowess. Lewis would let him go as far as necessary and then say "Well, stop, I happen to know something of that—I was on the ground" and then he would give his version of the current as entirely the reverse of what the other had said and in such a quizzical way that the soldier was finally glad to skulk off. Sometimes he would say something about our army to provoke a retort from us and then he'd drop his head in his hands and laugh heartily. He informed us this morning that Captain Stephens was playing a neat practical joke on Miss Hattie—passing himself off for a single man and *pretending* to be desperately smitten, while she seemed to be pleased in reality. I was astonished to hear that he was married, but he declared it to be a fact and told him he had been carrying on flirtations with the ladies in Page. I thought when I first saw him, that Captain S lacked in an eminent degree the elements that go to make up a true gentleman but I scarcely believed him capable of such duplicity toward one of his own set. If he had tried to raise expectations in me for the pleasure of disappointing them, I should not have been surprised, for he knows I'm an enemy and he might feel justified in punishing my heresies. But he and Hattie are fellow martyrs in the same cause, they are brother and sister Virginians and one would have thought, if he had possessed much of that chivalry of which he talks so much, he would have constituted himself her champion and resented every impuny, warded off everything painful that approached her as a brother would have done instead of making a sport of her womanly feelings and girlish credulity. But I wasted too much time and space upon the insignificant mannekin, one might know that a man who could default to his country might well be recreant to every other duty. Only I'm glad I bluffed him off as I did.

They all left by eleven—the colonel and staff taking lunch and declaring they expected to be taken by Jackson's advance guard. We had a paper containing an account of the "whitehouse" sortie a most gallant dash bravely carried out. Spent the evening in glorious repose, it seems so pleasant to enjoy a little quiet once more. Of course our men did not come in. I felt a little uneasy this evening when I heard that our cavalry were near town, for Shields' men had declared they were just going over the mountains a little way and when Jackson returned here they would fall back upon him in company with forty or fifty thousand that had come in during the night and were concealed in the woods around. We had every reason to believe the latter part of the information true and for a little while I felt afraid they might decoy our men—but presently I laughed at my fears, for I trust in Jackson and his God. The signal corps on the mountain have been making some demonstration this evening—of course entirely unintelligently to us.

June 22nd, 1862

Well this had been a glorious sunbright day of quiet and repose. Felt a little sick in the morning but as Father had the headache I exerted myself to read to him and presently felt better. Slept, read and ate all day. E Hope came in during the evening and sat a little while. Ma was out at Mrs H's at the same time. When she came home she told us that Mr. H told her the paper announced the recognition of the S C by France. I have lost all confidence and dependence in such rumors, but I would be glad if it were so. I was at the window this evening after tea and heard Grandma talking to someone, evidently a stranger, out in the yard. Looking out I saw a very youthful, boyish looking personage in the dark blue uniform, standing bucket of water in hand. I stepped out to know the meaning of a paper which he handed Grandma, and learned that it was a *girl dressed in Yankee uniform.*[1] She said she lived near Edinburgh, she had a stepmother who treated her so unkindly she was obliged to leave her home and went to live with her aunt. Here she and her sister assisted in washing and doing the housework; Fremont's disgraceful band came in, men very rude and they used the unruly member rather too freely for her pleasure, whereupon two of the soldiers led her off

prisoner, took her female attire from her and forced her to assume her present
garb with the name of "John Smith." They had even cut her hair off. She
traveled in the wagons and succeeded in a few hours in giving her captors the
slip in the confusion of passing trains, and joined another regiment where her
sex was not known. She went on to Washington, not being able to get
home,—returned to Linden and finally obtained a pass to Front Royal and
across the river. But she could not get through the pickets to her home. She
was afraid to appeal to any of the higher officers lest they should suspect her
of being a spy, afraid of telling her story to anyone for fear they should betray
her. She had been away from home just a week living all the time in the
wagons; at last she went down to Aunt Black Betty who lives in the mill, told
her story and begged for protection and had engaged to bring water and assist
her in washing to discharge her board there until she could get home—had
just come up now after some water and seeing Grandma had concluded to
tell her troubles. Poor thing, what an awful situation to be in—only sixteen
years old and thrown thus among strangers in the hands of cruel enemies
so far from home. She was evidently a rude, uncouth girl carelessly raised,
but I thought I could detect an innate delicacy of feeling in the blush that
mounted her cheeks when she looked down at her unusual costume and even
the bitter epithets she bestowed upon her savage captors were called forth
by a feeling of outraged pride and outraged propriety that I could approve.
When she spoke of home and of the probability of her sister sharing the
same fate I could see the tears well up into her eyes. We determined to adopt
some measures for her relief, and told her in the meantime to go back and
retain her present character until our plans were ripe for execution. In these
days of treachery and deceit there is no knowing whether there is truth in her
story—no knowing but she may be playing the spy—but I don't believe it.
I'm convinced that she is a female—her features are delicate, her hands even
or rather so for one working as she says she has done; her hair which is rather
long will not consent to part on the side as she tries to wear it, but persists in
falling asunder in the middle showing a straight, white line—and her voice
is clearly that of a girl. And if the remainder of her story be not true she is
one of the most consummate actresses I ever saw. I watched her narrowly and
could but notice how glad she seemed to be with her own sex once more,
how she shrank back when Father, who was passing by, stopped to speak to
her. And when she rose to walk, she seemed so much ashamed, said she did

not know how to move in those clothes and felt "very mean." She may be quizzing us, but I'd rather err on the side of mercy, than suffer a woman to want for any assistance which I could render at such a time. Poor thing! we must do something, I scarcely know what, but to be in her situation, would almost kill me I know and no doubt she suffers.

[June 23, 1862, entry omitted]

June 24th, 1862

Wrote all the morning. About eleven o'clock the provost marshal came over and Father took him down to the mill and laid the case of Nancy Jenkins— alias John Smith before him. He seemed to be very much incensed at the treatment she had received and vowed that the offenders should feel the effect of his wrath, promised to give her a passport home. This evening Father got the pass and we fitted her out with wearing apparel as far as we could but as our dresses were all too small for her we had to send her over to beg one from Aunt Betsy. She came back at sunset looking very happy and deposited some money with us that Aunt Betsy had given her, said she would call by early in the morning to see us as she intended starting immediately. I'm so glad the poor thing has thus far escaped so well and as she's homesick I hope she will soon get back to her friends.

It rained all the evening and I employed my time in trimming hats. Heigh ho!

June 25th, 1862

Nancy Jenkins came in this morning and having equipped her and given her written directions she set out on her return home. Poor thing she is very ill bred and rude, but I can't but help feel sorry for her and hope that she may arrive safely at her destination. . . .

June 26th, 1862

Repaired Grandma's bonnet this morning and we were busy all the morning laughing and talking. In the evening went upstairs and read and wrote, then

down to the cherry trees where we regaled ourselves with some of the fruit
and concluded by going out to the old seat at the stile to watch the sunset and
the stars come out and afterwards to the parlor where we sang and played till
after ten.

June 27th, 1862

Ma and Laura took advantage of this beautiful day to walk down to Rose
Hill. Allie came over and said they had news of Mr. Hope and I ran up there
to hear it. Found them all in great trouble, all the family in the kitchen
emptying a bee stand. They told me the Yankees had been out robbing and
plundering all the night—had taken every bee stand but that one they were
fixing. There had been great running to and fro during the night but they did
not know how to account for it all. Twas reported that Beauregard was at
Charleston and had whipped them all there. It was said that Jackson was
advancing down the valley in three different directions frightening the Yanks
terribly. The news came very directly—I wonder if it is so. Spent a very
pleasant day all by ourselves—Grandma and Aunt Betsy being at Uncle
Tom's. Two Yankees came in to take a five o'clock dinner and after they left
we missed a spoon. . . .

June 28th, 1862

This day one year ago dear Irvie had his picture taken in Baltimore for us.
Poor fellow! How little he recked as to his whereabouts the anniversary of
that day. Was busy sewing, reading and writing all day. Quite warm and
pleasant. Wonder if the Northerners enjoy it.

Played a little on the piano tonight.

June 29th, 1862

Read and talked with Father a good bit of the morning. Aunt L Buck
came in to dinner had been to church and heard a good sermon from
Dr. Hough—we wished to have gone too as the weather was so very pleasant, but Father dared not leave home to accompany us, and we dare not
go alone. Uncle Tom came over in the evening and said he thought they

saw some of our cavalry on the mountain today. Would be surprised from what I previously heard. It commenced raining about four o'clock and continued till after ten. Aunt L was obliged to stay all night she sending Jacquie home as a substitute. We had singing until bed time and after that sat up till late talking with Aunt L. This morning early we saw numbers of troops going out of town—cavalry and infantry in three different directions. What does it mean? We all think there will be a battle on the mountain very soon. I hope much from the result.

June 30th, 1862

We—Ma, Nellie, Aunt L and myself very early this morning dressed and went over to town—Nellie and I went to Oakley and the others to Captain Roy's. Ma came up after a while and brought us some very singular news. *Beauregard had taken, and was occupying Manassas.* We laughed at the idea, twas so absurd. Mr. F came in to dinner and told us that————certainly was on the mountain, that he had talked with him and learned from him that poor Ashby was certainly dead.—Was standing near him when he fell. It seems that cavalry could not be of service where the engagement took place. Ashby would be in the engagement and took command of an infantry company; his horse was shot from under him, and he then went on foot. Just as he waved his sword above his head calling "Come on, my brave boys!" one of the regiment, accidently discharged his gun and the ball took effect in his wrist passed through his breast and out the back of his shoulder. Poor fellow! He uttered not a word, but, turning and giving one look at his executioner fell to the earth.—Had a fragment of wood from the spot which was covered with blood. How I would like to have possession of such a precious relic.

Also told how Jackson actually rode into the Federal lines and impersonating a Federal officer ordered them to remove a cannon which commanded the bridge "to a more favorable position." He was obeyed, and then immediately turning to his own men, he told them to cross the bridge which they did before the Yankees could recover from their surprise and consternation. He whipped Shields, crossed the bridge, burnt it after him, drove Fremont back, forded the stream below and finished Shields, taking from him all his baggage, artillery, and everything. Shields himself was not there in person, and only a part of his division, but that was badly served up. Four thousand was their loss, one thousand ours in killed, wounded, and missing. Had gone back to the army. I pray he may be safe. We spent a most delightful day and were about returning home about sunset when the Yankee cavalry entered town *preceded by two ambulances.* We sat on the porch waiting for them to pass, Nellie had on a white dress and a hat trimmed with ribbon red, white, and red. Some of the creatures turned around waving their hands and calling out—"little Secesh in white dress!" and a great deal more which we did not hear.

It is thought they only went out on picket duty, had a brush with our pickets and returned *bringing their ambulances.*

Heard that poor Eltie Richardson was very ill today. Oh I hope she may be spared! Twould be a fatal blow to the family—her death.

Father commenced harvesting this morning.

July 1st, 1862

. . . An officer just from Winchester brought news of the capture of Richmond and the loss of Gen. McClellan and thirty thousand of their men—he stated that Gen. Banks had just received an official dispatch to that effect. This news was first brought to Rose Hill and had thence spread through town. I did not believe it because had it been true there certainly would have been more rejoicing among them when they came in today, yet I could not help but feel uneasy and sad.[2] Nellie and I concluded to go up to Mrs. Hope's to try and get something more definite if possible. They did not believe it at all and seemed in pretty good spirits. We spent a very pleasant hour and had a real treat in *real cake*—something which I thought had become obsolete in Virginia, or at least this portion of it. It has been quite a warm day and the hands of the harvest field seem to feel it very much. Poor Father, I'm afraid he's harvesting his wheat only for the Yankees to take it from him afterwards.

July 2nd, 1862

A rainy, disagreeable day.—Felt sad and unwell. No news. Mr. Berry came over at dusk and really cheered us so much that I retired to bed with quite a light heart. He stated that they had been fighting for several days at R but that so far from their having the place he believed the fight was still in progress and that we were giving them quite a distasteful experience in battle. He argues very hopefully from the disorder prevailing in every division of the Federal Army which had occupied the valley—Shields had resigned, Fremont been superseded and would do so and a probability of the removal of Banks—besides there were inferior officers innumerable who were tendering resignations and every kind of petty jealousy existing between the privates of the various commands. I have noticed the same thing myself and believe with him that these dissentions may prove a very fruitful cause of their final defeat. Oh! dear, would that it were already consummated!

July 3rd, 1862

Very unwell, was not down to breakfast. Mr. Allen brought very cheering news from town. Said they had been fighting at Richmond since Wednesday before the last and that we had given the enemy a severe repulse there, but that the battle still raged. I was nearly asleep when about ten o'clock Laura rushed upstairs exclaiming "Come girls, and hear the good news Mrs. Moffatt brings!" It was indeed glorious. We had turned the enemies flank, chased them over the Chickahominy—taking quantities of ammunition and a hundred pieces of artillery beside a large number of prisoners and there killed and wounded ever so many. Thank heaven!—and yet how do I know but in this horrid butchery I may not have lost some of my dear friends and relatives. Ah! "There is truly nothing sadder than a victory except a defeat." I was so surprised to hear that Jackson the dear "Old Stonewall" had worked his way around and reached Richmond in time for the fight. I hope he met Shields division again.

Mr. Berry was over to rejoice with us. He told us that the officers who promulgated that falsehood about the capture of R went back to Rose Hill that very evening and contradicted it. Inhuman wretch! Thus to throw the family and the whole community into a state of exciting and painful suspense just for the purpose of gratifying his love of tormenting! . . .

July 4th, 1862

The glorious anniversary! The day on which the enemy had promised themselves the pleasure of dining in Richmond—and they will, some of them in

the tobacco warehouses there. Perhaps it is very wicked of me to feel thus
exulted—but indeed tis not so much triumph in the defeat of our hard oppressors as joy at our success. . . .

The Yankees tried to celebrate today but the only demonstrations made
toward the object was the constant firing of cannon from the heights frightening negroes and children. We could distinctly see the bombs as they
ascended and then fell again and the reports sometimes were really very
heavy.

Mr. Berry dined with us and as Father was needed in the harvest field in
the afternoon I had to entertain him—or rather he entertained me and very
agreeably too despite the sharp aching in my head. After he left I had to go
to bed paying thus the penalty of yesterday's imprudence when in my exu-
berant experience I ventured through the wet grass in my thin cloth slippers.
Oh how I did repent of my rashness!

I've been trying to recollect the preceding Fourths of July as far back as
possible and find I could remember very distinctly five of them. The Fourth
five years ago, Cousin Sue, Nannie, Angie Smith, Julia Jacobs, Mrs. Smith,
Nellie and I spent very pleasantly together at Warren Springs. The Fourth
four years ago, we spent there with Katie, Alice, Gennie and other schoolmates. Three years ago—there was a Sunday School celebration on the green
at the courthouse upon which occasion the Front Royal Guards turned out
in all their "pomp and circumstance"—that was a delightful day. Two years
ago I spent it at Rose Hill having walked down the night before with Eltie
from singing school. Last year we spent the day at home and after tea
walked down to Rose Hill just as that memorable meteor fell and spent the
night there. Oh! the graduations of change that we may trace in five little
years!—my head!

July 5th, 1862

Had the headache all day and felt very feverish. Dr. Rixey called by in the
afternoon from Salem enroute to his sister's. He says he had seen a Richmond
paper giving an account of affairs at the seat of war. We have taken thirteen
thousand prisoners, thirty large siege guns, and one hundred and twenty
small pieces and "lots" of ammunition. The success, on our side is *for the
present* very decided. He also said he had met a man from Price's army

who stated that Beauregard with a portion of his command was certainly in Richmond—Price also was there. Their Maryland "News Sheet" which he brought confirmed the news and also confirmed the news which he brought of the recognition of the Confederacy by France and her determination officially announced at Washington, of putting a speedy conclusion to this war. Oh! this is all so encouraging it seems too much for us ever to have hoped for so soon. I don't believe a word about Jackson and Longstreet being dead and Magruder and Early and Stuart prisoners—no doubt the belief with them is offspring of the wish that it *might* be so. My dear brothers then are most probably on Virginia soil once more and feel as if they were almost home. Dear fellows, I feel so impatient to hear from and see them now that they are so near. But, wait, I will. For I believe this struggle will not continue many months longer.

(Later) Alice Stewart took tea with us. She is a sweet girl and I would like to have her visit us oftener. Belle Boyd and Mr. Jeffries came over and sat a while after tea and little as I felt like playing I exerted myself and undertook a piece when just then Grandma came in and asked if I had heard from poor Willie Richardson and then told me he was *dead*. Mr. Pettie had just come over to say that a letter had been received from a Dr. Ambler at whose house he had died announcing the fact. Poor dear, dear boy. I had felt uneasy and anxious a long time about him and had sometime almost feared something of the kind, and yet when the announcement came I was never more shocked in my life. It seems so hard to think of losing him thus—he so noble, so young and yet so brave and manly. I did not know how much I loved him before, and if I thought *we* were distressed, what a death blow it would be to his poor sick mother and sisters—poor Eltie ill even now. Oh it's all right! God knows what's best for us all, but it does seem hard for us to understand how so much useless and injurious lives are spared while those so much needed, the dearest and best are taken away. Poor Willie, he was kindly and tenderly cared for in his last hours. He was taken to Dr. Ambler's near Richmond where he lay sick until the 29th of May, when he died of hectic fever—produced no doubt in a great measure by his anxiety about his family. He was conscious until within a few days until his death and they had prayers for him until he grew so ill they thought best to desist, but he by his meek look requested them to continue the exercises. They buried him just as they had supposed his friends would have had him at home and "his grave was filled with flowers." I think these little details indicated delicate consideration and appreciation on the part of his stranger friends that soothed while it touches us deeply. Dear fellow—no one was ever more deserving of them and none more apt to receive them at home, and though stranger forms supplied the place of loved ones in the dread hour and stranger hands closed his eyes, yet their ministerings were so kindly that they comforted his death bed. He "wasted his life for his country's care, laying it down with a patriot's prayer," and I firmly believe that dear Willie has gone to a happy rest, that anxiety and pain will be his nevermore.

July 6th, 1862

Bank's army came in today and a brigade encamping in the back field we again had the officers here—Col. Schlaudecker and his staff—the former acting brigadier general. Genl. Cooper's brigade under Col. Schlaudecker encamped on barnfield burning remainder of fencing from barn to mill and around barn-yard—consuming 50 shocks of wheat and damaging tools and farming utensils. Our experience was but a repetition of our previous experience with the Union soldiers, raids on the garden and cherry trees, dairy and kitchen and entreaties for a meal as they professed to be starved and almost worn out. It has been a miserable day, very warm and such an incessant noise with the wagons and bands and shouting and running to the well for water. Gen. Banks came over in the evening but I had not the heart to see him. Poor Cousin Elizabeth, and Cousin Sue and Eltie! I've been thinking of them all day and how agonizing all this confusion would be to them. Uncle Tom was sick and could not go to them, but wrote them by Uncle Newton who disclosed the sad intelligence first to Cousin E who fainted. No wonder poor thing! for he was her last stay, her last hope and comfort and indeed in Willie seemed to center the affections of the whole family, and they all depended on him entirely for he was strong and matured beyond his years. And now he was gone—the last male member of his race gone just when he seemed to become almost necessary to their existence. They dared not tell Eltie, she was too ill, and yet I don't know how they can conceal it from her. Poor Cousin Sue Buck is with them and that will be a great comfort to all of them. I have remembered today so many of Willie's little gentle, kindly acts in days gone by. I remember too how eager he was to be in the service, how desperately he struggled between duty to his mother and sisters and duty to his country, and how much it cost him to stay at home for some months while his friends had all gone to the army. And then when he left again for the war how earnestly and affectionately he begged Nellie and me to visit his sisters and cheer them. I remember how rigidly and zealously he discharged his duty as soldier as well as son. And then I remembered the last time I saw him—last November how well he looked and how bright and happy he seemed as he dashed off on his pet Tom. Poor Willie, there are not many such as he was.

July 7th, 1862

Nellie was right unwell—we had a repetition of our former experience in Yankee officers—a continual tramping of man and beast through the yard and an incessant worry. Twas a very warm day and we spent it mostly upstairs growling at the hard Yankees. Old Gen. Cooper came over in the afternoon—a very well behaved old fellow apparently. The soldiers after the rain this evening amused themselves with carrying off Father's wheat which he had already cut and shocked. Indeed the Q. M. came over today and formally announced to Father the "military necessity" he was under of cutting and appropriating the remainder of the wheat standing in the field. I thought it quite a crude proceeding.

July 8th, 1862

Was aroused about four a.m. by a great hurrying to and fro and flashing of lights. Looking out the window I saw the encampment all ablaze that flickered about wildly and a busy hum proceeded therefrom. Presently the back door opened and Father and Col. Schlaudecker came out talking and then I heard boots hurrying down into the dining room and then the rattling of cups and saucers. I slipped down into Ma's room where was a light and seeing Martha standing there asked where Ma was. She confirmed my suspicions by saying the brigade had received marching orders four hours before and that Ma was down in the dining room giving the officers their breakfast. That's gratifying at all events. . . .

The surgeon came in the afternoon to see his patients and Nellie's throat being very much swollen Father called him in to prescribe for it which he did much to her discomforture for we teased her not a little about being attended by a Yankee doctor. He told Ma he would bring her a supply of medicine. Wonder if he will? . . .

Col. Van Buren showed us photographs of his family today—beautiful pictures they were. After night it was too warm to remain indoors and we occupied the porch and pavement. The Colonel gave us a description of his travels in Europe—had visited England, Germany, Switzerland and Italy, explored the ruins of Pompeii and Herculaneum and peeped into the crater of Vesuvius; admired the antiquities of Rome and reveled in the gayeties of Paris. Twas entertaining to listen to his accounts and we were thus engaged until bed time.

July 9th, 1862

Had a paper this morning in which was the name of Capt. Simpson mentioned among the prisoners taken at Richmond.

The day promised to be a fine one and Ma and I determined to go down to Rose Hill. . . .

I felt sick before starting to walk but hoped the exercise would prove beneficial. Found Cousin E's darkened and silent as a grave, but upon entering we saw her black clad figure at the bed side with her face buried in the pillows weeping. She bears her bereavement more heroically than I would have thought for, poor thing. Eltie she said was a little better. I could but notice what a deathlike quiet pervaded the house, broken only by the rolling and rattling of the army wagons that were every minute passing and repassing. Cousin E. was called from the room on some errand and Ma and I took our seats at the front window and looked out. Such a change as had taken place in that beautiful yard—since I had been there a short time before. The turf which was always so soft and freshly green was trampled and withered and brown and the shrubbery all utterly destroyed. The luxuriant myrtles that in rich masses covered the hill were all torn and sered. I thought how it would have grieved poor Willie to have known all this and when Belle came in and told me some of the insults and annoyances to which they had been subjected I felt glad that he had never known anything about it all. Poor

Cousin Sue! her heart seemed almost broken. She had grieved until she was faint and sick and when I asked her to take something to strengthen and refresh her said it was not worthwhile for she did not want to live now. We started up to see Eltie but I grew suddenly so deathly sick that I could not walk so I lay on the lounge by poor Cousin S and she told me all about Willie—talked all the time about him and it seemed really to relieve her to have someone to unburden her heart to. We were none of us except Ma and Belle well enough to eat dinner. Cousin Sue Buck did not come down at all until after dinner and then looked so pale and sad that I could not bear to see her. Went up into Eltie's room and sat with her a while. She looked badly but rather better than I expected to see her. I do not think she suspects anything of Willie's death—and they've been afraid to hint anything of the kind to her. They are cheerful as possible before her and yet it is strange they can keep the deception up so well. I was miserably sick all day and could scarcely manage to drag myself home in the late evening. Retired directly I got there.

[July 10, 1862, entry omitted]

July 12th, 1862

Sick, sick, sick! Oh me. Read all day when I could. In the late evening Belle Boyd, Alice Stewart and Mr. Jeffries came in. Belle told them all soon after she got here that she and Dr. Bogardus had traced up their relationship and found that they were cousins and when he came in they were evidently very well acquainted from the way they conducted themselves. This I learned from Nellie—I was fortunately confined to my bed. . . .

July 13th, 1862

Father and Uncle Tom were in to see me this morning, the latter very cheerful and hopeful. Father said he wished Dr. B. to see me and prescribe for me as he thought I needed a regular renovation of my system. So I reclined on the lounge in my wrapper and received the son of Asculapius in state. It seemed very inconsistent in me to permit the attendance of a sworn enemy in a professional capacity, but I felt desperate enough to try almost anything in hope of regaining health and strength. He seemed gentlemanly enough too and taking Father downstairs with him wrote out a lengthy prescription as to my diet, habits and exercise promising if I would obey his instructions to make me a strong healthy girl. Well I'm willing to try almost anything that will effect so desirable results for I'm weary, weary of feeling always weak and sick and unequal to any exertion.

No news.

July 15th, 1862

Too unwell to venture downstairs today. Ah me! What a great comfort it is to have kind good friends to attend you when sick, kind friends to prepare tempting dainties for a weak appetite, to administer the nauseous potion with a refreshing draught, to bring cool fruits and fair sweet flowers to cheer your solitude—and above all friends with ready sincere sympathy in your suffering. Oh surely I'm greatly blessed in this respect and I thank Heaven for it.

July 17th, 1862

Felt quite "sharp" this morning and undertook to sew some. Ma went over to spend the day at Uncle Tom's. It rained from noon all the evening. Arranged the book case in the passage. Ma came in at night saying they had many rumors in town, but it had been satisfactorily ascertained that few of the "rifles" were injured in the battle before Richmond and they none of our immediate friends. Captain Simpson, John Steele, J. T. Pettie and others were captured—Scott R and Smith T were very nearly taken but escaped in safety. Oh! I'm so glad tis no worse! This is more than we could have hoped for. Our men are certainly near here some of them and tis generally thought Jackson is advancing on Winchester.

They have given Eltie Richardson some intimation of Willie's death and she says she has seen and suspected something amiss ever since the family first heard it and she also said she believes if it were true it would kill her. Poor thing how I feel for her, she little knows how true it is.

The report of our Secretary of War has been seen and were astounded to learn that eight thousand would cover the whole loss of the Confederate army killed, wounded and missing during those dreadful battles. We had thought it must have been at least twice that amount.

July 18th, 1862

This is an anniversary—this day one year ago we struck our first fair blow for the freedom of the Old Dominion and I have thought of it all day, have remembered how dear Irvie and I walked down from the mountain and I commenced making his uniforms. I remembered how in the evening Mannie, Clara Taylor and Fannie Stewart came over and how we sang and played on the piano and by moonlight in the yard and after they left the vigil we kept waiting for the cars and my writing a letter at one o'clock A.M. and everything connected with it. Poor Irvie, where is he now I wonder. We heard some very unpleasant news with regard to Beauregard's bereavement and resignation. I hope and pray there may be no foundation for the rumor.[3]

Commenced raining this evening. Nellie and I had quiet nice practice on the piano all to ourselves tonight.

[July 20, 1862, entry omitted]

July 21st, 1862

I was so nervous and excited about that letter that neither Nellie or I could sleep much. Up bright and early to see if the day promised to smile on our intended jaunt and was gratified to observe that it did. On my way down to breakfast met the Dr. coming up with a frog in one hand and a magnifying glass in the other. He wanted to know if I had ever seen a frog eye magnified and being answered negatively asked me to step out into the sunshine and examine this one. I did so and was surprised to find that they were really beautiful looking like jewels of the finest, brightest jet set in chased gold. I had heretofore imagined that their eyes were the dullest most stupid things in the world but was mistaken entirely. Father told us not to start to Dr. T's until he came back from town and we thought it would have rained and spoiled our plans before he returned, but this was all forgotten when he came back with his hand full of letters—one from Cousin Kate B to Cousin Sue, one from Irvie to Cousin Horace Buck and from the dear boy to me—a great long nice letter dated from Tupelo, Miss., June 18th. They had received my lengthy letter written soon after Jackson's besom had swept the valley and seemed heartily to sympathize with and rejoice in our freedom. Said the climate agreed remarkedly well with them all—none of them having been sick of any consequence. Alvin had a few days before coming on to Richmond as bearer of dispatches and would not return before the first of July—but I suppose he did not return at all as Beauregard went soon after to Richmond himself. . . .

July 23rd, 1862

Raining—felt very unwell and slept the early part of the morning then came down and attempted to sew a little but did not get well underway with my sewing till after dinner. . . .

July 24th, 1862

Was up quite early. Sewed steadily all the morning, took my bath, rested a little, read and made an engagement to go over to town with Nellie in the afternoon. But an unfortunate cloud and shower prevented the execution of our plans and we were fain to enjoy the lovely evening after the rain at home on the porch. Gen. Augurs bodyguard took possession of the premises, barn, stables and all and broke into the granary. The Dr. told us that he heard in town today that they had recaptured the most of them. Don't believe him though. Sat out on the porch in the evening, writing. Miss Belle Boyd and the Dr. have quarreled, he thinks it "does not pay" to visit her.

July 25th, 1862

A very bright morning. Ma came into our room bright and early this morning and brought a note written by Cousin Sue B to Father at two o'clock in the morning requesting that Dr. Bogardus would go down to see Eltie. She was very ill and a messenger could not pass the pickets in going for any other physicians. The Dr. went immediately and had not returned when the break-fast bell rang, but when he did come about nine o'clock he said Eltie was better. Ma concluded to take one of the little boys and walk down to see her. . . . Monsieur Le Yank! Just to think they have issued a proclamation to the effect that for every Federal soldier shot by bushwhackers they will arrest the citizen nearest the spot when it occurred. And moreover that soldiers were to fire into groups of citizens collected at the corners for conversation "because it annoyed the soldiers who saw them." A beautiful state of affairs when men are prohibited the sidewalks of their native town. We had a news-paper of date of 28th containing some very caustic articles from London papers and also containing Lincoln's villainous order for the troops to rob the Secesh and subsist off them. Oh I'm so tired of tyranny! Ma and Carey and Dr. B came home at twilight Ma bringing me a beautiful bouquet and citron aloe. Eltie was much better and they were in better spirits than could have been expected. I am so glad.

July 26th, 1862

We—Nellie, Martha and I had a seige of it this morning cleaning and dusting the garret out. Was so tired after completing my task and was glad to sit down and enjoy a chat with Uncle Tom who had come over in the meantime. He was in fine spirits and made us feel quite cheerful at leaving. Dr. Bogardus came in about ten seemingly a good deal encouraged about Eltie, he walks down every night and stays until the next morning and sometimes goes down twice a day—is very kind and attentive indeed. Nellie and I concluded to walk over and spend some hours with Cousin Mary. Nellie had on her white dress and her hat trimmed with red, white and red and as we passed off the porch she stopped to pluck a pink oleander to put with a white rose bud on her bosom. I laughingly asked Father if he did not think those dangerous colors under which to make our entree into town? He jestingly referred us to the Dr. who stood in the door of his room—his advice very gravely given was that she should doff them but she resolutely declined to "haul down," whereupon he continued the jest by offering to act as guard and protector over to town. Of course his offer was not accepted. Found Cousin Mary enjoying a siesta—spent a pleasant time in her room and then went down to tell Mrs. R. goodbye, she took us out into the yard and showed us her flowers—some rare ones that I had never seen before—she gave me some plants and roots to raise for myself. As we returned home I stopped to inquire of Miss Sallie Kendrick how Mrs. Jackson was and after answering my question she told me that an order from Gen. Pope had just reached town commanding that the oath be administered to each citizen upon pain of their banishment from town and the confiscation of all their property.[4] This is what I have all the time been dreading and now it had come in a more hideous shape than I had ever anticipated. We met Mr. Hope and Mr. Hainie and the former had been weeping and seemed to be utterly bewildered by the shock. Oh how intensely I did hate the whole race of Yankees. Dr. B met us hurriedly just as we reached the bridge and we were not able even to return his salutation. . . . Tea was over and the family was assembled on the porch and such shocked faces was when I told them of the order. We were all eager to give up everything and go within our lines but Father soon proved the impracticability of this by telling how such a rush as would be made toward the most accessible points within our lines must necessarily impoverish the places, not only the inhabitants but the army which is worse, and the result a horrible famine. He said if it were not for his dependent family he would know quite well what to do—be shot first. As it was we must await the issue of events. Wait! Oh how possessed my soul with patience when such a disgraceful fate seemed waiting us—when men whose whole lives had been unblemished, whose lips had been blameless to be thus forced to perjure themselves in their old age—to be compelled to swear to support a government which their very souls abhorred, to seem to advocate principles from which their souls revolt in horror. Oh it does seem so hard, if our men would but come to our delivery. There is one consolation in believing that desperate diseases require desperate remedies and I think they must see that their cause is waning that they thus resort to warring against defenseless women and children. . . .

July 27, 1862

Dr. Bogardus came home about eight o'clock and said that poor Eltie was not so well—he feared she was taking diptheria again. I'm so sorry to hear it. . . . Dr. B and H have received their marching orders and leave tomorrow. Father had a conversation with the former regarding that order of Pope's and he pronounced it both iniquitous and impolitic. . . .

July 28th, 1862

Ma is quite indisposed this morning, Carey is little better, both Evred and the baby complaining. Eltie still suffering from her throat. Our boarders left immediately after dinner in an ambulance provided for the purpose. One of the Dr.'s last acts was to hunt for some lemons and fresh beef for Eltie and prescribed for Ma. When making his adieu he went down into the basement to look for Evred and then called for the baby. Nellie, Ma and I were in Grandma's room—I tying up a lunch for him when he coolly walked in and bidding us take care of ourselves and wishing we might soon be relieved of our present troubles shook each of us by the hands in adieu. . . .

Was very sick this evening and retired early, Ma sleeping with me in my room and Nellie and Laura occupying her chamber in charge of the babies.

July 29th, 1862

Ma and the baby both quite sick and I quite weak, we all stayed upstairs during the morning. Aunt Betty came in and sat a few hours with us. She heard that Eltie was very ill and said Uncle Tom had gone down to see her. Orville came over from Oakley after dinner and said that Uncle Tom had just come home and told them that dear Eltie was dead. Poor dear Eltie, gone from a troublous world, her brief span of life has been all sorrow and now she is happy. She expressed her resignation, her perfect trust; took leave of all her family, requested that they would not sorrow for her when she would be so happy and begged they would not reflect on themselves for anything they had ever said or done to her and left messages to each and all and made bequests. Then telling Uncle T that there was much she would like to say to him but had not the strength and folding her hands on her bosom expired today two months after Willie died. Two more dearly loved schoolmates gone making a happy exchange and I left to envy them their happiness. I do feel such sympathy for the family, twill be almost a death blow to them and I grieve more for them than for her though I know how sadly we shall miss her here and she has done a great deal towards contributing to my pleasure, still I would be selfish enough to wish for her back. . . .

July 30th, 1862

Cold and bright. Cousin Mary was going to Rose Hill and I wanted to go with her but was most afraid to venture so far on foot. Grandma concluded to go and while they were getting ready Uncle Tom came in and they all went together. Ma a little better, but the baby still quite sick and looks really emaciated, poor little fellow. . . . The poor little baby is very sick tonight and I must help Nellie nurse him. Belle Boyd was taken prisoner and sent off in a carriage with an escort of fifty cavalrymen today. I hope she has succeeded in making herself proficiently notorious now. They say they are going to put her within our lines and keep her there.

July 31st, 1862

. . . The little baby was so ill this morning that we thought he must have convulsions and Father had to go for Dr. Turner who took dinner with us. The baby was a great deal better when he came and he seemed to think that he was teething and did not require much attention from a physician. . . .

We heard this evening that there had been a great battle at Gordonsville and another at Warrenton Junction in which we were victorious. Oh if I only dared believe it! They have certainly moved a battalion from town to the river and commenced throwing up breastworks and planting cannon which looks like preparation for protecting a retreat. Oh I do want to hear some news so much!

A most ludicrous scene occurred today. Some Yankees bargained with Mahala for some bread, but upon handing her the money gave her notes which she refused to receive, whereupon snatching up the loaves he swore he would have them anyway and scampered off up the steps but she grasped him by the coat and stayed his flight, but he was not thus to be foiled of his prey, and tossing the bread up the steps to his companion called for him to make off with the prize. Mahala followed him out into the yard abusing him and charitably wishing he might have a cold bullet through him before he had a chance to repeat the act. The Lt. and Father happened to witness the scene and the former commanded the fellow to restore the stolen viands, but he only threw her a portion of what he had taken and while she was securing that made off with the remainder. How I would like to send the boys a sketch portraying this scene.

August 1st, 1862

Had a weary night with the baby who, however, seemed better this morning.

Arose at six o'clock, cleaned up my room, swept the passage out, ate my breakfast, took Ma hers and then with Nellie fell to work thoroughly cleaning out the basement presses and washing up and managing all the children. Completed by ten o'clock and was tired enough by that time too. Mrs. Moffatt spent a cozy day with us. Wrote in the morning and evening a little while. No confirmation of yesterday's reports, but another rumor of a battle at little Washington.

Heard through a letter received from Newt. Petty that only three of the Warren Rifles were killed before Richmond, none of whom were our own immediate friends. He said they were very badly off with supplies and almost starving but as he is something of an epicure I hope this is an exaggeration. He also said he had seen dear Alvin in R a few days before with dispatches from Beauregard and that he was well and had left his friends in good health. Oh sometimes I do grow so impatient to hear from the boys directly. To think that A was there a month ago and we've not received a letter from him yet.

August 2nd, 1862

Nursed the baby and read a book—Courtesies of Married Life which Laura had borrowed. . . . After tea E and J Hope came running up breathless to say they had received a late paper in which it was stated that ten of our iron-clad vessels had entered at Mobile and two more were on their way hither so that that port was now opened to the commerce of the world. And told us many more encouraging things. Oh! this, if true, will prove a great thing for us. Dr. M has come to board here.

[August 3, 1862, entry omitted]

August 6th, 1862

. . . I concluded to write to Jule so that with my diary and perusal of "Adile" kept me in employment all day. Was, I'm ashamed to say in a very bad humor tonight. Dr. Marshall came in at the tea table. He said that it was reported that Winchester had been burnt and gave other items of disaster to our army with such cool assurance that I could have choked him. Of course, we did not credit the rumors but I was infinitely provoked at his manner of reporting it. . . .

August 8th, 1862

Nursed the baby, practiced, did some clear starching, read, wrote, and sewed. . . . We were all sitting on the front porch talking when Dr. Marshall thought he descried a signal light which upon examination proved to be a singular star. This appearance led to a discussion of natural phenomena, spiritual agencies, dreams, etc., which occupied us pleasantly until twelve o'clock. Dr. M insisted upon our using his span of horses while he remains here and I think I'll gratify him.

August 9th, 1862

Busy sewing pretty much through the day. . . .

August 10th, 1862

Dr. M offered to stand on guard at home while Father went to church today, so we all went for the first time since the 25th of May and were fully repaid by hearing an excellent sermon from Dr. Hough. . . .

Aunt Lizzie called for us in the evening and took us home with her. Had a delightful ride and enjoyed it all the more because it was such a novelty. Reached the river about six o'clock in a dash of rain, but succeeded in getting to the house dry. Dear old Clover Hill! My thoughts and desires have been pilgrims to this Mecca a long time, and now to be there in person! Twas so pleasant. The house I found very much changed by late repairs, but the inmates were the same dear warm hearted friends that erst they were and welcomed us so cordially.

August 11th, 1862

Was up bright and early this morning after a refreshing night's rest. Went down into the garden and by the time the bell rung for prayers had a sweet little cluster of rosebuds glittering with dew for Aunt Lizzie. After breakfast we went out to look at the improvements and admired the quantities of beautiful flowers that ornamented the yard. How perfectly delightful it was to stand on the broad portico with the fresh dewy breeze of early morning laving my brow and bearing to me the grateful incense of a thousand flowers and reveled in the beautiful scene before me. The green hills sloping down gradually to the meadows that lay stretched along the bank of the river; the river flashing and dimpling in the sunbeams and reflecting back the beauty of the towering cliffs and wooded heights beyond. Then the picturesque old bridge with the white house by it and the cleft in the mountain side down which leaped the laughing cascade and the soft blue tint of the distant mountains just where it met the clear brilliant sky. All at one glance I took in and might have stood admiring it for an indefinite time had not Aunt Lizzie broken the spell by bidding us come and pick over some berries she was having dried for Ma. While thus employed Aunt Harriett rushed in and cried out that "our men were dashing down the road" and on going out we indeed saw horsemen moving rapidly on the other side of the river but could not at the distance distinguish them. Emma presently came in to see us and said she had met them, that they were our men and that they were going to Front Royal. Not long after, while playing and singing in the parlor we heard the children calling out that our men were coming and the Yankees in hot pursuit. And it was really the case. We saw our men plunge into the river and dash across laughing and shouting. On they came toward the house and just as they got opposite the house the Yankees came in sight on the other side of the river. We all ran out and the gallant fellows galloped up to the stile and shouted—"ladies we've been to Front Royal, taken two provosts and a captain and other prisoners—don't be alarmed for us, we have every advantage and apprehend no danger, go into the house please ladies, the Yankees will fire and shoot you." But we remained there long enough to give them some apples and hear that they had seen Henry Buck who was well. Then they rode up the lane to the barn and pausing there defied their pursuers and then disappeared behind the hill. The Yankees did not attempt to cross the river but moving about the river bank cautiously for a while returned to town. It was the most daring feat to be sure, twenty-one men to venture to Front Royal where was an encampment of men sufficient to have taken the whole party without using guns at all. Only seven went into town, went into the Provost's office, took his excellency, took Dr. Marshall, went a quarter mile out of town for another prisoner and starting with the officers and *thirty* other prisoners left town just as the Yankee cavalry were preparing to pursue them. Owing to their haste they were compelled to abandon the thirty infantry prisoners and taking the officers on horseback made good their return. Dr. Marshall came back but tis a mooted question whether, as he said, he escaped, or being a surgeon, was released by our men. . . .

Commenced reading the "Heir of Radcliffe" but did not progress very far. Took a charming ramble this afternoon over to the cascade gathering ferns, flowers, etc., etc. and then back again crossing the river by twilight.

Had music and singing and a very novel and grotesque entertainment after tea. . . .

[August 12, 1862, entry omitted]

August 13th, 1862

We all—Em, Ju, N. L., N. E. F. and myself walked over to Mrs. Hall's this morning. Found Alice able to sit up and come into the parlor. We heard this morning that the Yankees were to be up and arrest all citizens within five miles of the scene of that exploit and we did expect them all day but they did not come.

Went down to Flint Run in the evening and after rambling along its banks for a time Nell, Julie and I, at Mrs. Hall's instigation doffed shoes and stockings and waded the stream—a very undignified but not less delightful proceeding on our part. . . .

August 15th, 1862

Wrote a letter this morning and sent out by Uncle Fayette. Sewed a little and read a good deal. Was on the bed too a good deal for I felt so unwell. The

remainder of our party had a great game of romp on the grass before tea
and after I tried to sing but was taken so sick that I had to take medicine and
retire before prayers. Heard the Yankees were preparing to leave Front Royal
and do wonder if it can be true.

August 16th, 1862

Was down again this morning a little weak but much better. Kept very quiet
with my book all the morning till about eleven o'clock when Jule came in to
my room with a glass of sangaree in her hand to strengthen me for the trying
scenes which she said were about to ensue.[5] Pointing out the window she
showed me about seventeen Yankee cavalry just crossing the river toward the
house; and Nellie came hurriedly in bidding me conceal my diary and letters
as they certainly make a search. But they did no such thing, only rode up to
the house and made enquiry as to the number and movement of the "secesh
cavalry" that had gone over into the "Fork." The servants and children assured them that there were hundreds of the most ferocious kinds of bushwhackers over there which intimidated them so much that they would penetrate no further than to the barn-field. When wheeling their horses they
dashed back to the house, some of them coming in to get bread and milk,
some searching the outhouses and some trying to capture two little ponies
feeding in the front meadow. . . .

The girls walked over to our old "Sunset Cliff" this evening but I did not
feel well enough to go with them and so stayed with Aunt Lizzie going around
with her and talking to her while she watered the flowers. Then went on the
upper porch to wave to the party on the cliff across the river, and drink in the
loveliness of that river scene which was even more to be appreciated in the mellow subdued tints of the evening than when radiant with the light of the early
sun. Dear old Clover Hill! How quiet and what an atmosphere of tranquility
and peace hovers ever around here and how often during the turmoil and confusion of the last months have I thought of this almost paradise on earth. Ah
me! I must tomorrow go back to the oppression of Yankeedom.

August 17th, 1862

Nev. rode down to Mr. King's before breakfast this morning to ascertain
whether or not we could get into town and returned saying the enemy had

evacuated the place. Glorious! immediately after breakfast the light carriage was harnessed and Julia, Nellie, Neville and myself set out. What a delightful ride we had along the cool shaded banks of the river laughing and talking merrily and anon relapsing by tacit consent into silence enjoying the beauty of day and scenery. But in the midst of our fully blown pleasure we were suddenly disconcerted by the breakage of one of the shafts and as it was impossible to repair damages then and there nothing was left for us but to "foot it" to town, the distance of two miles. Found no pickets at any of the posts and when we came in sight of the place we *knew* the Yankees had left. Such unbroken deathlike stillness as reigned around was never known while their hated influence extended. We walked through the streets without encountering a soul until nearly out of town when we met Uncle Tom who told us all the Rose Hill family—Cousin Sue B included, were very sick; he had just come from there. So sorry. He gave us the particulars of the dash and it was even a more daring achievement than we had first thought for only seven of our men came into town and three of them rode right down to the Yankee camp and were fired on. One went into the hotel and broke up the rests there, and another went a half mile up the creek and yet all escaped. "Twas gloriously done."

Found the family all better except Willie who is quite sick—all seemed so glad to see us. Aunt Betty and Uncle Tom spent the evening with us and I hoped Jule was going to stay too, but she went home with Nev. promising to come down again during the week.

Felt quite unwell tonight. We have whipped Banks again at Culpeper and the 102d New York Regiment which had been here, was cut to pieces.

August 19th, 1862

Father proposed a ramble to the river this morning to see the formidable fortifications there. We had a pleasant walk and a hearty laugh at the abortive attempts at defense made by the Yankees. To think of a mud embankment and rifle pits at the *foot* of the hill, protected by an abatis of saplings about as impregnable as a box-hedge which commanded nothing but Mr. Weston's garden. Such a farce! Such a farce! . . .

Poor Willie is quite sick and Uncle Newton was to see him today. They are all better at Rose Hill.

August 20th, 1862

Was very unwell this morning but Ma persuaded me that I would feel better if I would walk out. So I got ready and went over to town with her and Aunt L. Went to Capt. R's and found Cousin Mary in bed and Mrs. R too. Mrs. Miller and little Walter were there—the first time I've seen the latter since he was a month old. He's a bright saucy little fellow. After sitting an hour Ma and Aunt L arose to go up to Uncle Tom's and I to come home, but I found my headache and faintness had increased so much that I could scarcely walk and was forced to accede to Cousin Eve's repeated requests that I would stay to keep Cousin M company in bed and promises to nurse me very nicely. Sure enough I went right to bed and stayed there until late in the afternoon and although I was so nervous and suffering so intensely the day was not an unpleasant one, for Cousin Mary was glad to have some one talk with her and entertained me so well and Cousin E nursed me so to my satisfaction that it relieved me half the pain I felt. Dr. Dorsey was surprised though when he came in and found two patients instead of one. . . .

August 21st, 1862

Managed to drag wearily through the day. Willie still so very sick and Uncle Newton to see him. The latter told us he had heard from Charlie and that he had been accidently shot in the foot and that the foot had to be amputated in consequence. Poor Charlie! a cripple for life, how distressing it will be to him. . . .

August 23rd, 1862

Felt brighter today, busily engaged sewing all day. Heard that Capt. Simpson had been exchanged and was in town. Brought cheering news from all our friends. Aunt L Buck called by this evening on her way from up the river, and told us that Walter had started to see us but been persuaded not to come by some officious friend. He sent some saucy messages to Nellie and me. Aunt L says he was in the most hilarious spirits imaginable. Dear fellow! How I should like to have seen him. Through Uncle Newton we learned that Capt. S had seen Cousin Alex Blakemore in Rd. and Uncle John too. Cousin

brought news from our boys—he had just left them at Chattanooga, Tenn.
They were with Col. Jordan under General Bragg who intended retaining
them in his employ come what would. All were well. Beauregard had neither
lost his life nor been deranged but was on leave of absence at some spring to
recoup his health. We were so delighted to hear it. Cousin E Cloud wrote me
a note this evening to the effect that Capt. S was to leave for Gordonsville in
the morning and would carry out letters if I had any to send the boys. I
thereupon sat down and indited what dear Irvie terms one of my "four story"
epistles to the boys and dispatched it by Allie. Uncle Tom came over and told
us of that glorious "back down" of old Pope. After issuing the most infamous
proclamation tending to the inhalations of the secessionists he comes out in a
recantation—prohibits the administration of the oath under compulsion and
expressly provides for the protection of secession property and all just because he was afraid of our dear old President. Well, it is too good.

Kattie Samuels went to Strasburg this evening to see her husband who has
been exchanged and is there. . . .

August 24th, 1862

Very cool this morning. Quite early we heard heavy cannonading from the
east. Uncle Mack came in before church and brought me a message from
Mr. Jamieson who was at his house a few nights since. He sent his compliments and regrets at not getting to see us—being afraid I suppose to venture
out of the mountains. Father, Nellie and I went to church and just as we
entered the church yard I noticed quite a distinguished looking stranger sauntering slowly toward us in whom I presently recognized the redoubtable
Capt. Simpson who came forward and spoke to us quite cordially though he
as well as ourselves were constrained. While Father was talking with him we
went into the house. Dr. Hough preached poor John Steele's funeral sermon
and I think there were few dry eyes in the house. The text was—"I will
patiently bear the indignation of the Lord for I have sinned against Him and
He will deliver me"—and "Rejoice not over me, oh mine enemy. Though I
am fallen yet shall I rise again, though I sit in darkness yet shall He show
me His marvelous light."

Found on coming out the church that the cannonading was more distinct
and heavier. On passing down the street learned from a soldier who professed

just to have left the scene—that Jackson had beaten the enemy back from Culpeper and that they were in retreat for Washington—our men hotly pursuing. Went up on the house when we reached home and could clearly distinguish cannonading from two directions and the heaviest I ever heard. It seemed singular that we should feel so calm with the thunder of artillery shaking the very ground and knowing as we did that the fate of the valley, if not of the capital itself depended on the issue of the conflict. . . .

This has been a sad, sad day to me.

August 25th, 1862

Was awakened about twelve o'clock last night by hurrying to and fro and opening and shutting doors. Feeling uneasy I glided downstairs and met Father at the foot of the steps who called out to me not to be afraid that Uncle John, Alex and Horace had just come home from Warrenton. I asked when they left and how went the day. He replied that all was well. At the breakfast table this morning we met all together and Uncle John confirmed all we had heard through Capt. Simpson concerning the boys and told Ma over in what high estimation they were held by their superior officers. It is so gratifying to hear it and Gen. Gordon says he'll not give them up under a commission. . . . After breakfast Uncle J had his beautiful little pony brought to the stile and proposed that I should take a ride. So I told him I'd go out and invite our friends to meet him here. Took Carey behind me and had a most charming ride upon the little jewel of a nag. . . .went on down to Rose Hill. I dreaded this visit so much—dreaded so much to go where the footsteps that were wont first to meet me and the voice that ever was present in welcoming were now still and silent in the grave. They all looked so sick and so sad—four dark robed, wan figures all that were left of the once large and happy family. Cousin Sue and poor little Belle were both in black. I did not stay long, but after telling the news Uncle John brought and trying to interest them in foreign subjects I started home. . . . I could not but be amused this morning, while giving the baby his breakfast in the dining room Horace and Alex spied me and in they marched to shake my hand cordially and receive my congratulations on their safe return and prosperous appearance. They evidently considered themselves heroes in their fatigue uniforms and———but they were very respectful though cordial and replied

to my questions very proudly. Alex assured me he had assisted in lifting
Gen. Ashby into the ambulance after his death and Horace dwelling on the
great battles they had witnessed. I was right glad to see them.

Was lying down upstairs in the afternoon when I heard a bustle below as
of arrivals and soon distinguished Cousin Betty R's voice and Mr. R's, then
presently Uncle Mack and Uncle John, then Uncle Fayette, Aunt Betty's,
Uncle Tom's, Uncle Newton's, and little Belle Richardson's. Dressed and went
down where they were all sitting at the door looking so happy and chatting
away so merrily congratulating themselves upon this pleasant reunion and
regretting that Uncle John must leave during the night. Suddenly in the midst
of it all came a cry—"the Yankees!" We sprung to our feet and looked out
in time to see in truth a company of about thirty horsemen dashing gallantly
into town. Immediately all was confusion, we knew they had come for our
soldiers, some few of whom with Capt. S were with their families in town,
and we were for getting Uncle J out of their clutches. So thrusting some of
his things into his carpetsack we started him on foot across the field sending
his horse around to meet him and telling him to strike for the pine thickets.
As soon as he was off the remainder of the party dispersed like a flock of
frightened partridges. Some of us went up to the dormer window on the roof
to watch the proceeding of the Yankees. Saw them go out to Mrs. Simpson's
and return minus the Confed. Capt. Then saw them go into the private
houses we knew for the purpose of searching them and expected a squad of
detectives over here every moment but they did not come—and about dusk
they left without having taken a single prisoner. . . . Horace and Alex seemed
so adverse to returning to their military duties that Father permitted them to
remain at home. Oh how I do long for the time when our friends may visit
us at will and not be afraid of staying overnight at the same house twice in
succession as is now the case.

Tis said Capt. Simpson was concealed in the cornfield near town today
while they were looking for him and that he ruined a very handsome uniform
presented him while a prisoner by a lady of Boston.

August 26th, 1862

Ma and Aunt Letitia went to Rose Hill today. I felt very unwell all day but
did some little sewing besides teaching the boys. Was in the parlor practic-

ing this evening when hearing Nellie exclaim "Oh they'll get our cavalry"! I went to the door and she pointed out the same company of Yankees riding swiftly into town pursuing two of our cavalrymen who had started out to the river a short time before. We watched them until they were concealed by the houses. . . . The Yankees did not get our men and really looked mean when they went out of town a second time foiled of their prey. There is clearly a traitor among us, else how did they know any of our men were in town.

August 27th, 1862

Felt quite sick this morning but as Grandma and Laura were away I had to exert myself to help nurse Willie and the other children. Willie was more unwell and the children as bad as they could be, so we had a fatiguing day of it very, Father too was complaining. When they all came home————late in the evening Laura brought me from Ellen Brown a song that I had long coveted—"We Sleep but we are not Dead"—Alvin's song. Heard today that Jackson was at Salem. Longstreet holding the Yankee army at check at Warrenton. . . .

August 28th, 1862

Heard a confirmation of the capture of the brave "Baylorians." Jackson is said to be at or near Manassas and to have completely surrounded the Feds. . . .

August 29th, 1862

Aunt B sick and Willie little better. While trying to write this morning Mrs. Hall came in and I had to stop. Very soon after, the children came in to say a company of our cavalry was coming in town. We saw them—a goodly sight. Three of the number came over to dinner. . . .

. . . Mrs. Moffatt and E came in late this evening and Mrs. M told us she had heard from one of our soldiers that skirmishing a preface to a general battle was going on at Gainesville and a great fight was hourly expected—the Yankees are surrounded completely and we hope and trust we may be successful.[6]

August 30th, 1862

Felt sick this morning but heard the boys' lessons. . . . Father came home
to dinner and told us he had seen a Balto. Sun which spoke of an irruption
of some of the Indian tribes upon some of the northwestern states and
twas feared they were backed by the Mormons. So Uncle Sam will have
an occasion for the use of some of his surplus soldiers—volunteers. The
paper also contained a rumor that Sturgis' command (which had been sent
to quell the rebels who made the raid upon Bristoe Station) was taken by
those very rebels. Then the news from England was not at all comfortable.
So glad! . . .

August 31st, 1862

No service in the churches today. I read aloud to Father until Uncle Mack
came in and then went up to my room to take a nap. Was very unwell and
so silly as to cry ever so long after dinner just because I did not know what
else to do.

   Uncles Fayette and Newton were with us a little while in the evening and
after they left Ma, Nellie and I walked up to Mrs. Hope's. While we were
there Father came in and said he had just seen a reliable German up the street
who was just from the scene of action and he told him that Jackson had
repulsed Pope's whole army at *Manassas* with great carnage, had taken a great
many prisoners and vast amounts of army stores—enough to supply our men
during the coming four months. But we had lost much too, the "Stonewall
Brigade" was terribly cut up and Ewell had been wounded and had his leg
amputated and many, many a noble Southern sleeps silently on that sangui-
nary battlefield. It was a glorious victory though over the enemy and we felt
very very hopeful and cheerful for our cause. We came home and found
Aunt B and Uncle T there and soon made them participants in our joy. Oh
it seems all so great a mercy that I can scarce realize or understand it. To
think how it has all changed since six months ago. Then, we saw nothing
but disaster and destruction before us. We had lost our stronghold and permitted the enemy to penetrate to the vitals of the country with his desolat-
ing armies, laying waste the land with fire and sword. Then his ironclad
gunboats were swarming on our coast and port after port, city after city

were occupied by his ruffian horde and the whole South was being drained of its substance. So that there was nothing but starvation and ruin for the inhabitants. Our capital was menaced by a vast army of exultant and victory flushed foes. Our army seemed to have melted away or were within the coils of a mighty serpent that must soon crush them—oh it was all disheartening enough! and I have wondered how we ever struggled through such depths of gloom. But the day I trust has gone on our midnight, how it has all so changed I can't understand, but surely God has been with us. Tis He that arrested the tide of Union successes and nerved and inspired our men to such deeds of daring heroism. Oh! may we never forget to whom we owe it all and weakly give to erring impotent man the need of thanksgiving and praise that belongs but to the Maker!

September 1st, 1862

"The summer is past, the harvest is ended," and today beholds the dawn of the autumn. I wonder how the summer has gone by I can scarcely tell I'm sure. It has seemed such a short one, and even with all our troubles and annoyances it has not been a joyless season; for those few pleasures we had were all the more keenly appreciated for their rarity. But I fear I have planted few seeds of improvement in the meantime and that this autumn will prove very barren of the fruits of high resolve, self-conquest or anything of good. I believe though that I *have* learned to be more useful to myself and to others for which I'm thankful.

Ma, Aunt L and myself walked over to Mrs. Cook's where we spent quite a pleasant morning admiring her flowers, reading Giles' letters and eating apples. Found Mrs. Morehead at home when we returned and not very long after Uncle Tom came in and then Aunt Betty so we had quite a gathering. . . .

September 2nd, 1862

Father came over from town this morning and told us that Scott Roy had come home the night before—was wounded in the forehead and the blow would probably have proved fatal had he not happened to have his face averted at the time. He brought news that poor John Simpson was killed, Sam missing and Robt badly wounded. Saml. Spingler was thought to be mortally wounded. Tom Santmyers has his finger shot off. None of our immediate friends were injured. Scott's wound was a mere scratch—only a passing compliment from a saucy bullet. How I would like to see him and hear him spin some of his "camp yarns."

Nellie and I spent a very pleasant day at Oakley. . . .

September 3rd, 1862

Ma and Aunt Betty and Laura walked out to Dr. Dorsey's today. Spent the day sewing and nursing. Father remarked at breakfast this morning that he had heard a very singular noise during the night and on looking out saw in the direction of Winchester a brilliant light. We were at first apprehensive of a general conflagration of the town, but afterwards heard that it was the explosion caused by the enemy destroying his magazines there. They had evacuated the place at two o'clock this morning. Good! I hope the valley is clean now! . . .

Scott left this evening without calling. Unsociable fellow!

September 4th, 1862

. . . Just as I came up to my room tonight Father called to me from the door and bade me guess who had arrived in town a few moments since. Of course, I guessed Dick and correctly too. Bless his life, I'm so glad. Father had just returned from town where he had seen Dick who had only then reached town walking from Strasburg. . . . Ma, Nellie and I sat up in our room a long time tonight talking in the moonlight.

September 5th, 1862

. . . We were all sitting in Grandma's room sewing and chatting merrily when we heard a light but firm step and a dear familiar voice exclaiming "How are you all!" and in a moment Dick was in our midst giving and receiving embraces and kisses. We were so glad to see him and spent such a delightful day with the dear fellow who has improved and looks wonderfully well. He with a friend of his Lt. Timmerman are recruiting for the regiment and will be with us probably some time. Father was at the mountain all day so we had Dick's conversation all to ourselves and he told us so much about the army that we had never heard before. I'm sure I had no idea the battle of Williamsburg and Seven Pines were such important conflicts till hearing his accounts of them. I never till today noticed the striking resemblance between our dear Irvie and Dick in manner and conversation and it has if possible endeared him all the more to me—indeed several times today I've been cheated into addressing him as "Irvie." . . .

[September 6, 1862, entry omitted]

September 7th, 1862

A bright and beautiful day—no service in the churches. . . .

Mr. Hope came up to see us this morning to impart the news which he had brought directly from the army the night before. He had seen some of our friends and all in the army were well. He also saw Jackson's army cross the Potomac. The old Genl. had outwitted the enemy most completely as he always does. By marching a portion of his forces toward Arlington and making a great ado with his artillery he induced the Yankees to believe he intended making an attack there while all the time our troops were wading the river at Edwards Ferry above Leesburg. What must have been the feeling of those men particularly the Marylanders themselves when they first set foot upon the Maryland shores—the longwished for goal of their fondest hopes. I think they must have saluted ground with almost the same reverence that Columbus did when he landed in the new world. As the men gained the opposite banks they struck up My Maryland accompanied by the bands. Then I think the sternest heart must have throbbed in sympathy and the most unimpressible of Maryland's exiled sons must have wept like children. Oh it was such a scene as one witnesses but once in a life time and I would have given much to have seen it. And we certainly are there to help her "burst the tyrant's chains" and rescue one other bright star of the Southern constellation from the gloom of tyrannical oppression. Oh I sympathize with those who welcome the freedom which our army brings them, with them I've tasted the bitterness of slavery, with them I've welcomed deliverance which only we could appreciate. . . .

[September 8, 1862, entry omitted]

September 9th, 1862

Well, its all over thank goodness! I never want to sell another sheet, pillow slip, towel, table cloth, or napkin as long as I live. . . .

Cousin E Cloud went home this evening. Cousin Mary remained and very soon Alice Morehead, Aunt Betty, Uncle Tom, and Chris Lane came in—the latter has been sick at the mountain but is now on his way home. I don't know when I ever enjoyed anything so much as I did the bantering which he and cousin M kept up all the time he was here, it was one continued round of retort and repartee. Dick had also come to tell us goodbye for he is off to-morrow on a recruiting expedition to Fauquier—will return on Friday. He no doubt anticipated a great deal of pleasure from his trip notwithstanding the responsibility.

Nothing authentic from the Army.

September 10th, 1862

Cousin M left quite early and I spent the morning in a desultory kind of way, sitting with Aunt B, reading, sewing. . . .

Cousins Ed and Emma came in this evening to my great surprise. I was so glad to see them though. But Cousin E brought rather unwelcome tidings if true—it seems that the Winchester people are apprehending an advance from Harpers Ferry and that there is quite a formidable force at the latter point and also at Edwards Ferry which will cut off our communication with our army. However, I believe our Generals will soon remove this inconvenience—at least I trust so. I've noticed a number of army wagons passing through town today and numbers of soldiers enroute for Winchester. . . .

Nellie and I did enjoy the moonlight so much tonight—we sat out on the hill a long time watching the effects of the silver light on the cloud and seeing all sorts of fanciful images on the clouds.

Father commenced threshing his wheat today and seems to be getting through with it very smoothly. . . .

September 12th, 1862

. . . There are so many broken down soldiers passing through town en route for Winchester. We had some seven or eight to supper and two of them stay here tonight—one a very handsome little captain—a Georgian and his Lt. D. H. Hill has command at Winchester and tis said has cut off the supplies for the Yankees at Harpers Ferry. *Such*, says Ma, is the news current in town. Stay with Aunt B tonight.

September 13th, 1862

Had a number of soldiers to breakfast this morning and after breakfast at Father's request Nellie and I sang and played for them and for a wonder they seemed to enjoy it very much. One of them sat as near as he conveniently could to the piano and Father says he scarcely moved all the time. I could but notice how much more like gentlemen they behaved than did the Yankees. Loyal blood will show itself in any guise. The little Capt.—Watson came to tell us goodbye and expressed himself in a very gentlemanly manner. Taught the children, sewed, read and wrote. In the afternoon Aunt B and Uncle Tom came over, but did not remain long. Pleasant day altogether.

September 14th, 1862

Was very unwell this morning and did not accompany Father to Rose Hill. Father returned and Uncle Mack came over and they said it was rumored that Wirt had surrendered Harpers Ferry and we had taken a quantity of arms and "contrabands." . . .

[September 15, 1862, entry omitted]

September 16th, 1862

Father topped those old locusts in the back yard: was so sorry to see them thus mutilated. J. T. Petty, A's familiar friend, called by this morning on his way to Winchester. We had heard of his having received a letter from Alvin and sent to know about it. He told us he had not had a letter from him in a long time but expressed the greatest affection and esteem for him. I had never before met with the gentleman and was agreeably surprised by his easy graceful manner and fluent conversation. He told us Scott Roy was in town again, being unable to march for his sore foot. . . .

September 17th, 1862

As usual had soldiers for breakfast. Poor souls! They've almost starved and the inhabitants will soon have nothing to give them. I have written to Aunt Lizzie for her and her country neighbors to send supplies to the hospital in town for their benefit and know she will do it. . . .

September 18th, 1862

A pleasant morning. Neville came in about ten o'clock with a wagon load of supplies for the soldiers. Kind Aunt Lizzie! I knew she would do all she could toward feeding the poor things. This was Thanksgiving day and we went to hear a Thanksgiving sermon.[7] On our way to church saw Scott at the gate. Dr. Hough delivered a most excellent discourse from the text——"vengeance is mine, I will repay, sayeth the Lord." I liked his views with regard to retaliation so much. Ma and Father were both at church but they went home and we up to Oakley to dinner. Spent a pleasant afternoon and came home about dusk, Aunt Betty accompanying us to the store. Found upon reaching home a pretty calico dress for Nellie and myself, a present from Uncle John and one that I indeed prized very highly. No news.

September 19th, 1862

Grandma went to Oakley and Ma to Riverside today. Were busily engaged sewing this morning when Scott came in to bring Nellie some late periodicals which he promised her yesterday. He behaved so strangely—sat some ten minutes and then suddenly rising bowed himself out of the room. Wonder if he is hurt at anything.

Commenced making my Lovars jacket this evening.[8] Uncle Mack came in about dusk and told us there had been a most terrific battle at Sharpsburg, Maryland in which we had nearly been defeated but had succeeded in driving the enemy from the field and then slowly fell back ourselves.[9] It is represented as a most disastrous battle to both parties in loss of men and very little advantage to either. . . .

September 20, 1862

Ma still at Riverside. Heard yesterday that Cousin Mack Blakemore was there having arrived very unexpectedly from the West. Jule left us this morning. We went together to town but the streets were so densely crowded with soldiers that we had to turn back and she took another route. The reports concerning the Sharpsburg battle are confirmed—Kattie Samuels told us her Father was an eye witness of the affair and he says our army are certainly recrossing the river. It looks rather gloomy for our prospects in Md. and I cannot possibly understand it all. Went to town this evening shopping, and upon my return saw a strange soldier sitting upon the porch who proved to be Cousin Mack. He greeted me very cordially and I soon felt very well acquainted with him tho I've not met him before since I've been grown. While we were all chatting Mrs. M came up bringing a letter they had just received from G dated from Charleston. All the boys were well. It is strange we can't hear anything from Alvin and Irvie direct. Heard cannonading and went on the house after tea to listen to it. Sounds very distinct and from the direction of Harper's Ferry. Sat up until quite late listening to Cousin Mack's description of his visit to Mobile and his account of the life the boys all led together at Tupelo and Chattanooga. He had not, however, seen the boys for three weeks before he started for Virginia and they know nothing of his coming.

September 22nd, 1862

Aunt Betty and I spent the day at Rose Hill, on our way thither we met Ma, Laura and Cousin Mack returning from Riverside, and with unanimous will they said Nellie and I must go down and help Cousin Bet wait on the soldiers.

I consented and Cousin Mack promised to call for me with Nellie in the evening. It was very sad at Rose Hill, but not quiet for all day there was a continual stream of soldiers coming for a meal. In the afternoon, too we had such a scene with poor Eliza who had heard that her husband Jim was among the contrabands taken at Harpers Ferry and that Dr. D his master intended selling him. . . .

September 23rd, 1862

Soldiers coming in from the time we were up, till this time. Such numbers of wounded as have been passing. I would not live here for the world to see all the poor wounded fellows dragging themselves wearily along. Nellie dressed the wounds of a poor Alabaman today and did it bravely while I turned faint and sick while merely holding the basin for her. Spent the day laughing, talking, reading, and singing and playing. Cousin Mack is devoted to music and it is a pleasure to sing for him. I do like him so much—much more than I ever expected to like him, he is so gentlemanly and seems so well to comprehend what is due a lady. . . .

September 25th, 1862

My birthday! Twenty years old! Oh how long a time have I lived in this world for the good I've done. Older than wise and wiser than good what a record I have to confront me today! What a summing up of a life of twenty years! And I'm a woman, repel the unwelcome thought as I will, close my eyes to the fact—say passionately—"I will be a child careless and free!" Nevertheless by this very feeling of care that is clinging about my heart is the truth made apparent—"I *am* a woman in *feelings* as well as *years*. A woman by this passionate longing and yearning—this hunger of the heart: a woman by this sensitive apprehension of my own unworthiness, of my deficiencies in every respect, in my loneliness, awkwardness and temper. I can't bear to think or write about it.

Cousin Mack and Dick were with us till late and we had a merry time writing consequences and playing "what's it like" and most amusing games all of them. Father made us all a little present of some money, most acceptable.

September 29th, 1862

News came in this morning to the effect that Longstreet's Corps was to cross the river at Confluence, and marched through town enroute for Warrenton. We were so glad to hear it and concluded we should see some of the Rifles. The troops commenced passing through in the afternoon and in the late evening some officers—Captian Luckadoo and some others took supper with us. Aunt Letitia dined with us today and Grandma as well as Ma were absent. Tis said General Lee passed through town today but he came so quietly and unobtrusively that scarcely anyone knew it but he till he had gone. Longstreet too is reported to have gone by us incog. It's too bad to think I've missed seeing these two brave chiefs. The Rifles are in town but have only leave of absence till ten o'clock tonight so we shall not see Scott or any of the boys. It's right provoking. . . .

October 31st, 1862

A bright beautiful day. Father invited me into the parlor directly after breakfast to hear Capt. Peyton's account of the boys; he only had time the night before to tell us they were well, but now how much good it did us to hear him tell how cheerful and happy they were—how much esteemed and respected. He also spoke in a most complimentary manner of Maj. Roy, Capt. P, Maj. Hardee, Gen. Chilton soon bade us a most kindly adieu and left and Capt. L too went to Strasburg. Troops pouring in all day. About noon a courier dashed up and enquired for Gen. Longstreet, seemed very much surprised when told he was not here. Then the General's bodyguard came in and encamped near the barn. We had not expected Gen. Longstreet till tomorrow but now concluded he could not be far off and about four o'clock they all rode up Capt. L among them. Mrs. Moffat was here and just before she left we concluded to make the best of the pleasant evening by a walk to "Point of Rocks"; as we were standing under the aspen trees when Capt. L came out and commenced a conversation by enquiring how I liked Gen. L. This led to a discussion of the comparative merits of our Generals when upon my enthusiastic admiration of Jackson he thought I detracted from Longstreet's fame and he was greatly picqued. I was so much surprised that such a quiet self possessed individual should have been startled out of his usual equanimity thus. Had a pleasant walk and returned to tea. . . . The General retired early and Capt. L. then requested Nellie and myself to play and sing "There's Life in the Old Land Yet" for him. We went in and found Capt. Young there— sat down and played and sang until we were tired and then entered into a sociable conversation. I did enjoy it so much—I never have met with two such refined polished gentlemen, they exactly realize my ideal of the chivalrous knights of yore, so courteous and delicate in their manner. I do wish the world were composed one half of such men. Did not retire till quite late. Jimmie Blakemore rode through the yard this evening and did not call— what a cold strange boy he is to be sure!

November 1st, 1862

Was up bright and early this morning. Started upstairs to get something out of Father's room knowing he had come down, but upon opening the door saw a pair of spurred boots on the floor and concluding the owner was not far distant I beat a hasty retreat. I was startled truly. Wonder what Capt. L would have thought of such an early call had he seen me. Just before breakfast Cousins Mary and E Cloud came in to see the General and very soon after Capt. Simpson, though I fancy the object of his visit was quite a different one than theirs. I was amused at the conversation which ensued at the breakfast table. Neither Cousins M or E was there nor yet Capt. S. Father, Capt L and myself discussed natural scenery and the old General spoke never a word save to keep up a desultory fire of inquiries concerning Capt. S and when he arose from the table he remarked briefly in reply to some information given him—"Then tis time he was promoted." What a very quiet, dignified old gentleman he is—very fine looking though and with a countenance full of benevolence. He is fond of children too, another trait which I admire. A courier arrived from Jackson about midnight last night which seems to hasten their movements for they announced bright and early that they must be off immediately and off they did go about nine o'clock. Capt. L remarked when he left that he would certainly return to the valley if it ever were in his power to do so. They one and all expressed themselves as delighted with this part of the country. . . . Sat in the yard some time watching the troops pouring in as they have been doing for the last four days and listening to "Mocking

Bird" being played so sweetly by the passing bands. I have a peculiar fancy for hearing that air performed by the band, not so much because of its plaintive notes as that it is dear Irvie's favorite and reminds me of that ninth of July at Manassas. . . .

November 2nd, 1862

Grandma and Aunt Betsy went to Oakley this morning. I went over to the store to make some little purchases. . . . Felt quite unwell this evening. . . .

November 3rd, 1862

. . . Ma and I concluded to spend today at Mrs. Cloud's. Received a warm welcome and found Mr. Daniel Cloud there. While chatting cozily up in Mrs. C's room we heard an unusual stir in the street and upon looking out we saw a train of army wagons dashing through at a furious rate and the street which had all the morning been thronged with soldiers were soon without the appearance of any military personage whatever. We could not learn anything definite however—only wild rumors of the enemy's advance, the evacuation of the town, etc. After dinner we noticed the troops were filling the roads leaving the town in different directions and looking over toward Bel Air we noticed horsemen hurrying in and out the gate and a general appearance of confusion. Had just taken my seat at the piano to sing a Southern song for Mr. Cloud when the door opened and Nellie walked in. She told us there were batteries on the hills back of the house and at one time during the afternoon our men were in battle array in expectation of the enemy. The persons we had seen riding about the yard at home were sundry officers who had called for various purposes. Mrs. Cook called in after a while and we should have had such a pleasant evening but for the confusion and excitement around. The streets about this time were crowded with soldiers, infantry, artillery and cavalry with a long baggage train all passing at once. As soon as these had dispersed a little we concluded to return home and upon reaching there found Uncle John. He explained the movements of our army by saying our troops were falling back and that the valley would probably be evacuated ere long. Such a damper to our spirits as it was to hear this!

He seemed in pretty good spirits though and told us that only D. H. Hill's division was near here now but that all Jackson's army would probably pass through soon when we would have an opportunity of seeing our friends in his corps. . . .

November 4th, 1862

Had some sewing to do for Uncle John and after he left was busily employed when Father came in and brought us a letter from each of the boys. Dear, dear boys! They wrote so cheerfully and hopefully. He also told us that they were expecting an attack here and that Dr. T. had warning to leave home lest their house should stand a chance of being shelled and their lives endangered. He wished to know what we should do as there was probably as much danger in our remaining as there was in Dr. T's family. All was turmoil and confusion in the midst of which I sat down to indite a letter to the boys which letter I suppose would be the last we should be able to send them as the mail communications would necessarily cease; it was, I'm afraid a most erratic composition and if the boys do not feel too much for our troubles they'll have a good laugh over it. In the midst of our perplexity the dinner-bell sounded and Mr. Berry came in looking so placid and tranquil that his very presence acted as oil in stilling our troubled spirits—he brought later advices from town of a more specific nature than Father's and assured us there was no need of excitement or alarm. So we concluded by settling ourselves quietly down. . . .

A gentleman rapped at the door about eight o'clock tonight and Father ushering him in, introduced to us Dr. Clarkson of S. C. an officer in D. H. Hill's division. He had come at General Hill's bidding to request Father to go down to camp and give some description of the topography of the country—his headquarters were near the old Lehew place and Father was to ride the Dr.'s horse and the Dr. await his return here. Found our guest a clever little fellow with the slightest symptom of the South Carolina boasting propensity—but intelligent and well bred. . . . Father returned after ten o'clock delighted with Gen. Hill whom he pronounced a thorough gentleman. His information was of considerable importance according to the general. Dr. C returned to camp immediately. Yankees said to be near town. Such numbers of soldiers as we have had to supply with meals today! Poor creatures, I do pity them so and I wish I had a great big larder at their disposal.

November 5th, 1862

The forenoon was pretty much spent in feeding soldiers, running up and down stairs, and harkening to numberless requests from them. Each one of them brought some different rumor with regard to the movements of the enemy but all concurred in the belief that they were not far distant and that an attack would soon be made here. About three o'clock p.m. Father came in and in a tone of intense excitement told us that the pickets were coming in and falling into line of battle above Rose Hill, that the officers said there would certainly soon be a fight here and some of them advised him to remove his family as they could not answer for what mischief the enemy shells might do the house, as it would be within range. So he advised us to put on our bonnets and as soon as he could he would have the wagon at the door to convey us to Clover Hill. Even while he spoke we heard the booming of a cannon but a few miles distant coming from the direction from which the enemy were to advance. Nellie and I did not believe there was as much danger as they all thought for and begged to be left with Father to take care of the house, promising to hide in the basement when the shelling commenced, but they would not hear of such a proposal and bade us make ready as speedily as possible for an onward move. Father then came in while we were dressing the children and told us not to wait for the wagon but put on our bonnets and hurry over to Oakley where he would order it to call for us. We hastily threw a few garments and necessaries for the children into a sheet, did not wait even to tie the corners, but Father taking Aunt C on his arm led the way. I followed with the dear little baby in my arms, then Orville and Carey, Nellie, Laura and Evred and Grandma and Ma while Martha and Eliza Ann brought up the rear with the baggage. Poor Father how it hurt me to take leave of him when he returned home. He is not often so much moved and when I see tears in his eyes as then I know his spirit is deeply troubled. It did seem so selfish to leave him alone although it was his own wish. We hurried through town with the cannon booming loudly and hearing as we passed all sorts of wild rumors. The cavalry were dashing through the streets and a long line of infantry pickets were being marched to their position on the hill. Aunt Betty, bless her big warm heart, received us with open arms and a cheerful face, not in the least frightened. Aunt Betsy and old Mrs. Childs who were there seemed both very much composed. The cannonading ceased soon after our arrival here and now everything seems comparatively quiet. The wagon was detailed until very late and we concluded not to go to Clover Hill at least tonight. Father has just written a note for the boys to go home for tonight; he says there is an attack expected very early in the morning when we can start in time to be out of danger. Nellie and I have determined not to go another yard from home, Ma has made us promise not to go home while there is a battle impending but we are determined to remain here with Aunt Betty that we may be near enough to Father to hear from him if anything should happen and see him. Oh dear I'm so tired of this running from home—tis very well for Ma and Grandma to take the children away for I believe the little things would be frightened almost to death during the bombardment, but Nellie and I are older and have reason to understand that it would be better to stand by our old house as long as we have one. Dear old Bel Air! I looked at it after leaving there and wondered if I should ever again recross its threshold or stand by the old hearthstone. It would almost break my heart to lose the old place of mine nativity, the place hallowed by the recollection that the sweetest, most precious hours that I ever knew or will know were spent within its precinct, that the dearest ties of our lives have been formed there, the best loved friends grew with me there. Dear, dear old home! But hark there is some excitement, they say there is a large fire seen in the direction of our encampment across the river, a signal light I suppose. An officer has just come in and says tis reported our army is retiring across the river.

Since writing the above Willie Buck has come in from Strasburg and confirms the report—he saw the army crossing the river and now I hear the shouting and ramping of a passing brigade which has been stationed just beyond the house here—they are, I suppose, the rear guard of the division and are falling back with it. Ah me what a thrill the sound of those passing footsteps sends through my heart, like the heavy lingering tread of departing hosts, for surely after they leave our day of grace will have ended and we be delivered up to the Phillistines again. Heaven protect us! But we won't despair yet, we may be going to give them battle on the other side of the river in a more advantageous position. I hope so, for a desperate conflict were preferable to desertion by our army just now. I can't help but think "Longheaded" Jackson is prime mover in these affairs and I've confidence that he will make it tell in some ways. Meantime I'll eat an apple with the circle about the fire and woo "tired nature's sweet restorer" that I may be fresh and strong for the enactment of tomorrow's tragedy or comedy as the case may be.

November 6th, 1862

Twas cloudy and bitter cold as I peeped out of my window early this morning, but all was quiet. The wagon came before breakfast but as there was no sign of a battle they concluded to await the issue of events. Nellie and I concluded to go home, the others would wait at Oakley until they could with entire safety return home. . . . I thought I would have frozen almost in my walk home, found the boys at the woodpile and Father at the barn. The house did wear a most deserted aspect but I was so glad to get back. E Hope came in to say they had letters from George and that all were well. Had a big fire kindled in Ma's room and everything very cozy by the time Father and the boys came in. They seemed glad to see us indeed. Father told us we had better remove the things from the store room into the basement, the Yankees were said to be entering town. Went to work and soon had everything moved and then put some dried fruit on to stew. Martha came in just as it commenced snowing, saying Ma had sent her over to take care of us and to insure our returning to Oakley in the evening. It snowed so hard that Father was weatherbound to the house and we had a cozy time of it—Nellie read one of Charles Lewis' novels—"A Day's Ride or a Life's Romance" aloud to us while I made gloves for the boys. They were down at the mill where they were butchering pork. I could not help but be astonished at ourselves when I thought that there we were sitting placidly before the fire reading a novel while every moment we were expecting the advent of our bitter foes and not knowing but they would burn the very roof over our head. Thus fortunately we learned to accommodate ourselves to circumstances. There were startling rumors all day. Sometimes the Yankees were said to be in town, sometimes near; our troops have fallen back some miles in back of the river. Fancied we saw a cavalry picket in the lane beyond the house. I should like to see one more Confed soldier indeed. Snowed so hard that I was afraid to venture out and was very glad of an excuse for remaining at home. Commenced making myself a bonnet. A quite nice little supper we had of it and then sat up reading until quite late. Bitterly cold it was and desolate enough looked Grandma's room when we had a fire made before retiring for the night. Poor soldiers! How I pity them in this piercing enemy weather. Another night of freedom.

November 10th, 1862

A beautifully bright morning. Started on our walk, Cousin Mary meeting us at Mr. Glasscocks and Ma accompanying us as far as Rose Hill. Arrived at the river and found the boat on the other side and the ferryman non est. Some soldiers soon crossed over in it though and they were so polite as to assist us in, arrange the seats and carry us over—it was well they did too for had it not been for the helping hands of one of the gallant souls I should have been most indubitably precipitated into the river. As it was we had a merry but somewhat hazardous ride, the soldiers not understanding the management of the boat very well, but we arrived on the other shore safely and enjoyed a good laugh at the discomfiture of some of the poor fellows who were in recrossing incontinently jarred into the water, only however receiving a slight wetting. Received a hearty welcome from Cousin B and Aunt L and then from Miss Sallie Kendrick who is boarding with them. Nellie soon commenced one of her confidential strains and kept them all convulsed with laughter of her account of Father's maneuvers for her and myself. Mack came in after a while—his camp is only a few miles distant and he is frequently at home. . . .

The railroad was torn up and burnt tonight—twas right painful to witness this destruction knowing as we did that twas but the forerunner of an abandonment to the enemy.

November 11th, 1862

We had a merry time this morning wandering from parlor to porch, from porch to stile in the bright sunshine laughing, talking, singing and playing. Sam and Lt. Eyster left about ten and the brigade which encamped last night near Front Royal recrossed the river and passed right by the house. . . . Nellie and Mack had a great romp all to themselves which I was too unwell and Cousin Mary too dignified to participate in. Mack goes to camp in the morning.

November 12th, 1862

Saw Mack off before breakfast. Busied myself hemming some handkerchiefs for Cousin Bet. Heard Kate Long was very ill, poor thing, with typhoid fever. Not many soldiers passing. Maj. Howard again dined with us and Nellie made him the bearer of a very saucy note to Maj. Snowden emploring him to give Mack leave to return and inviting the Major himself down, offering as an inducement some "very nice sausage" which Cousin B had just made. We looked for Mack all the evening but he did not come. Miss Sallie, Cousin Mary and myself took a walk about twilight to the North River and visited the railroad which was still burning. Twas right sad to see the ruins of the road which has been traversed so often by dear ones some of whom had gone the long journey through the dreary way. Mack did not come at night either—but we had a merry time making off lists of names for each other to dream on as Mrs. Kendrick had given us some bridal cake at the tea table refusing to tell us where it came from though. No news.

November 17th, 1862

A dark, gloomy, disagreeable day. Was busy all day sewing. . . .
Had a spell of the blues today.

[November 19, 1862, entry omitted]

November 21st, 1862

Cold, disagreeable day. We were all sitting reading and sewing in Ma's room when the door opened and a young officer presented himself—Capt. Boswell, chief engineer in General Jackson's corps—a handsome little fellow. He had come to borrow the spy glass for the use of the signal corps on the Fort Mt.—and left immediately after getting it—gave us no news from the army.

Poor Uncle Ben died last night and was buried this evening. He has been a great sufferer but I hope it is all over now—a faithful good old servant he has proved. They say Aunt Betty is very much distressed at his death. Cousin Mary left this evening.

November 23rd, 1862

A cool but bright morning. . . . About ten o'clock two soldiers came in one of them bringing the spy glass with a polite note of thanks from Capt. Boswell. Went to hear Dr. Hough today and a most excellent sermon it was. Ma and I went up to Oakley where we spent a very pleasant quiet afternoon. Father came over and walked home with us after night. Heard today that all our forces had left Winchester with exception of Hill's division which will be left there as rear guard. Jackson is reported to be up the valley somewhere near New Market.

November 25th, 1862

The Stewarts have sold out and are going to the country to live. Alice sent a message to Nellie and myself asking us to call and see her before she left. So we concluded to make our visit this morning. Found everything at sixes and sevens there and the room into which little Nettie ushered us seemed to have served the purpose of dining room, chamber, parlor, pantry, laundry and lumberroom.

Alice came down after a time apologizing for her own appearance and also for the disorder of the room—said they were preparing to sell out their household effects—that Fannie had gone over to the farm to prepare for the reception of the family and that she herself—was suffering from the tooth-ache. Sat there an hour and then went on up to see Cousin Mary. . . .

November 27th, 1862

Aunt Betty sent a message begging us to dine with the Misses Cloud and Mrs. Hough at her house, but as Ma was not at home we concluded we could not go. Father handed me a pacquet today which upon unsealing proved to be a letter—six pages of foolscap from dear Irvie giving me an amusing account of his moving experiences since he left us—I never was more amused in my life and could scarcely read it for laughing. Bless his dear life! I must answer very soon for it has been already written a month. Ma came home late in the evening.

December 6th, 1862

A bitter winter day—snowing, blowing and freezing—finished my letter and dispatched it—wrote, sewed, read aloud to Father. Oh poor, poor soldiers my heart aches for them. No doubt there will be numbers frozen to death this inclement night. Heaven help them.

December 8th, 1862

Had a quiet day today. Ma came home late in the evening and said Uncle T had just arrived from Richmond after meeting with no success whatever in his efforts to obtain our supply of salt. I don't know what in the world we are to do for salt when tis sixty and ninety dollars per bushel. Old Gov. Letcher ought to be starved a while himself and then perhaps he may be less chary of making promises that he will not fulfill—for he did promise Uncle T most faithfully that this should be one of the first counties supplied and now after decoying him into making several bootless trips to Richmond he comes boldly out and declares that we can "learn to wait as well as other counties." Unmitigated old quizz that he is.

Uncle T brought me a tiny letter from Nannie dear. Says all are very cheerful in Richmond. No movements of the armies on the Rappahannock. Heard that Walter came home last night and Dick yesterday evening.

December 9th, 1862

Ma and I concluded to take advantage of the pleasant weather and to go shopping. Called in at Mrs. Jones and sat an hour and then went up to Capt. Roy's. Nothing would do but we must take off our bonnets and spend the day. . . . Ma knit a pair of cuffs for S tonight. Walter is getting well. I'm so glad to hear it!

December 12th, 1862

A lovely day. Aunt Betty, Uncle Tom and Allie dined with us and in the afternoon Walter and Dick came in. At night we banished the noisy children to the basement where they consoled themselves with blind man's buff, and Ma, Walter, Dick, Nellie and myself had the cheerful fireside in Ma's room all to ourselves till nine o'clock. Dick went over to the office and brought us the papers by tonight's mail and Walter edified us by reading aloud Lincoln's last message.[10] Truly tis a most sublimely ridiculous composition—so exquisitely nonsensical—so different from the messages of our own Davis—surely men must see and contrast the two men and—taking the Presidents for a type of the people—contrast the————————————conclusions. . . .

December 15th, 1862

. . . Walter came in during the day and we had quite a sociable confab—he and Nellie, I suppose, interchanged confidences this evening—they were closeted for a long time and after Walter left when I went into the parlor to play on the piano she sat there and cried and cried and would not tell me what the matter was. Dick was with us at dinner too and they stayed till quite late telling anecdotes of their campaigns. Father went to the office but we received neither letters nor papers—too bad indeed. Rumors of a battle at Fredericksburg and a glorious victory indefinite and doubtful.

December 17th, 1862

A quiet day. Walter came in the afternoon and about dusk Mr. Berry came. Then while sitting about the candle discussing our recent victory at F who should walk in but Cousin Will Cloud. Walter did make me behave too rudely but I could not help laughing when he sat right by my side and kept up a running fire of sotto voce comments upon everything that was said. I know Mr. Berry must have been shocked at my ill-manners. . . . The battle of F must be of much greater importance than we had at first imagined—we had thought only a skirmish on a large scale but if as I hear the Yankees admit a loss of twenty thousand men it must have been a terrible conflict. And oh how many of our own gallant spirits may have shed their life's blood in the struggle. Fredericksburg is said to be burnt too. Poor inhabitants! . . .

December 18th, 1862

Walter came over to breakfast and we all sat in Ma's room during the morning listening to his accounts of the horrors of the field of battle. Truly tis not much wonder boys so soon become men in such trying times. . . . Heard that the 17th Regiment was not in the late battle—so glad! Poor Generals Cobb and Gregg both fell in the engagement though. Weighed today—111 lbs.

December 19th, 1862

Was quite busy all day—was up to my elbows in flour this afternoon when I heard a well known footstep and a cheery voice and Walter was in our midst jesting and caressing in a breath. Put my bread to bake, washed my hands and brushed my hair, settled myself down to enjoy his society—Uncle Tom came in and we had a most pleasant time of it. It was late when they left and Walter promised to call by as he leaves tomorrow. Had papers today giving an account of the three days battle at F. Ah it must have been horrible—and then the shelling of the town and the suffering of its exiled inhabitants. Something must be done for them if possible. Our army reoccupied Winchester, thank goodness.

December 20th, 1862

. . . We were wondering all day why Walter didn't come by this morning and to our surprise he came in this evening quite late. Said he would not go until tomorrow. Sat with us till nine o'clock and then went home. Was making preparations for going to bed when Martha came in with a message from Father to the effect that there was a soldier just come in who would be glad to have his supper. Went in the room and was introduced to "Mr. Maury"—he seemed to be a very gentlemanly little fellow, a cousin of Lt. Maury and while he sat at the table he gave quite an interesting account of that gentleman's resignation and escape from Washington. Mr. M's a chaplain—does not look much like it though.

December 21st, 1862

Mr. M left early—attended Mr. Berry's church—he made a touching appeal in behalf of the suffering soldiers and the exiles from poor ill-fated Fredericksburg. Aunt Betty and I are going to raise a subscription for their relief. Was introduced on my way from Church to a Dr. Williams from Maryland. We were to dine at Oakley and he walked up there with us. . . .

. . . Just as we were preparing to leave for home Walter came in. He immediately stated his intention of remaining over night so I concluded to remain too and Ma said she would go over and send Nellie—Walter went with her and presently he returned with both Nellie and Nannie Buck. We had a most delightful evening—Uncle Tom went to sleep on the sofa very early and we gathered before the great blazing fire with an immense waiter of nuts and apples and talked and talked a long, long time so cozily. The Yankees are said to be very near in quite a force and our army has left Winchester. Dick Bailey came in very unexpectedly this evening—he looked so well. Will be up again tomorrow.

December 22nd, 1862

. . . We were all in Aunt Betty's room—Nellie and Walter "billing and cooing" and I copying advertisements for Uncle Tom when Dick Bailey and soon after Alfred McKay came hurriedly in and told Walter he had better hasten away with them to Luray as the enemy were said to be near the river. But Walter was not to be thus easily moved and they concluded to go out toward the river and see for themselves while Walter would await their return and leave with them in an hour's time. So he coaxed me to write him an introduction to Kate Chapman and proceeded to copy a song for Nellie when the two boys with Mack Wells and young McKay returned saying the Yankees had crossed at McCoy's Ford just above and if they did not "fall back" very speedily they would be cut off from the army. Walter quietly took his pipe from his mouth—proceeded to twist Nellie's curls about his fingers and finally was induced to don his overcoat. We buckled his pistol and saber about him, brought him his gauntlets, tossed him his cap, filled his pockets with apples and bidding us "goodbye" too vaulted into his saddle and they were off cheering and waving their caps as they went. Poor fellows! We watched them as far as we could see them and then went to reading a "History of the Mexican War." . . .

December 23rd, 1862

Father remarked at the breakfast table this morning that Mr. Richards had arrived with his goods. He had gone a week ago to a store in Loudon kept by the Quakers who had obtained from the Yankees every sort of supply and were selling them out at very reasonable prices. Father had loaned Mr. R a horse and carriage and sent an order by him. Directly after breakfast Ma and I went over to look at the goods. He had only opened a few of them but those were quite at reasonable prices. I got a pair of lasting kits for two dollars quite a miracle such a chance these times.[11] To our great delight Father managed to get a half bush. of salt for $1.10, thirty-two lbs. loaf sugar for 20 cents per lb. pepper for 20 cents, soda for 37 1/2 cents, indigo 12 1/2 cents, etc., etc. Since May last I have eschewed coffee except————————occasionally a cup of that beverage minus the sugar. Indeed for two months the whole family have been drinking their coffee unsweetened, for sugar has been from a dollar twenty five to a dollar fifty per lb. and almost impossible to secure at that. Coffee has been proportionately dear and so for pepper, soda, indigo, etc. We were nearly out of them all and knew not where the next were to come from. Ma got from him a supply of sewing materials too, just as she had almost used the last she had. Sewing silk is ninety dollars per lb.—spool cotton fifty cents per spool, needles fifty cents per paper, pins fabulous in cost but she got it all for much less. He sold calicos for fifty and seventy-five cents when it has been selling here for a dollar fifty and two dollars. Oh it's a great thing for the community and they're disposed to avail themselves of the advantage.

After leaving Mrs. Richards we went up to Aunt Betty's and spent the day. It has been one of the loveliest December days I ever saw. Carey came over while we were here and told us twas rumored down street that Mr. Samuels had fallen in the late battle and when Uncle Tom came to dinner he confirmed it. Poor Kattie! How I do feel for her—so young to know so bitter a sorrow.

She has been very uneasy and distressed about him ever since the battle, and was quite sick all last week. Her mother even is not here having gone to Loudon for goods. Poor girls! I wonder who will break the news to her and comfort her in her distress. . . .

Laura expects to start to Clarke tomorrow—was busy sewing for her tonight.

December 24th, 1862

Laura did not go today—had a letter from Jule stating that they would go down Friday or Saturday next. Was busy all day baking cakes for the children out of sorghum molasses and honey and making pies—they were very nice too when done. Father told us that a Yankee paper had brought to town the intelligence of Burnside's removal, Seward's resignation and a quarrel between Chase and Staunton. Glorious! With division in their councils— disorganization of their army and dissatisfaction among the people I think their prospects of subjugating us a very poor one.

Poor Kattie has heard of her husband's death and is almost broken-hearted. Oh I do pity her from my very soul.

It is very late—the children's stockings are all "hung by the chimney with care in hopes that Saint Nicholas would soon be there." And he has been here, in the person of Laura who has filled them with cakes and some candy and toys which Uncle Tom brought from R.

December 25th, 1862

Was awakened at two o'clock this morning by "Christmas Gift!" being shouted in my ear by Carey and Orville who had stolen in my room unheard. Then at four o'clock they were at it again. Orville, Carey, Annie, Willie and Evred and such chattering and shouting and running about as there was. They were perfectly delighted with the contents of their stockings.

Ma and I walked over to Oakley at eleven o'clock—met the Misses Marshall in the meadow and they walked nearly there. Found Aunt Betty entirely alone and apparently very glad to see us. The weather was so pleasant that we soon quitted the house for the porch. Twas a glorious day. There was pervading everything a soft, peaceful Sabbath like influence so soothing and delightful—even the sunshine so beautifully bright had a chastened, subdued brilliancy. I did so enjoy sitting there listening to the notes of an enterprising bird perched on a neighboring tree and thinking, thinking so much of the past with its mingled web of events. I employed myself meanwhile with sketching Bel Air on a bit of cardboard making a picture just large enough to send in a letter to the boys. . . .

The guests left early in the evening but Nellie and Laura came over then and we did not go home till after the moon rose. Such a charming walk we had of it too in the pleasant moonlight. The boys were exploding bombshells in the field when we came home and we witnessed the bursting of one or two. Sat down and wrote a long letter to the boys when I got home. The news from the Washington Cabinet has been confirmed.

Mrs. Boone came home last night—does not believe the news of Mr. S's death. Kattie went to Woodstock today.

December 27th, 1862

Father's throat nearly well. Nannie Buck, Bob and Jacquie all here romping with children here this morning. Dick Bailey came in very unexpectedly, sat an hour, and then left for the regiment. Ellen Brown and Sallie Kendrick were over—made themselves quite agreeable—brought a subscription for the Warren Rifles. Twas a pleasant evening and Nellie and I went down into the meadow after sundown and perching ourselves in the branches of the old fallen sycamore tree had a delightful swing. A right proper amusement for the dignified Miss Lucy Buck. Tis said our army has fallen back to Newmarket. Kattie Samuels sent down a letter from Mr. S so he's not dead at all—I'm so glad.

December 31st, 1862

Baked some cake and pies for the children in the morning. Father told us at dinner that there were news of Stewart's presence in the valley and tonight told us that there was a report of a victory achieved by Morgan in East Tennessee. Grant was at Holly Springs, Md. retreating down the Miss.—that Gen. Johnston was about investing Nashville and etc., etc. Oh it is so much good news if only it were *true*.

We were sitting by the candle stand in Grandma's room tonight when Father came from the office bringing a paper and two letters—one from Nannie Taylor to me—one from Irvie to Nellie. I was almost beside myself with joy at their arrival particularly when upon reading Irvie's we learned that he had been promoted to the rank of Captain and ADG on Gen. Cleburn's staff in Gen. Hardee's corps. He has richly earned his position and I'm glad his efforts have met with approval and reward. Dear boy! I hate the idea of his being exposed to the dangers consequent upon active service and am so sorry he and Alvin will be separated, but he has one kind Protector as Omnipotent to save on the field of battle as in the quiet of home, and as Alvin has gone on to Bragg's army strongly recommended by Gens. Beauregard and Gordon for a like position and I sincerely hope he may succeed for he richly deserves it too, I'm sure. "Capt. Irving A. Buck" how ridiculously it does sound.

Am determined to sit up tonight and "watch in" the New Year. Laura will keep me company in my vigils. Will answer Irvie's letter tonight and send by tomorrow's mail.

Chapter Four

☙☙☙☙☙☙☙☙☙☙☙☙☙☙☙☙☙☙☙☙☙☙☙☙

And Now a New Page Is Spread Before Us

☙☙☙☙☙☙☙☙☙☙☙☙☙☙☙☙☙☙☙☙☙☙☙☙

January 1, 1863–June 8, 1863

January 1st, 1863

Glorious dawn of the year which is destined to form an epic in the future history of our young nation. All hail to thee sixty-three radiant in thy youthful hours, bright with an atmosphere all sunshine and beauty, clear in the light of thy declouded sky; melodious with the minstrelsy of thy rippling waters; glad in the joyous harmony of nature! May the radiance of thy dawning hours be an earnest of the full fruition of the glory of light that shall grace thy crowning days. May thy suns never behold the scenes of bloodshed and darkness that have shamed the earth in the past season of strife and conflict. Ere thy days shall have sunk into the ocean of eternity may the noon tide of peace be abroad over our land—may our nation worship under its own vine and fig tree with none to vex or make them afraid—and peace and tranquility reign where now riot and confusion hold high revel.

Last night after the children were in bed Grandma, Aunt Laura, Nellie and myself had a petite supree—apples, nuts, cakes, pies, bread and butter, and the rose leaf to the feast was a cup of coffee concocted by Laura and myself. It was my first attempt at distilling the beverage and I had quite a time in accomplishing my task, and when I did it was so strong that it intoxicated me fairly and I was like something wild for the rest of the night. Wrote dear Irvie a long letter and commenced one to Nannie Taylor. Our vigils were not gloomy but still I often cast many a retrospective glance into the far past—the past of trials and suffering. There were woven with my reflections visions of two dear faces that had faded from our midsts, of two lives blotted from existence—one blighted in her youthful being by the poisonous breath of disease and the sickening anguish of bereavement and distress—one in the young bloom and vigor of manhood in the noontide of his usefulness smitten on the red field of the fight at his post of duty toiling for the maintenance of honor and right—battling in defense of country, home and loved ones—

> Wasting his life in his country's care,
> Laying it down with a patriot's prayer.

I saw a vision of two fresh made graves and a vision of their bereaved and desolate homes a living tomb almost. They were two of the brightest links in our chain of dear associations and I felt that they never could be replaced. Yet their memory was a bittersweet, for I knew how infinitely our loss was their gain—how it "has not entered into the heart of man to conceive" of the blissful exchange.—Then the thoughts of the many, many noble and precious lives that had been offered up on the altar of their country in propitiation for a nations sins—of the torrents of blood that had been poured out a priceless oblation to liberty. I thought of the passionate sorrows,—the weary heart struggles, the trials, the hardship, the suffering, the sacrifices that were mingled like gall and wormwood in our cup during the past years. And yet I remembered the sweet drops of comfort and hope that had been wrung into the bitter draught—the comfort of knowing that our trials were perhaps sent as a test to our faith, that as we had come out unscathed from them we might hope for fruition of our trust. That we had learned—

> "How sublime a thing it is
> To suffer and grow strong"

we knew of our powers of endurance—our own strength, our own weaknesses—knew whom to trust, whom to fear. We had the hope in the future that our country would profit by the severe lessons she had conned—that our liberty when achieved would be the more deeply cherished because of difficulties overcome in its establishment. I remembered how much we had to be thankful for in the successes with which God had blessed our efforts so universally. I remember the beginning of last year—how fearfully I tried to scan the blank page of the coming twelve months to learn the lesson therein contained—I remember questioning the future————of events—tried to prepare myself for meeting and defeating its difficulties ere they were upon me. How little I knew of its bringings, how little guessed the fiery ordeal stretched before us, how little we guessed of the depths of the troubled sea through which our barques were to steer, how often times we were well nigh wrecked on the breakers or swallowed in the storm. But thank God that our strength was equal to our day—that we have come forth from the fire with, I hope, our garments the whiter for the burn—that our barques are floating in calmer seas and that the sun will shine through the mist around our path. And now a new page is spread before us in which the ensuing year will write its record—the little page is open and 1863 inscribed thereon in characters of radiant sunshine and gladness—oh may no unsightly blurs of darkness, no tale of crime or shame, no deeds of guilt be registered thereon when time shall stamp his seal of the past upon it!

We retired after two o'clock but owing to my unusual dissipation it was a long, long time before I slept. The children were up quite early and I followed their example—dressed and fixed Irvie's letter for the mail. After breakfast wrote a note to Rose Hill and then finished writing in my diary.

Such a beautiful day I felt ought not to be spent indoors so, gathering the children together, Nellie and I went down to the old sycamore tree and had a merry time swinging. Father invited us to walk with him—so we set off— Carey with his gun and had a tramp through the old fields and spicy pines the distance of two miles. I have often heard of profound silence and audible quiet but I never before realized it. The afternoon was clear and cloudless and delightfully soft—we paused upon an imminence in an old field covered with dry, rusty grass, before us lay the tiny valley through which wound the little brook like a bright erratic fairy, there was the little village nestled so lovingly at the foot of the great, brown mountain, over it brooded the light haze of smoke wreath and the smile of the sunlight. Beyond was a chain of blue mountains like great walls shutting us out from the turmoil of the great busy world. We stopped to enjoy the pleasing tranquility of the scene—not a sound was to be heard—the brook was too distant for its murmur to reach us, not a breeze rustled the coarse dry grass, not the chirp of an insect, not the note of a bird disturbed the deep quiet. The silence so unnatural grew absolutely oppressive till suddenly a deep, booming sound reverberated through the mountains followed by the rush of air. Twas a cannon—the spell was broken thus rudely—we descended from the hill and turned our faces homeward. Found Ma, Aunt B, and Uncle T, Belle and Sam there—had come in our absence. They all remained till after dinner and then went their several ways. Nellie had a fancy to be weighted and we threw our shawls about our heads and ran up to Mr. Hopes mill where she was informed that there was just ninety nine pounds of humanity comprised by her frame.

The servants had a surprise party tonight and we witnessed some of their terpsichorean performances from the window—they did enjoy themselves so much and it was most amusing to note how faithfully they aped the manners of the "white gentry." [1] Retired quite early feeling completely worn out.

January 5th, 1863

A charming morning. Went early over to Aunt Betty's and we started out on our expedition. Went first to Mrs. J. W. Mcs, found her busily engaged making socks for the "Rifles"—she very readily promised us five dollars and seemed to be pleased at our having called. We next went to Mrs. C's and sitting there an hour discussing the current topics made known the object of our visit and received hearty cooperation in a fifteen dollar note. Went then to Mr. C's—Mrs. C was absent but Mr. C was busily engaged teaching his little daughters. He expressed himself pleased at our efforts to aid the poor destitute citizens of F and gave us five dollars. Walked out to Dr. T's—he and Mrs. T were not at home but found Cousin Mary C. making one of her pleasant circles and spent a pleasant hour receiving from Miss C five dollars. Went over to Mrs. R. T's but she had already contributed through another. On our return called at Mr. F's—had never been there and felt very much like I was venturing into a lion's den but soon felt quite relieved at the peaceful aspect of the interior of the house—was ushered by a tiny colored portress into a cozy room where upon a comfortable sofa before the blazing fireplace reclined the mistress of the house in her neat wrapper and at her feet on the rug slumbered a great white cat. It all seemed the most perfect embodiment of quiet comfort. Mrs. F. received us very graciously and to my very great surprise we left with a promise of another $V. Went to Col. J's found the small family of four persons sitting at the dinner table spread with the luxuries of the season, but they had not a farthing of all their plenty to bestow upon destitute misery. "Blessed are the merciful for they shall obtain mercy." Went next to Mrs. Jones—and after sitting a space made known our mission which was cordially approved and testified by another $V. I was so much pleased with Mrs. Jones—she is so quiet, so dignified and ladylike and so different from the mass of persons with whom one comes in contact. Proceeded to Dr. Brown's—met the family in full conclave assembled—had a merry chat and soon had the Dr.'s name subscribed for $5.00. Went to Mr. Jackson's—found Roxie there and Mr. Hill. Mr. J. of course willingly aided us with five dollars. Next dropped in at Mr. Weavers where were a number of gentlemen. Weaver thrust his hands into his pockets, set his teeth firmly together and declared himself unable to contribute "Charity begins at home, etc." Mr. F. thought his wife "had given enough for both." Dr. D. leaning carelessly on his gun with his game in a net at his side drew out a five dollar note and wished he could do more for our object. Poor old Mr. J. Trout was standing near but knowing his losses and the many claims upon his charity we refrained from making any demands on him but he never the less slipped two dollars into our hands with regrets for the insignificance of the sum and his good wishes for the success of our enterprise. Good old man! I valued the donation much more for the spirit which prompted it than for the value of the sum itself. Mrs. Mck's was our next point—did not go into the house but Miss M and Mrs. T met us at the door and promised us something. To Mrs. Stimpson's next we declared and here found Mr. S transacting business with his *hands full of banknotes* but as soon as we mentioned our purpose he declared himself an object of charity and fled the room, but we aroused Mrs. S's sympathies and she handed us two dollars. Twas nearly sundown and having fasted since breakfast Aunt B and I concluded to adjourn our proceedings till tomorrow morning. Met Mr. L on the street and he gave me five dollars. Returned home and found twenty dollars there just sent me from Clover Hill. Sat up quite late writing to Mack Bailey—feel quite tired. News tonight of a great battle at Murfreesboro—the contest not decided but advantages decidedly in our favor. No letters—so sorry. The Yankees have been all day expected in town but up to this hour "all's well." Thus has closed my first day at begging contributions.

January 6th, 1863

. . . Read an extract from "Howsins History of the War" for Father and then addressed myself to the task of finishing the socks commenced for the "Rifles." Grandma came home in the evening bringing me twenty-five dollars from Riverside. Feel quite unwell tonight.

January 8th, 1863

Father told me at the breakfast table that news had been received the night before of the repulse of the Fed Army at Murfreesboro. But the battle was still raging. . . .

January 9th, 1863

. . . Was busy all day sewing and making out my list, collecting money, etc. etc. Scott came in about twilight to say goodbye for he leaves tomorrow. . . . When Father came home he brought a confirmation of the news from Murfreesboro but it was not fairly a retreat of our army—we had a large number of prisoners and twas not deemed advisable to remain when the enemy was constantly receiving reenforcements, but we had till the time of our falling back repulsed the enemy in all his attempts. There was, he said, a rumor of the presence of the Yankees a few miles distant but he did not seem to apprehend much from their advance.

I feel a little cross tonight but I'm glad at all events that we've gotten the full amount of our Fredericksburg fund $259.00 to send by Scott tomorrow. I'm glad to think our citizens out of the little they have left are yet willing to do their part toward relieving those more destitute than themselves. Still no letters from the boys. Miseracordia.

January 10th, 1863

Chill and cloudy. Sent my pacquet to Scott and my letter to the office. No Yankees and Scott has gotten safely away with the supplies for the poor "Rifles"—so glad. Raining and sleeting alternately, very disagreeable. Sewing all day. . . .

Wrote tonight. Heard that 7 of Buck's Company were captured two days since—hope tis not true.

January 12th, 1863

Ma and I concluded to spend the day at Mrs. Cloud's—ran over quite early and had a cool yet pleasant walk for the day though frosty was clear. Received a hearty welcome and spent a delightful day. There were constantly callers coming in—Uncle Tom, Aunt Betty and Mr. Hall met us there and dined with us. Came up from dinner about four o'clock and going to the window looked out on the street where just opposite stood a group of soldiers and citizens—among the former Newt. Petty, Captain Jacobs and Joe Miller— talking idly. We had but just taken our seats when there was a rushing sound like a hurricane and the ground shook with heavy tramping. Miss Matty R. sprung to her feet with a startled look and exclamation of surprise and we followed her to the window and looking out saw a cavalryman dash around the corner, another and another. We at the first moment imagined they were our own men but a second glance showed them to be a body of Yankees cavalry, 25 in number. They divided into three squads, one dashing each way up the street and the third drew up before Weaver's store and proceeded to take possession. They looked like demons as they galloped through the streets every man with sabre brandished above his head or his pistol pointed at the windows by which they passed—many of them were bareheaded and with their harsh laughter they seemed like nothing human. I cannot think any town was ever so taken by surprise and had it not been serious twould have been quite amusing to see into what a consternation the whole town was thrown by their entrance. The groups of citizens scattered like chaff before the wind—the soldiers all escaped excepting Newt Petty who was captured before he left Weaver's store. When they entered the store it was with a perfect rush and presently we saw them pour forth with their hands, arms, hats and handkerchiefs full of cakes and candy. It seems that Weaver had a supply of both these scarcities which his exhorbitant prices prevented being sold and it was so vexatious to see these brutes wasting and enjoying these luxuries that many a poor little child had regarded with longing eye and vainly desired. They packed their knapsacks, fed some to their horses, threw some away and finally one of them called all the schoolboys around him in the street and threw handfuls at them having a regular scramble. From that time until dusk it was a perfect harvest of sweets for the little fellows and they made good their opportunity. The Yankees took everything they could lay their hands on—tobacco, blacking brushes, boxes of little fancy notions and finally the mail bags. Oh it was provoking to see them pulling out letters and papers reading them and then tearing them into fragments and scattering them over the muddy street and at this very time too when we were expecting a letter from dear Irvie with his photograph. I was so excited and vexed I could scarcely restrain myself. They captured both the Culpeper and Luray mail carriers just as they were entering town and must have been led in by some traitor who knew of their expected arrival—indeed we saw one of their guides as he entered with them dressed in Confederate uniform. Villain that he is! We saw them capture some of the citizens and their horses. Uncle Mack and Jacquie were there and their steeds were immediately seized upon and they actually made Uncle Mack take the very spurs off his foot and give it to them. Ma and I kept waiting thinking they would leave town immediately, but presently Allie Ashby called by and said they had taken their horses to the hotel and seemed to be applying for a nights lodging. As it was dusk we concluded we had best leave at all hazards and seeing Carey on the outside the street called him to accompany us home. We left Mr. Hall at Mrs. Cloud's all anxiety for a fine horse which he had ridden to town and which was in Mrs. B's stable. Just as we had crossed the street an officer called by calling out to one of his men "They're coming!" and a servant boy passing just then told us that "a whole regiment of infantry with artillery were coming up the street"—and true enough through the gathering twilight we could descry the dark mass just entering the street and only managed to get out of town at exactly the right moment to avoid them and as we crossed the field we saw the "Star-spangled Banner" borne aloft through the town. . . .

We have had a merry time of it tonight notwithstanding their presence among us and no one to have heard the wild bursts of merriment from the rooms where we were assembled would have guessed that we were again at the mercy of a bitter and remorseless enemy. Found at home tonight a letter from Alvin of December 8th so of course it contained no news. Oh! dear I wonder what tomorrow will bring forth.

January 13th, 1863

A cool bright morning. We were up quite early. . . . Neville went over to town to see if there was any probability of the Yankees leaving and presently returned saying there was none and that he had just heard an order issued by an officer commanding a vigorous search of all the houses, and advising us to conceal what we could as they were also ordered to seize upon everything contraband—letters, papers, etc. We immediately went to work and sugar, coffee and sweetmeats, letters, papers, money, etc. were secured. The turkeys were put in the dark cellar next to Harriet's room and the bacon in a packing box under the boy's bed. The horses had already been spirited away by Father's directions. The morning passed in expectation then but it was not until four o'clock until Father came in and told us that a file of the Yankees was approaching from Mr. Hope's. We went to the window and looked at them as they stood there on the pavement with their guns on their shoulders. I had my hand on the door knob to unclose it when it suddenly opened from the outside and I was astounded to find my face a few inches from the great, rough phiz of one of the soldiers who was swearing a great big oath in reply to a remark from Father declaring that he "never went anywhere without his gun." Father assured them that there was only a house full of little children and some ladies and that they would surely not harm them. Presently they came in—a portion of them remaining as guards about the doors. They looked into presses, cupboards, trunks, pantries, closets, cubbies, drawers, wardrobes, lofts, boxes and baskets and at Nellie's earnest solicitation they even peeped into our bandboxes and Ma's dress pockets. They even crawled under the bed and found the bacon which they however did not disturb. They went down into the basement and searched the servants' things and found a blanket which had belonged to Ambrose and which, after his death, Dr. Bogardus gave Martha as a reward for her attentions to him. This they took and also tried to hook a watch belonging to Horace which attempt he detected and frustrated in time. In passing to Harriet's room they found the turkeys and grew quite facetious over their discovery but did not seem to take a fancy to them. Once I had occasion to pass out the front door and around to the "west end" where Ma was alone and I wanted to be with her. Upon opening the passage door I found it full of soldiers standing idly by their guns whistling, singing, and spitting amber all over the floor; they had formed a file on the porch on either side the door with their guns crossed. I doubted whether they would permit me egress—so called Mack Erwin to escort me through them. He stepped before me and bade the men move aside and let me pass—this they obeyed so far as to shuffle themselves into a better position for looking and stared and shuffled as rudely as possible while I had literally to walk over their feet and I know in my progress they must have been made acquainted with the huge pocket of valuables which I wore on either side of my skirt. Oh! but I was angry. They went to the smokehouse, the granary, the carriage house, the barn and the mill and finally departed with two old worm eaten haversacks, which the little boys had found on the deserted campfield, an old shot gun of Mr. Hope's which was here, and a musket which the boys had also picked up on the field—together with a shot pouch of Father's which was presented him by a friend a long time ago and which Irvie would want to use in his hunting excursions. I felt as if I could shoot the man who carried it off myself. I don't think they will re-pay for the trouble of their search here unless the knowledge they gained of the extent of our possessions and wearing apparel availed them something. A pitiful business, thus brutally investigating ladies wardrobes and dressing bureaus—I've no doubt they would have made their visit a more profitable one had they not been so strictly watched. As it was they were accompanied by a crowd of children as well as by others wherever they went. I hope they did not go to Rose Hill and alarm them there. They promised Father not to do so but their pledges are good for naught.

After they left this evening we had quite a time relating individual obser-vation of all that had occurred. We fared much better though than some of our neighbors who were robbed of meat, etc., etc. They quartered in all the unoccupied houses in town and that accounts for our not seeing their campfires—we did see where the artillery is encamped though. We went into the parlor this evening and had a cotillion and after tea Jule, Nellie, Mack, myself, Neville, Laura, Orville and Carey went into the basement and had a regular old fashioned game of "Blind man's buff" and "Tap the rabbit"—then some of them proposed a game of cards which I declined participating in.[2] We enjoyed ourselves so much and I feel quite worn down with the unusual excitement and exertion. I'm uneasy about "Sky Lark"— Father sent Alex to find him this morning but he was not at the place designated. I hope, however, that the boy only carried him to another of greater security. Twould be a great pity to lose so fine an animal and such a pet too as he is of Mack's.

January 14th, 1863

The first thing I heard upon awakening this morning was Father calling out—"The Yankees are gone!" and looking out saw the last of the cowardly crew disappearing over the hill. Oh such a sense of relief as we experienced at their departure!

. . . Mack returned in the afternoon with his horse which he found in the mountains. He and Jule determined to go home and begged me to accompany them—concluded to accept their invitation. Had quite a cold drive and reached Clover Hill about sunset—found Neville awaiting us there. Jule had the headache and we retired early.

The Yankees went to the Academy and broke the school children's desks and tore up their books—and yet they're the pioneers of civilization and enlightenment and religion. A meek act for such reformers.

January 15th, 1863

Bright pleasant morning. Commenced reading "Charms and Countercharms." Was deeply interested in the book when the sitting room door opened and "Lt. Baylor" ushered in—the same individual who led that daring charge into Front Royal last summer. He referred to it very pleasantly and then said his battalion was on its way now upon a similar expedition into Clarke and would presently pass down the road. . . . Took a walk in the afternoon and although the atmosphere was oppressively warm still it was grey and cloudy and quite blustering. Tonight it is raining and blowing in good earnest and I'm afraid our anticipated visit to Emma tomorrow would be frustrated. Ah well-a-day!

January 17th, 1863

Bitter cold but bright. . . .

We spent the day coqueting with some light sewing and pleasant books and in pleasant conversation and jesting.

In the afternoon we, by general persuasion, induced Emma to accompany us to Clover Hill. The stars were shining cold and bright when we reached there, and who should come out to assist us off our horses but Walter. Dear fellow, I was so glad to see him—he had been to Front Royal on business and was now returning to his regiment. . . .

We are all very stupid in our room tonight, the effects I presume of our ride in the sharp air. I'm so sleepy—tis bitter cold and from my soul I pity any who are exposed to the atmosphere this night. Poor sentinel on duty!

January 18th, 1863

Intensely cold and bright. Walter and Mr. B left early and then I proposed going home and Mack was to drive me in his rockaway. Neville went with us and we had a pleasant ride discussing persons and places. We were told by groups of cavalrymen whom we met coming from town that the Yankees were crossing the river and when we were within two miles of town a dragoon dashed by telling us they had already entered the place. We concluded we would be in danger of participating in a skirmish by proceeding further and concluded to retreat in good order to Clover Hill while we could. They were surprised to see us return and thrown into consternation by the news. Emma instantly fled home and Aunt L made preparations for enduring a search. But the evening waned and they did not come. At last we were led to conclude from all we could learn that twas a mistake as to their having been there at all. Jule and Mack, Neville, Lillie and I had a long pleasant walk on the river bank this evening—did not get back till near dark. Had a reading circle tonight but that incorrigible Mack would not permit us to profit much by it all. Wish I could hear from home.

January 19th, 1863

Clear as a crystal. The boys informed us at breakfast that the ice on the river was fit for skating on and insisted on our accompanying them across to witness their performance. I felt so low spirited that I was disinclined to any movement but knowing Jule wished to go I consented to the arrangement and went. The bracing air invigorated body and spirit, and I felt a great deal better when once skimming about over the glassy ice looking through the clear water beneath to where great shoals of fish were gliding and darting about as though skating too. Climbed up on the high cliffs towering over the river and sat there under the pines and looking down on the river murmuring and flashing along between its ice bound shores I wished oh! so earnestly, that my life were such a sunlit softly flowing stream. There was all the time hanging over me some presentiment that it would never be thus that even then some gloomy "event was casting its shadow before." We went home about twelve o'clock and I had sat down to write the boys a letter which Jule would forward by some passing scout. . . .

Court had to convene out in the courtyard today and they had to station pickets upon the surrounding hills. Very primitive proceedings!

January 23rd, 1863

Cleared off cool. Father came in this evening bringing a letter from dear Irvie dated from ———— ————. Poor fellow, he was in the late dreadful battle—how glad I am that we were unconscious of it till it was all over. He writes very despondingly and seems almost to wish himself back at Charleston with Alvin whom he says has returned thither. He says our friends all escaped unhurt and almost as if by a miracle. The battle must have been much more deadly than we had thought for. Must write to him soon. Ma wrote to Alvin tonight.

January 24th, 1863

. . . Commenced writing a long letter to poor Irvie tonight.

January 26th, 1863

Ma absent all day, Nellie and I housekeeping alone. Made Salt rising and was writing all morning. In the afternoon the Yankees were said to be entering the town—we were destined to an agreeable surprise for they did not come—but Ma and Grandma *did* about five o'clock and soon after they came I heard Carey shouting from the porch—"Two letters! Two letters." I presently found myself on the porch contending with him for two pacquets which he held tantalizingly above his head. I succeeded in capturing them and saw my own name on each written by two hands dearest in the world. I immediately commenced a succession of ecstatic gyrations which were suddenly put to a dead stop by an assault made upon my treasures by Ma, Laura and Nellie combined. We compromised by settling ourselves down on the front step,— Father, Ma, Grandma, Laura, Nellie, myself, Carey, Orville, Nannie, Willie, Evred and Frank—Ma read while we listened with absorbing attention. The first was Irvie's dated from Tullahoma and giving us some account of himself since his last letter—this was dated the 13th. Seemed better reconciled—said he was working very hard but is pleased with his brother officers which is a great thing. Dear fellow, he writes so cheerfully and affectionately, I'm so glad to see it. Tis a pity there's so much dissatisfaction against Bragg—I hope it may be removed however. Irvie sent me the promised photograph so like his own dear self and yet so unlike with that grey, earnest face and that officer's uniform. We have been looking at it through a magnifying glass and every eye I believe looks on it through a glaze of tears. Alvin, dear brother as he is, wrote me such a long, long letter—five pages of foolscap— such a *good* one, such a one as only a great, warm heart and comprehensive judgment could have dictated. Twas written from Charleston where he had just arrived from Tenn. After witnessing that battle which from his description must have been most appalling and deadly. To think too how near he was participating in its horrors and we did not know it! He writes in such good spirits and is very sanguine of receiving an appointment. I think I was somewhat intoxicated with the delight these letters afforded me. I might have stood *one* but both together were more than my weak head could bear and I scarcely knew whether to laugh or cry and so compromised by doing a little of both. Wrote an addenda to Irvie's letters thanking him for his letter and photograph—will write to Alvin too, in a few days. . . .

Had a suspicion of headache from today's excitement.

February 3rd, 1863

Found upon awakening this morning that it had snowed some during the night and grown very cold. Cousin Mary left soon after breakfast and Aunt

Betsy walked over to town with her. Father butchered his hogs today and just as each swineship had been executed news came to town that the Yankees were crossing into town. Knowing that they would appropriate or destroy the pork if they chanced upon it he had the bodies removed to the house and upon going down into the dining room I was forcibly reminded of the old Revolutionary times when I saw the porkers stretched at full length upon the floor. However, the Yankees did not come with the exception of four who came as far as Rose Hill to reconnoiter. . . .

Mr. Berry came in this evening but as I had a headache and felt very "blue" I did not make my appearance. He brings cheerful news of the confidence and good spirits of the troops around Richmond. In the Yankee army Gen. Burnside is deposed and superseded by "Fighting Joe Hooker."

February 4th, 1863

. . .When Father came from town this morning he brought news that the blockading squadron at Charleston had been sunk or driven away by some of our "ironclads." Oh! I do hope tis true—what a great advantage it would be to us if we can only keep the port open for sixty days as they say we will be able to do according to maritime law. Oh for a letter from Alvin now!

February 5th, 1863

The most pitiful cold weather and snowing steadily. Read aloud to Father until about ten o'clock when Uncle Tom came in. After he left came Henry Buck who spent the evening and was with us tonight. He told us that Harry McDonald had just come out of Winchester on business for his mother and brought dreadful tidings of the state of affairs there. Milroy had issued a proclamation to the effect that no citizens should be allowed a pound of flour unless upon condition of his taking the oath of allegiance. Mrs. McDonald's family had been living on bread and water for weeks. It was truly pitiful to hear the account he gave. . . .

February 6th, 1863

A very deep snow on the ground. . . . It cleared off beautifully about noon. In the afternoon Father came in bringing a letter from Irvie to himself giving a more minute and interesting account of the battle. He writes in good spirits but nevertheless thoughtfully. He enclosed two letters from George Wms. to himself—both very "spicy" and one containing quite a compliment to Irvie.

Gus Tyler came in tonight with Henry and sat till nine o'clock. He has grown and improved very much—from being silent he has become quite loquacious. Gave a most interesting account of the battle of F. and related a variety of anecdotes. Among other things told us of a mock battle which our soldiers fought with snowballs during the late snows. It was conducted according to strict military rules—the officers playing a prominent part in it. One of the colonels was standing on a stump trying to rally his men when Scott Roy struck him in his mouth with a snowball. It must have been rare sport—and as usual the Seventeenth distinguished itself. He also spoke of an instance of their cruelty. An old Negro in the Yankee camp had the smallpox and the miserable miscreants put the poor creature into the river to swim across to our camp that the disease might be introduced there. But he was drowned in attempting the passage. The very men who were guilty of this inhumanity were themselves drowned the next day in crossing in a boat to exchange papers. Righteous judgment.

Wrote a long letter to dear Alvin tonight.

February 12th, 1863

. . . Read the President's message today for the first time.[3] Surely it is a masterpiece of composition worthy the source from which it emanated. If "Neutral Europe" does not feel ashamed after the perusal of this document I do not know what is to prevent them. . . .

February 13th, 1863

Pleasant morning. Commenced making my wrapper. Taught the boys—told Nellie and Laura a story. . . . Nellie received a quizz or valentine this evening. Twas a letter purporting to emanate from Giles Cook requesting the privilege of corresponding with her, but it was too evidently Scott's handwriting and style for it to be mistaken. Saucy boy!

No letters for us tonight and no papers. Nellie and I sat up till quite late devising a retaliatory valentine for Scott.

February 14th, 1863

Was busy all the morning manufacturing valentines (at Horace's request) and sewing on my wrapper. Commenced reading the life of Patrick Henry aloud to Father. Dr. Rixey dined with us but left immediately after dinner. Was reading aloud to Father this afternoon when Laura summoned me to Grandma's room where I found Ma and Nellie curiously investigating the superscription upon the outside of a huge fancy envelope bearing my name. Opened and found it to contain a very pretty valentine embellished with some sweet little verses. The handwriting and style of composition would indicate Scott as the donor, though twas postmarked in F. R. . . .

Read aloud to Father till ten o'clock—am delighted with the book—so clearly and concisely written—so interesting withal, so clearly forshadowing the present aspect of the political condition of the country. Sewed a little while—commenced a letter to Alice Morehead and did not get to bed till twelve o'clock.

February 23rd, 1863

Cloudy and snow falling. Cleared off in the afternoon. Father found among the papers sent by Uncle John an Examiner giving an account of the battle of Murfreesboro in which mention was made of the different Generals engaged and their staff. Among the officers upon Gen. Cleborn's was mentioned "Captain I. A. Buck" as having behaved with others with great bravery and done good service. It was such a surprise and pleasure to see it. Ma and I went up to the dormer window in the attic and sat a long time looking out on the beautiful snow scene. Were immeasurably happy, all. *Felt entirely well—did not feel a single pain.* And that of itself was a delicious novelty. My pleasure was considerably dashed by the non-appearance of the mail. Wrote a little while tonight and then sat up and talked a long time to Laura and Nellie about my winter in Baltimore.

February 25th, 1863

This was one of King Winter's gala mornings—such as he sometimes vouches us as though to reconcile us to his harsh and generally unlovely aspect. He had exhausted the contents of his jewel casket to give brilliancy to the scene—his mantle of ermine was sewn with rubies, amethysts, and diamonds, every tree was encrusted with rich seed pearls and every branch, every twig seemed a constellation of tiny star gems that glittered and flashed in a blaze of regal splendor in the bright clear rays of the morning sun. In the distance the trees looked white as with myriads of blossoms lending an appearance of enchantment to the fairylike scene.

We all went to the mill to be weighed. I counted the same as upon a former occasion—111 lbs. Mr. Hope conducted us through the mill and took a great deal of pains to explain the whole mechanism. I was very much surprised to find it so very complicated and to see how much velocity might be involved in a simple grist mill.

Was busy all the morning writing and sewing. . . .

March 9th, 1863

Had made an engagement to spend the day with Emma at Mrs. Cook's—so, although quite unwell I made ready to accompany Nellie—the morning was bright, the air bracing. Called at Mrs. Cloud's where Emma soon joined us and then went on down to Mrs. C.'s. Received a hearty welcome and spent a most delightful day. In the afternoon Mr. Berry came down and sat with us. Seemed to be enjoying the greatest flow of spirits—was full of merry anecdotes. About four o'clock Scott came in. He is so kind and thoughtful—went in the parlor to hear the "Officer's Funeral" which he says he learned for me—'tis a sweet, sad thing and reminds me so much of Willie R. Scott says he has ten days to remain at home—so glad! He saw the Taylors when in Richmond—seems to like them much. Told us some very pleasant anecdotes and then left. Mattie and Mary sang a new song for us "The Pirate" a very pretty thing and very well sung by them—mean to learn it—if I *can*. We all called in at Mrs. Jones and sat an hour after leaving Mrs. Cook's. Heard that Van Dorn had captured an amount of supplies and prisoners from Rosencrans the other day. Had a long letter from "Nannie Dear" tonight—*such* a nice one. Laura and I were reading aloud alternately to Father tonight—"The Greyson Letters" a book handed him by Dr. Hough the other day. Like it very much—tis a perfect mosaic of humor and philosophy.

March 17th, 1863

Clear this morning. . . . Laura came over bringing a little microscopic collection of our Generals' and statesmen's photographs—Davis, Lee, Beauregard, Jackson, Hill, Morgan, Price, Bragg, and Semmes—all composed in the space of a large sized pin head. The collection belongs to a refugee Marylander, Mr. Winchester, who is staying in town. . . .

March 19th, 1863

Felt better this morning than for some time. . . .

Received tonight a "Southern Illustrated News" from dear Irvie—not a very interesting number though. Was sitting up till late tonight reading the Lamplighter. Heard that Scott was going tomorrow. Do wonder if he *will* go off without coming to tell us "goodbye."

March 20th, 1863

Snowing this morning. Ma quite unwell—slept but little last night, so did not dress till noon. Father came home and told us that Scott did not go today. He also said it was rumored in town that all of Jones Brigade would be through town tomorrow—destination unknown. . . .

Scott came over tonight and has just left after eleven o'clock—he's such a social, good fellow. We had music and singing and a discussion of "old times," very pleasant it was. At parting he promised me the photograph which I asked him for last spring. He thinks he'll never come back, poor fellow.

We were disappointed in getting our mail this evening again.

March 22nd, 1863

Clear this morning but very muddy. Nellie would insist on my accompanying her to church till I was forced to go in self defense—felt quite sick in church but the walk upon the whole was of service to me. Dr. Hough as usual gave us a most excellent sermon. Scott was not at Church but I sent him his book and a card through Cousin E. Cloud. . . . Was lying down on the bed by Ma when some one ran in to say Scott was coming—was surprised to hear it as Cousin E. told me he would leave this evening. He immediately proposed going up on the house top—twas a lovely evening and everything looked so beautifully springlike. He gave me a little verse, a waif he had culled somewhere—a sweet, plaintive little poem—and then sitting down talked a long time so much more kindly and unreservedly than he had ever done before. Bless his great warm heart! He's a dear good boy. I'm so sorry he's going away so soon now that I know him so much better than ever before. He left about sundown and does not expect to be back for a long, long time, poor fellow.

The different regiments have been passing by all day today—the Seventh is in camp only about a mile and a half from town and all the others scattered around. I'm so glad to see *our* soldiers about now instead of the Yankees whom we had feared would have been here ere now.

Feel tired and *so* sleepy tonight.

♦

March 27th, 1863

The day appointed by our President for humiliation and prayer.[4] We observed it strictly so far as fasting and attending divine service was concerned. Just before the church bell was rung Henry B. and Charlie R. called. They both behave very singularly—don't know what to think of them. Henry told us that Cousin R. Helms' wife had just arrived at Rose Hill—had been forced to flee from home by the threats made by a negro servant formerly belonging to her. Her husband is with his regiment near town and I suppose will be gratified at her arrival. . . .

March 28th, 1863

Cloudy and rainy in torrents. Uncle John tapped at the door soon after breakfast and being admitted inquired who among us would undertake to renovate his slender wardrobe. We all unanimously declared our willingness for the task whereupon he succeeded to allot to each her work—with the which and listening and talking to him we whiled away the hours till noon. Mack has a cold—could not venture out, so he read aloud to Father all day. . . .

[March 30, 1863, entry omitted]

April 1st, 1863

Bright and pleasant but quite cold. In the afternoon Ma and I concluded to go up to see Mrs. Hope. Spent a quiet pleasant evening but I felt very sad from hearing them all talking about the military movements and discussing the probability of our army having to leave this part of Virginia. The thoughts of it haunted me like a nightmare all the time. Mr. Berry came in to tea and while sitting at table Father told me he had a letter from Irvie with one enclosed to me but would not let me have it till after all had finished eating. Of course, I have not much appetite for the repast and of course I hastened upstairs to read them. To me he writes very softly, very amusingly—to Father thoughtfully and seriously. His letters were dated the ——— ——— ———. So Father *did* write him about Captain Latrobe really. It's right funny! Opened and added a postscript to my long letter which I must mail tomorrow. Ma writes to Alvin too. While sitting about the stand writing, who should walk in but Walter. So glad to see him. We sat up till eleven o'clock talking. He is so cheerful and confident that I almost wonder at my allowing myself to grow depressed this afternoon. Truly Captain Mosby is making to himself a name and bids fair to rival Ashby. Poor fellow. Tis said all of Aunt Cattie's servants have left her—poor thing I wonder what she will do, for she is more dependent for their services than almost anyone I know of.

April 2nd, 1863

Clear and warm but quite windy. . . . Called to see Miss Tensia and Belle Ford and spent a pleasant hour with them. Then went over to see Mrs. Robert Turner whom we found quite sick. Mrs. Dorsey with her but she remained only a short time. We did not leave until sundown. Mrs. T. made herself very agreeable and poor woman I do pity her—sick and entirely alone with the exception of her servants and two little children and such a dreary house to be confined in, so dark with the wind whistling and shrieking around. She told us that Monroe Tyler had died from his wounds—poor fellow! I'm afraid he was not prepared for death than life. She loaned me the "First Year of the War" and a volume of Southern poems. . . .

April 3rd, 1863

Such a lovely morning such as we've not had in a long time. Nellie and I were seized with a violent desire to take a ramble to the river and made angling the ostensible object of our expedition. Nellie went up and got E. Hope to accompany us, with Orville for guide we stepped forth—(Carey was sick and could not venture). We struck a new path through the fields and climbed the high hill directly opposite town from which we had a charming view of the little valley that intervened between us and the mountains stretching away in smooth meadows that were just changing their russet winter garb for the soft velvety green of early spring. The little creek dancing amusingly along seemed brimming with sunshine, and the woods wore a soft, hazy appearance, the state between leafless branches and full foliage. The mountains had drawn about them a transparent azure veil—all save one a far distant peak that reared itself in sharp outline against the clear sky glittering and white with ice and snow, lending an agreeable diversity to the scene. We crossed one field which had been last summer the site of a Yankee encampment and where we still saw half hidden under the brown, crisp grass traces of their presence in the fragments of boxes, old canteens, tin cups, broken bottles, bits of rope, odd shoes, dismanteled huts and all the etcetera of one of their lairs. Once we paused upon a breezy hill just above the river and sat down to rest. I felt as if I could have spent the day there in the tall dry grass with the warm balmy sunshine falling goldenly like a shower of loving smiles around me: with the river flowing near murmuring its soothing lulling lullaby; with the sunny hillslopes forest bound looking rich and green with their beautiful mingling of evergreens. Ever and anon the soft, plaintive cooing of a solitary dove came to our ears. Sounding so sadly weird—for from my earliest childhood has been associated in my mind something unearthly, something unreal in their sweet notes—a something that awed by its very sweetness. I was sorry when my eager companions proposed the descent to the river bank that they might begin their arts of blandishment on the finny tribe. . . .

It became oppressively warm and we were hungry, tired and footsore upon reaching home about two o'clock p.m. Bathed our heated faces, rearranged our disordered dresses, ate our dinners and then I lay down and was on the bed nearly the whole of the afternoon so weary and stupid. Was preparing to disrobe tonight when they came in to announce that Messrs. Yates, Alexander and Crane were in the sitting room. Johnnie Yates was one of the principal actors in that raid into Front Royal last summer and I was anxious to see the redoubtable young soldier. Great was my surprise therefore upon being introduced to a delicate youth scarce as tall as myself, with a round child face and a hand that looked much better suited for playing on the guitar than wielding a saber. And yet this boy soldier had been engaged in some of the most daring feats imaginable—had been captured and imprisoned in Fort McHenry for five weeks—the idea of confining such a child in a military prison—it seemed *too* cruel—he is the same who captured our Provost in town last summer. . . .

April 4th, 1863

Very cold this morning, but clear. Nellie and I arranged the floral trophies of our yesterday's expedition in a large vase the first thing—and they really did look lovely. About eleven o'clock two young gentlemen Mr. Williams of Winchester and Magruder of Woodstock came in and remained to dinner but not feeling very socially inclined, I did not make my appearance. While they were all at dinner I was sitting in Grandma's room reading when a tap at the door was followed by the entrance of Walter. He was very much hurried and would remain long enough to go down to the second table and dine with me. He was very serious and taciturn and at leaving he gave Nellie his saber and pet merschaum to take care of till his return. We knew he was bound on some dangerous enterprise, but knowing equally well that he did not wish to reveal his object we made no enquiries concerning his movements. I hope poor fellow his intrepidity will not lead him into needless peril. In the afternoon Father was summoned away and Ma and I had to entertain the young gentlemen. They were very agreeable and amused us very much with fighting over their battles like any experienced veterans for our benefit. They left about four o'clock. Carey quite unwell.

Laura came home this evening bringing me the first violets I've seen. Planted potatoes today.

April 5th, 1863

Found the snow deep on the ground this morning, and the trees were heavy with their white burden. Allie came over in the morning. Read aloud to Fa-

ther. Dick Bailey called in the afternoon and confirmed the reports we have
been hearing from the servants during the day of firing of musketry over the
river. A body of Yankees had come down the river and had been shooting
across from Guard Hill with their long range guns at our pickets at this side.
Cousin Horace Buck, who was staying at Mr. Richards started to come over
in the boat when one of the scoundrels fired a bullet so close to him that it
almost grazed him.

April 10th, 1863

This lovely day promised to be a quiet one for the inhabitants of Bel Air. But
about ten o'clock Cousin E. Cloud came in and then Uncle Newton and
finally just before dinner Cousin Will Cloud, Willie Buck and Dick Bailey all
came in—had just returned from scouting in Loudon—bring cheering news
of the abundance of provisions and forage in that part of the state. They say
they are really going tomorrow and when they are gone there will be no
troops left in this part of the valley. We were singing and playing for them
after dinner when in the midst of our glee Mrs. Cook and Mattie and Mary
came in. The boys left and scarce had their footsteps grown cold on the
threshold when Cousin Mount hurriedly entered. We were asking him something about Walter when a loud shout startled us and one of the children
rushed in to say "Cousin Walter's coming at last!" In he came laughing and
jesting, just took time to tell us that he's been to Clark, had seen Uncle Larue
who told him that only four of his servant men had left him. He said he had
been all day dodging the Yankees, running out of the back door when they
came in the front one. He had been to see Josey Grantham and as the Yankee
picquet post was just at the house he had great time hiding from them once
even getting in the bed—and the scamps had pursued him as far as the island
ford and then fired at him after he crossed the river. He seemed in a great
hurry for he soon called Cousin Mount out. They held a whispered consul-
tation and then mounted their horses and rode off in great glee. W. telling us
he would be back sometime tonight to take his supper. But tis eleven o'clock
now and thus far he did not eat. I've no doubt they went to camp to try and
get reenforcements to go and capture the pursuing party at the ford. After
they left Misses James Paget, Maggie Myers, Mattie Reynolds and Julius Riles
and a Mrs. Griggs from Clark came in and sat till sundown. All left us after

tea and I felt so completely worn out with the confusion and with nursing poor little Frank who has been sick today, that I would fain have gone to bed directly, but the mail goes out tomorrow mayhap for the last time and I felt bound to avail myself of the opportunity of sending dear Alvin one more message from home. Ma is writing to Irvie too. We were surely disappointed when Father came in tonight and told us the mail had brought neither letters nor papers. It's very plain that Scott has forgotten to keep his promise. Uncle N. left me some nauseous powders to take tonight. Ugh!

April 11th, 1863

Another fair day. Slept till late this morning but was in the garden in time enough to get a violet to enclose in Irvie's letter which with mine was sent early to the office. Walter came in a little before nine o'clock to say good-bye—it seems they have changed their program after leaving here last evening and didn't after all go after the Yankees. He gave us a more minute account of his trip into the Yankee lines and then with many injunctions to us "keep brave hearts" he vaulted into his saddle and galloped away—he with all the rest of the troops will return himself to Luray tonight. Squads of cavalry were continually passing this morning and we cast after them many a wistful glance for each company that passed seemed like a funeral cortege carrying away the dead body of another and another bright hope. We had flattered ourselves that some few of the different regiments would remain but it seems now that all are gone.—We are wholly deserted. . . .

Tonight while we were sitting at the supper table it seemed so pleasant to have no one but our own immediate family together—such a thing had not occurred before in a year. Father remarked as he arose from the table that he thought some one of the family would be apt to receive a letter tonight saying which he proceeded to draw from his pocket two missives, *one*, at least, of which I felt sure was for me—either a letter from Irvie or the package from Scott—but no, both were addressed to Nellie one in Dick's handwriting—the other in that of Giles—both were in good spirits and dated their letters from near the Blackwater. I was so disappointed, but my chagrin was some removed by the news contained in the papers—*we have gained a glorious victory at Charleston* and completely repulsed the enemy.[5] Thank God! And next to Him, blessings be to our blessed Beauregard for I'm convinced tis greatly to his energy and ability under Heaven that we owe this glorious success. Oh for a letter from Alvin now!

April 12th, 1863

A most lovely springlike day has this been—a perfect April day variable with smiles and tears like any capricious beauty. It was delightfully quiet and pleasant this morning. No one at the breakfast table but our own immediate family. . . .

Father returned after night—says he noticed a great commotion and moving of lights at Dr. Turner's when he passed—am afraid something has happened there for we have heard Mrs. T. was very ill again this evening.

[April 13, 1863, entry omitted]

April 14, 1863

Nellie, Dick and myself called at Oakley and then at their earnest solicitations I consented to call in at Captain Roy's to see something Cousin E. had promised Nellie. Found Mrs. Dr. Hough there and we all had a merry time over looking Cousin E's daguerreotypes—and I saw Scott's miniature—the very best I ever saw and so handsome. Oh!—I was more than ever provoked at his noncompliance with his promise. It's too bad of him! Cousin E. does act very strangely—I wonder where was the use of her making that display of her letter in Mrs. H.'s presence.

Feel very tired tonight and cross too—think I'm a much injured individual and the injury inflicted by hands from which I had little expected it.

[April 16, 1863, entry omitted]

April 18th, 1863

Toujours le meme

A bright beautiful morning. Cut out a pair of gloves to make for myself. The second anniversary of the day the poor boys went into the war. . . . Father proposed that I should "press" Jacquie's idle horse into service and take a ride. Willie rode with me as escort and a delightful canter we had of it

all over the high hills east of town from which we had such a charming view
of the mountains—arms stretched embracingly around our little valley, looking so soft and blue in contrast with the mellow richness of the sunset sky; of
the little glimpse of river scenery the bits of water looking like truant lakes
hiding behind the intervening wooded heights; of the little quiet "dulce—
far—niente" looking village nestled in the valley; of the green rolling meadows, the dancing, singing brooks leaping and flashing over their brows. A
calm, sweet prospect it was over which the very genius of silence seemed
to have woven its spell. . . . Aunt Betty told me a great deal of good news
too, only I'm afraid tis not true, about Longstreet having surrounded sixteen thousand Yankees in Suffolk forcing them to surrender, of our having
achieved quite a little victory at Kelley's Ford, of a second success at Charleston and of Stuart's having been promoted and assigned the command of the
valley—but this, the most cheering piece of intelligence to us seems to bear
the stamp of authenticity—oh if it be but true. How I wish it may be! Called
by Mrs. Hope's and then reached home just as the bell rang for tea. Felt
positively happy—too much so to talk, so stealing off into the parlor I sat
down to think with my piano—memory and fingers talked to the keys of
bygone hours until Nellie came in to tell me of her evening at Mrs. H's—she
soon went out though leaving me to the twilight and the society of my own
thoughts. I was thinking of this ever to be remembered anniversary—playing
half unconsciously the "Farewell to Mary Queen of Scots" when just then Ma
called me in a quick eager voice. Closing the piano I hastened to her room—
she and Father were sitting by the candlestand inspecting the contents of the
mail just brought in. She held up to me a letter—one glance sufficed. Snatching it eagerly I ran off into Grandma's room to open it and was there ever
anything so like another as that miniature like Scott?—the same candid,
manly face, kind in expression and to my eye handsome too. And his letter
so frank, so mischievous, so characteristic withal—I almost cried in my excess of delighted surprise and scarcely know yet how to behave myself. The
day's pleasure has quite turned my head and I shall have to hasten to bed that
sleep the "kind restorer" may set me all right again. Ah me!

April 25th, 1863

Windy but bright and warm. Ma and I were clear starching our laces and
muslins in the morning. Father came in about eleven o'clock and told us that

Mr. Thomas had arrived in town from Richmond bringing the news of a battle at Suffolk in which both Giles and poor Scott were wounded though only slightly. Poor fellows! I do hope they'll come home now until fit for duty again. Could hear no particulars of the battle at all. . . .

April 29th, 1863

A shower this morning. After it cleared off I went into the garden and was weeding the flowers when hearing the children shout a welcome looked up and saw Walter riding in at the yard gate. We were as much delighted as surprised to see him and to hear that he had been again to Clarke. Remained long enough to give a very stirring description of the late affair at Fishers Hill in which he was engaged and to tell how near he was being shot (his horse was killed) and then left. . . .

April 30th, 1863

Tonight Ma, Father, Cousin E., Nellie and I went into the parlor and had a private concert—a very pleasant one til bed time. Just as we were going upstairs Ma whispered to me that father heard in town of a battle in which the Seventh Regiment had been engaged losing very heavily but she bade me say nothing about it to Cousin E. lest she should be alarmed about her boys. Since coming down we have been discussing the matter and are seriously afraid some of our friends and relations must have fallen in the fight, but nothing definite can be learned of it.

May 1st, 1863

A beautiful morning befitting the advent of a beautiful month, balmy and bright. . . . My headache is terrible—am afraid I shall not sleep much tonight. No further news from the seventh. No mail.

May 2nd, 1863

Lovely weather. Felt very badly after my feverish, broken night's rest. Finished the gloves I was making for Aunt Bettie and did little than read all the morning. Allie came in and told us the report of Willie Jackson's death had reached town. He was mortally wounded in Jones late engagement, charging at the very head of the regiment and being ridden over by the rushing Cavalry charge. Poor boy! so young, so brave to be doomed to such an early and horrible death. I trust the news is without foundation. To think he should fall in his first engagement, while so many of his comrades have passed unscathed through the shock of many battles. . . .

. . . It is generally believed that the Seventh was not as much injured as we had feared at first. How well I remember this day, year—the anniversary of our investment by the Yankees.

May 6th, 1863

Raining and sun shining by turns. Early this morning Alex came in from home bringing a note from Ma and letter from Irvie received yesterday afternoon. The letter was evidently written in the greatest haste and he poor fellow perfectly absorbed in the gayeties in which he had been participating. Reading the letter struck a chill to my heart for I thought how soon he might be summoned from the festive hall to the deadly conflict and how poor a preparation he was making for the change. . . .

Uncle Tom came in and told us there had been a terrible battle at Fredericksburg in which we had repulsed the enemy both sides losing very heavily—Genls. Jackson, Hill, Heath and Paxton were said to be wounded I trust only slightly though.[6] Oh how thankful we should feel for having been once more able to repulse the enemy in mortal conflict. Emma and Cousin Sue and I stood on the front porch a long while talking this afternoon and then after tea we got "Hyperion" and Emma and I read it together til too dark to see the letters. Sang again and sat up talking some time after retiring to our rooms tonight. Raining hard.

[May 7, 1863, entry omitted]

[May 8, 1863, entry omitted]

May 9th, 1863

A most delicious day, so warm and so bright. Taught the children, sewed some and read some. In the afternoon father invited us to walk down to the old "tank" with him. We went, he, Orville and Carey went on down to the river to fish while Laura, Willie and I returned through the meadows home. Stopped on the rugged wooded hill below Clifton and gathered some new violets and dug for "Crowfoot" for Ma. Had a pleasant walk home, sat and chatted a while with Ma then read in "Alone" and finally went with her out on the old stile about sunset where we sat cracking nuts and watching them fixing the foot bridge swept away by the high waters of the last few days. The boys came back exhibiting a little string of fish of which they seemed to be extremely proud. Mr. Berry came in before we had left the tea table—brings only a confirmation of what we had already heard of the late affair at F. Had seen General Lee's report—did not learn the list of casualties. Jackson, it is thought, is but slightly wounded. So glad! Ma and I came upstairs and lying down on the bed talked until bed time—it made me so sad. I feel like crying tonight. Ah me!

[May 12, 1863, entry omitted]

May 13th, 1863

Carey carried our letters to the office this morning and came back telling us that intelligence of Jackson's death had reached town—we did not credit it at all though. But alas! Emma and Nellie came with sad faces and told us that it was but too true, a Richmond paper all heavily in mourning had been received in town announcing the melancholy event—though giving none of the particulars. Oh what a blow is this—Our bravest and best, the most devoted and earnest in the cause in which we all have staked so much—the truest and noblest, our christian patriot. Gone! Everyone seemed stunned by the news—and it has been a mournful day with us—nature seemed even to partake of the general gloom, for the sun although shining in a cloudless sky seemed sickly and wan. During the morning Willie Buck came over to tell us goodbye preparatory to going into the army and then Mack Irwin called and they both left together. Received a new "Messenger" and after having finished writing in my diary we went upstairs Emma, Nellie, Laura and I and read it. Ma went up to see Mrs. Hope who is sick and we had intended going over to see Mrs. Cook's flowers but it clouded over and grew so grey that we did not venture forth. Oh me! I can't realize that dreadful story of General Jackson's death—perhaps it may be after all a mistake.[7] I hope so, Oh I hope so!

May 15, 1863

The papers bring additional particulars of Jackson's death. I never fully believed it before—but I've read it now.

May 16th, 1863

Was aroused from a sweet dream by Nellie's voice in the early dawn crying out—"get up girls! I've bad news for you—the town is full of Yankees!" Not crediting the tale I turned my head to a more comfortable position on the pillow intent on resuming the thread of my dream, but she finally succeeded in convincing me that it was my duty to believe and obey her. Had not completed my toilette when I heard a knock at the front door and then the clanking of sabres as the owners were admitted. They inquired for father and were directed to the stables, where he had gone to send the horses off to a place of concealment. The household was wide awake and stirring though not excited, and Emma, Nellie, Laura and I sat down by the window to finish "Alone" and were at an interesting crisis of the fascinating narrative when the door flew back and in came two Yankees with father. They had come to search for "rebel soldiers" and upon being told their trouble would be fruitless they said there certainly had been some in Front Royal last night. They did not prosecute their investigation quite as rigorously as their predecessors though, only peeping under the beds and making father unpack the large box of Table and Bed linen in the upper passage—provoking wretches! to give so much trouble. The gallent officer in command was dressed in full Confederate Uniform. There was a box of bed and table linens in the hall which they insisted upon overhauling for "contraband goods"—they had their troubles for their pains as there was nothing suspicious contained therein save a piece of cotton which had been bought before the war and this they did not take. There were only two of the sinners who came in the house the Captain and a young, well dressed seemingly mortified sort of Yankee Boy whose office seemed to be to watch the expression of our countenances to ascertain our opinion of their proceedings—he was gratified and edified I know at the curled lips and contemptuous smiles of some of his spectators. They behaved very well for Yankees, only one of them was drunk and indulged in very free use of oaths to his companions while relating to them how he would have burned Mr. Hope's house to the ground but for the sick woman in it. They were members of the famous "Jessie Scouts" of Fremont notoriety.[8] About eight o'clock we were dismayed at seeing a body of Infantry—from one to two hundred marching in preceded by their baggage wagons. After they came in the Cavalry went across the mountain on some secret embassy. We spent a very quiet day—not another Yankee appearing on the premises the whole day. They did not form an encampment but bivouacked in the public square in town. . . .

May 17th, 1863

Our first inquiry—"have the Yankees gone?" was answered negatively. Of course, Sunday School was not to be thought of or church either for that matter. We wandered listlessly about all the early morning, first in the parlor playing and singing hymns, then in the garden gathering flowers and awakening the lazy bees, next upstairs, then on the porch until we finally settled down in something like the following order: father went to town to get the news, Ma, Nellie, and Emma committed themselves to napping and I had resource to reading and writing. . . .

Was sitting on the porch reading aloud to Father about three o'clock this afternoon when looking out we saw the Yankee Infantry marching quietly out of town—minus their Cavalry escort. We soon learned that they had heard of the loss of their troops and that fear had hurried their departure. Mr. Berry came over soon after they left. Very soon after their exodus a body of the officers came galloping back and scattered over the suburbs of town as if in quest of something but soon collecting they took a final departure. They had returned vainly hoping to capture some of our men who might have crept from their hiding places but in this they were disappointed although there were several in concealment there.

Father says they injured his store somewhat having taken the drawers out to feed their horses in and burst some of them besides scattering some of father's old receipts about in the upper store room. They took, in the post office, yesterday a letter from Scott Roy which had been overlooked in the distribution of mail matter on Friday—Don't know to whom it was written but they read it publicly in the street and threatened to publish it. It's too bad indeed. We all, Ma, Emma, Nellie, Laura and I sat upstairs a long time at twilight talking—Emma speaking more of her early life—of her mother and little sister than I ever knew her before. . . .

May 18th, 1863

All busy with spring cleaning today. That was all a mistake about the Yankee Cavalry having been captured. This is the summary of their proceedings. Our Cavalry—Fifty in number went down to Charlestown a few nights since and captured some sixty Yankees and with their prisoners were returning by the Piedmont Route via Delaplane. The Yankees in Winchester hearing of this feat vowed vengeance and retaliation and sent forth this detachment to intercept them. They surprised our men in a very disadvantageous position—a skirmish ensued in which they retook all the prisoners and four of the Confederates but not the arms which we had taken from the prisoners and with which we made our escape. Twas a miracle that all our boys were not captured—Poor Charlie Richardson was among the number taken. The Yankee Cavalry in returning to Winchester did not come through here but took the "Island Ford" Route—which accounts for their not being here when the Infantry evacuated the place. . . .

May 19th, 1863

Pleasant this morning. Still engaged with spring cleaning. Had a wearing time nursing Frank. Repaired a bonnet for Eliza Ann. . . .

[May 20, 1863, entry omitted]

May 21, 1863

All the hands busy planting corn and as Father seems so anxious to get well through with the job the house servants were also engaged in it. So Nellie and I had the children to attend to. Grandma went up to the Hope's in the

afternoon and while she was there Eliza came in and sat some time with us.
Nellie and I went in the garden in the evening to help Carey water the plantes.
The flowers are beginning to bloom beautifully and there is such charming
weather with so much of beauty around the very fact of existence itself almost
seems a pleasure.

May 25th, 1863

Had commenced writing this morning when quite early Aunt B. came in to
fulfill her engagement with Ma and begged me to make one of the party.
Twas chill and disagreeable without—misty and grey and I had a suspicion
of the neuralgia—but Ma, Grandma, Nellie and Aunt B. were bent on it and
go I must. We were to walk until we met our conveyance which father had
sent for from Mr. McDaniel's where it had been concealed from the Yankees.
Father went with us—we met the wagon only after we had, as we thought,
arrived nearly at our place of destination and we decided to continue our way
on foot. Father put us into the wrong road though and we had a pleasant but
a very long weary walk. I found some strange wild flowers in the woods
through which we passed and some pretty leaves. When we arrived at Happy
Creek (twas my first visit there though living in sight of the place twenty
years) a little urchin directed us around to the front entrance. I could but be
struck with the air of dilapidation and desolation that reigned over everything
despite the natural beauties of the place. The whole appearance of house and
grounds reminded me of descriptions of the old "Halls" of some of the im-
poverished English gentlemen. The porters lodges looked but the shadow of
what they were intended for, there was no gate—scarcely any inclosure
about the lawn, the hedges were beautiful in their wild luxuriance but un-
clipped and ragged, the grass tall and rank growing even in the walks and
drives. There were flowers and blossoming shoots though that gave a pleasing contrast in their neat arrangement to the general neglect visible everywhere. Old Mr. M. was standing on the stone steps of the great hall door to
receive us and give us a cordial welcome. We were ushered into an immense
hall and thence into the sitting room where Miss Mary soon made her appearance apologizing for the temporary absence of her sisters and inviting us
to her room where we laid aside our bonnets and shawls and rearranged our

toilettes before going down to see old Aunt L. who has been sick so long. She was apparently very glad to see us, and sitting up in bed talked a great deal. I never saw such a looking object as she is—almost a skeleton, her livid brown skin falling in loose wrinkles over the projecting bones—her mouth all drawn—lips thin and eyes bleared with age yet quick and restless and yet there she sat and talked as clearly and distinctly of her situation—spoke so calmly and happily of her removal to the "Happy Mansions" as if twas a journey to her native land and early friends on which she was going—even chiding herself for her impatience to be off. How I envy her quiet happy confidence!

Misses H. and M. had returned home in the meantime and after going back to the house we were invited in to luncheon and then shown into the parlor. There we spent the morning talking, admiring the pictures, listening to a long letter from the Rebel Brother in Wheeling. Then we went into the great old garden and out among the flowers.

While at dinner the boys—Orville, Carey, and Allie came in with our spring wagon in which we were to return home. They having left no one at home "on guard" in case the Yankees should come in, Father had to hurry home. Old Mr. M. is a hospitable courtly old gentleman in his house and took more pains to amuse me than I deserved—even bringing a volume from the library—"Froissart's Chronicles" for me to look at to compare the "art in its infancy with its present state of perfection." They were grotesque, stiff, droll looking figures on the yellow parchment very unlife-like and very in-sipid. In course of conversation today "the Antiquary" was spoken of and learning from me that I had never read it she promised to loan me it as soon as she could find it and just as we were leaving putting on our bonnets in the chamber, I took up a couple of books laying on the bed—"Dynevor Ter-race" by the author of "The Heir of Radcliffe" and Miss Mary noticing me with it remarked that twas interesting and if I had never read it I should take it home with me. I accepted the offer delightedly promising to send her an exchange in the shape of my "Messengers." We had spent a very pleasant day not withstanding my aversion to going and I discovered to my surprise that Miss M. instead of being the sour, silent being she appeared in public was a most talkative merry creature imaginable, Miss Hattie not near so un-couth as one might imagine but a notable, kindly, intelligent housekeeper and Miss Ann Maria—the quiet bird-like pet of the household. It won't do to judge from appearances and I am glad my many false opinions of this family have been rectified by this day's visit. Found Uncle Tom taking tea at home. Emma had been there too during the day. Tired and sleepy tonight—very cold and damp.

[May 28, 1863, entry omitted]

May 30th, 1863

The papers came tonight and my June "Messenger." The papers confirmed the welcome tidings we have just received of the late Confederate victory at Vicksburg.[9] Thank heaven! tis more than we could have hoped for.

June 1, 1863

Was lying half asleep on the bed when Laura rushed in with two huge envelopes saying something about Alvin and Richmond—I sprung to my feet and snatched one from her—"Miss Lucie R. Buck" in Scott's familiar handwriting and the postmark "Richmond"—was a little disappointed but 'twas the next best thing to being from Alvin himself. The other pacquet was for Nellie containing a note and a piece of music—"Her Bright Smile Haunts Me Still"—mine also a note and "Rock Me to Sleep, Mother"—which no longer than yesterday I had been longing for. Bless his life!—'twas so kind of him to think of it. He has rejoined his regiment and is doing well.

[June 4, 1863, entry omitted]

June 5th, 1863

Writing to Alvin. Interrupted by a visit from my little Sunday-School Scholars. They went with us to visit the bird's nest—to the flower garden, then into the parlor where I told them stories and played and sang for them. Their visit was brought to a very abrupt termination by the report that the Yankees were in town. They hurried off but it was soon ascertained to be a false alarm—twas only some of our own picquets galloping down the road. . . .

June 6th, 1863

. . . An amusing incident occurred tonight. Just as we were preparing for bed there came a knock at the door—we were all in our night clothes and every one made a simultaneous rush for the little room. I had fortunately presence of mind to open the door a few inches and peeping out inquired "who's there?" The answer came—"Nobody." Twas very indefinite so the question was repeated and then came—"No Yankee nor nothing of that sort." That was all sufficient and E. Ann was dispatched to admit him. Twas a member of Captain McNeil's Company and we could hear him through the door giving Father an account of a skirmish in which they were engaged yesterday near Winchester—they must be a brave band.

June 8th, 1863

After retiring at ten o'clock Alex came in and told us that a company of Yankees had come into town. Uncle John immediately got up and dressed and went away and Alex took his horse and some baggage after him. They all seemed a good deal excited but I did not believe the story Alex told at all. This morning, however, twas confirmed—There were some four or five hundred—they came in from below, got in the rear of our picquets, captured them and left unmolested. They did not know even that our men under Captain Stevenson were encamped near town—and they did not know that the Yankees were here.

Chapter Five

❧❧❧❧❧❧❧❧❧❧❧❧❧❧❧❧❧❧❧❧❧❧❧❧❧❧

Very, Very Footsore and Weary

❧❧❧❧❧❧❧❧❧❧❧❧❧❧❧❧❧❧❧❧❧❧❧❧❧❧

June 9, 1863–December 31, 1863

June 9th, 1863

Awoke about five o'clock this morning and came in Grandma's room to dress. There was no fire made, no water brought, no movement whatever below stairs. Just then I heard Father enter Ma's room and exclaim—"all gone horses and all." Throwing on my shawl I stepped in and inquired what was the matter when Ma told me that the servants had all left in the night and carried our three horses with them.[1] We every one of us made a dash for our clothes, hauled them on, kindled a fire, brought water and Laura and I went to milk the cows while Ma, Grandma and Nellie cleaned the house, got the breakfast and dressed the children. Old Uncle Gilbert came and declared his ignorance of the exodus—and to do him justice I don't believe he did. Immediately after breakfast Mrs. Moffatt came in and then Uncle Tom and Uncle Mack and Allie and Elliott and Aunt Bettie and Mr. Kiger—Poor Mr. Kiger's servants went too. When they all came to us they kissed and cried over us but we laughed and told them twas more than we had done for ourselves as yet. Indeed tis surprising with what calmness one learns to bear all such sudden shocks—now my sensations when first becoming cognizant of their flight were a mixture of wonder at their dexterity in baffling so successfully all suspicion of their movements and indignation at their ingratitude in taking the horses when they knew they were our main dependence of support. The first thing we did after cleaning the breakfast things was to clear the trumpery from their various rooms and truly Hercules' labor in the Augean stables was the only thing it could be compared to. Mrs. Moffatt very kindly sent us Matilda and Miss P. Haynie, Caroline and Aunt Bettie contributed Lucy and we fell to work in good earnest, never thinking of such a thing as sitting down to rest during the day. The servants took apparently nothing with them but their finest clothing and in the midst of trumpery left we had an opportunity of discovering various articles hitherto counted among the missing. Father and Mr. Beecher started about twelve o'clock to Winchester to attempt the recovery of their horses—poor Father his loss is the heaviest of all, amounting, it is thought, to some sixteen thousand dollars. Well tis all right doubtless though we can't now see it just so. Mrs. Hope sent us some dinner and we did not stop to have any cooked—I just frying some meat and putting down a hoecake for the servants. While making up my biscuits for supper in the afternoon Cousin Sue Buck, Belle Richardson, and Aunt Eliza came in to condole with us—Eliza to assist in our labors. Twas fortunate for me, we're all well nigh exhausted with our unwanted exertions. After the kitchen and basement were put in order tonight we all agreed it looked comfortable enough down there to tempt us to take up our abode there. Fastened doors and windows and came up in the house where we found Mr. Berry just arrived to stay with us as protectors for tonight. We have just had prayer and are ready for our much needed repose. Wonder where Father is—wonder if the servants don't some of them feel a little homesick. Poor creatures! They little know the fate in store for them. Tis said Belle Boyd is in town tonight. What next? My biscuits were pronounced faultless tonight.

June 10th, 1863

Rising and working before sunrise this morning made me so deathly sick, but soon wore it off. Mr. Kiger came in to breakfast—said he had been patroling the premises all night. One of his servants, the mother of the family, didn't go with the others—remained behind to sell out and wind up business intending to follow after them. Eliza came up from Rose Hill this morning and milked and made the fire for us and cleaned up the kitchen, put on meat for dinner and everything we couldn't do for ourselves. She's such a good, able servant—if we only had such! Uncle Tom was over this morning and Aunt Letitia Buck too surprised us by coming in very quietly quite early—she helped us churn and take up the butter—gave us some instructions in cooking and after cheering us very much took her leave with the promise of a speedy return. Em. came over this morning with a sympathizing note from Cousin E. Cloud and a nice, white silk handkerchief from Mrs. Roy for me to wear about my head to protect my "Neuralgia"—so kind and thoughtful of her. My pea soup was pronounced at table to be excellent. Aunt Eliza came back from home in time to take up dinner and assist us very much. Tis our wash day. Mrs. Normal took the clothes to the mill to wash them—we think of hiring her to come and do the work next week. Old Uncle Gilbert looked sorely distressed and lonely. I feel sorry for him—particularly as he has been making himself so useful since they all left. Uncle Tom and Uncle Fayette came in this evening, the latter remained to tea and I made some biscuits and curd—my first curd for the occasion. I really enjoyed the day—hard as the work was, but in the late evening twas very trying when the children were crying to be put to bed and dishes to be washed and put away, milk to strain, water to bring, chips to get, plants to be watered, kitchen to clean up and candle sticks to set up. Mrs. G's. Eliza milked for us tonight. Charlie Richardson rode into the yard about sundown and Uncle Mack too—they brought us news of a skirmish between Jones' brigade and some of the Yankees. They say there will before one week be the greatest revolution in the state of affairs here in the valley that we could conceive of. There's evidently some tremendous scheme in course of culmination. Would it were developed!

Mr. Berry came over again tonight. Just as we arose from prayer some one called out—"Father's come!" and to our great surprise he was in grandma's room, having just gotten home—bringing with him his two horses. We were so glad to see him and hear him give an account of his interview with old Milroy who consented to his receiving his two horses upon condition that the third should be given the servants as their "lawful" hire since the first of January.[2] Father saw the servants—all save Horace and Marshall—they were all together in a crowded, close shanty with not a single convenience of life.

Miserable creatures—there's no doubt but they wish themselves back in their comfortable home many times ere this. They tried to brave the matter off very bravely when they met Father—told them they had had no idea of leaving until about noon that day before, when Martha said she had overheard Grandma tell Mrs. Hope that all the servants ought to be sent South (which was palpably false) and that they took the alarm—knowing Mr. Kiger had bought a wagon to take his servants there and concluded to start right off. They sent for *Allfair* that night upon the plea that her sister was dying—so she went with them and all of the twelve (including Rob Roy) went on the three horses and carried their baggage—how they ever managed it I can't conceive, and they did not start either until just about dawn. They said they would like to have all their plunder if they could get it but Rob Roy confessed he was almost afraid to return on this side of the river fort. They asked no questions whatever but told that they were enroute for Alexandria where they expected to meet their mother. To think that Mahalla even went off without taking John Henry, her pet child—he being not quite so convenient as Allfair but I suppose she thought he could come on at any time with old Aunt Hester. Poor Miserable creatures! I do pity them rushing so blindly to a fate that they little foresee. We are so thankful that Father made all the trip without taking any pledge or any way compromising his principles—truly tis more than we could have reasonably expected.

June 11th, 1863

Cloudy and damp this morning. Aunt Eliza milked the cows for us and very soon Aunt Evelyne came down from the mountain to iron for us and Armanda saying Mrs. Roy had told her to come over and do what she could for us. We concluded however that was better not to have all our assistance at one time and then at another to be entirely without any, and as Aunt E. had come such a distance we retained her and sent Armanda home with a note to Mrs. R. explaining our reasons. We girls assisted in ironing and getting dinner too. Quite early Miss Betty White came in to bring butter (the idea of such a thing!) and regaled us with a dash of gossip. Then Uncle Newton and Aunt Jane and Mr. Kiger were to dine with us. Laura made a valise dumpling which elicited general commendation. Aunt J. assisted in washing up the dinner service and while cleaning the dining room we were summoned to the top of the house to see a long wagon train of pontoons that were being brought into town. We instantly conjectured the purpose for which they were intended, and as it had cleared off Ma and Father rode down to the river to see them thrown across after Uncle N. and Aunt Jane left. Mrs. Moffatt came up to see us—says tis generally believed in town that a portion at least of Lee's army is advancing on Winchester through this way. After Ma and Father came home Uncle Fayette and Uncle Tom came in but they would not remain to tea. It rained right hard a little while about sundown and we were just in the act of having a new stove put up in the kitchen and there was such confusion and trouble and we were so worn out as to be almost ready to give up. Tis more quiet now and I hope a good night's rest may quite restore strength and spirit. Oh me! what would the boys think to see us now in our several new capacities.

June 12th, 1863

This has been a most glorious day, weary and footsore as we are. Armanda came over quite early though Eliza milked and made the fire in the kitchen before she came. Mrs. Normal also came to finish the ironing. Aunt Eliza went home after breakfast and Armanda proceeded to scouring and cleaning. One of the little boys having gone to town in the morning returned with news of the near approach of the expected army. About half past ten o'clock we heard music and looking out saw the van guard of Jackson's old corps entering the place—in advance of old General Ewell in his carriage surrounded by his escort. Oh how the gallant boys cheered and shouted—Ma and I went up on the house and when they saw us they waved and hurrahed to us. Oh! it was glorious! Column after column filed past with glistening bayonets, flying colors and rolling artillery, while the strain of martial music and their soul burning shouts mingled in one unbroken, soul thrilling volume of sound. I felt almost frantic with excitement and delight. The soldiers commenced stopping in for milk. Presently a servant came with "Major Roger's compliments to the ladies" and a request that they would send him "a lunch." I arranged a beautiful bouquet of roses and Nellie made up a box of bread, butter and chipped beef and honey and milk and sent him. His reply to the courtesy was an assurance that he was "everlastingly obliged" and would "never get done loving." While getting dinner a messenger came over from

Mr. Cook's to inform Father that the Reverend Mr. Lacey was there and would be glad to see him. He returned about an hour before dinner accompanied by Mr. Moreton, the gentleman who breakfasted here the morning after the battle of Front Royal. Making arrangements for my dinner I gave Armanda directions accordingly and left it in her hands and dressed myself and went into the parlor to welcome our guests. He was most cordial in his greeting and seemed really glad to see us again—said he had been some time anticipating a movement in this direction and resolved in his own mind that he would call on us again. He was so cheerful, so hopeful and so agreeable with all. Charlie Richardson soon came in and after him Young Sheppard. It was amusing at the dinner table to notice the efforts the gentlemen made to wait on themselves and how they disliked being recipients of our attention. Nellie and I enjoyed it—particularly as our exertions received so much unmerited praise. Cousin Mount came in directly after dinner and we all went up on the house to watch the troops coming in and waved to them. Mr. Moreton and I were discussing books and I mentioned "Tannhauser"—he had never seen it. When he came downstairs I handed him the volume and told him he should glance over the contents while at camp that night. (His brigade was in Cousin R's field). He begged for some music and he, Cousin Mount and I sang and played till the latter left with Charlie. Nellie being dairy maid was much engaged in giving the soldiers milk. Mr. Moreton left about four o'clock promising to come up again from camp this evening "should his Brigade remain where it was" and bring to hear some music a young Dr. Cannon from S.C.—a gentleman whom he represented as illustrating in an eminent degree the "Chivalry" of the Palmetto State without its "bombast." He professed to be very anxious to procure for his friends a young Va. wife and wondered if we would not one of us "take him in."

Lucie came over from Uncle Tom's to help us get supper—while Armanda assisted Nellie to clean the churn. Mr. Moreton returned just before supper to say his brigade had moved off and he would but just have time to bid us goodbye. We persuaded him to remain to tea to eat some of my biscuits and all the time at table he kept us in a roar of laughter with his rich, spicy anecdotes. Upon leaving he expressed his gratitude for what he termed our goodness to him and begged to know in what way he could serve us—offering to do all in his power toward restoring to us our property. He likes "Tannhauser" very much—reviewed it this evening. I do think he is one of the noblest specimens of manhood I ever saw—so earnest yet unaffectedly pious, so intelligent and refined in nature. It is a treat to meet with such a being.

Had a hard time milking tonight—Armanda and I were both inexperienced hands and "Criser" was most refractory. We've gotten through our day's work at last though and now are quite welcome "Tired Nature's Restorer." The troops are still passing through and *have* been in an uninterrupted stream since this morning. Their shouts and cheers are making heartful music to our ears as they ring out in the stillness of the night air and their watch fires gleaming from every hill are so many beacons of hope to our anxious eyes. God bless the dear, brave ones and make us thankful for His enduring mercies.

June 13th, 1863

Aunt Eliza came up again this morning, but not before Ma had made the fires and we commenced milking. She finished this and then Armanda came in and she left. Finished ironing, got dinner and did some cleaning up. In the afternoon there were pies to make for tomorrow, salt rising to bake, and supper to get besides milking, and washing the children. Oh such a weary time as we had of it—the children were sleepy and fretful, the stove *wouldn't* get hot, the bread would not bake and the cows *would* run. Uncle Tom and Aunt Bettie and E. Hope came in in the midst of all the confusion until I felt almost crazed. Just as supper was put on the table Father came in bringing with him two letters from both Alvin and Irvie. Bless their hearts. How affectionately and cheerfully they do write—tis as cordial to our drooping spirits to have such pleasant tidings from afar. Could not eat a bit of supper— indeed I've not eaten two full meals since our labors began. After much tribulation we succeeded in getting the children washed and put to bed— then we brought in wood and water for the night for Armanda had left after supper—cleaned up the kitchen and arranged to have a nice bath. The kitchen floor being partly brick we moved in buckets and tubs, filled them with tepid water and proceeded with our ablutions—Ma, Nellie, Laura and myself. Feel greatly refreshed by the operation but am still very, very footsore and weary. The soldiers all left for Winchester this morning save a few broken down ones and the sick in the hospital here. Tis said cannonad-

ing was heard up the valley today—no news from Winchester though or
from any other place.[3] Oh me!

June 14th, 1863

Up bright and early. Aunt Eliza milked and cleaned the kitchen while we
cleaned the house and dressed the children and helped get breakfast. Had
everything in "apple pie" order directly after our early meal. Concluded
to have a cold dinner and make the day truly one of rest. Went in the garden to get a bouquet, and was dressing myself when they came in to say
Uncle John has come. So he had and with him a young Captain Armstrong
of Maryland, an acquaintance of Irvie's. They remained but a short time,
Uncle John doing a great deal of talking though, asking questions, condoling
with us, prophesying brighter times and telling us the news. Tis only within
the last few days that we've heard of the Cavalry right over the Ridge in
which there was more Cavalry engaged than has ever been on this conti-
nent before. Uncle John tells us Cousin Sam's son Willie was quite severely
wounded, poor fellow—thought dangerously so. Father went to town immediately after breakfast and did not return until after Sunday School and
then went back to church and dinner out. I betook myself to the kitchen
where I quietly spent the morning writing till about ten o'clock, and Belle,
E. Hope, and Nannie Buck and Allie came in. All save the latter and Belle
soon went to Church though and we were engaged in getting dinner—we
were all cooks, Ma made bread and fried meat, Grandma prepared onions
and lettuce, I dressed the latter, brought water and arranged table, Nellie and
Belle brought milk, cream and butter and Laura warmed the pies. We did
enjoy it so too—it seemed so sweet after working so hard for it. While eating
Aunt Eliza came in and then before we had cleared the table Charlie Buck,
Orville, Carey and Allie came. Aunt Betsie spent the day at Mrs. Glasscock's.
Charlie is a great boy—remained down in the dining room after dinner and
helped Nellie to wash the service and clear off the table—all the while talking
so cheerily. There has been the heaviest cannonading heard in the direction
of Winchester. I never have heard such a succession of rapid and heavy firing
in my life—we all went out to listen and felt very anxious to ascertain the
cause of it. Twas the day reported by some that Milroy had made good his
escape—by others that he had been captured, etc. etc., Charlie stayed all

the evening with us telling anecdotes, helping drive the fowls from the garden and walking around looking at the growing vegetables, and lastly going into the kitchen while we toasted bread for supper. Aunt Lizzie and Mack Irwin were here to tea—truly our friends have been thoughtful and kind. Just as supper was over Mr. Berry came in and then two soldiers who wanted bread and milk, so twas quite late before I had the dining room cleaned up. Our company was all gone and we were sitting at the back door listening to the cannons which were still booming more loudly than ever when the gate opened and Uncle Mack rode in. He had just returned from Winchester— told us that Ewell had succeeded in completely surprising Milroy, had surrounded, cut off his reinforcements and supplies, and driven him with his ten thousand troops within their entrenchments beyond the town from which we were endeavoring to shell them. Their fortifications seemed almost impregnable but there was no doubt of our being able to oust them very soon as we had already seventy huge pieces pointed on the fort and were mounting some immense "parrotts." Uncle M. seems very confident that all of our servants will be retaken for they had not left W., when he was there. Oh! it was glorious, glorious, beyond measure—never was presence of men more welcome, never tidings so rejoicing. Thank God! Father had been in the mountains with the spy glass to endeavor if possible to discover the locality and exact position of the battle and had only just returned to hear from us the grand news. Grandma has been suffering so with toothache all day and Nellie has a very sore foot—am afraid they will both be unable to be about tomorrow. The cannonading still continues without intermission.

June 15th, 1863

Very early astir. With Aunt Eliza's assistance we soon had our work completed. Uncle Newton, Bobby and Jimmie were in this morning—the former extracting Grandma's tooth and prescribed for Nellie's foot. Had a season of rest in which I sat in the kitchen and wrote. Just as dinner was ready to be sent to the table Lucy came in bringing a note from Jule who said she had sent her maid to render us what assistance she could—truly it is kind of our friends to interest themselves so in our behalves—may heaven reward them for it. Mrs. Normal did not come today as she promised, so we've had all the work to do since Aunt Eliza left. Father came in to dinner with news of the fall of Winchester. We had heard cannonading early this morning and when it suddenly ceased were convinced that they had surrendered, and so they had. Milroy and all his minions—not a man escaped and we took supplies, three thousand horses, ammunition, arms, etc. Delightful. Nothing could be more charming than this capture of Milroy—May his deeds be visited on his own head now. I guess they find that although our Jackson is ascended his mantle has fallen on a man most worthy to be his successor.

Twas very sultry and by time dinner was over and the basement cleaned I was almost broken down with heat and fatigue.

. . . The report came to town about sunset that Milroy and three thousand of his troops escaped from the fort early this morning before it surrendered, but we did not credit it at all. While sitting in the back door after dark we heard a step on the pavement and looking out saw Father pass with a cavalryman who proved to be Charlie Richardson. He had just returned from Winchester *bringing Horace with him*. He confirms the report of Milroy's flight but states the number of those escaped to be much less than was at first supposed. It is too vexatious to think that cowardly old villain has outwitted us thus and how pitiful of him to go off and leave his remaining men alone in such a perilous situation—never mind Providence permitting we'll get him yet. Charlie says Horace and Alec were in attendance upon Yankee Officers, which accounts for the capture of the former. The latter left, it is supposed, with the fugitives who accompanied Milroy. Of the other servants we could learn nothing but that they had left Winchester for Martinsburg a few days after Father saw them and are probably by this time beyond the arm of justice. Horace had been put in jail but Father and Charlie soon went over and brought him home. He looked humble enough when he stopped at the door to get a candle, but no one knows whether he will not make another attempt very soon to follow his kith. Father has determined to keep him at home if he will remain and behave himself.[4]

June 16th, 1863

Nancy came in to work this morning and we had Aunt Eliza too, so things were soon put into shape. There were soldiers in quite early for milk. Charlie showed us the beautiful horse which he yesterday captured from the

Yankees—'tis a spirited, beautiful animal, truly, but has some star artillery gaits. C tells me he captured some writing paper for me.[5] Glad of it—very!

. . . Felt stupid, tired and worn today. While sitting in the parlor writing this evening, Aunt Bettie, Nannie, Mollie and Miss S. Thorpe came in and told us Longstreet's corps was expected through town either during the evening or early in the morning and they had brought us a basketful of beautiful bouquets to throw them. While they were telling us this some cavalrymen rode up to the gate for milk and they told us 'twas a mistake as their corps would certainly cross below at Berry's Ferry. Oh, it was provoking to have them coming in every five minutes with contradictory reports— sometimes we were wild with delight at the assurance that he certainly would come—then disappointed beyond measures by the assurance that 'twas altogether impolitic for him to do so. . . .

June 17th, 1863[6]

Nellie's foot was so painful this morning that I relieved her of the office of dairymaid while the others cleaned the house and cooked. Was at the dairy extremely early and yet there were already numerous applicants for milk. While filling canteens a courier rode up and inquired for Father and when he came informed him that he had dispatches from Ewell to Longstreet desiring the troops of the latter to form a junction with his own at an early date and to accomplish this they should take the lower route and the courier wished to intercept them at Berry's Ferry and called to obtain directions as to his way. We knew then that our boys would not come through town and Oh! we're so disappointed. After we had finished breakfast there were six or eight applicants for a meal so the dining room was not ready for dinner til late. The gentlemen begged for music and Nellie and I played and sang for them some time. . . . Charlie Richardson came in and sat a little while—brought me my Yankee paper—'tis such a prize. After he left went into the garden and gathered peas for dinner. Ever since day break a portion of Longstreet's wagons had been passing til about nine o'clock when the artillery followed in their wake. Passing as the soldiers did, right by the house, we of course had a continuous stream of the weary, dusty, travel-worn fellows calling for milk, bread, water,—everything that could be imagined in the way of refreshments. We sent buckets of water down to the road from which the children supplied the thirsty, and those who came to the house were furnished with every drop of milk that could be spared—and indeed more than could conveniently be spared from the family rations. It was a pleasure to see their faces lighten when we would answer in reply to the invariable question "What do I owe you for this?"—"Nothing"—or "You are paying what you owe us every day you are in the Army." They continued to come in so rapidly at last that we had to take food out of the stove which was being prepared for dinner and give them. So constant was the excitement—so fatiguing our work, (for Nancie having the washing at the mill, Grandma, Ma and I got dinner) so warm the day that I could not eat a morsel. They were all at dinner and I was in the kitchen cooking, attending to my "salt rising" when two soldiers called at the door and begged for something to eat. Without thinking what I did, I invited them to take a seat in the kitchen while I went into the dining room to ascertain if there was anything that could be gotten for them. While setting their dinners for them I saw they were perfect gentlemen to all appearances and presently when Ma came in they told her they were members of the Washington Artillery which was just going by. The spokesman was a delicate featured, slight and graceful youth and conversed fluently and elegantly. . . . His own name was Herbert and he seemed to feel almost as if he had met with friends and commenced telling of a young brother of his who died in Warrenton a year ago and I'm almost sure 'tis the same young Herbert of whom we before had heard. He was tenderly nursed by a lady after receiving his wound and when he found himself dying he called her to him saying—"You have done for me all that my mother could have done save one thing—you've not kissed me for her, will you do so now?" She bent over him and pressed her lips to his while his arms closed about her neck—then sinking back on his pillow he said contentedly "I'm ready now" and soon died. 'Twas so sad and sweet. In taking leave of us the young man very cordially invited us to visit them should we ever go south. Was busily engaged in making up a batch of bread about three o'clock this afternoon when Nellie came bounding in with "Lucie, Mr. Macarley is here and has asked for you!" 'Twas such a surprise, for we had well nigh forgotten the little fourth Alabamian who called to get his breakfast that first morning when Longstreet passed through last Autumn. I was busily engaged making up a batch of bread when he came and could not appear but after having inquired for me once or twice I sent an invitation for him to come in and *see* my excuse for not being visible. Into the kitchen he came laughing and expressing his pleasure at returning to Front Royal again. He watched the process of bread-making with great apparent interest and when all was ready helped me prepare the oven, draw out the fire, etc. etc. very much as he might have helped me furl my parasol or tie my overshoe two years ago. Invited him back to the parlor, came up into the house, arranged my dress and went into the parlor myself where were two nice looking soldiers who were introduced as the Messrs. Baker from N. O. members of the "Washington Artillery" and acquaintances of Cousin Cornelia Buck's. They were fine young fellows, intelligent, well bred and agreeable, having evidently seen a good deal of fashionable life. The elder sings very well and we had quite a concert—then followed a discussion of music and poetry and novels. That Mr. Baker was thorough with all standard publications of these classics. I felt convinced but was somewhat surprised to find that Macarley appeared equally well informed. He's a singular compound anyway. My own impression is that he's a spoiled boy—the son of an easy southern planter who has been allowed the alternative of study or amusement and has preferred the latter in the shape of lying on his back in the woods and reading romances, or hunting game in flood and forest. How surprised Mr. Baker seemed when I expressed my admiration of Tennyson—he says he is one of his favorite poets but can never get anyone to agree with him and in leaving remarked that he should remember me as the young lady with whom he could express the merits of his much maligned favorite. He gave us his autograph as did his brother and Mr. Macarley. When Mr. McC heard that Irvie was in such constant communication with his place of residence, Huntsville, Alabama, he begged that we would write him and insist upon his visiting his home averring that his family would be glad of the opportunity for showing kindness to one whose friends had extended the rites of hospitality to their absent "romping Bob" as he says they dubbed him. He seems really grateful and in a degree attached to the family just because of the two meals furnished him when hungry and tired. The long "Reed like Alabamian" who was here yesterday and the little half demented Creole who got his luncheon here were both of them hanging around the house today. Don't know what to make of their singular movements. The Q.M. who was here this morning left a quart of spirit which he told Father to use until he should send an order for him. We are so glad—'twill be a perfect treasure—there was also a mule left upon the same terms but 'twas so unmanageable that they could not get it into the field. Amanda was over again this evening. We begin to think there is a powerful magnet in the kitchen here now in the person of our returned fugitive.[7] This fugitive I'm afraid is not a willing captive restored. There is an air of discontent and unrest about him that is very suspicious—it may, however, be only the effect of mortification and loneliness—time will prove.

June 19th, 1863

The morning bade fair to be a quiet one but about ten o'clock we were surprised by a visit from Jimmie Blakemore and his cousin Captain Mc-Willie. . . . We've learned from Jimmie that A. P. Hill's corps would pass through town during the day and Anderson's Brigade was hourly expected. About eleven o'clock the broken down poor fellows commenced dropping in and they came in a perfect avalanche until about one when there was a cessation with only an occasional caller. Captain Grey and Captain Spann of S. C. dined here. A gentlemanly old bachelor he is. Had a hard time cooking supper this evening. Soldiers still coming in—while I write their shouts are ringing in the air.

June 20th, 1863

Damp and misty. Allie, Charlie and Jimmie over to play with boys. Busy all the morning putting away clean clothes. Nannie and Charlie over in the morning. At ten o'clock A. P. Hill's Corps commenced marching through town and there was an immense sensation.[8] Children all went over to see troops—bad to worse. Commenced letter to Irvie. Miss Betty White here to dinner. Mr. Berry over early in the afternoon. No news. Our army is in Md. and Penn. now though. Was working up in salt rising in the evening when a drunken soldier came into the kitchen from out in the rain—represented himself as one Captain Carey of the Madison Artillery—commenced swearing—was frightened and sent for Father who came and settled him. . . .

June 21st, 1863

Cold but clear. Nancie left quite early to go home. Pender's Division passing through—bands playing and colors flying. We were on the house a long time watching them. . . . Ma did not get home until late—two soldiers to supper and had to go into the dairy after dark to skim milk for the sick at the hospital. There's a rumor of a battle at Upperville today. Scarce believe it though.[9]

June 22nd, 1863

Soldiers in to breakfast early. Had settled quietly to work when Cousin Mary Peirce walked in. Had a cozy time laughing and talking til about noon when Father walked in looking pale and excited. At table he and Ma both looked much disturbed and in reply to my question as to the news from the army he said the news of the battle of Upperville had been confirmed and that 'twas reported that Jones Brigade had suffered severely in the action. After dinner Ma called me out and told me that dear Walter was said to have fallen. Oh! such a shock!—it seems as if my heart had stopped beating and my limbs stiff and cold—still I did not credit the report—first news was always so exaggerated. Cousin Mary went home as soon as she heard it and we were all alone with our sorrow and suspense. In the afternoon cavalrymen coming directly from the scene of action confirmed all we had heard til there was left no room for hope. Father had written for Uncle Mack to come down as soon as he heard it and about three o'clock he and Jacquie rode up to the gate. Father told him all—he did not come to the house at all, but sending Jacquie with a message to Aunt L he started immediately for Upperville to learn what he could with regard to the fight and tried to recover his body. This is what causes us such grief, to know that the dear fellow was shot and instantly killed was bad enough but to have no assurance that he might not have been mortally wounded and left in the enemy's hands to die a cruel death and then his dear form cast a mangled and disfigured heap under a pile of their own unhallowed slain—'twas distressing beyond measure. Ma and Nellie went on immediately to the Mountain to stay with Aunt Letitia during Uncle M's absence. I do feel so much for her, poor thing! Uncle Tom, Aunt Bettie, Charlie Buck and Mack Irwin came in this evening—the two former remained to tea. Uncle Tom will mail my letter to Alvin in Richmond as he goes tomorrow.

A letter has just been brought in by a cavalryman from Cousin Horace Buck announcing poor Walter's death and tendering sympathy to his parents but giving no particulars as he had not been able to learn any himself. This destroys the very last vestige of hope. Oh! I'm so sick!—so sad at heart!

June 23rd, 1863

Early after breakfast this morning they told me Uncle Mack had come. Presently Father came in and said he had recovered the poor boy's remains, which would be here in a few moments. How like a knell those words sounded! till then I had not altogether resigned a hope that the evil tidings might be groundless or exaggerated. Now the sad truth was established beyond a doubt. And yet with this great sorrow mingled a feeling of earnest gratitude—he should have accorded us the sacred privilege of performing for him the last sad duty—his dear form should not rest in an unknown and unwept grave, but we should lay it with kindred dust where we could plant over it flowers and tend it with the loving care that we delighted to bestow upon him while he lived. I went out and gathered some beautiful jessamines, lilies, and roses and some ivy for a wreath and while twining these for his bier, Nellie came in. In a very little while the house was thronged, ladies bringing baskets of wreaths and flowers and all with sad, tearful faces. They brought dear Walter in about ten o'clock, Cousin William Cloud coming with him. I saw the black great wagon drawn slowly along and thought how often we had watched for his coming as for a ray of sunshine and had seen him dash up to the house so fearlessly looking so handsome and graceful, so noble—and now to think of his being brought so sadly, so unconsciously back to his second home which he entered for the first time in his life without a tender greeting. Ma soon came home and after awhile they called us into the parlor to see the dear boy once more. Never shall I forget the sight— there lay the still white figure under the southern window, the attitude one of such perfect, majestic repose as seems to quiet and subdue my grief. The face that lay there among the wreaths and masses of lilies and jessamines was the most beautifully placid one that I have ever seen and so natural, so free from the usual ghastly terrors of death that I could almost have imagined that the dead was breathing as the wind stealing through the window just lifted the hair from the pillow. There was something almost holy in the expression of that loved countenance—the hair was brushed back from the broad smooth brow, the lids just closed as in gentle sleep while about the mouth hovered an expression of high resolve just softened into a peaceful smile. Never have I so realized the beauty of Bryant's words————

> "Approach thy grave as one who wraps the drapery of his
> couch about him and lies down to pleasant dreams."—

As when looking upon this very embodiment of the sentiment. Dear Walter! how I looked on those mute lips and thought of the gentle, kindly voice that should cheer us no more, on the closed eyes and remembered that never again should they look with their *warm* light upon us and those footsteps forever still with their familiar music. Oh! it was hard, hard to think of giving him up in his glorious full flush of youth, in the full tide of honorable fame—hard to give him up who had been so true and dear a brother in the absence of those who had hitherto been all this to us. I know he died as he often expressed a wish to—the pang of death was short—his transition from time to eternity a quick one, and his summons found him at his post of duty gallantly defending the soil of his dearly loved state—nobly vindicating the cause to which he has devoted his every energy for the last two years. And in his death we have nothing painful to remember of his unworthiness and yet, oh! yet—all cannot reconcile us to giving him up so suddenly, so unexpectedly just as we had begun to believe that he bore a charmed life—that he was destined to the glorious making of being one of the deliverers of his country, of rescuing—name from oblivion. Dear boy! how gratifying it was to see the universal respect and attention shown him—unaffected regret expressed by everyone at his loss—he was regarded by the mountain people as a kind of Sir William Wallace—his adventures and associations with them last summer when scouting endeared him to them so much—as indeed it did to everyone. There were persons present today who could have appeared upon almost any other occasion and, looking out of the windows I saw an old hoary bearded man sobbing like a very child as he stood under the trees in the yard. There were those present whom I suppose were never known to attend funerals before scarcely. Uncle Mack, Jacquie, Mary and Eltie came down just before Mr. Berry arrived. Poor Aunt L could not bear to see her poor dead boy and remained with Gussie at home. Mr. Berry read the 90th psalm, sang and offered up a petition that strength might be granted the afflicted to bear up under the great sorrow. Then we went in to take our last leave, to press unheeded kisses upon the cold white forehead—to look our last upon the dear familiar features. I led little Mary by the hand and after she had kissed her poor brother took a spray of jessamines and rose buds and gave her to keep as a memento—poor little thing! she little comprehended all the great loss she had sustained. Cousin Sue Buck told me there would be a seat in the Rose Hill carriage for one of us if we wished to attend the dear boy to his last home. I persuaded Nellie to go knowing as I did that could he have had a wish upon the subject he would have said—"Let Pa, Jacquie, Uncle William, Nellie and Cousin Sue be there."—And it was just as he would have had it for very few others could go for want of conveyances. The coffin when carried out seemed to cast a shadow over the house which is lying there still—it seemed so lonely and sad when one knew he had crossed the threshold never to recross it again. Tonight I went into the parlor where the moonlight was lying on the floor just where *he* had been laid this morning and it seemed almost as if his gentle spirit had stolen back to brighten the old home with its presence.

Cousin Mary, Ed, William, Evred stayed with us today—the latter is here tonight—he gave us the full particulars of dear Walter's death. It seems that when the Colonel became aware that a desperate struggle was intended feared for Walter's daring, impetuous spirit and detailed him to act upon some duty relating to the QM department, thinking thus to detain him from the battlefield. But he could ill brook inglorious ease at such a time so he quickly transacted his business and took his place in the foremost rank. The enemy were overwhelming us with superior numbers—our men wavered and seemed upon the point of falling back—Walter cried out—"Boys, don't let them do so! Let's charge them back!" They swept on and just as they reached a yard belonging to the house of a Mr. Thomas, our poor boy fell pierced through the throat with a ball—He exclaimed when first struck— "I'm a dead man!" His companions saw his horse give a few bounds and he reeled from his saddle just as they were forced to retreat before an overpowering number of the foe. His horse was found riderless after the fight all bloodstained but no trace could be discovered of Walter. At last the Yankees abandoned the battlefield and Monday evening while Cousin Will was looking for him he made inquiries at Mr. Thomas and the ladies of the house told him a young Confederate Lieutenant had been shot in their yard—that the Yankees said he was on Gen. Stewart's staff but they thought his name was Buck. They had begged for his body but the Yankees refused their request and had buried him in the yard. Cousin W opened the grave, recognized the body then covered it again and went away to procure a conveyance for it. He met Uncle Mack who had just gotten into Paris—informed him of the recovery and having procured a wagon returned to the place and proceeded to disinter the remains. The inhuman Yankees had robbed him of everything—Porte—Monnaic, papers, boots, clothing, arms, the little ring which he had worn until it seemed almost a part of himself, and even cut the buttons from his coat, after doing this they wrapped a blanket about him, scooped out a little hollow and covered him over. Dear, dear boy! to think of his being subject to such indignities from such hands. And yet, he was unconscious of it all for he could not have lived many minutes after receiving the fatal wound and I'm glad he was spared the knowledge. There was a cut on his head but 'tis thought was inflicted by his falling on the sharp rock and not a saber cut. Oh, what would I not give to know what his last thoughts were when he knew that eternity with all its mysteries lay before his gaze, that the next hour all would be revealed to him, how I would like to know whether he had time for a thought for us all, whether he realized the fate which was his! But this is vain, vain! he cannot come to us "Let us strive to go to him," and together decipher the mysteries that have so perplexed us here. Oh, if he could only have been happier here! but he suffered as only such sensitive, passionate natures do. Suffered like the Spartan boy while the wolf gnawed at his vitals beneath his cloak. Dear boy, how often he has said that life was a valueless gift, how often has he asked "Lucie, what have I worth living for?" He had an insatiable yearning for tenderness and affection such as few men ever experience and with it a firm conviction of his own inability to win it that was touching to see.

But he is quaffing now, I humbly trust, the pure water from the fountain of Love, his restless, troubled spirit like the sea has grown quiet, tranquil in the smile of the god of Peace and Love and his repose is one of unbroken blessedness. We all can remember his having expressed his unshaken trust in a merciful God, his resignation to his will—and this more than anything on earth has consoled us in our great sorrow—'tis a blessed, blessed knowledge.

Nellie and Father did not return till late—Jule met them at the burying grounds. Cousin Will with us and a Mr. Carter, a wounded soldier.

Dear Walter—a lonely slumber will be yours tonight—all with the silent dead, but you will not heed—'twould be all the same to you were it the snowdrifts instead of this soft moonlight that mantles your grave. Your head does not ache as mine does now and you have not dreary, heavy sorrow at your heart. Poor Aunt Letitia! what a sad, sad night for her. And Dick, poor boy—I cannot bear to think of the blow that must soon fall upon him in this sad knowledge.

June 24th, 1863

Nellie and I spent the morning gathering up and putting carefully away all our little mementos of the little lost brother—the letters, locks of hair, and flowers, and trying to recall his every look and gesture in his last visits to us. It seems so very lonely now, as if a greater part of the family was gone. Ah me! I scarcely feel an interest in any news from the army now at all, with Walter's death has died my interest for his branch of the service to a great degree.

Ma spent the day at Oakley, the evening at Captain Roy's. Nancie was washing and we had to cook dinner. The supper I got myself. Em. came over about two times. Wrote Irvie an account of poor Walter's death—poor fellow! how it will distress him to hear it.

June 25th, 1863

Cloudy and damp. Grandma and Aunt B at Oakley. Writing, reading and working all day. Finished Irvie's letter. Was in the garden entwining white roses and thinking that I never should see one or a lily or jessamine without thinking of that flower strewn bier. When Laura handed me a letter from Nannie Taylor—It had just arrived by mail. Dear Nannie! how sadly she writes. My heart aches for her in her sore distress and we are indeed sisters in affliction. There was also a letter from Irving. Poor Fellow! He writes so gleefully, little dreaming of the shadow that has fallen over us all.

How much I've been thinking of that lonely grave of poor Walter's lying out in all this dreary rain and cold—just as if he were conscious of it, dear boy. Cousin Will called by this morning on his way to the regiment. Never saw him as sad or as reluctant to say good-bye.

June 30th, 1863

Writing. Uncle Tom returned from Richmond yesterday and came over quite early. Says he saw poor Dick at Hanover Junction and told him all—that he was deeply grieved and said he would willingly have laid down his life for Walter—poor dear fellow! . . .

Poor Walter, buried but one short week and yet seemingly absent a long, long year.

July 1st, 1863

Nancie went to the mill early to do the washing and left us the kitchen to clean up. Someone hurt my feelings very badly and I went upstairs and took a good cry. . . . Report of the route of the enemy at Vicksburg—hope 'tis true—but fear. Amanda came over to help Nancie this evening and we had some little leisure—they all sent us an invitation to go over to Capt. Roy's. Think we will tomorrow. Have had the "blues" miserably the greater part of the day and tonight I feel sick.

July 3rd, 1863

Father told us at breakfast this morning that he had heard through a cavalryman from a part of our servants—Mahala and her children had been captured—he was ordered to guard them with some thirty others as far as Green Castle, Penn. She recognized in him a young man who had lived in town, made herself known to him—said she wished she was back in her home, that 'twas a good one and that now she had spent all her money and was without food and had no one to provide for her. The children next she said—crying and in great distress. Poor things! I feel sorry for them because they are the innocent sufferers by their mother's folly and I'm afraid this will only be the commencement of their suffering. The men had all been sent to Richmond to work on fortifications.————————nothing was known of Harriet and her clique.

Father was riding to the Mountain and invited me to accompany him. Did not care to go but he seemed to wish it and I accompanied him with Ma. My horse was a delightful one and the ride was charming. Ascending the mountain through a wild, solitary road dark and cool in the shadows of the over arching trees I for the first time in my life heard the wood robin—there was something almost supernaturally sweet in the liquid, flute like notes that seemed to ripple down from the hills upon us. It was perfect to be out in the woods once more, careless whether or not the fire was burning in the kitchen—riding along on a freely ambling pony, breathing the fragrant, spicy breath of the woods, listening to the soft murmuring flow of the brooks way down the mountain side and to the rustling leaves and the many birds. We went to Mrs. Fox's—dismounted at the old spring under the cherry trees and quaffed the clear, ice cold water that bubbled up from their roots. Mrs. F. came down and invited us up to the house—found everything looking cool, clean and sweet about it. Presently Father proposed that we should go about fifty yards from the door to gather raspberries from a mass of bushes that grew by the fence—we went but 'twas so intensely warm, and the place presented such a tempting rendezvous for serpents that we were afraid to venture where the ripest fruits were to be found. Father, with two soldiers— boarding at Mrs. F's sat under the shade at the spring all day, and Ma and I in the parlor. I was thinking so much all the time of dear Walter for here was the scene of his adventures last summer. Every foot of ground passed over in the morning, every rock and shrub and tree seemed in some way associated with him—indeed there's scarcely one of them that were not intimately known to him I'm sure, dear boy. . . .

July 5th, 1863

Father left this morning before breakfast. Finished up our work in good time and dressed myself, took my book and daguerreotypes upstairs for companions and addressed myself to rest. Ma and Laura went to church although it was showering. Grandma, Nellie, Lucie and I got dinner—dressed the wild duck which Orville shot—and very nice it was too. E Hope came up in the afternoon—was asleep though and didn't see her. . . .

July 6th, 1863

Ma, Laura, Frank, Willie and Carey went down to Rose Hill this morning. In the afternoon Carey and Willie came home and returned carrying Evred with them. So quiet a day as never before been known within the memory of the oldest inhabitant of Bel Air, for when Orville and Lucie went for the cows there was not a child white or black on the plantation and indeed we sat down to tea with only five at table and they all grown up females. Uncle Mack called in about dusk to take a luncheon and told us of a battle fought at Gettysburg, Penn.—a desperate conflict not at all decisive but resulting in heavy losses on both sides—feel very anxious as to the particulars of the struggle.[10] Ma and the children came in late. Mr. Berry just before ten o'clock brought confirmation of Uncle Mack's news and the additional intelligence of Corse's Brigade having been ordered into Maryland. Heaven forbid it! for Pickett's division is said to have suffered severely in this last battle.

July 8th, 1863

Very pleasant. Grandma and Aunt B spent the day in town. Looked all day for Father but he did not come. All sitting on the porch after tea when Uncle Mack came in to say Victor and Charlie Brown were at home and brought news that the Warren Rifles would *all* be in tomorrow enroute to rejoin their division in Penn. Our joy was too deep for words mingled though it was with sadness with the thought of meeting poor Dick again. Feel so nervous and excited at the thought of their coming. Mr. Berry did not come over til quite late. Very, very sultry and oppressive.

July 9th, 1863

Quite warm but pleasant. . . . We were sitting in the door after tea when Dick rode through the gate. Poor fellow! how he struggled to be calm and how thin and pale and sad he looked. After sitting a few moments on the porch where his pa had just come, he got up and went into Grandma's room and we followed him. Then he commenced talking over his great loss and wept so sorrowfully. Lifting up his head he said "Well, I would have given my life a willing sacrifice for his!". . . Dick says Scott's in town. Wonder if we shall see him. All have furloughed til Sunday morning. . . .

July 10th, 1863

Worked very hard this warm morning. Was almost exhausted when about four o'clock in the afternoon they sent me word that Scott was in the parlor. Made a hasty toilette and went down to see him. He looks thin and pale, poor fellow! could only remain a few moments as they had just secured orders to report at the McCoy's Ford about six miles distant this evening. It really distressed me his visit so short and unsatisfactory and I almost wished he had not come at all—pleasure though it was to see him again. How disconnectedly he talked and how fitful his manner—no wonder though when he was so hurried. Was sitting upstairs trying to compose myself to writing in my diary when Mrs. Moffatt came in. . . . While discussing the unpleasant news of the fall of Vicksburg (which by the way, we didn't believe) when Father came in quite tired and with headache. . . . Uncle John has sent me a new calico dress, a perfect beauty—so neat and clean—'tis very kind of him. Laura and I attended by Lucie took a bath in the creek tonight down under the willow trees. Ah, me! I'm so distressed about the poor boys.

July 11th, 1863

Finished my work quite early this morning so as to be ready for dear Dick when he should come. Uncle Mack was soon here but we waited some time for Dick. . . . Poor Dick struggled bravely with his feelings and strove while with us to talk and appear cheerful. He was with us about an hour and then bade us farewell with brimming eyes and husky voice. Dear, dear boy, it seemed like giving him up as we had never done before. We went on the house to watch for them as far as we could see them. Ma and Father went to church. . . . A terrible storm burst upon us while we were sitting at the tea table tonight. The older ones left the dining room going upstairs while Nellie and I attended to the children. Suddenly there was a blinding flash and such a deafening crash as I never before heard—the lightning had evidently struck near the house—we at first thought 'twas the house *itself.* The children were dreadfully frightened but we finally quieted them and finished supper and cleared the table. Time has been when such a shock would have put me in bed—particularly as I felt the electricity tingling in my arm, but my nerves are growing stronger and I am, I hope wiser now.[11] Poor boys! were they in this terrible storm I wonder?

July 12th, 1863

Raining. Busy all the morning—had a note from Cousin E. Cloud making a request relative to dear Walter's uniform—answered it and complied with her wish—we've three buttons and the two shoulder straps as mementoes of our dear soldier's services to his country.

Reading a "Harper" of sixty-three which Father brought home with him—quite a novelty these times and interesting from that very fact. Never saw it rain harder than it has done all day. . . . Everything seems dark and threatening, yet I will not despair but commit our cause to His hand who "out of chaos" brings forth order.

[July 13, 1863, entry omitted]

July 16th, 1863

Father had a general clearance and ventilation of the dining room—it having been so damp for the last fortnight that everything had grown moldy there. Worked pretty hard til after ten o'clock and then sat down to sew on my dress. All tranquil. Nancie's sister came over to help her iron today. Wrote in my diary in the afternoon. . . .

July 17th, 1863

Rumors of our Army falling back this side the Potomac. Don't believe it though.

July 18th, 1863

Anniversary of the "Battle of Bull Run." Working very hard cleaning up etc., etc. Many soldiers here in the afternoon for milk. Can't help but feel a little anxious as to Lee's army. What can it have crossed the Potomac for? Perhaps 'tis a feint.

July 19th, 1863

Our army is certainly all on this side the Potomac. What can be the cause of it I wonder—so sorry. And we'll not have Baltimore after all. Wonder when Mr. Morton will get to Boston. Willie Buck's come home. . . .

. . . heard of the grand anti-conscription riot in New York.[12] Nemesis is awakening. . . .

July 21st, 1863

Anniversary of the great Manassas Battle. Corse's Brigade commenced arriving quite early—about half past nine o'clock. I went over with the children to the shop to see the 17th. Met there with Willie Buck. The 17th was next to the rear regiment in the brigade and as they filed by us I felt as if they were somehow dearer to us than those who had preceded them albeit I saw not a familiar face in the regiment—not one save the "Warren Rifles" and but one or two there—poor worn, dirty fellows. While trying to distinguish some familiar countenance I heard a "Hello, Lu! Where's Nell?" Turning about who should I face but dear Dick, dusty and bronzed with the sun. My hand was again grasped and this time 'twas Smith Turner whom I've not seen for a year. They were so hurried that they could only exchange greetings with us and say they hoped to remain near and see us again after a little and then off they went. I never shall forget how disappointed I felt when they ran on to rejoin their regiment and I saw their receding figures gradually lose themselves in the throng of martial forms. I looked after the regiment as long as it could be seen through tears and then we turned and retraced our steps homeward. All the forenoon there came rumors of the advance of the Yankees into town. Father came in about noon and told us the 17th had engaged the enemy near Mr. Armistead's and 'twas reported they were surrounded and would be captured unless Pickett's division, which was expected, should arrive in time to relieve them. We were quite anxious and restless listening for the discharge of musketry which was ever and anon heard and wishing so much we could only know our poor boys were safe.

The division came in about four o'clock and we soon ascertained 'twas as well with our friends in the 17th—that they had succeeded in repulsing a body much larger than their own, of dismounted cavalry—old U.S. Regulars. Huzzah! bless our glorious 17th! how they have longed ever since the war for a brush with the foe in the valley and near their homes and now that wish has been gratified they've whipped them bravely and well and now they no doubt feel more exultant than they've ever yet felt after a miniature battle. 'Twas said Gen. Longstreet passed through town and about five o'clock one of his Aides, Col. Sorell called to inquire if the General had stopped here— said he had expected he would have done so. A little later Maj. Latrobe's groom came in with the Major's horses to be stabled for the night but still too—shall I say it?—my disappointment—they didn't come. We had scores of soldiers though begging for milk, bread and every imaginable article of food—poor fellows—I wish our ability to serve them only equalled our will. . . . Just as we were washing the last cup and saucer after tea who should walk in but old Major Moses, Gen. Longstreet's "aide" who was here last fall.

What a cordial, jolly old soul he is—how warmly he greeted us and recalled every little incident of his short sojourn here. Have just been sitting in the porch watching the cordon of camp fires blazing on the brow of the hill and listening to his account of the incidents of the Gettysburg affair. He explained to us the probable object of this rapid falling back of all our Army of the Potomac. Says he thinks the valley will be deserted by our troops but does not think we will suffer any from the incursions of the enemy. Says that the desire of both the Confederate and Federal Army seems to be to reach the line of railroads between here and Richmond—that the two armies are running a race, that Meade has sent a detachment of Union troops to hold these mountain passes just long enough to detain our men til he shall have accomplished his object, but as we have the advantage of the shortest routes and have possession of one of the passes—"Chester's Gap"—he thinks we will be before them. It does grieve me so to think that we are to be left unprotected again so soon just as we had begun to feel secure once more too—however, if Gen. Lee so orders it, of course 'tis all right and we've nothing to do but await results.

It is now nine o'clock at night and I'm almost broken down with running to and fro waiting on the soldiers. Poor fellows, I don't mind this though as long as we've anything for them. The last squad of applicants have just departed and I must confess one of them provoked me not a little when I told him we had just given away the last bits of bread and would not be able to get them supper as we had but little help—our servants being all gone and he thereupon replied—"Ah, well—that's always the case, we can't *expect* you *ladies* to *trouble* yourselves in providing for *us*. Were your servants here I should *insist* upon having my supper gotten at any rate." That too after I've been doing my very utmost to minister to their wants! Well I suppose there are some unreasonable ones in every Army.

Dear Walter! This day one month ago—how I've thought of it.

July 22nd, 1863

Was awakened by hearing Nellie called up to supply the soldiers with milk this morning, but what chagrin was ours when as we were dressing Father came in and told us the dairy had been broken into and robbed of everything except the jars and little Britannia cream jug. Here was a predicament, a large family with guests in the house and not a drop of cream for coffee or ounce of butter for breakfast. Laura thought some could be procured of Aunt Bettie and started off upon a foraging expedition while we proceeded to clean up and get breakfast. Just before the meal was ready she returned with dress draggled in dew and laughing heartily—said she had passed through a whole brigade, infantry, artillery, baggage wagons and cattle in going to town, and coming back had discovered a soldier in the middle of the field below the house paying his respects to our large cream jar, which lay there half empty. She demanded it as her property—he yielded very meekly saying he had found it there not knowing where it came from, and she hid it well, we could send for it. Uncle Gilbert, too, soon came in bringing a missing crock and plate. We had a number of soldiers to breakfast; Mr. Moore, a courier of Gen. Longstreet's—old acquaintance of Dick Buck's and a young artillery man from Richmond—an invalid. I was quite sick all the morning and 'twas with great difficulty I succeeded in getting through my work. Had to go to bed finally. Meantime Mr. Berry and Capt. Marshall came in—the latter having just made a narrow escape through the deception practiced by the Yankees upon his children. Was feeling a little better when Nellie rushed up to my room bidding me "Get right up" for a servant of Gen. Longstreet's had just come in and said the General and staff were to be here in a little while. This information was a powerful tonic and restorative. I dressed myself and then Ma came to tell me Mr. Herbert, my kitchen acquaintance, was here and had a surprise for me. Going down we found him with a friend Mr. Stone. They sat a couple of hours chatting most pleasantly, telling us anecdotes of their sojourn in Yankeedom. They are my ideal of the genial frank Southron—are well educated, refined and polished in their manners—don't know when I've seen two more agreeable gentlemen. By the way,—what a beautiful face Mr. Herbert has!—eyes like liquid violet and sunshine. They heard cannonading and thinking was perhaps their batteries they took a cordial leave and departed. We were sitting waiting for a summons to dinner when Dick dashed up to the stile—he disclaimed against dismounting declaring he had but two hours leave and must go immediately home for his clothes. Poor fellow!— what joy it was to welcome him back from the battlefield and hear him tell the news from the fight. He says Scott Roy is prisoner—can't say I regret it, for he is at least safe and it may be the cause of preventing his being in a more dangerous engagement and perhaps shot. The 17th acquitted itself gloriously being for the greater part of the fight unsupported and opposed to thrice its number. Dick was soon off again and we went to dinner—still no Gen. Longstreet. 'Twas very warm and I was stupid and tired. Ma went over to town—had a troublesome time with my "salt rising"—yard thronged with soldiers—poor fellows—so hungry and we with not enough in the house to feed the half of them—it's impossible to keep a supply of bread on hand when they are continually coming thus. A little after four o'clock the boys went over to town to see Gen. Lee who was expected in and Father down to the river to see the pontoon bridges. Presently one of the little children ran in to say Father was returning with Gen. Longstreet. It proved however to be Gen. Lee with his staff.[13] They dismounted, some of them walked out under the shade of the aspens, some went to look at little Frank asleep in his wagon under the trees and the General with his chief and one or two others took his seat on the porch. Father stepped to the door and called Nellie and me and introduced us to him. The old gentleman greeted us heartily with such a warm, fatherly manner and then turning introduced us to his staff one by one. He then said to me—"Won't you sit down, my daughter and let us talk some?" I laid my hand on a chair standing near in compliance but he made room for me on the seat by him and said "No, not there, but here close by me." When I was seated I told him how much pleasure it gave me to see our defender—the Father of our State—he replied—"Oh, No! my daughter. I only wish he were more worthy of being seen. There! Look at those young rebels (pointing to his staff) they're a great deal better worth your looking at—gallant young beaux that they are." They asked for a rebel song and Nellie and I played and sang for the first time since dear Walter's death—the excitement and embarrassment caused a great difference in our singing, I knew. General L wished to know if we were not afraid to let those treasonable songs resound beneath our roof such as the "War Chant of Defiance." They remained but a short time and just as they were leaving the old gentleman hoped we might not be troubled much more by our enemies and bade Nellie and me by all means not to "let any of those fine young Yankee officers carry us off." We replied that we depended upon him to prevent such a possibility. Before leaving he enriched Nellie's autograph book and mine with his name at the same time protesting that he knew we would much prefer having our sweethearts' there rather than his. Dear old General! how I've always admired and loved him, but what a filial reverence mingles with that feeling now and how much more the father than the general he seems. How his hair is silvered and his brow marked with thought and care, yet what a noble, benevolent spirit looks forth from his brown eyes. What an air of dignity about his every movement. Gen. Chilton was with him looking very natural. He told us that *Major Peyton* had gone by another route which accounted for his not being with them. Not long after they left, Cousins M and E Cloud came over bringing with them Amanda to assist us in getting supper and was glad to see her for we were sorely harassed by calls for refreshments which was impossible to furnish to more than half of them. Indeed I've had my feeling so wrought upon today that I've almost wished I had no heart. To see the poor fellows coming in worn and weary and with tears in their eyes begging for something to eat. We had tried to provide for such demands, but where hundreds were coming in, 'twas impossible. Even now they are still coming late as it is.

We've a guard for the garden tonight. Gen. Lee says we've good news from Charleston—he having received a dispatch from Gen. Beauregard stating the repulse of the enemy at that point.

No Gen. Longstreet. Well, never mind—who cares? A. P. Hill's Corps came in today—Ewell's tomorrow—wonder if we'll see any of our friends.

July 23rd, 1863

. . . Received two long letters—one from Irvie to Ma and one from Cousin Mack to Nellie and me. They were at Chattanooga whither Bragg had retreated. Irvie writes in bad spirits, attributable to some very hard travelling through rain, some unpleasant indefinite skirmishing and a deprivation of his accustomed creature comforts—and the society of his lady friend. These letters were dated the 7th but Mrs. Roy sent one of the 15th and one of the 16th from Benton in which he stated—that they were just ordered to Jackson, Miss.—so there's no knowing where they are now. *Scott Roy* passed the road early this morning leading a horse which he had just captured. Father saw and talked with him and learned that last night while they were encamped near Linden he rolled himself through his guards, found a horse worth $1,000 and decamped but the owner of the horse awoke just as he was leaving and he quietly left the horse and went on til he found another horse near the outposts which he possessed himself of—and taking a route directly opposite to the one he intended pursuing, travelled all night and had just arrived. Oh, I'm *so* glad!

We had numbers of cavalrymen to dinner—among them young Holman who was here last spring.

Early this afternoon we heard heavy musket firing in the direction of "Green Hill"—we had heard that Scott Roy had brought from the Army some important information with regards to the Yankees and that Gen. Stuart had gone up to see him about it. Scott had sent over for a saddle to accompany Gen. S on a reconnaissance. So we at once concluded that Gen. S had gone with the detachment of his command and attempted to surround and capture the part of Yankees at Linden. The firing continued pretty regularly all the afternoon. . . . we all went upon the house together. There we could distinctly see the flash of the cannon, see the smoke, and see the shell when it exploded—could see the troops moving about the pieces. We at once concluded the Yankees were forcing a passage through the Gap there and that our forces would oppose it to the bitter end, that we would have a general engagement during the next 24 hours.

We saw Gen. Johnson's Division marching in that direction and a battalion of artillery went by the house toward the scene of action. But toward dusk the firing gradually ceased and now all is calm—the calm that precedes the storm, I'm thinking. Broken down soldiers are still coming in although it is now nine o'clock at night—some just from the fight. Poor fellows, poor fellows! my heart aches for them. . . .

July 24th, 1863

We were awakened several times in the night by soldiers passing through the yard some inquiring directions, some begging refreshments. Gen. Johnston himself was down in the hill and he and Father rode out to select a site for an encampment. There was firing too about 11 o'clock at night. We expected to be awakened by cannonading this morning but nothing unusual occurred so soon. From the constant rolling of wagons last night and the scarcity of troops this morning we were inclined to believe there was some important movement on hand. There were soldiers in for breakfast before we were dressed and from that time forth. Just as we had gathered up the breakfast things to wash they came to say Scott was here. We went on the porch where he was sitting, found him looking very well and just his own kind, cheerful self. He gave quite an amusing account of his capture, how the officers in command treated him so well taking him into their tent and giving him the most delicate bits for his breakfast. How he told Major Hazeltein that he was going to escape and invited him to call at his father's when they came to Front Royal. What a boy he is to be sure! to think of his having taken leave of his fellow captives and guard not long before he left and then having come out scatheless. I really did enjoy the hour that he spent with us—there are some persons whose mere presence exhilarates us as mine is said to do—and 'tis very seldom the case that I do not feel happier and better from his visits unless 'tis the regret at his departure mars it. He spoke something of leaving for Luray this evening but as his going seemed doubtful we expected to see him again before he left. He had been gone but a little while when old Mr. Marshall came in and while the old gentleman was sitting on the porch talking, our men were thrown into line of battle on the hill just south of town, skirmishers thrown out, videttes stationed and in a little while the irregular discharge of musketry was heard on the hill near Dr. Turner's which was quickly followed by the opening of a battery upon the hill south of the place. It was very exciting, very exhilarating, too much so to permit of our remaining in the basement where Ma and Grandma carried the children and even they remained there but a short time. Some of the bullets and shells passed near enough to whisper some confidential messages to us. The firing continued about three quarters of an hour, then gradually ceased. Then some of the cavalrymen who had been stationed in our orchard, came in. Next we saw the line of infantry on the hill move off and the cavalry from the surrounding hills gallop off toward the river and a few moments after—while our videttes were yet on the hill by Rose Hill the Yankee Cavalry dashed into town. A few shots were exchanged without any effect on either side. They only pursued our men a short distance. Captured but two of them while we took three of their's. There was a brigade of infantry in town all day—Yankee Gen. Jones' Brigade was on the opposite side of the river and there our cavalry retired—the remainder of our army went on up to Luray. There were but two of the Yankee wretches on the premises and they were infantry who called at the pump to get water. There were nondescripts in the yard this afternoon—professing to be Confederates who were cut off from their regiments and dressed partly in Confederate uniforms—but I never should be-

lieve they were anything but Yankee spies—they carried the mark of Cain
in their faces. The whole party left about 3 o'clock and Ma went up to
Mrs. Hope's to learn the news. Very soon Uncle Tom came in and told us
they had committed few, if any, depredations in town.—Had taken Col. Ja-
cob's meat, searched a few houses, etc. etc. But they went into Mr. Cook's,
saw Giles at the dinner table, learned he was a soldier, yet never attempted
to molest him. They went to the hospital, and though they cursed the poor
wounded and sick who were unable to move, they didn't take one prisoner
nor parole one of them. They went to Rose Hill though by a traitor, who had
been there the day Gen. Wright stopped there and professed to be one of his
men. They took off her two only horses, leaving one sore-footed one in their
stead at the instance of a former acquaintance of the family who happened
to be with them. Took all her meat excepting four pieces, searched the house
and behaved most insultingly. They went to Dr. Dorsey's, near which place
the fight occurred and stripped him of everything—all his horses, save one
which happened to be in town, all the cows, sheep, hogs, poultry, destroyed
his garden, stole everything they could lay hands on and even went to the
basket of newly washed clothes and took Ginnie Jones' night-dress which
they put on and told Mrs. D. they intended tearing them up for towels. There
was one of our wounded soldiers there whom they dragged into the yard and
threatened to kill before her eyes, but she cried and begged them not and
they at length desisted. There was a poor man living near there—Kenney
by name, who had a number of children—they went to his house, cut up the
furniture, tore every stitch of clothing save what they had on at the time,
destroyed all his garden, leaving him nothing but the roof and walls of his
house. This was their mode of proceeding wherever their steps led, we would
all in town no doubt have shared the same fate had they not been in great
haste and fear all the time. Mr. Berry, Mrs. Moffatt and Julia Hope came in
after tea. Mr. B says we lost about 150 killed and wounded Thursday evening
and the Yankees from three to five hundred. One of their captured officers
declared that one of our shells exploding in their midst killed 13 and wounded
fifty of their men at one time. Nellie, Evred and I walked nearly home with
Mrs. M and J but before reaching there they called out to us that the Yankees
were coming into town and as it was nearly dark we concluded to hurry home
for fear of a re-encounter. They encamped at Perry Criser's tonight. Tis such
a lovely quiet moonlit night and very difficult to realize that our fiendish foes

are couched in their lairs a few hundred yards distant ready at the first signal to spring upon their prey. Oh, dear! Such vicissitude! One day in the very heart of our army the next abandoned in the hands of the Yankees. Would like to understand the movement of the troops today. Scott made his escape, but lost his horse by one of our own men.

July 25th, 1863

All quiet, Yankees non est. Two soldiers came in this morning in Confederate uniforms—we at first suspected them but they showed us their credentials til we were convinced they were the genuine Simon Pures—members of the 4th Georgia Regiment cut off from their commands. One of them wrote a letter to his mother while here and left it with Father to mail. This is one of the most unpleasant phases of our present situation, we cannot distinguish friend from foe and ten chances to one if you aid a poor distressed looking soldier today tomorrow he will return at the head of a band of ruffians to murder and plunder you. This evening just before tea a little Yankee strolled into the yard—gun in hand took his seat by the pump where Father was and commenced a stupid conversation. He was left behind by his comrades yesterday—so he says—I believe he's a "decoy" nothing more nor less. Father gave him no encouragement and finally succeeded in ridding himself of so unwelcome a guest. Wonder which it will be next—Yankee or Confederate or a mixture of both. Rained hard this evening.

July 26th, 1863

Pleasant. Father carried some milk over to the hospital and brought back a favorable report concerning the patients there. He learned too from conversation something of the purport of the fight on Friday. It seems that Meade's whole Army was just below the Ridge and he had thrown them forward to intercept Ewell, cut him off from the main body of our Army, compelled him to fight here under great disadvantages and after defeating him going on and whipping our Army in details—the vanguard of his army was the portion that advanced on Friday to capture our pontoons and baggage trains—but they were moved on Thursday night which accounts for all that stir and rolling of wagons which we heard. Had Meade been one day earlier, had

Ewell been a day later, had our Generals been less prompt and energetic, our gallant Stonewall Corps must have been compelled to fight ten to one and defeated and cut off, our baggage trains lost, our pontoons captured and our little Valley and village the seat of a deadly struggle and destructive conflict. Thank Heaven for so miraculous an escape. Our men accomplished on Friday all they intended. They held those mountain passes and kept the enemy at bay til our army was safely distant—and then made good their own escape. 'Twas a masterly movement—that escape—executed in a very Jackson-like manner. Nellie and I went to church today—the first time I've been there for seven weeks—it made me sad to think of the many changes since then. Saw everybody—came home with Bobby Buck—Father dined at Oakley—spent a quiet pleasant evening. Nancie came home this evening, had passed over the battlefield of Thursday, saw numbers of our poor dead yet unburied, says the track of the battle can be traced for several miles by the earth plowed up by shot and shell, dead horses, broken guns and equipages of every description.

Ma, Father and all of us walked into the garden after tea. Rumor of the battle at Culpeper C H in which Gen. Longstreet repulsed the enemy—Jones' Brigade crossed at McKay's ford yesterday and has gone on to rejoin the army at Luray. So we shall see none of the boys.

July 29, 1863

Last night we were awakened by the arrival of Sallie, our new cook, with her two little children. Like her appearance very much, she seems accommodating and pleasant. Experienced quite a sense of relief in view of this assistance. Mrs. Marshall and Miss Betty in about noon to borrow the spyglass. No news. Rained this evening.

August 9th, 1863

Very sultry tonight. Took Evred and Frank down to the creek this evening and let them have a play in the water, they looked like little Cupids—so white and plump they looked under the shade of the trees. They've been talking so much about robbers and mad dogs tonight—from all accounts both are very rife. These same robbers may prove very formidable annoyances. I'm afraid there is quite a number of them—deserters from both armies, armed to the teeth, who have taken up an asylum in the mountain fastnesses from whence they descend upon unprotected farm houses, plunging the wilds. Several of them were captured the other day among whom was the leader and a young female in masculine apparel. This captain represents himself as a Mississippian—our men have opened negotiations with the lawless band proposing that they shall give themselves up to justice in order to save their chief from death—otherwise he will suffer the extreme penalty of the law. Of course, though, they will never have the generosity to do *that*. Wonder what will be the next phase which this state of society will assume.

[August 20, 1863, entry omitted]

August 21st, 1863

Day appointed by our president for national fasting and humiliation. We all decided to observe it.

[August 22, 1863, entry omitted]

August 25th, 1863

Was lying on the bed about dark trying to get some relief from my miserable toothache when a hard rap at the door was followed by Father's entering to announce the arrival of a gentleman and lady with their two children to stay all night. I sprang to my feet picturing in my imagination some weary, desolate refugees, homeless and friendless on such a night, and I thought to do my utmost to make them comfortable and easy, but my ardor was considerably abated upon learning that they were persons of wealth—travelling in easy style with their three servants on a pleasure tour—'twas right provoking to have them come in with such easy assurance—such calm indifference and have all the household thrown into a state of unutterable confusion—supper to get at such a time of night, bed linen to be changed and a thousand and one inconveniences and annoyances to be suffered and all because Mr. and Mrs. Pegram are fond of travelling. And then the insufferable

assurance of that lady nurse of theirs! I do hate to be made a piece of convenience of! Oh, me! How my tooth aches and how I wish I might go to bed,
'tis nearly eleven o'clock and yet I can hear that woman's laugh ringing as
loudly through the house and her talk as uninterrupted in its flow as it was
an hour ago.

August 26, 1863

Up early—tooth better—cleaned up—helped dress children and made my
own breakfast toilette. The Pegrams left directly after breakfast with cool
acknowledgment of our hospitality—so glad to have them go for I'm so sick
of confusion and noise. Mr. Armistead has sent over the girl, Lucie, whom
we intend hiring. The other girl, we will send home.

August 28, 1863

Mrs. Armistead's girl Lucy has come to live with us and the Clover Hill Lucie
went home yesterday. They tell me the present arrangement is quite an improvement upon the old one. Glad to hear it very.

August 29th, 1863

Busy, very, this morning—fixing the parlor, arranging evergreens and bouquets in there. Papers came this evening up to the 21st—news from Charleston, heavy bombardment there—Fort Sumter almost demolished but we've
still possession there and there's no probability that the Yankees will get the
city even admitting the Fort falls.

[September 9, 1863, entry omitted]

September 10, 1863

In the afternoon we were sitting in the door reading aloud to each other when
a stranger rode up to the stile and Dick introduced him as "Dr. Menafee"
whereupon the gentleman proceeded to inform me that he had come to examine Miss Buck's tooth. It directly occurred to me that Father was going to
have my offending masticators extracted. Father was absent and Ma spending

the afternoon at Mrs. Turner's. I nerved myself to the trial and just as he was in the act of having the first one drawn Father came in and so quietly was it done that he knew nothing of the operation till it was over. But the second attempt was more trying and I thought it would almost kill me. It was an immense relief to have these annoyances gone.

September 12th, 1863

This morning after breakfast Dick beckoned Nellie and me out and carried us to see poor dear Walter's horse—"Belle"—it seemed almost like looking at a part of himself so often had I seen him mounted on her looking so proud and bright and to see Dick caressing her so sadly. Then he shewed his saddle and all blood stained. Poor dear, dear boy. . . .

September 13th, 1863

. . . Dick sat in our little room and we entertained him showing all our little mementoes and treasures and talking over days of lang syne till dinner time. Just as we were going down to the basement he slipped a fragment of paper in my hand and bade me read it when I left the table. Father and Uncle John dined at Oakley. When I opened the paper it proved to be a little poem clipped from the paper—"The Empty Saddle" and had it been written for Dick and Walter it could not have been more appropriate, so sadly sweet, so touching. I copied it to send Irvie. I don't know when I've enjoyed anyone's society as I have Dick's this evening. He seems not changed one iota since the first day he enlisted save that he's more subdued and affectionate as a general thing. We gave him melons, pears and peaches just to enjoy seeing him eat them as he used to so long ago. He seemed loath to leave and lingered at the stile as late as possible til five o'clock. . . .

September 15th, 1863

Very busy all morning. Laura canning peaches—I sewing. Mrs. Moffatt, Uncles Mack and John here in the morning. Uncle M is uneasy about Dick as he is gone to Fauquier and will probably meet with the Yankees' reconnoitering parties—Oh, I hope not. There's a report of a battle at Culpeper and that our forces have fallen back from there. Grandma and Aunt B came

home after tea. Dr. Hough over in the evening. Received a "Messenger"—
busy reading it tonight.

September 16th, 1863

. . . Uncle John came home tonight. Nellie and I played for him in the parlor
and then we had a chat together. He confirms the news of the fight at Culpeper with no additional particulars, though. . . .

September 17th, 1863

Bright and beautiful day. Uncle John left about nine o'clock for the Mountain.
Copied some songs and then sewed steadily til dinner—after dinner read
Mrs. Rises letter to Father and took up my sewing again. About three o'clock
we were agreeably surprised at a visit from Cousin Will Cloud. He told us
about the battle at Culpeper, was in it himself, and with Cousin Ed, when
he was struck in the head by a spent ball—had brought Cousin Ed home
with him for the wound was fortunately not a dangerous one. He says twas
only our cavalry opposed to three corps of Yankee Infantry in the fight on
Sunday—that we had no intention of giving battle but the enemy pushed
on so madly as to give us no time for retreat without fighting our way
out—he seemed to think the casualties on our side very light.

September 20, 1863

Mrs. Kiger was at church, she told me she had tidings from Missouri and that
"Angie Smith was married to a gentleman from near Plattsburg—a Mr. Lincoln." Poor Angie, to think of her going through life encumbered with such
a name.

September 21st, 1863

Mack, Irwin and Mr. Luke came in to tea—just from Clarke. Bring the news
that all are well and the additional good news of a victory by Bragg over
Rosencrans in Tennessee. Oh! I pray it may be true. Played and sang for
Mack til he left, then came upstairs and sat at the window writing.

September 22nd, 1863

Had a tiresome time cleaning this morning. Dick came in to breakfast but left immediately after. Did not get through with the work til late. Repaired my old hat. . . . Was sitting at my window trying to write by the poor light when Ma came in bidding me guess who had come and ended by saying Mr. Bowman from Charleston and he brings news that Alvin is well and getting on finely and that he has had no letters from home for three months. Father went to see Mr. Bowman to try and learn some particulars of the siege at Charleston and he's just come home quite elated by the cheerful strain in which Mr. B. discourses of the defenses of Charleston. He leaves tomorrow and Ma and I are going to write tonight—late as it is, and send Alvin letters by him.

September 23rd, 1863

The news from Tenn. is not so flattering as at first account—yet we've whipped the enemy in an engagement there.

September 24th, 1863

Heard there had been a great battle in Tenn.[14]—dear Irvie! What of him I wonder.

September 25th, 1863

My birthday—twenty-one years old today—free, white and twenty-one! Heigh-ho!

A miserably, cold, wintry day—making Frank a pair of shoes. . . . Father told us at the tea table that Gen. Bragg's official report was received in town and that the battle in the west had been a great though not decisive victory on our side but that we have lost largely in officers among whom Gen. Hood was killed and Gen. Cleburne wounded—poor Irvie!

Tonight while Nellie and Sue were on the house talking, I have been sitting at the window not looking at the beautiful moonlight silvering the aspens but living in those thirty minutes the past fifteen years of my life marshalling all the brightly tinted pictures on memory's wall and basking in their light, turning over the leaves of the past to read what of me was there recorded and alas! humiliated at the sad array of wasted hours against me—standing like accusing spirits with glowing pictures of the "might-have-been" confronting the dreary prospect of the present. The hour was not spent without many resolutions of amendment and yet alas! those resolves are often but ropes of cobweb to constrain the habits of a lifetime. Twenty-one and free! Free indeed, why tis reversing the order of things when every year since I was a little child the shackles of care and anxiety have more and more closely clasped about me confining and restraining even the natural impulses of my heart. Free forsooth! I could laugh the idea to scorn were it not such a sad—such a mournful burlesque.

[September 26, 1863, entry omitted]

September 30th, 1863

Oh, I'm so tired—almost worn out. Nancie at the mill washing and we've had all the work to do. Was busy making some Confederate cake and getting dinner when Cousin E. Cloud came in—was glad to have her come for we had been feeling so sad about dear Irvie for Father heard in town that in the late battle of Chickamauga our loss in officers was very heavy and have no reason to suppose we are to be exempted from bereavements which others better than we are enduring. God grant our fears prove groundless yet I feel very, very sad. We had thought Cousin E might be able to throw some light on the subject but she told us she had heard nothing at all from our Western Army. . . .

October 1, 1863

Went over to spend the afternoon with Mrs. Wheatley. On our way passed near the old graveyard and Cousin Mary wished to visit her father's grave. It was a sad, sad scene!—the sky covered with drifting gray clouds through which ever and anon burst fitful gleams of sunlight, the long, sere grass rustling and the trees shivering in the wind that sighed low and mournfully through them. The enclosure of the graveyard was all dilapidated and gray and moss-grown. The tumble down gate half off the hinges and grating harshly as we tried to open it, then the graves themselves overgrown and almost concealed by the tall rank grass and briers, the walks between full of goldenrod, blackberry bushes and sumac shrubs—such a desolate, desolate place as it was—the white tombstones looked ghastly and the crickets made a sad weird sound in the leaves. I shall never forget the appearance of the neglected resting place of those loved and gone before.

October 4th, 1863

Bright though cold. Reading in the Bible. . . . Nancie left us this evening— was obliged to go and we had to get supper and shall have to do our own work now for two weeks to come—which I, for one, am very willing to do though we did have a time with the milking tonight because Horace didn't come home in time to do it. Nellie has tried her hand at making up light rolls tonight for the first time. Tomorrow night will try my hand.

October 6th, 1863

Was up by five o'clock to make up my rolls and helped dress Father's foot which gets no better. Aunt Eliza up early to milk for us. Horace and Uncle Gilbert went up to the Mountain to dig out potatoes. Nellie's day to cook but we helped her and I helped to churn and twist yarn too. Upset the churn and inundated the kitchen with sour cream. . . . When Horace and Uncle Gilbert came home tonight they told us that of the 20 bushels we planted only ten were realized, the robbers and deserters in the mountains having dug the remainder of the crop. There goes our dependence for next winter. Thus it is "unmerciful disaster follows fast and follows faster."

October 7th, 1863

At work very early and at it pretty much til the dining room and kitchen were cleaned after dinner. Ma went to town in the morning. Uncle Fayette came in to dinner. Had the dinner things cleaned up earlier than usual and had from that time til time to go about supper for writing in my diary. . . . Ma says a letter has been received in town from Scott Roy but that the Warren Rifles are certainly in Tenn. having taken part in the late battle there. Only a few of them were hurt, thank Heaven. Made up the bread tonight while Nellie read aloud "Marmion." Pouring rain.

October 13th, 1863

Finished Irvie's letter this morning and sent it off. Cool and damp in the morning but weather more pleasant in the afternoon. Went up on the house to see the cavalry come in to town. . . . Had a message from Mrs. Roy to the effect that Miss Mary Simpson had a letter from George Williams in which he stated that I. was safe but with a *bullet through his cap*. Thank Heaven that twas not an inch nearer the head. Oh! it has made me so happy to know that our dear one is safe and well.

[October 23, 1863, entry omitted]

October 25th, 1863

Bright but cold. Wrote a note to Emma by Cousin Newt who left quite early. Grandma and Aunt Betsie went to town. Tried to read—attempt a failure on account of the children's noise and constant call for attention. Nellie and I went over to hear Dr. Hough. Had a good sermon from 13th Corinthians. Saw everybody at church. Sue and Cousin Mae told us they will be over tomorrow. Reading to Father a short time in the afternoon. Then commenced writing some when Charlie Buck came in. . . . Nellie, Laura and I came upstairs after tea and sat a long time in the cold moonlight discussing the "Messenger." Then we went into Aunt B's room and read aloud to each other. Then I went down into Grandma's room, got Frank to sleep and read in my Bible. Every one in bed, I the only being in the house astir.

October 27th, 1863

After breakfast this morning we were sitting quietly at work when they ran in to say the Yankees were coming—sure enough there were parts of two regiments of cavalry. Laura went in a great hurry off to Mrs. Hope's to tell

Mr. Moffatt and while she was gone one of the scamps dashed up to the door where Father, Sue, Nellie and I were standing and, without a word of greeting demanded "Where that man was that came up here." Father told him that there was no one here to the best of his knowledge. He in the most insolent manner said he knew there *was* and he would find him in this house before he was done. Father then turned to us and inquired if we had seen any man here—Nellie replied with a mocking laugh that "*he* was the only man she had seen come." He turned with a most fiendish look and said—"I 'spose then the nigger lied—he's here and I'm going to find him." With that he commenced blustering around with his hand on his pistol and marched into the garden where sure enough he stumbled over a Confederate soldier lying under the syringa bushes near the gate—twas John Taylor who had taken refuge there unknown to one member of the family. The Yankee brought him triumphantly forth and went off with him to town. They all very soon after turned and left town in a violent hurry—stopping as they went at Rose Hill! We heard after they left that they had taken Uncle Tom's last horse, Charlie Buck's pony and five of Mr. Richards besides twelve barrels of corn and all Cousin Bet's turkeys. . . .

October 28th, 1863

Very cold and clear. Nellie and Sue went to spend the day at Oakley. Repairing some old corsets. . . .

October 29th, 1863

Up and had breakfast very early. Confusion and trouble. Sat upstairs reading in my Bible, then came down and wrote in my diary. All the whole family from Mrs. Childs and Grandma down to Frank and Lucie went down to the mill to see the process of molasses making. Aunt and I had the house to ourselves and I improved the delightful quiet by writing. They did not return til dinner time and then Nellie came bounding in with face full of excitement to say George Hope was come home. . . . Ma and I walked down to the mill talking all the way about the probability of having the boys with us once more, for George tells us Alvin can have a furlough if he wishes it and he will either come home or go to Kentucky as he prefers. Spent an hour at the mill watching the boiling and talking to Mrs. Richards—got back about tea time—went upstairs after tea and had a gay time til time to go to bed.

November 7th, 1863

. . . About twelve o'clock Father came in to say the Yankees were coming— and there were four hundred cavalrymen. Such a time as we had putting away things! Laura ran off to Mrs. Hope's to warn George and came back almost dead with the fatigue. They passed the home repeatedly but not one was in the yard. Mrs. Marshall called in to rest and told us they had taken Mack Bayley, who had gotten home the night before, and John Boone and John Sumption. They remained til a little after three o'clock and then left town whooping and singing like demons. Ma came home after they were gone and told us they behaved unusually well—searched Mrs. Hope's house for George but did nothing brutal. They invited themselves to dine with the citizens—took as much as they wanted of hay and corn for their horses and got the Luray mail—this was the "most unkindest cut of all." Well I'm so very sorry for Mack and Cousin Bet and yet tis laughable too to think of his riding in town behind the Yankees! Well, it has all settled down into comparative quiet now and I'm glad tis no worse. Busy sewing on those interminable shirts. Grandma and Aunt Betsie came home.

[November 8, 1863, entry omitted]

[November 12, 1863, entry omitted]

November 14th, 1863

Lovely—spring like. Headache—tired. Arranged the vase of flowers in the parlor, finished crocheting my case, read and wrote a letter. Mrs. Moffatt up in the morning. Had a note from Millie Bowen, replied to it and wrote in my diary in the afternoon. Ma, Grandma and Aunt Betsie in town. Russell Richards and Neville Buck here and Gussie came down about four o'clock bringing with her a letter from Dick in which he stated that poor Scott had been captured while scouting near Norfolk on the second of this month. Poor fellow! To think how we have been looking forward with so much pleasure to his visit to us in December and now he's in the hands of the enemy and there's no exchange for prisoners either. Vile wretches! these Yankees I wish—but no matter, that won't give poor Scott his liberty. What was the use of my learning the song, I just don't believe any of the boys are coming home and oh! me I've got the blues.

Raining hard—eleven o'clock p.m. Ma and Laura preparing to start to Clarke in the morning but fear they'll be disappointed. I'm so sleepy and sad.

November 22nd, 1863

Bright.—Finished cleaning up, gave Sue her breakfast—she seemed better and brighter in the morning. Sat by the window and wrote Mollie a note and also wrote in my diary. Father went over to Uncle Tom's. Grandma and Aunt Betsie to church. Aunt L Buck returned with them from church but only sat a short time—she and Sue had a letter from Dick brought from the regiment by Major Simpson. He spoke of Scott's escape from the Yankees—then they told me they had heard how he effected this. It seems there was a blockade runner in the same apartment with him and he told in the course of conversation that he had a little skiff not far distant which, if he could reach it would enable him to run the blockade free of his captors. Scott asked for a sketch of his plans which the man readily placed with his pencil on a bit of paper. The captain of the guard had reason to suspect Scott of having designs of escape and had him up before the Provost Marshal who tried to convince Scott that twould be very dishonorable to attempt any such thing, but Scott very properly told him that he was not on his parole of honor and that twas perfectly fair for him to go if he could—that were the Provost in his place he would do the same thing. The officer then ordered that he should be more securely confined, but the order from some cause was not put into effect that night and Scott persuaded the young man who accompanied him to try to give them the slip. They climbed out of a window over on a beam projecting from it, from there they descended to the roof below them, from the roof they slipped down by means of the lightning rods to the ground—made good their way to the place designated by the "Blockade Runner" as the harbor for his little skiff, found the boat, boarded it and turned their backs on Norfolk, and all this in the face of an order from the Provost that they were to be shot in case they were detected in any such attempt. They rowed for 28 or 30 miles between two light houses and finally succeeded in reaching a point of safety from which they made their way to camp. Bless that boy! This is only the third time he has taken French leave of his captors. Oh I'm so glad for now he'll be home Christmas and I do think he deserves promotion for the evidence he has given of strategical abilities. What would I not give to see him and hear him talk about it all now, though he is too modest to say much for himself I know.

November 30th, 1863

Bitter cold—up early and had the house in order betimes. Busy with my hat. Uncle Tom in to dinner. Rumors of the defeat in Tennessee. Hoped tis false though. Sitting all of us before a bright fire in Grandma's room, I with Frank on my lap feeding him preparatory to putting him to sleep when we were startled by a sudden knock at the door which proved to proceed from a wagon driver who enquired if we would give lodgings to Mr. George Burwell, his wife and daughter. It was very inconvenient yet how could we refuse shelter such an inclement night? They came in almost frozen. A fine looking old gray haired gentleman, an energetic lady in black—his wife, a lady-like looking little niece and daughter and son respectively thirteen and fifteen years of age. We proceeded to make them as comfortable as possible. Great was our consternation upon finally discovering that they were attended with a suite of twelve servants, three white drivers, eleven horses and five or six conveyances. Made the best of our bargain though and got on very comfortably, the night cold as it was.

December 3rd, 1863

Made a mistake this morning and was up two hours before day. Wrote a song and by that time the house was astir. Watered and aired the geraniums and verbenas, read in my Bible, and after breakfast came upstairs to my window and wrote in my diary. Warm as a spring morning. Busy during the day. In the afternoon late Nellie and I were practicing for some time and then went down in the dining room preparing for supper when we heard a shout which we recognized as Neville's and going to the door saw the wagon driving up with Ma and the goods. Such a time as we had hearing the news. She had been to Harper's Ferry and bought her goods and returned safely without having to take even a pledge—had had a delightful trip and seemed cheerful and well. After supper we overhauled the goods and were delighted to find something for each one—for Nellie and me dresses—beauties—trimmings, balmorals and belts.[15] Then shoes, hats, aprons and cloth and yarn for Father and the children and some little articles for Grandma besides groceries. Poor Laura, I know she has a heavy heart tonight. Ma says she made a mighty effort to suppress her tears when she left. Commenced making my balmoral tonight—we have been sitting up talking to Ma—now it is twelve o'clock and I shall not have time to make up for lost time.

December 5th, 1863

Very unwell this morning but accomplished my usual duties. Sewing. Was lying down when Nellie came to say that Aunt Letitia Buck was down in Grandma's room on her way to Riverside. And she—Nellie—was going with her. Went down to see them off and was just preparing some medicine to take when a note came from Cousin Mary Cloud begging me to come over right away. I knew from the manner of writing that she had heard the report, so although really unwell to turn out I made ready and accompanied EM to town. . . . Parted with Cousin Mary partially promising to see her again tomorrow. Did not get home till after dark—met Orvie and Carey coming over after me. Repaired Annie's skirt for her, read aloud to Father in the "Bachelor" and wrote to Laura tonight. Tis eleven o'clock—am tired and sleepy. Heard that three of Mr. Richard's servants with two horses, a mule and several of Mr. Petty's servants fled to Yankeedom.

[December 10, 1863, entry omitted]

December 11th, 1863

Ma heard through Harry Roy this evening that he had seen our servants in Chambersburg when he was in—that Mahala was doing finely keeping a boarding house—Eliza Ann living with her, and Martha married and settled down. Must confess I've my doubts about it though the servants will all believe it and twill have the effect of inducing numbers to leave home.

December 15th, 1863

Grandma brought me a "Record" when she returned containing an account of the campaign in Pennsylvania written by an English officer who accompanied our army thither. They say tis very graphic and interesting but I've been too unwell to read it.

December 16th, 1863

Commenced the "Campaign in Pa."—most amusing and entertaining—particularly so to us as the writer was quartered with Gen. Longstreet's staff and the names he mentions among the officers are, many of them, very familiar ones.

[December 17, 1863, entry omitted]

December 18th, 1863

Cool and windy. Fitting my dress. Mr. Berry over a short time this evening. Writing some. Felt better tonight and was just having a quiet game of romps with the children in Grandma's room while Ma and Father talked in the sitting room.—There came a loud "Holloa" from the yard and going out Father was confronted by a cavalryman who asked if supper could be obtained here for Major Harman, Adjutant Nott and some other officers who were coming in. Being answered affirmatively he then informed us that the whole of Rosser's Brigade was passing the house and so it was though we knew nothing of it before. Dear Walter! I thought of him immediately and remembered how—at any other time we should be looking for his coming with them and now he would never come again. Had not much time for thought though for, the soldiers came pouring in and we had to attend to getting supper for them. Poor creatures they were in all that storm night before last and in a skirmish last night—some of them were perfectly stupefied with cold and fatigue and had water in their boots which they got in crossing the river at Fredericksburg. They had come from there and gone entirely around Meade's army—were enroute for Clark or Frederick but diverted from their course by the high waters. Being at the doors on an errand I met face to face a poor fellow who had just dismounted—he limped terribly and I asked him if he were wounded—he told me that he was crippled with rheumatism. Indeed he could scarce move and we told him he must stay in the house tonight although he said it had been a year since he slept under a roof before. There were at one time twenty or thirty horses before the door at a time. All settled down by eleven o'clock.

[December 19, 1863, entry omitted]

December 24th, 1863

Very busy cleaning and finishing my dress till after eleven o'clock. Then Father came in bringing a long, long letter from Alvin to Nellie of the twenty-ninth sent through Miss Kate Graves. Bless his soul! It is such a treat and he is well and cheerful as usual and he's heard from Irvie and he is after the battle. Thank Heaven! There was a letter for me too from Scott—a good long, saucy "Scottish" letter. Such nice Christmas gifts as they are! Busy down in the kitchen baking cakes till after eight o'clock. Lucie went home this evening; we hated so to give her up and she cried bitterly.

Tonight got the children washed and put to bed and after they went to sleep filled the stockings and boiled some molasses for taffy. Father attempted to attend to the boiling but after waiting till ten o'clock he gave it up in despair and left Grandma, Ma and me alone in our glory. Did not get through till after twelve o'clock. Poor children! I contrast their limited means of enjoyment now with our former happy life and it makes me sad. Ah! Dear, tomorrow will be a lonely, dreary day for me with none of the dear ones we were expecting—not even Nellie and Laura. There are only five pairs of stockings over the fire-place tonight and there are five of our house circle absent—five hearts are no doubt turning longingly this way tonight. God bless them! One of the very loneliest nights I ever saw.

December 25th, 1863

Children up very early. A lovely day clear and bright. Helped the children with the contents of their stockings and then proceeded to clean up. Dressed after breakfast and went off upstairs to take a good cry for my heart was full of sad and pleasant thoughts and memories and I was so lonely—missed the dear absentees. Felt better after crying a while and went downstairs with Ma and Grandma. Uncle Newton sick. Father went out to see him. Charlie Buck spent an hour or so with us. Cheery boy that he is—tried to play and sing for him but had to give over the attempts in despair. Then Uncle John came. He was not well and lay down. Then Uncle Tom who remained to eat our orthodox turkey and mince pies. Wonder where the poor boys got their Christmas dinners this year or if they had *any* poor fellows? and Nellie and Laura and Orville?

Frank fretful and sleepy this evening and I felt really worn out. At twilight when Ma and Father were talking by the firelight—I laid on the bedside and thought, thought and cried. Ah the sad, sad changes that are more and more apparent every year! how much more they depress, how much less able I feel to bear them—our dear lost Walter! Let the seasons roll around as they *will*, *he* will never come to make glad the festive times for us. And yet tis wrong to grieve thus when we have so much more to be thankful for than to complain of. Our other dear ones are spared to us. I think how this house might now be shrouded in sorrow as thousands and thousands of Southern homes are—how our hearts might be writhing in anguish had a hostile bullet laid low our darling Irvie in that last miserable battle. I think of poor Mr. Smedley—of his son—so young—so cruelly deprived of his useful young life—think of the sad households there and feel that we are blessed even more than we could reasonably hope for.

We are anxious about the children but look for them tomorrow or the day after.

December 29th, 1863

A bright beautiful day. Father went down to the river to hear from the children. Playing and singing and telling Gussie stories all the forenoon. Aunt Letitia here. Feeling quite unwell tonight. Aunt Letitia has letters from her son in Philadelphia who has heard from Cousin Alex. He's in Chicago. Of course he would not *say* if he *was not* well treated. They have also letters from Mack Bayley who is at Camp Chase and doing well. They had a letter from Cousin Mack and Dick but don't know the contents of them.

December 30th, 1863

Ma sick in the night and I scarcely able to drag myself about. Still there was a great deal to be done as twas wash day and few to do it, so I roused myself and managed to accomplish my usual work and then went to work knitting. . . . Had a letter from Nellie—written the 24th. She says the children were to have started yesterday so I presume they'll be here tonight. Father and Carey went down to the river to meet them. While washing up the dinner things Uncle Tom came in bringing a package of letters—some seven or eight from Alvin, Irvin and one from a Mr. Dore of Richmond to father and an enclosure from Benton to myself, an old one. Indeed nearly all letters were old ones dating back—some of them as far as August—some were more recent and all of them as welcome as could be. How we devoured their contents learning from them many little incidents which we probably could otherwise never have obtained. This outpouring of the post office is probably owing to a letter which Father wrote the P M General some time since. It's high time there was something of the kind done for we've been badly enough treated by the mail boys. The letter from Mr. Dore was written informing Father that his young son had stopped here going and coming from Maryland, that he had spoken in such warm terms of his kindness to him and this had prompted him to make the request he did of him. He said his poor boy had fallen at Williamsport and was buried in the Lee cemetery there— his headboard bearing his name—"Leslie C. Dore." He had heard there were blockade runners constantly plying between here and Maryland and he wished to know if they could by any means procure the remains for him and bring them in. He wrote so touchingly—it made me sad to think that this was but one incident out of a hundred such occurring daily in our Confederacy and that this appeal was but one out of many heart cries coming up constantly from bereaved households. Ah me!

December 31st, 1863

Miserably sick but managed to drag through my oppressing work and then went to bed with a nervous headache. Uncle Tom came in about eleven o'clock bringing another pacquette of letters which came by this redundant mail—three from Irvie to Nellie and three from him to Ma and two from

Benton to me—one dated 29th November, the other December 5th, the latest one we've had from them. Poor fellow! he is in no happy frame of mind—so depressed by the defeat there—seems so desponding—complains of hearing nothing from home. Read the letters all through. Suffering very much all day—towards evening felt better and took a cup of tea. Determined to watch in the new year though it was only by dint of persuasion I could get permission to do so. Filled the children's stockings after they went to bed—undressed—got my portfolio and went to writing. Grandma sat with me till eleven o'clock and then left me alone writing to Scott. It seems so lonely—so isolated sitting there waiting for the last few sands to drop from the glass and watching for the burst of another year of trial—even as I watched the advent of the last year—little knowing, little dreaming what that year the great move of time would sweep from me—how much of life's brightness it would dim—how it would sweep away to the dim shores of eternity the form of one so dear to us—one of the brightest lights of our darkened days of time. How little I had dreamed of the toil, the trials and the care that like a blight had come over me. And yet how little there was to complain of in comparison with the blessings that have been showered upon my unworthy head—and can I not trust for this coming year to the same kind hand that has guided me through the darkened paths of life heretofore? Yes, surely. It is raining and the drops fall like great drops of tears—the old year is weeping his inevitable death. Poor old year! Why should he wish to linger in a world where his eyes behold only the fading and blight of all things bright and beautiful, rather let him close his eyes to all the sorrow and care of this trying season and fold his hands softly and lay his old weary, white head down til it rests upon the bosom of oblivions' stream—thus—while we mortals turn to hail the incoming of the new "eighteen hundred and sixty-four!"

Chapter Six

᚛᚛᚛᚛᚛᚛᚛᚛᚛᚛᚛᚛᚛᚛᚛᚛᚛᚛᚛᚛᚛᚛

One Day in the Very Heart
of Our Army the Next Abandoned
in the Hands of the Yankees

᚛᚛᚛᚛᚛᚛᚛᚛᚛᚛᚛᚛᚛᚛᚛᚛᚛᚛᚛᚛᚛᚛

January 2, 1864–June 6, 1864

January 2nd, 1864

Uncle John left before breakfast. Had a great deal of work to do. Soon finished though. Uncle Jim came in from Clarke and said the children had started home and were at Mrs. Painter's where they would stay until the weather moderated or the river fell. Uncle Tom came over. Father went to the river to try and hear from them. Was just bringing in the wood and chips when I saw Laura coming in the back door and then Orville and Jacquie and Dumb Mary. They had left their baggage at Mrs. Painter's and *walked* over having crossed the river in a skiff at Hans Ferry. Such a noise as ensued among the children—so many questions to ask and answer! Then there was a letter from Nellie. Poor thing! She was evidently loath enough to have the children go and will, I'm afraid, be sad enough. Laura our new "help" came in this evening—a delicate looking, unsophisticated individual. Hope she'll be able to do more than her appearance indicates. Very cold tonight. A great crowd about the fire. The Yankees are in town—came in very unexpectedly from Warrenton—a body of Meade's troops come to cut off Early's division and reinforce Averill at Martinsburg. From the appearance of the camp fires tonight there must be infantry with them. I feel perfectly at ease tonight but am afraid tomorrow they'll commence their plundering though. Well, they won't get my "treasures" I guess.

January 3rd, 1864

Clear, bright and cold. Did not get through with my work as soon as usual. Soon after breakfast we saw the Yankees filing out of the woods and forming into ranks, went out of town the way they came carrying with them *one* poor little prisoner. They said the mail—containing those letters I've been writing—have been captured. Ma and I were so provoked that we bundled up and went over to see Uncle Tom about getting a postmaster who would attend to his business and hide the mail when the Yankees should come. There was no church and we would spend the day with Aunt Bettie. Saw where the wretches had been in the Baptist church killing chickens. There were the feathers and blood on the floor and everything in sickening disorder. Indeed it seems they confined themselves to warring on fowls. We found Father at Oakley when we got there—Aunt Bettie was looking better than I expected to see her. It seems there was a whole division of cavalry with artillery—the greater portion of them encamping between Drs. Dorsey's and Turners's. They had come thinking to cut off our troops and reinforce Averill but the high water proved an insurmountable obstacle and they had to return as they came. They searched Uncle Newton's house for guns—taking from there one ham. Charlie had fortunately escaped up the river. Uncle Tom says they went to Rose Hill and took every turkey and ham they had besides nearly all their other meat. Poor Cousin Elizabeth. She gets it on every side and is so little able to stand these losses and annoyances. Green Samuels was at home and made his escape by adopting female costume and walking out after dusk. Dr. Leech sent his little son off to the woods with their horse. The animal refused to move after getting on the hill and as the Yankees were pursuing the child, the child had to surrender. Was taken to camp when Miss Lizzie hearing of it, went and begged him and the horse off. One of the girls then led the horse into the dining room where holding him by the reins—holding in her hand a pistol and keeping at bay the miscreants who came to take him. Dick Bayley came in about noon—said he stayed at home last night and *talked* across the river to the Yankee picquet on this side knowing that the river was too full for them to cross, the boat was destroyed and the night too dark to admit of his being recognized as a "Rebel." . . .

January 12th, 1864

Father took Laura and me down on the ice and gave us our first lessons in skating. It was a magnificent morning and I felt so invigorated by the bracing air, the bright sunshine and the run through the crisp sparkling snow. Then the ice formations at the dam were so exquisitely delicate and beautiful. We were there about two hours—Father predicting that we will make expert skaters—did not get one bad fall though Father did. Returned to the house with tired ankles but in a perfect glow. Read in the *Journal*. Sewed a little. Ma home to dinner.

January 24th, 1864

Up very early but oh! such a time as we've had getting breakfast. The fire place is a very different matter from the stove when it is used for cooking by, as I soon discovered. We were—all of us combined—till after nine o'clock getting breakfast. While preparing for dinner, Aunt L. Buck and Jacque came in—persuaded them to remain all day. Sally very sick. I had toothache but working over the warm fire seemed to relieve it somewhat. We had a jolly time getting dinner. Could not get the pots and kettles off the hooks—had to send for Father to come and help us. He was so much alarmed at seeing me about the fire with my calico dress that he insisted on my resigning my office to him but I trembled for the fate of my biscuits. We had sausage and hominy and the nicest biscuits and boiled beef and lamb and coffee. Aunt L. soon went home after dinner. Grandma came home tonight. Very warm and close. Feel tired and unwell.

February 11th, 1864

Bright and keen. Busy after breakfast preparing Laura's costume and making a "Bonnie Blue Flag." Then writing in my diary. Ma was taken suddenly sick about noon but being better in the evening Laura, Orville, Carey and I walked over to Dr. Leache's. Met everybody there and had the greatest time selecting subjects, costumes and rehearsing. All seemed "Merry as a Marriage Bell"—but my heart was very, very heavy—thinking of Ma and all at home.

February 12th, 1864

Cloudy. Up and at work busily making off programmes and sending bundles. Nanny and Mollie came about eleven o'clock. Had everything prepared and went over to the Academy about four o'clock to assist Miss Lizzie in preparing for tonight—found everything bustle and excitement—went to work with the rest smiling as brightly as they did and I know not one of them suspected what a heavy heart I carried in my bosom. . . . Arranged the stage, pinned on the wreaths about sunset—came home and dressed. By dent of persuasion induced Ma to go with us. There were six of us. Found them waiting for us. Such a babble of confusion as I entered into behind the scenes! My name was called till I almost regretted having one and the boys were noisy but these being gradually arranged things passed off very nicely, "Drilling Conscripts," "Examining Conscripts," "None but The Brave deserve the Fair," "Come spin My Dearest Daughter," the "Interview between the Pickets" and above all the "Bonnie Blue Flag" sung in person were admirable. After all our dread the affair passed off quite creditably and we realized quite a nice little sum—$94.00 for the benefit of the poor soldiers. Got home about half past nine o'clock. . . .

February 20th, 1864

Beautiful day. Spent an hour this morning on the ice. Little Leaches and then Poor Charlie came in. He was in high spirits and would have me in the parlor to play for him. Father came in about two o'clock to say, if Charlie had no objections, he would ride his horse to Mr. Forney's. Before he started the children ran in to say the Yankees were coming. Charlie sprang to his feet, flung me his overcoat, mounted his horse and at father's directions galloped across the orchard toward Green Hill. They proceeded and pursued them but he managed to elude them that time. While waiting the denouement of this move one of the children cried out—"Oh they've got poor Old Sam!" and sure enough Horace had started off towards the thicket with the horses and was overhauled by the Yankees and forced to give up the best of the two. We saw them cantering across the fields towards town leading with them our main dependence for future bread and fuel. It was with a mingling of consternation and anger that we saw the robbery committed. We waited some time for the main column to approach—Carey finally concluded to go over and try to get the horse returned to us. Father soon followed him and just as he started some one remarked they "did believe there was Charlie Buck upon the hill looking down upon the Yankees now." Sure enough we descried two horsemen on the brim of the hill near the thicket where Charlie *should* have been concealed but could not believe that it was Charlie till by looking through the spy glass we recognized him beyond a doubt. We at first concluded that he was a prisoner and the other horseman with him his captor but closer inspection convinced us that they were both of them of the same "Stripe." It was very rash of Charlie, and Laura and Orville concluded they would run across the field and give him warning but after they started we recollected the Yankees might be led to watch their transit across the plowed field in full view of town and thus their attention be attracted to Charlie when otherwise he might escape notice. Just then the whole column appeared coming over the hill and we saw Carey and Father returning from town leading "Old Sam"—we were as much surprised as delighted at the success of this expedition. When they came up to the stile where we were standing Carey told us he had asked the man who took the horse to return it to him, the man appealed to his Sgt. to know what he must do and the Sgt.—"Oh! give him up, he's not fit for Cavalry service." "But," turning to Father—"I return him only on condition that those two men on yonder hill remain where they are: if they leave I shall take it for granted you have warned them, and in that case I will take your horse from you again. I have already sent my men to take them." And while we were hearing this account one of the servants said "The Yankees are after Mass. Charlie!" And we saw them dash on him from the thicket in his rear and all disappeared together over the hill. Presently we saw them coming back and Poor Charlie with them. We ran down to the fence as he passed and I just had time to say "Oh Charlie, have they got you?" and "have you any message home?" But the tears leaped into his eyes and he could only compress his lips and shake his head. He is strong and brave and so far as the consequence to himself is involved could have borne his misfortune unflinchingly, but alas he knows the sorrow that it will bring upon his home,—upon his poor old father. Laura and I determined to go to see him and if possible obtain his release from the Colonel. We wrapped him up some apples and pies and took his overcoat, Carey going with us as escort. When we reached the camp heard that Misses Lizzie Leach and G. Petty had been before us and with a great deal of trouble succeeded in obtaining permission to approach to the prisoner *in presence of an officer.* We threaded our way through the wall of soldiers and horses and approached a group in the center of which we soon discovered the poor boy standing on his wounded foot. His eyes filled with tears as he saw us and still he seemed glad. He was surrounded by a whole bevy of little boys who were heartily abusing the Yankees and Miss Lizzie and Miss Gennie stood near besides a whole lot of his captors. When we gave him his overcoat one of the creatures remarked facetiously "he shows the 'spread-eagle,' don't he?" The officer who had him under guard—a Capt.—seemed somewhat of a gentleman and he said "My boy if you were not in Military service you should not be wearing those buttons" alluding to the U.S. buttons on the overcoat. A third chimed in with—"Oh! he's put half and half seccesh uniform with Yankee buttons. You are not much of a rebel are you my fine fellow?" Charlie in reply positively affirmed that he *was* altogether a rebel! They all then unanimously agreed that they honored him all the more for fearlessly declaring his sentiments. The Capt. now came forward and remarked that he was under the necessity of placing him with his guard as he should be compelled to leave him. So we kissed the poor boy "Goodbye" and they carried him off. Miss Lizzie heard me inquiring for the Colonel and went with me to find him. He had just ridden out of town, so we waited at Dr. Leache's till we saw him dash in town. Then we followed him immediately down to camp. As we were walking around looking for his Colonel-ship I heard someone say "Are you looking for me, Cousin Lucy? Here I am." and peering through a group near the wagon saw Charlie sitting near one of the fires surrounded by his half dozen guardsmen. Passing him we came upon the Colonel standing just in the rear of the wagon surrounded by his officers and reading what I supposed to be a letter which he had purloined from the P.O. He was magnificently equipped but was one of the most cruel looking beings. Very tall, finely formed, a red head surmounted with a fine laced hat, a very red face, a beak-like nose, ugly blue green eyes, a sinister mouth and long, red side whiskers. He pretended not to see us approaching and resolutely turned his back but our friend the Captain announced us to his Lordship and he then looked over his shoulder and growled out—"I *told* you might speak to the prisoner, why don't you go on?" With this he sharply confronted us, when Miss Lizzie stepping forward said "Colonel, the young ladies with me are relatives of the Prisoner—we wish to speak to you about him." I then told him that Charlie was lame and would never be of any service to the Confederate states as a soldier any more. He asked then "why did he run?" We told him "for the purpose of saving his horse." "He did not act much like a man trying to save his horse—sitting there right in full view of our force and in company with another soldier too. He was spying our movements and communicating with the Rebel army." "But"—we argued "there are no Southern troops near for him to hold communication with." He looked very knowing as he replied—"*you pretend* not to *know* there were twenty Rebels in town last night—nay, twenty left the place this morning? They are here and you know it. Plenty of troops in this place." We asked him how that could be when his own soldiery occupied the town. "Why" he said, "if they are not in town they're somewhere near—you know where as well as I do and you'll know more in a few hours about them than you do now. I've been out myself reconnoitering." He was such a coarse kind of wretch and every time we attempted to combat his arguments he would arrest our speech by some lame attempt to act facetiously and then look around to his officers as if appealing to their admiration and they evidently regarded him as an Oracle. At times, he would try to entrap us into some betrayal of the knowledge we supposed to possess of our army. Finally I said "Colonel, if you are not attacked by our forces before you leave town you have no reason to suppose this young man has given them any information detrimental to you, if he has given no information he has not harmed you—surely you will release him?" The rude churl turned his back coolly upon me and thrusting his hands into his pockets shrugged his shoulders and looked oh! so mean. Finally he faced about and remarked contemptuously—"Well, my *good woman*, I don't think I shall take the fellow, of course I cannot decide as yet though." This was said in a manner which plainly implied a dismissal but just as we left his Lordship's presence Miss Lizzie in an

——— ——— proposed that we should invite him to our home. I felt as if this was too much of a condescension but while I hesitated she continued—(for the sake of getting Charlie off—*I* will!) I then turned about and remarked to the officer that if he would come to my home that evening I thought I would convince him of the truth of what I said, at the same time pointing to the house just across from camp. He muttered something about "seeing about it" and with this we were obliged to be contented and left camp. Had scarcely gotten home when the sergeant who had returned the horse marched up to the stile announcing that he had been sent by the Colonel to see into the case of the young prisoner. He then went on to say there was no use talking about it for there was no hope of his release—he "felt sorry for him" had "been a prisoner himself" and "knew the sweets of captivity" and so on. At last turning to us he said "Good evening ladies. I hope the old gentleman will be able to keep his horse which I returned to him this morning. Can you give me a little bit of something to eat?" So I had to go off and get him some bread and butter and milk. He seemed determined to give us no comfort at least. We persuaded Father to go over and see the Colonel himself—he went and presently returned saying they were about all starting—not having received the reinforcements from Cole's Battalion which they professed to expect. He had seen the Colonel, he promised to release Charlie after they crossed the river in case he was not attacked by our guerillas. There were two or three other prisoners besides Charlie and Newt Broy—the soldier who was not taken with him—young Bartlett and Mr. Sheppard. We watched the column as it left town as long as we could see it and then went into the house to canvass the day's events. Presently came a knock at the door and a request that Father would meet Aunt Jane at Dr. Leech's. He went and on his return said that Aunt J and Nannie had come in just a few minutes too late to see Charlie and that he—poor fellow—had gone off without so much as a change of clothing. Oh, I'm so sorry. I certainly thought they would be long enough here to allow him to see them all at his home and knew that they would furnish him with everything. How thoughtless of me to let them pass by, go off unprovided for. Yet I hope he has not gone far either—surely they'll let him return as they said they would. Cousin Sue Buck and Nannie and Mrs. Armistead and Mrs. Wheatley walked on down to the river hoping to overtake them but only reached the bank in time to see them crossing to the opposite side. Poor Charlie, how much he is in our thoughts and hopes tonight. Surely he will come back.[1]

February 21st, 1864

My first thought upon waking this morning was of our dear Charlie. "Would he come?" I asked myself over and over again. We heard that poor Uncle Newton was well nigh frantic and Ma concluded to go out and see him—Laura and Willie went with her. . . . Father and I went to church—had a good sermon. Was surprised to see Aunt Jane at church—asked her if Charlie had returned but her tears were sufficient to give the sad negative. She said Cousin Sue Buck had proposed her going to Harper's Ferry to try if possible to communicate with Charlie—at least to send him clothing. . . . Dear Charlie, he has grown to be such a comfort to us all—and like all who have become a consolation to us is snatched from us by these ruthless vandals. Aunt Jane and Mr. Berry are gone to the Ferry and will, I hope, succeed in at least learning something concerning him. We will at least trust for the best.

February 27th, 1864

Warm and smoky. Ma and I and the children all unwell. Lounging about and sewing at intervals. Father came in the afternoon bringing me a nice, long letter from Alvin. Mr. King had been in to Charleston—saw the boys and brought this letter with him. Dear boy! I believe he does love me better than I deserve any way. . . .

March 4th, 1864

Bright. Frank very fretful after me. . . . Was busy fixing for Laura's company—Annie Buck came home from school with Laura and very soon after Nannie Buck and Jessie Leach came. Very busy getting things in order. The children romped. . . . As it grew later I persuaded Emma to go upstairs and dress to personate "Miss Duechenberry." While preparing her Jule and Annie Ford and Neville came; then the parlor rapidly filled. I went in with the girls and found Sallie Petty, Sallie Leach, Lottie Blathis, Lucie Overall, Mollie

Barber, Mollie and Mattie Cook, Wythe Cook and Hennie, Allie Ashby and
Bob Buck, Vivian, Willet and Engie Leach, Willie Davidson and Neville.
Presently Emma knocked at the door and being invited in created no small
sensation. After playing a few games in the parlor they all adjourned to the
basement where game after game followed each other in quick succession—
"Blindfold," "Fox and Goose," "King William," "Jugging along," "Travellers," "Pleased and Displeased," "Smiling Angel," "Clap in and Clap Out,"
"Drunken Sailor," etc., etc.[2] When they became uproarious below we "old
fogies" as they voted us went into the parlor and had music. I thought so
much about Nellie and wished for her tonight—know she would enjoy it all.
Had nuts and ginger cakes. All left a little after eleven o'clock—Jule, Annie,
Anice, Emma, Cousin Lucie, Jessie, Nannie, Bob, Nev, and Allie remaining
with us. We had music and a game of "Lawyer" after all the others left and a
snack so that it was near two o'clock a.m. Well, I'm thankful everything
seems to have passed off happily and well. Had a note from Cousin Mary and
heard of the raid on the Central R.R. tonight.

[March 10, 1864, entry omitted]

March 11th, 1864

Alternate sun and showers. Pouring down a little after five o'clock when we
were sitting talking about Nellie and the first thing we knew the door flew
and in walked the lady herself followed immediately by Aunt L. Buck—such
a delightful surprise. Aunt L. and Jacquie went home when it cleared off but
as for Nellie we have just had her singing and talking ever since she came
home without a moment's intermission. Dear old thing. She looks so well.
'Tis after eleven o'clock. Oh me, I'm so glad she's come home again.

[March 16, 1864, entry omitted]

April 20th, 1864

Ma quite unwell. Did not get through with my work til late. Felt unwell.
Mending Father's coat, cut out a pair of shoes for Frank. Grandma went to

Oakley, Aunt Betsie to Mr. Glasscocks. Reading "Woodstock." Cloudy in the evening. Listening to Nellie and Laura playing on the piano. Wythe Cook came in to bid us farewell as he goes tomorrow with Uncle Tom enroute for his brigade. Poor fellow! it really grieves me to see him, the last of our old social circle, going from us into this cruel work. He too, seems sad. Nellie and I played and sang for him and he left about ten o'clock. Mattie Cook dined with us too, she came to hear another story and I related "Opicciola" and "Rip Van Winkle."

April 30th, 1864

Very busy. Sweeping off the pavement when Dick Bayley came over to get me to go out with a fishing party to the river. Did not feel like it but they persuaded me and I had a pleasant walk. Found at the place of rendezvous Kate Greene, Mollie Barbee, Sallie Leech, Jennie Jackson, Sallie Petty, Charlie Barbee, Welton Greene, Allie Ashby, Henry Cooke, and a host of "lesser fry." Caught no fish of course. They would have been very daring fish who ventured to nibble a bite amid such a tumult as was kept up with tongues and oars. We soon wearied of fruitless sport and adjourned to the mill to weigh. I made out a hundred and thirteen pounds. From thence Dick took us out boat riding in detail. Sallie Leech and I were last—we sat on the grassy bank and gathered apple blossoms chattering like two magpies while Sallie's cavalier Charlie looked woefully on from a distance doubtless most jealous of my proximity to her. Had a delightful row in the boat firing a salute from Dick's revolver to the party on shore but a sudden shower cut our sports suddenly short—we landed and took refuge in the little veranda of Mr. Weston's sweet little cottage—tis my ideal of a home. . . . Found Ma out in the garden dropping seeds. Poor little Evred scalded his foot terribly—sitting before the fire a kettle of boiling water overturned on his right foot and took the skin off. His screams of agony were awful and twas some time before he experienced any relief but I held him in my arms and told him stories and finally he proclaimed himself ready to sit up and take some supper. Poor child! I'm afraid he's going to have a bad time of it. All were very tired tonight and twas some time before chaos reduced to order. I'm tired and sore enough tonight. Had a note from Jule and poor Tell was dead.

May 3rd, 1864

Better this morning but far from well. Commenced a pair of drawers for Evred. His foot is not so well this morning. Ma went to Oakley. Father and the boys digging in the cornfield trying to make us some bread for next year. Very gloomy day and the children, Evred and Frank, almost crazed me being confined to the house and so fretful. Dick Bayley over to say goodbye. Wrote Uncle John by him. Stole off upstairs in the afternoon and wrote a little while. . . .

May 6th, 1864

Father is very busy in the garden—has finished planting corn and now making great exertion to have every vegetable in the ground before another rain. The children have actually taken off their shoes and stockings, 'tis so very warm.

So many Yankee deserters passing constantly in squads.

May 9th, 1864

Jule better—up at breakfast. After washing the breakfast things we adjourned to the parlor and read the "Messenger," gossiped, sewed and played on piano til dinner time. Julie Hope up in the early afternoon to tell of the news that had just reached town—glorious news of a victory at Chancellorsville by our intrepid and peerless Lee! Poor Gen. Longstreet wounded though not seriously and Gen. Jones killed.[3] Just one year tomorrow since one of our brightest military stars paled and faded from our firmament—our noble Jackson went to his rest! So rejoiced are we at the good tidings and yet so anxious as to its individual result. An alarm of Yankees coming and Julia fled home. Seven of the enemy's cavalry did advance into town but made the visit brief. . . .

May 10th, 1864

Lovely. Up early and had everything nicely cleaned up. Went into the garden and gathered lilacs and into the porch reading and then with the girls into the garden again before breakfast. Lolling around generally after the things were cleaned up in the dining room. A report of 2,000 Yankee Infantrymen at the River en route for town—didn't come though—at least only a small squad to the hill near Rose Hill. . . .

May 12th, 1864

Raining. Cleaned up some time before breakfast. After breakfast in the parlor practicing and reading. Then upstairs writing an hour, then mending my calico dress and had just commenced making a pair of pantaloons for Carey when he ran in to say the Yankees were coming. There was, sure enough, a regiment of cavalry and we had a time pitching about trying to get things arranged for their reception. Seven of them came to get something to eat and informed us the whole army would soon pass through. Sitting upstairs this afternoon heard someone talking in a rude voice and going to the window found a Penn. Dutchman on horseback parleying with Father about corn to feed his horse with. Impudent churl! I was angry enough to shoot him when he tried to frighten Father into giving him the little corn he had saved for bread by telling him he would bring his whole company to search the whole house if he complied not with his demands. Father compromised by giving him some refuse feed for the fowls and the wretch chuckled gleefully over his success. About four o'clock they suddenly left town in a hurry, at least the greater number of them—some remained in camp and some went to Luray. Scarcely had they turned their backs on town before one of Mosby's officers rode up, then while upstairs writing to Scott in came Capt. Montjoy and four comrades to tea—we had come from the table and everything was in confusion so we had to go to work and fix the things on the board and in a great hurry. The soldiers had just commenced eating when Father called me out to reconnoiter the premises with him and suddenly a troop of little boys came from town to inform the Confederates that there were a hundred Yankees in town. We gave the alarm and they made the most rapid exit I ever saw from the dining room and mounting their horses rode in the direction from which the enemy were expected. Capt. M rode off to town and presently a troop of twenty came by and we waved and cheered them so heartily. Oh! I do hope as Mosby is here he will "hurt somebody" before he's done. Great excitement. Reaction tonight and I'm low spirited and tired. So "coming events cast their shadows before"? I wonder.

May 13th, 1864

Raining. Writing after breakfast. Making a pair of pants for the boys. Sitting upstairs all day writing and sewing. Father came in at noon and brought news of the advance on Staunton and sad news of the slaughter at Chancellorsville. Feel so sad—it seems as if the very air were rife with bloodshed and wailing. Oh the weary, weary days—when will they pass? . . .

May 14th, 1864

Raining hard. Restless and unsettled. Sitting upstairs all day doing work. Writing. Sallie Leech came over in the afternoon to apply for a home in person—poor child! We all of us feel so deeply for her and large as is our family and inconvenient as twill be to have an addition to it, we must take her and make her as happy as we can. Her father is to be married tomorrow evening to that hateful woman and they're all going to scatter wherever they can find homes. Tis one of the saddest cases I ever knew. Have read of such things but never witnessed anything of the kind before. To think she has already commenced management of his home and making him whip Ninian like a dog. Then for her to boast of how she's going to arrange things and above all things her great impudence. Tis enough to disgust anyone in the world.

I was very sad tonight. Have just heard that Lt. Wells was mortally wounded, poor fellow. Mr. Gold of Clarke with us. Saw prisoners who were captured by Mosby's men brought in today.

May 16th, 1864

. . . Annie, Minnie and Lizzie Leach over in the evening and told us all the sad tale. How it made my heart ache to see those pale delicate girls in their sombre robes standing and telling to strangers the story of their wrong. They are bitterly afflicted indeed. Did not eat supper, had not the heart. Got Frank to sleep and then sat on the front porch til Jule came home. Aunt Eliza came up after Cousin E Cloud's letters and I had to write her a note tonight. Ah me! My heart is so heavy. Jule and I have been sitting at the front window in our room looking at the moonbeams gilding the aspen leaves and sparkling the creek and talking about the stars. The quiet loneliness of the scene and the talk have done me so much good.

May 18th, 1864

Clear. Cleaning up Grandma's and the boys' rooms. Took my first lesson in whitewashing. Very busy. Father came in to give us some additional particulars of the battle. It must have been a most desperate one and poor Gen. Stuart was certainly killed.[4] Irreparable loss to us! Five of Baylor's men came in to get dinner and told a great deal about it—they said Rosser's Brigade repulsed three brigades of the enemy.

That old villain Dr. Leach actually had the bare-faced assurance to tell Father today that he would "shoot him" if Sallie were not returned to him within 24 hours. I can't find words to express my contempt for and detestation of him. Poor Sallie came home about noon. . . .

Just as she was leaving she received an imperative summons from her father to come over and have an interview with him and she left pale and trembling just as a terrible storm of wind and rain came up. Miss Lizzie had to dismiss school for several days til she could make some arrangements for herself. . . .

May 20th, 1864

Pleasant very. Doing job work. Ninian Leach over to say "Goodbye" preparatory to leaving for the Army—poor boy, he looked so young for such a rough, trying life.

May 22nd, 1864

Such a bright morning. Quite busy til after breakfast. Horace brought news of a skirmish between Mosby's cavalry and a body of Yankees picketing over the river. Went into the garden and gathered flowers to put in all the rooms. Then went upstairs and sat by the open window breathing the air heavy with the rich fragrance of the locust blossoms and listening to the birds and leaves and waters making music. Ma, Grandma, Father and I went to church. Heard Mr. Berry. Was told that a body of Yankees having heard Major Turner was at home, went to his house last night to search it and there was no one at home but Lucie and her protectress, Miss Roberts. How frightened she must have been! The major had taken the precaution to spend the night with a friend but the thieves got his watch and boots though he escaped himself. Conflicting rumors as to the skirmish at the river. . . .

May 23rd, 1864

Anniversary of the "Battle of Front Royal." Pleasant. Repairing my silk dress. Ma spending the day at Mrs. Roy's. Uncle Tom over in the afternoon and told us the Yankees, nine in number, had been in town in search of "rebels." Charlie Richardson *had* been there but was gone in time to elude them. Neville and Charlie down today. Lucie Jackson and Jessie Leach over after tea. Sang tonight; Laura and all of us.

May 26th, 1864

Damp and gray. Very unwell. Laid down a little while after breakfast with Frank and read Franklin's "Essays." . . .

May 28th, 1864

Unwell. Have eaten scarcely one full meal for a week. Ma, Grandma and Mrs. Moffatt walked down to the Forney's this morning. Put away the clean clothes and sent up to Mrs. Hope's for the muslin for my Garibaldi.[5] Cut it out and mended a pair of pants of Father's and just as I commenced sewing Nev. Buck and Cousin Tom Buck rode up. The latter would not dismount but sat talking in his own noisy fashion at the stile. He seems to think there is no doubt of the western army having come on to reinforce Lee at Richmond. Oh! If we could hear something definite. . . . Mrs. Moffatt came in looking agitated and said Ma had been taken very sick at Mrs. Wilkinson's and the wagon would have to be sent for her—just as I feared when she left this morning. Went into the garden and told Father, laid by my work to prepare things for her reception. Gave out tea for her and then had the water heated and bathed Frank and Evred. Still they did not come and I felt perfectly miserable—everything horrible suggested itself to me—perhaps Ma was too ill to come or they had started and she had fainted. Waited supper til nearly dark when the wagon drove up with Ma in it looking very pale but otherwise much herself. Very soon after Grandma and Nellie came in—the latter having at the river heard of Ma's indisposition and returned with Grandma. Oh! I'm so thankful that it's all no worse—my heart has been so heavy all the evening. Laura returned about the time that Ma did.

May 29th, 1864

Anniversary of Shield's second occupation of Front Royal and Jackson's retreat from Winchester and anniversary of poor Willie Richardson's death. I've been thinking of it so steadily. Within the garden a long time this morning gathering some of the abundance of exquisite roses there for the purpose of replenishing my vases. Father left quite early for town and after making my toilette read some. Then laid down and slept with Frank—felt very tired and weak having fasted so long. Ma lying about all day more languid and listless than I've seen her for a long time. . . . Left Father on the porch repeating an account of the battle which he had from Lt. Samuels and came up to my room. I felt deeply sad all day. Everyone seems to believe that our army as well as those of the enemy are massing at Richmond and that a most hideous and stupendous struggle is impending—if this be the case what vital interest we have involved in the issue, both nationally and individually—how entirely are we severed from all communication with the seat of war and in what suspense we must exist for the coming week till all is over. . . .[6]

May 30th, 1864

Quite cool. Up early at work. Went into the garden before breakfast to gather Sallie Leach a bouquet of roses. After breakfast Ma and Grandma went to bid Mrs. Childs goodbye and I sat in Grandma's room with the children writing. Ma returned about ten o'clock. Busy sewing. Very unhappy. So much confusion and Ma not well. In the afternoon Mrs. Keiger passed on horseback—just in from town bringing tidings from Washington of a glorious victory gained by Lee over Grant last Friday in which we captured a hundred pieces of cannon. So glad! Father brought us the news just as Ma and I were starting to Mrs. Hope's after tea. . . .

June 4th, 1864

Cool, but clear. Up later than usual. Tired—busy til late. Grandma went to Forney's and Riverside. Busy packing and making preparations all the morning. Wrote to Jule by Fettie who came down. A slight headache. Had a fright this afternoon—thought Evred was lost. Felt sad. Had a nice note from Jule. Tired and sad tonight. Have heard through Laura that Major Simpson was certainly dead and that General Cleburn had had a desperate fight and my heart ached for my poor Irvie as well as for Mrs. Simpson's family.

Chapter Seven

༾༾༾༾༾༾༾༾༾༾༾༾༾༾༾༾༾༾༾༾༾༾༾༾

Wish I Could Hear from Home

༾༾༾༾༾༾༾༾༾༾༾༾༾༾༾༾༾༾༾༾༾༾༾༾

June 7, 1864–August 26, 1864

June 7th, 1864

Up at four o'clock. Flying around as busy as could be til seven. Kissed little
Frank and Evred goodbye in their sleep. Thinking so much of what Cousin
Mary told me last night about poor E. Jacquie down to see us off and Uncle
Tom. Felt very sad at leaving. Met Aunt Bettie on the road and at Rose Hill
Ginnie and Cousin Lizzie and all of them out to see us. Father went with us
across the river and told us goodbye at Riverside. Had a charming ride—the
sweetbriars in the road were still sparkling with their morning dew bath and
looking so rosy and fresh while the perfume from the roses with the odor of
the grapevines was perfectly intoxicating. The horse moved with great spirits
and although the day was clear twas so cool that we did not have to hoist our
umbrellas. At one o'clock we stopped in a beautiful grove of trees and spread-
ing out our lunch had a most charming little picnic. Gathered mosses and
flowers while the horse was eating. Left in an hour and had a pleasant evening
ride. Did not meet a living soul from the time we left the river til we entered
Berryville and then a very few of them. Reached Bloomfield about six o'clock

and Cousin William met us at the wagon and conducted us into the house.[1] Found old Mrs. Allen and Miss Lucie there taking tea and Mrs. Pittman staying with Aunt Cattie while Miss Julia was at the store inquiring for their tobacco. Did not go into tea but was introduced to them afterwards. Fannie and her mother have not returned yet—so sorry. Felt less fatigue than I expected from my journey. Chatting tonight and Cousin Nellie playing some for us. Up in our room early. There are no Yankees in the neighborhood. I felt so thankful and am so grateful that we've gotten through this far safely. Mack's a great boy. Wonder who got little Frank to sleep tonight—dear little fellow.

June 9th, 1864

Gray and threatening. Mrs. and Miss Pittman left early. Played a game of checquers with Nev and beat him one game but he beat me twice. Cousin William and I then had a game which proved a drawn one. Went in and made off a memorandum and wrote a note for Aunt Cattie. Nev, Irvie, Aunt Cattie out and Uncle Larue went out to hear the news. Ma, Cousin Nellie and I had the day to ourselves. All returned at noon just escaping a heavy shower. Ma was all day trying to make arrangements for getting to the Ferry but they told her they were very strict there and dissuaded her from going. A showery evening. Mrs. Davis and Martha called to tell Ma the difficulties to be encountered in an excursion to Harpers Ferry. I was perfectly enamoured of Martha—she's so sweet and pretty. Quite a heavy shower this afternoon. Ma is making arrangements to go to Van Cleersville tomorrow and cousin Nellie is to go as far as Tudor Hall with her. Cousin William and Nellie playing for us tonight. Wish I could hear from home.

June 10th, 1864

Bright, but cool. The travellers off soon after breakfast. Had a message from some gentleman who passed the gate informing me he had brought us a letter from home, but not knowing he would come this road had left it in Berryville. So anxious to get it but see no chance of doing so. Mrs. Luke called and spent a couple of hours this morning. A report of the fall of Staunton but don't believe it. Altering my blue gingham dress. Was preparing to start to

Rippon this evening when old Mr. Paige came in saying there had been a squad of Yankees at his house during the day. So Aunt Cattie sent Francis with me as a "footman" and Walker and I had a glorious canter on old Saltman through the dim cool arches of the woods. Went to Mrs. Phillips and tried to learn some news but she had heard but little save the confirmation of rumors already heard. A woman had just come in and was telling us of a reported battle which had been fought by the Yankees with some of Mosby's men in which a Confederate officer, Captain Gleason was killed, when a rushing sound was heard and presently a squadron of Yankees dashed by. Francis flew out to protect the house. They did not molest anything though and passed on to join the main column just beyond. I started back to Bloomfield after they left and had to wait some time in Mrs. Davis' meadow for Francis to come up. While Saltman was browsing on the white clover, old Mr. Strother came out and chatted till F came. . . .

Talked Walker to sleep in the lounge. Occupied the little end room for the first time tonight—it's to be my domicile while I remain here.

June 12th, 1864

Very cold. Stupidly lounging about on the sofa all the morning trying to read. Went upstairs to take a nap—had nightmare six times and finally gave up in despair. Cousin George Carter in to dinner. Expected the travellers home but they are still non est. Got my letter today—a mere scrap but very welcome nevertheless. Mrs. Coyle brought it down. Cousin William asked me to walk in the park to see his wild geese and the deer. While there Walker found a little fawn only a day old—the prettiest most graceful little creature imaginable. . . .

June 13th, 1864

. . . Cousin William was sitting with me on the porch speculating as to the cause of the detention of our absentees and proposing to go after them tomorrow when he sprang to his feet with "Hist! I hear the sound of wheels" and then hurried off into the gathering shades of evening to look out for them. Presently Aunt Cattie came out and we heard them coming down the hill. Arrived all safe and well. Ma had been unable to accomplish anything by the trip both on account of scarcity of goods and difficulty of getting the check acknowledged. Was detained by news of a difficulty persons had in getting through. . . .

Commenced teaching Walker this morning.

June 14th, 1864

Damp and cool. Darning for Walker and teaching him. Reading and writing to Nellie and running about the house all the morning on errands. Old Mr. Van Meter in gathering roses. After dinner writing in my diary. . . .

June 16th, 1864

Pleasant. Busy sewing for Ma on the boy's shirts. In the afternoon Aunt Cattie and Ma rode down to Mrs. Van Meter's to see about sending to Harper's Ferry leaving Cousin Nellie and William and me in charge of the house. We closed the shutters of the chamber and betook ourselves to the parlor and Cousin N and I coaxed Cousin W to play on the violin while we sewed. Had scarcely gotten settled when Uncle L called me hastily into the passage and going to the front door saw two ladies standing there, and peering into the hat of the first lady caught the merry gleam of a pair of sparkling black orbs and a glitter of white teeth and to my immense surprise recognized Maggie Mohler—the very girl of all others in Page County I would like to see. She introduced the other lady as "Mrs. Long." They were accompanied by young paroled soldier, a Mr. Foreman. We invited them in, gave a round introduction and learned that they were "running the blockade" with tobacco and had been directed here by Mr. F, they having no acquaintances elsewhere in the neighborhood. . . .

June 17th, 1864

Very warm. Sat on the porch steps after breakfast and talked with Maggie and showed her some little bits of poetry which I thought she could appreciate. Heard quite a heavy cannonading in the direction of Martinsburg. Dr. Osborne came in—brought no news. Dogs fought and frightened me. When it became too warm for the porch we adjourned to the cool parlor and Maggie played and sang for us. Had some very nice lemonade. After dinner adjourned to our room for a nap which we however did not take as our tongues ran away with our fatigue and we talked as if for dear life till late in the afternoon. When did ever I say as much before in as short a time? Ma got hold of my COMMONPLACE BOOK and we had a review of it. Dressed before tea in time to go down and look for the fawn but although Ma, Mrs. Long, Maggie and Walker and I all spent some time searching for it, it was now gone. The others gave up the hunt and retired to the house but we two girls sat on the ledge of rocks and told our Leap Year's experiences. Mr. Foreman came in tonight while Mag was singing and playing for us. We came up to our rooms at ten o'clock and Ma and Mrs. Long went to bed but Maggie and I sat up reading letters when there was heard the clatter of hoofs on the road above the house. Our first impression was that the Yankees had come after Mr. Foreman and we were consulting as to what we should do for him when Cousin Nellie came in with a shawl around her to say she did not think they were Yankees. We looked so ridiculous all of us standing up on the floor with wild, staring eyes and disheveled tresses and certainly we would have been in no costume for receiving the Yankees. My first thought was for my daguerreotypes and letters which were in a drawer in another room of which I had misplaced the key. However, we soon found that they were Confederates who had come by to get Foreman to go on a scout with them. Captain James Bailey, Jim Williams and Webb Maddox and a Mr. Brown. We went over into the room adjoining Cousin Nellie's and looked out of the window beneath which they were standing and I thought Maggie Mohler would have made us all hurt ourselves laughing at her mischievous comments upon the conversation that ensued below. Cousin Nellie and I donned our wrappers and went down to get the gentlemen something to eat, and when it was prepared, nothing would do but we must go and peep through the curtain of the dining room window to see them eat. When they came out on the porch Maggie got her satchel of luncheon and pelted them with ginger cakes. They declared that 'twas the first country they had ever visited where it "rained gingerbread." They remained so long before starting on their scout that Ma and Mrs. Long went to bed but Maggie and I sat on the garret steps by the window in the moonlight and talked of everything. Poetry, theology comicalities, human nature and the usual themes of very young ladies generally. She has always possessed the greatest fascination for me—I can't account for it unless it be the influence of a stronger, brighter nature over a weaker, dimmer one. She has more depth and warmth of feeling than any casual acquaintance would suspect her of possessing. I do love her dearly.

June 18th, 1864

Had a slight headache upon awaking this morning. Went down to help Aunt Cattie as Dummy is sick. Mr. Foreman back to breakfast. Did not succeed in their scout last night. Aunt Cattie expected Mr. Edgar Allen to spend the evening with us and I had to replenish the vases in the parlors and attend to Delphi while she repainted the hearth. All of us went to the park and Cousin Will finally succeeded in finding the fawn much to Maggie's delight. About eleven o'clock we took a stroll into the garden and I made Mag a wreath of red roses which she declared made her look like a "calf looking through a rose bush." We came on the porch and Aunt C had some cherries for us—but my head ached badly and I was forced to lie on the trundle bed and Maggie undressed and took her place beside me and she copied while I read from my book and we discussed the pieces together. Presently Ma and Aunt Cattie and Mrs. Long came up and the merry girl kept us all laughing ourselves almost sick till the dinner bell surprised us in the midst of our fun. Did not go down to dinner and Mag soon finished hers and came back to her place by me. We read and talked all evening—some time all would be with us, some time we were alone. Aunt Cattie about four o'clock made me drink two cups of tea and go and lie down quietly a while till I felt better. In an hour's time I was ready to dress for the evening. We went into the parlor and commenced a game of draughts when Mr. Allen came in. I beat Maggie and gave her over to Mr. Allen who also beat her and then me too. Tea bell rang. After tea finished our game and then Maggie and Cousin Nellie sang and played. I escaped this duty upon plea of headache. Mr. A left about ten o'clock and we soon afterward came upstairs but not to bed for Maggie and I sat up till twelve o'clock in our room talking earnestly save when her irrepressible mischief brimmed over into words and glances ever and anon. Ah! Well, the two past days have been happy ones—it is so pleasant to have someone to talk cordially and freely with as I can with this singularly fascinating being.

June 19th, 1864

Still warm. Sat on the porch after breakfast and then Maggie and I went to pay Dumb Mary a visit. She and Eliza seemed glad to see us and showed us all their little possessions. We then went to the garden where we sat under the "snowballs" on the grass making wreaths and talking seriously and Maggie sadly until the dinner bell rang. After dinner Maggie proposed going under the beautiful horse-chestnuts in the front yard. We took a knife and carved our names on the trunk, then sat on the grass till Aunt Cattie called us to come away lest we should take cold. We went upstairs and lay on the bed and fairly talked ourselves to sleep. Mrs. Long soon aroused us and said they must be going. It really gave me the blues to see them preparing to start—Maggie seemed almost as sorry to go. They will go to the Foreman's tonight and on to the store tomorrow, and will return here on their way home. I made them leave some of their clothing as hostage. . . . Reading in Testament. All of us tired and sleepy and retired early.

June 21st, 1864

One of the first things I thought of this morning was that this was the anniversary of our poor Walter's fall. All day the recollection haunted me, making me so sad when I thought how

> "One that I loved grown faint with strife
> When dropped and died the tender bloom
> Folded the white tent of his life
> For the pale Army of the tomb."

I know Nellie was thinking with me of our loved and lost and wanted so much to talk with her.

. . . Felt so unwell that I had to go to bed in the afternoon. Mr. Allen in to confirm the good news. Very unwell tonight.

June 24th, 1864

Ma has concluded to go with Mrs. Van M to Harper's Ferry tomorrow. Busy making preparations. She wrote to Cousin M Woodson and I to Charlie and

Mac to send through flag of truce. Very tired and sleepy tonight. Warm weather is pleasant but so enervating.

June 25th, 1864

Up by four o'clock and Ma and Walker mounted Saltman and left quite early for Mrs. Van M's. Cleaning up the rooms and putting away clean clothes, then reading and writing till breakfast. . . . Sewing steadily and finished Eliza's dress early. Was in the garden making a wreath for my hair when Walker called me in to say there was a note from home. Twas from Father—very brief but most welcome for it brought us tidings of both Alvin and Irving— the former in Petersburg, the latter in Georgia. There was a letter from Uncle John—poor Wythe Cook and Jimmie Brown are wounded and Cousin Mount is with his command again and General Rosser is reported dead. Ah, me!

. . . Have felt so uneasy about Ma all day. The fatigue and heat may make her sick or they may force upon her that horrid oath. Do wish I could hear from her.

June 26th, 1864

So warm. Up and dressed early. Thinking of Ma first thing. Cousin Wm. informed us at the breakfast table that he had heard of their safe arrival at Mrs. Van M's last night. Visited the sick and helped Aunt Cattie and took my Bible on the porch but the flies and heat drove me to the sofa in the parlor. Had not been there very long when Ma came. Was so glad to see her all right again. She seemed not to regret having gone in the least as they did not propose the oath at all, not even questioning her. Chatted on the porch and went upstairs and undressed. Dr. Osborne in to tell us of Fannie LaRue's return from N. York. So glad. She'll be here now, I hope. A week today since Maggie left.

July 2nd, 1864

Rather cooler. . . . Mr. Thompson came in to tea and then Mr. Sidney Allen and both affirmed the news which we had for several days past been hearing of the advance of an army. Some of the young men from the neighborhood had already come in and reported EARLY twenty thousand strong marching upon Martinsburg. So enraptured to hear it! If Beauregard just be coming with Alvin now it would be too much glory. . . .

July 3rd, 1864

Pleasantly cool. Awoke quite early and Uncle LaRue came out in the yard and called out to me to listen to the cannonading. Sure enough discharge after discharge was heard. There was a cessation about nine o'clock but the firing was soon after resumed and more violently than before. Writing and reading. Perry quiet and very pleasant. Was lying down upstairs about twelve o'clock when the door opened and in marched Fannie LaRue. So glad to see her. She heard that the firing was at Smithfield beyond Berryville—A diversion to deceive the Yankees as to Early's real intent. . . .

July 4th, 1864

We have Harper's Ferry, thank Heaven.

July 5th, 1864

The Yankees have still possession of Maryland Heights.

July 6th, 1864

An invitation came from Mrs. Van M this morning for Ma and me to accompany her to the Ferry. Delighted by the idea. Repaired ourselves, took a hasty breakfast, mounted old Saltman and rode down to her house. She did not get the wagon she expected and could not take us both. Ma insisted on my going. A young Reb by the name of Moore drove us. Enjoyed the drive but wished much for Ma. After passing Charlestown we came in view of the Heights about the ferry and I had enough to do looking at them, tracing the road winding like silver tracery up the sides of the green purple mountain and the white tents of the Yankee Camp about the summit, and thinking of all the various incidents connected with this classic ground of our ———— history. There was still some firing and as we reached Hall Town a few miles this side of the ferry we met numbers of soldiers who warned us against venturing into the place telling us that the Yankees were shelling it and had already killed several ladies and torn the arms off a little infant in one of the doomed houses. Indeed, they had thrown shells into Hall Town itself. Each one we met told us the same story. Finally when we were within three miles of the ferry we met a surgeon who told us we were already further than was prudent, but on we went till met by a squad of Rebs direct from there and they told us there was momentarily expectation of an attack as the Yankees were said to be heavily reinforced and advancing to cross the river. We concluded "discretion was truly the better part of valor" and turned about to the house of an acquaintance of Mrs. Van M. Found a little musical box in the parlor and amused myself playing on it. About noon squads of Rebs commenced dropping in for dinner. There was a loquacious young North Carolinian who proceeded to acquaint me with the "situation."—We have but one brigade there—Hokes—it seems. . . . About three o'clock it was currently reported that the Yankees were advancing to the attack in heavy force and that if they did so our men would have to evacuate the place. So the wagons which could not be gotten out were arranged in close phalanx filled with fine new axes and harness and saddles—hay was spread all around them and the Quartermasters stood awaiting the order to fire them. The order, however, did not come and when we left after four o'clock our sharpshooters were said to be crossing over to attack the Yankees and there was heavy cannonading heard from the Yankees on South Mountain. Had a pleasant ride home and met, to my great surprise, with Dr. Turner on the pike and heard from home. Was really glad to see him—he expects, I believe, to go home tonight. It was dark nearly when we reached Mrs. Van M's and looking back towards the ferry we saw two large fires near the Yankee camp in the mountain, and they were sending up rockets from there. Wonder what it all means. Found Uncle Alex waiting for us with horses and we rode immediately on home. Found the parlor brilliantly lighted and Maggie and Mrs. Long and Fannie there— so glad to see them. Felt very dusty and heated but washed and arranged my dress, drank a glass of milk and went into the parlor to hear Maggie sing and tell some of the adventures that befell them. They've been consistently successful in obtaining all they wished and seem really to have enjoyed themselves. When we came up to our room we three girls undressed, put on our night-robes and laid on the floor till after twelve o'clock chattering. Old Mr.

Taylor had just come in late as it is. They say our vanguard is at Gettysburg and Early's headquarters are at Boonsboro.

July 7th, 1864

Slept late and woke with a headache in consequence of late hours last night. . . . Ma and Aunt C and I were invited to spend the day at Mrs. Davis'. I had the headache so badly that they concluded to go by themselves and send back for me after I should have taken a nap and refreshed myself. The horse came a little after eleven and Walker and I had a pleasant ride over. Enjoyed the day very much despite the oppressive heat. . . . Found Cousin Mary reclining on the sofa in the parlor overcome with the ride. They had brought us a bundle of papers and letters and Ma and I sat on the porch steps and read the welcome missives then and there. One from dear Nellie to me telling about the children being sick and poor thing I know she's had a time of it with them. Then there were three from Irvie and one from Alvin—written, all of them, in good spirits. It was almost too much joy getting them all at once though. Nellie's was not near long enough. She sent me "Macaria" a novel too and I'm so glad of it. . . .

July 11th, 1864

We were invited to spend the day at Mr. Luke's. . . . All dinner parties are stupid and this was no exception to the general rule, though twas not *quite* so bad as I had anticipated. Mr. and Mrs. Luke are so kind that they will make you enjoy yourself. They had a sumptuous dinner and for dessert there was frozen custard and cream, a thing which I've not seen before since the War. There seemed to be a universal headache prevailing in the afternoon. Had a pleasant drive home in the twilight, found Cousin James going about and apparently "all right." Ma's not going tomorrow. So glad of the respite.

July 13th, 1864

Ma left quite early. Felt so sad about her going that I took a good cry instead of my breakfast. Felt stupid and unwell all day. Cousin Kate and Cousin James left in the afternoon for Tudor Hall.

Sitting on the porch in the moonlight thinking of home and the happy faces then brightening at Ma's arrival. Old Mr. Taylor came in and said twas reported that our army was falling back to this side of the river. Don't believe it though.

July 14th, 1864

Warm and bright. . . . Heard that Early was shelling Washington City at a great rate.[2] Coming home had some laughable encounters with Cousin James' old acquaintances—family servants. Helped Cousin James drive up some young colts. Did not get home till after supper. Reading "Dollars and Cents." Francis sick.

July 16th, 1864

Still so sick. Living a most indolent miserably useless life today—not well enough to be up or sick enough to be in bed. Writing to Alvin out on the porch this afternoon. . . . I suppose we're to be given up to the Yankees again sure enough for our army is leaving the Potomac. Wonder what it all means—this short and bloodless campaign in Maryland and the present return of the forces to Leesburg. General Early has an object in it, no doubt, and fully understands all he intends to do. Wish I did too. Saw some beautiful little rabbits.

July 17th, 1864

Pleasant quiet morning. No one in this morning save old Billie Galloway. Read two sermons aloud to Aunt Cattie and read in the Bible myself. Went upstairs to lie down and on coming down to dinner found six soldiers there on the porch who had come in to dinner. They belonged to Early—Hoke's Division—and the army was all coming back in this direction. We were so surprised but had not long to indulge our astonishment for the poor fellows kept thronging in for their dinner and it required all our united efforts to supply them. I washed dishes, went to the garden for onions—sliced these and carried pickles from the cellar to the dining room all the afternoon. Had fifty in to dinner and then after a short respite there were ten more in for tea.

Major Thornton, Dr. Bizzel, a captain on Early's staff, and a couple of young Marylanders and a young lieutenant were really the only fairly civilized specimens of humanity that we had. . . . Am really tired out.

July 18th, 1864

Soldiers in bright and early for breakfast. Down before breakfast helping Cattie. . . . Darning socks for the soldiers. Dr. McM. in to dinner and a number of others beside. Busy feeding the Rebs till three o'clock—then played and sang some for the doctor. Then wrote a little and finally put on my riding habit to accompany Cousin Kate and Cousin James by invitation down to Rippon. Had a pleasant ride, transacted our business and started home just before sunset. Heavy cannonading in direction of Castleman's Ferry. They say the Yankees have crossed to this side of the river and are charging our batteries on the mountain. We could see the folds of heavy smoke clinging about the mountain gorges and all the way home through the dim woods in the shadowy twilight the heavy boom of the cannon fell like the voice of Doom. Twas dusk when we reached home and Cousin James and Kate went on to Mr. Luke's, and we sat on the porch tired and dispirited for all seemed to think our army will have to retire up the valley if the Yankees advance. Oh, me! Whither are we tending, I wonder. Old Hunter has burned Andrew Hunter's home in Charlestown.

July 19th, 1864

Not all the soldiers gone yet. Seventeen came in for breakfast. Aunt Cattie laid down about nine o'clock and I performed divers little jobs and finally sat down to writing. Soldiers in frequently during the day and among them a poor sick fellow who remained till the afternoon. . . . I heard that the army was falling back and Cousin James took a sudden fancy to fall back with it, so after dressing this evening I went to work and wrote home and finished my letters to Alvin to send to Warren by him. . . .

Memorable day for Bloomfield.[3] Last night just after Cousin Mary and I were comfortably ensconced in bed we heard Cousin James come home from Mr. Luke's and Cousin Kate said something about his leaving before day in the morning as the army was certainly falling back. Cousin Mary and I both had left our letters unfinished and concluded to get up and complete them, make up our budget and give it to Cousin James right away. Stole across to Cousin Kate's chamber and got a light and there we sat in our night dresses on the floor writing away as if for dear life. Finished and I carried the package across the passage and laid it on the desk for Cousin James in the morning. We couldn't go to sleep. The dogs barked so and Cousin Kate was flitting about in the moonlight like a restless ghost—poor thing—while Cousin William and Cousin James were constantly moving up and downstairs. I was up a half dozen times looking out the windows to see if the Yankees were not coming. Finally about midnight I dropped into a doze which was broken by Aunt Evelyn coming in with a candle to get something for Cousin Nellie who she said was sick. Felt very uneasy and did not sleep until nearly day. Was up by five o'clock and downstairs to see Aunt Cattie whom I found quite unwell. She got up though and very soon Cousin James left. Dr. Osborne and Mrs. Luke were sent for and soon came in—and when Aunt Cattie sent for Cousin Mary and me to take a private breakfast Cousin Kate met us on the staircase and told us Cousin Nellie had an "immense daughter." Was so glad she seemed to be doing so well. Spent a quiet morning. Went up to see the stranger—a very fine specimen of infantile femininity. Repairing Aunt C's riding skirts all morning while she tried to take a nap. Had a glorious rain in the afternoon and got myself nicely "ducked" putting Aunt Cattie's flowers out for the benefit of the shower. Finished my work and went upstairs to writing and job work. Heavy cannonading all evening in direction of Bunker Hill. Mr. Sidney Allen and Mrs. Luke to tea. Latter remains tonight.

July 20th, 1864

Aunt Cattie quite unwell. Cousin Mary too. Mending shoes—making needle books. Old Mr. Lee in this morning to tell us that the Yankees had burnt his house and he and his family were at Mr. G. Pendleton's houseless and without any of this world's goods at all scarcely. Poor old man. He wanted Nellie LaRue but I'm afraid won't get it. Faulkner's, Butlers, Dr. Byington, Dr. Tanner, Mr. Huntley and Mrs. ——— ——— houses are all said to have been burnt and this dense smoke that fills the air seems to indicate that the work of destruction continues. Father of Mercy, where is this all to end?

Mrs. Luke left this morning and we all spent a good portion of the day in Cousin Nellie's room. She continues quite well and the baby decidedly improving. Mrs. Luke back tonight. All sorts of rumors from our army but none reliable. . . .

July 21st, 1864

The nurse Cousin Nellie had engaged—Ann Eliza—came this morning. Aunt C and Cousin M still complaining. Dr. Osborne said the other day there was a letter at his house for some of us and we expected him to bring it but he didn't and was rude when we asked him about it that in a fit of indignation I begged Aunt C to *let me* ride down to Rippon and let me get it. After some hesitation with regard to Yankee troops passing up the road she consented. Called at Mrs. Van M. but the girls were away from home. Mrs. Osborne met me at the stile and gave me a package telling me at the same time that an ambulance train had passed down last night with four hundred wounded en-route for the Ferry, said wounds having been inflicted they said in Loudoun. And a large baggage train had gone up in direction of Yankee Army. Our troops were supposed to be somewhere in direction of Front Royal. Was afraid to open the package on the pike, but we turned off into the woods, I unfastened it and found within a paper of the 12th, the ———— for Uncle L and in the envelope directed to me was a letter from Ma, one from Nellie and one from Nannie to me, besides one from Ma to Aunt Cattie and a note from Nellie to Cousin Mary. I was so overjoyed, so bewildered with my good fortune that I scarce could sit on my horse, but for all that made out to read them before returning home. . . . Attending to Cousin Nellie and the baby after tea. My letters have made me almost wild but I begin to want more already.

July 24th, 1864

Mr. Page, Mr. Luke and Mr. Senter in. Latter brought good news, our army again in this vicinity—Early had whipped the Yankees near Winchester and driven them back to the Potomac. Mulligan certainly mortally wounded. So delighted. Dr. Blackham in to tea. Beautiful evening. Cousin Mary had letters from her ma. Poor Emma!

Had a sad dream about poor dear Walter and Alvin last night. Poor boys!

[July 31, 1864, entry omitted]

August 1st, 1864

. . . Spent a pleasant day chatting and reading and watching the soldiers passing. Had an immense glass bowl of frozen custard placed on a stand in the parlor after dinner and we ate our satisfaction of the cooling refreshment. Went upstairs to lie down and read "Henry St. John. Gentleman" when Nellie came up to say Bettie Moore was down there on the porch. Went down and chatted with her awhile and then Mr. Allen rode up. Bettie left before tea but the latter remained until bed time. The Army is *not* falling back.

August 5th, 1864

Soldier here getting provisions for hospital in Winchester.

[August 7, 1864, entry omitted]

August 10th, 1864

Oppressively warm this morning. Heard before breakfast that the Yankees had been up to Mrs. James LaRue's yesterday and captured Arnette and were advancing on Winchester and I supposed Cousin James was cut off from returning home.

Had such a sweet dream last night. Felt nervous and badly all day. Uncle L carried Cousin James' clothes over to him and the latter soon left. Sent out a letter home by him. Old Mr. Lee in a little while this morning.

Was sitting in Aunt Cattie's room after dinner when a loud Hallow was heard and Aunt Cattie went to the porch just in time to see a Yankee dash up to the little front gate. He instantly ordered her to bring that horse (Saltman was grazing in the yard with his saddle on) out to him in the most peremptory manner. She, as peremptorily, refused and by this time Uncle L came out and the wretch then commanded him to bring it out. In answer to this Uncle L deliberately led the horse around the corner of the house and Aunt C told the Yankee she thought it was too impudent in him to talk to her in that style— if he got the horse he would have to come after it and he shouldn't have it then either for twas *her* horse and he shouldn't have it. With this the cutthroat flung the gate open and dashed up the gravel walk shouting "D——n you, I'll shoot you and the horse too" while he brandished his pistol in a frightful manner. Seeing Uncle L leading the horse away he ordered him to stop and with an oath that made me shudder he cocked his pistol and aimed at him vowing he would shoot him down and so determined and blood-thirsty the villain looked I was sure that he would carry his threat into execution and closed my eyes to shut out the dreadful scene. Uncle L was as bold as a lion though and resisted to the last. The villain even tried to ride over him and knocking his hat off his head endeavoring to fell him with a blow of his pistol on the head. A scuffle ensued in which it seemed as if Uncle L must be killed and Aunt Cattie called for Cousin Will who was upstairs with Cousin M to come down and protect his father. He came down and with Cousin M and me in the passage Cousin N was afraid for him to go out and entreated him not to show himself as he would augment the disturbance and at last grasped his coat to detain him. Both were pale as ghosts and I felt that my face was but a reflection of theirs. He broke from her and rushed out explaining to the Yankee that the horse was blind in one eye—still the caitiff persisted saying he was ordered to bring to headquarters all horses found with saddles on them.[4] Uncle L was the best man though and carried the horse off to the garden leaving the Yankee swearing that he would report him to Headquarters. I never was so alarmed in my life for I was sure the fellow looked as if shooting a man would be an interesting amusement to him. After he went away I went upstairs to sit with Cousin Nellie and wash and dress. Had just completed this operation when a great slamming and locking of doors brought me downstairs and they told me the Yankees were coming and just as it commenced pouring down rain three of them rode up and demanded something to eat. One of them, a tiny, beardless boy, was spokesman and very saucy after satisfying his appetite he turned his attention to some colts in the park and proposed going out and getting them. They found out they were unbroken colts and impracticable and they then chased the deer, and finally ended the entertainment by running after the geese and knocking them on the head with their pistols, killed four of them. It was so provoking. The Infantry were in camp in the Page's yards and we had a benefit of all the stragglers that passed. We had to keep up a perfect system of picketing on the porches to watch lest they should steal something. They applied—numbers of them—for milk and butter and were refused upon plea of having none to spare. Upon sending down to get milk and butter for tea it was discovered they had broken in the back window of the spring house and rifled it of its contents. Such confusion, such excitement! I was almost crazy. Uncle LaRue had imprudently left Saltman in the garden instead of the cellar where Cousin May and I begged him to put her and about bedtime twas discovered that she had been stolen through the back of the garden. I could have cried to think of them getting the poor little pony particularly after Uncle L having struggled so for her. The baby was better tonight and the excitement and fatigue and exposure to damp air has brought on such a miserable headache that I can scarce breathe. Oh, me!

August 11th, 1864

Oppressively warm. Had a miserable night last night—so sick and nervous—not much better this morning. Dressed and took a cup of coffee and heard Walker's lesson then laid on the sofa in the parlor. Uncle LaRue finds he has lost a half dozen of his sheep and one hog and I think has come off pretty well considering all things. . . . Felt so wretched all day—in the late afternoon Fannie L surprised us by coming in in a state of excitement to say she had been obliged to come up from her aunt's on business and a Yankee had halted her and when she refused to do so fired twice at her. . . . The Corps that passed us was Sheridan's and I would not be surprised if Lee's army comes through the valley again this summer and if so they will seem dear friends to home. I felt almost crazy today at times when I do think of home and remember how completely I was cut off and no prospects of Mr. Taylor's coming now either.

August 12th, 1864

Much better this morning. Quite busy making a Garibaldi this morning. Baby not well all day and Fannie nursing it a great deal. Fannie and I went up to our room this afternoon and lying on the bed had a merry time reading aloud and talking to each other. Took a walk after tea, visited the Clenobs—house, and played and sang. Heard a great rumbling of Yankee wagons on the pike tonight. Feel anxious to hear what it means. Hope Mosby is after them and will take them by surprise just to spite them for taking away all our butter and condemning us to dry bread for four days. Lovely night.

August 13th, 1864

Was awakened by Fannie coming to my bedside and bidding me listen to the cannonading. Sure enough there were sound of artillery and small arms firing coming up through the still morning air. After breakfast heard that Mosby *had* pitched into a train of 150 wagons going up to the army and taken them from the Yankees and sending them off barehanded. Old Mr. Lee in a little while. Aunt Cattie not very well and quite busy helping her keep house. Writing some in the morning, and then Fannie and I with the assistance of Izaac and Cousin Will erected a seat in our bower and made it look beautiful. . . .

August 15th, 1864

Felt stupid and badly. . . . Aunt C had me helping her take a comb of honey a while after tea and then Cousin May and I walked out to find Fannie. She did not come back till near dusk and as we walked home she told us there was a rumor of Longstreet being at Fisher's Hill. Oh! My prophetic heart! Want to go home!

August 17th, 1864

. . . Old Mr. Taylor came in to a late supper and told us he was unable to return home today, the Yankees had fallen back to Berryville and infested the place refusing ingress and egress to all. So distressed about not getting my letters. Preserved some blackberries for Aunt Cattie today.

August 18th, 1864

Damp and grey. Went down with my wrapper on to see Aunt Cattie quite early. She was well and I went into the bath. Cousin M better. There was a Yankee to breakfast, quite a civil being he proved to be. Raining in torrents all morning. Was upstairs visiting when Fannie came up to say the

Yankees were searching the servants' rooms. Down I went and found they had searched under their beds and in to all their little boxes for Government property and ended by demanding Alex's money, knife and comb out of his pocket and Aunt Evelyn's clothing and all of Dan's money. They then rode away without deigning to enter the house. They had not been very long gone when three cavalrymen rode in to the front gate and up to the porch where we sat. One of them remarked in an insolent tone "I want to search this house,"—upon which Fannie stepped forward and inquired: "By whose authority?" One of them, a pert little stripling, answered "By authority of this officer," pointing to one of his comrades as he spoke. *Officer* indeed!— No more officer than Fannie herself. In they came and the little malapert commenced upon Aunt Cattie's dresser drawers, running his fingers into the little memorandum books and spool and work boxes for "Government Property!"—"arms" and "rebels." Aunt C had neglected to conceal a little casket of jewelry belonging to Aunt Millie and slipping it out of the drawer handed it to Fannie to carry away. The wretch must have seen her in the glass for wheeling about just as she reached the door he shouted "What's that you're carrying off there? Bring it here!" Not heeding him she hurried on through the hall and he went after her trying to grasp it out of her hand. She resisted and he raged threatening her in a loud voice at last drawing his pistol and taking deliberate aim he swore he would shoot her if she did not deliver it. She never quailed but facing him with her back to the parlor door held the casket behind her refusing even to let him see it lest he should wrest it from her. He then fired his pistol or rather snapped a cap right full in her face without producing any impression. Rushing forward he attempted to gain possession of the coveted box and a rough hand to hand scuffle ensued in which Fannie dealt the miscreant such a blow as sent him reeling from her. The soi disant officer who with his companion had been an amused spectator of this scene now came forward to interfere.[5] Telling Fannie that she had better be quiet about the matter and if she would let him just notice if the box contained nothing contraband he would release her. She had told him previously that there was only some trinkets of a dead friend but to prevent further annoyance she hastily flung the lid open and giving merely a glimpse of its contents marched triumphantly off with her treasure. The wretches showed conclusively that they were looking for booty, money and the like for they did not so much as look into any place where there was any possibility of concealing arms and rebels but drawers and trunks and desks were ransacked.

Going upstairs they noticed Cousin Nellie's immense traveling trunk standing in the hall near her door. This immediately attracted their attention and they demanded it to be opened. They were told it belonged to a sick lady but it mattered not who the owner was and they were evidently skeptical of the invalid. To convince them the door of her room was thrown open and there was Dummie with the little infant on her lap just in the act of bathing it. Fannie warned them against venturing into the room lest the "little rebel" should have some design against them. She called them poltroons and the little imp who had been most forward all the time told her if she persisted he would burn the house just as soon without as with orders.[6] They were informed that she was not an inmate of the house only a visitor from New York. They immediately wanted to know what a New Yorker could be doing here and were informed she had come down on a visit. Something was said about her being in Middletown and they immediately mistook it for Middletown, Virginia and told her with fiendish delight that she had not a roof to her head as they had burnt M and would burn Berryville and Winchester too. One even went so far as to say B had been already destroyed. Finally, after a deal of impudence from them they departed having found nothing they thought worth taking in the way of money or jewelry thanks to our foresight and their footsteps had not grown cold on the threshold before two Yankees were after the white mare in the park which Cousin Will had protected and cherished so carefully. Off he went through the falling rain and Fannie, unwell as she was, after him. After divers fruitless efforts the horse was at length secured and Fannie not being able to do anything in the park came out on the road near the carriage house endeavored to twitch the bridle out of the Yankees hand. Both of the wretches endeavored to ride over her but she sprang into the carriage house door and picking up a rock struck the wretch a telling blow on the shoulder with it. He was angry but the captured colt was restive and he hadn't time to give vent to his anger. There was a half hour's truce during which time and indeed all the morning they were pouring in in squads. They said Mosby's having taken their wagon trains had cut off their supplies and they were starved. Some of them were civil and offered to pay. Others and the majority of them finished eating and went right out to the park to take the seven young colts grazing there. Some would ask for milk and butter and Fannie very cordially invited them down to the spring house that they might help themselves—the milk and butter had previously been removed to a place of safety and the door flung wide for observation.

About twelve o'clock they commenced swarming in by myriads—dirty, barefooted wretches and the first thing was to break the iron bars of the meat house window and climbing up on each other's shoulders enter the place and pitch out the meat—ten or twelve pieces and proceed, some of them, to devour it raw. Two pieces fell into a dark corner and these Uncle LaRue and I discovered and slipping around secured and brought into the house and hid. Then while this robbing was going on others were scampering like madmen over the yard and through the porches after the fowls till the whole air for hours was sounded with cries of the poor geese, turkeys, ducks and chickens. They got all the geese and turkeys save the old gobbler and a little wild turkey and nearly all the chickens and ducks. One old rooster they pursued for a half hour straight ahead and Fannie and I stood on the porch and laughed at him, she remarking that if he only would pursue a rebel with as much pertinacity he might stand some chance of catching him. The fellow sullenly replied that he did not care for the rooster and he had seen the rebs run as fast as the rooster ever did. "Yes," replied F "You looked over your shoulder." All this while there was an excessive fire of musketry going on and we knew the sheep and hogs were suffering for it. Dinner was not to be thought of for the imps thronged the kitchen and stole the food from the fire where it was cooking. Presently Delphie ran to me for the key to the cellar press and going down with it as fast as I could I found two miserable wretches had already broken the doors down and were running their fists down into my nice preserved blackberries and raspberries and Aunt C's pickles. They had not finished searching when Aunt Cattie and I got there and laid hands on a box of candles on an upper shelf. Aunt C insisted on their not removing it as it contained nothing to eat but the ringleader swore he would see in it so I said to Aunt C "Do let him have some tallow candles—no doubt he can digest them." The fellow turned on me with a scowl and said savagely "Don't want to eat none o' yer candles." As the wretch was stooping down to carry his investigations further I noticed an immense excrescene on either side of his back bone showing through the folds of his loose flannel shirt, which I at first imagined to be a natural deformity but the bump commenced a bitter struggling and kicking and proved itself to be a captive duck which had been consigned to his novel haversack. I could not help laughing angry as I was. After rifling the press they insisted on breaking into the other part of the locked cellar, but we diverted their attention and succeeded in getting rid of them. Coming up out of the cellar I found Cousin W leading old Fan the last riding horse up to the house and Fannie and I concluded to put her in the cellar. It was the longest time before we could succeed in eluding the Yankees so as to lead her through the kitchen and back into the cellar. A couple of Yankees caught a glimpse of us as it was and almost hurt themselves laughing at the experiment. Providence seems to protect the horse for they did not break into the back cellar though repeatedly in the act of doing so and did not find in the house the bacon and other supplies concealed there. When remonstrated with in regard to their depredations their invariable reply was, "This is nothing to the way the Rebs did in Maryland." False cravens! They wanted honey and threatened and coaxed for it. Finally two or three of them proceeded to make a raid on the ice-house where the bee stands were. Uncle L very quietly walked up to the door sill and mildly suggested the propriety of evacuating the place. They answered him with oaths and jeers and he took his cane and punched into the hives stirring up the little laborers most unmercifully. Then he retreated while the Yankees enraged at the coolness of the proceedings as well as the stings of the bees—

August 20th, 1864

Felt unwell and blue. Went upstairs to write. Helped Aunt C. hide her meat and blankets. Mrs. Van M came in just from up valley. Told of Longstreet's corps being between here and Front Royal and of a battle near F. R.[7] Our troops only ten miles from here. It almost set me crazy to hear of it. Went upstairs to take a cry but Fannie danced me in her arms and got me in a good humor. Sidney Allen and Edgar here—latter brought late newspapers. Had a great romp with F in the parlor. Mr. Taylor brought my letters—one from Ma, Cousin Mack, Scott and Benton. It almost crazed me. Had no appetite at all for my supper.

August 21st, 1864

Heavy cannonading all day. Yankees driven out of Berryville and Fannie and I went over to Clifton to see the soldiers pass. Had a great many Rebs to supper. Sixth Regiment suffered severely but no friends hurt. Longstreet's coming!

August 23rd, 1864

Very unwell. Went to bed about eleven o'clock. Cousin Mary unwell too. Tom Conrad spent the day here. Had a chill and fever. Cousin James came. Said something indefinite about Ma's starting down which raised me off my bed. Went down and met Chris Larue. He told he'd seen Alvin a short time since and that he spoke of coming home. Just then they said the wagon was coming and sure enough there was Ma and Orville. Was almost wild with delight at seeing them. Tom C left but returned after dark. When Ma told me I must get well because Alvin was at home I felt as if I should faint. And General Anderson and Longstreet's old staff—Major Latrobe and all. Cousin Mae in bed and I very unwell but so happy.

August 26th, 1864

Had a nervous spell last night and very unwell this morning but the thought of dear Alvin and home nerves me to make effort to come and I stood it better than could have been expected. The children met us beyond the mill and then Alvin and Nellie at the barn. Almost broke down at the meeting with all the dear ones. Alvin is thin but so natural and so cheerful and all the rest seem just as usual save that Frank is grown more saucy and intelligent than ever.

At home once more and now I feel like I could be perfectly contented.

August 27, 1864

Cool and bright. Got up and went around. Played and sang for Alvin, all went in the garden to gather grapes and finally I went to bed with another chill and fever. Got up in the afternoon and crept downstairs but tonight felt weak and when Alvin came to the sofa where I lay and kissed and caressed me I had to cry like a baby. Dear, dear fellow!

Chapter Eight

❧❧❧❧❧❧❧❧❧❧❧❧❧❧❧❧❧❧❧❧❧❧❧❧❧

Given Up into the Hands
of Our Foes

❧❧❧❧❧❧❧❧❧❧❧❧❧❧❧❧❧❧❧❧❧❧❧❧❧

September 1, 1864–April 15, 1865

September 1st, 1864

All went to spend the day at Oakley save Laura and myself. Nellie returned home to dinner. Tried to write to Scott but was too weak and unwell. There was an alarm of the approach of Yankees and after Alvin and Cousin Mack came home we persuaded them to go on up to the "Mountain" to spend the night. Tis too provoking to have the boys go off when there's no earthly foundation for such report.

September 2nd, 1864

The boys away all day. Alvin J. T. Petty and Cousin Mack in to tea and after tea Mrs. Moffatt walked up to invite us spend tomorrow evening at Mrs. Hope's. While sitting on the porch all of us laughing and talking a soldier walked up and inquired if Captain Irvin Buck's father resided here. He introduced himself as Lieutenant Crittenden late of Claiborne's staff and we welcomed him as a fellow officer of Irvie's—though it has been two months since he saw Irvie. Playing and singing in the parlor all of us till bedtime. It reminds me so much of the last night I sang and played for Alvin, but dear Irvie was with us then and now we miss him all the time when with him. Dear, dear boys.

September 3rd, 1864

. . . We started up to Mrs. Hope's about five o'clock under a very threatening sky. Soon after we arrived Lucie Weaver came in and then Dr. Mitchell and Mr. Hutchins, a little wounded soldier. Were having a quiet, pleasant time—had gotten up from the tea table and standing in the front parlor door when Mrs. M rushed in and said Carey had just come from home to say the Yankees were coming and the boys must run to the thickets. We just pushed them out of the house without their hats and they waded across the creek and scampered up the hill into the corn field in an incredibly short space of time. Alvin laughed heartily all the time. Carey went after them with their hats. Twas a false alarm we learned at nightfall and were chagrined enough at having our pleasant party broken up and suffering such uneasiness all for nothing. It commenced raining just as Father came up for Ma and they told me I must stay all night but they went home. Talking to Mrs. Hope till bed time.

September 4th, 1864

Eliza told me early this morning that Mr. Lake had come in to inform us that the boys spent last night at his house and to ascertain if the Yankees had really come. Went home early and soon afterwards Cousin Mack and Alvin came laughing over last night's adventures. Cousin M and Aunt L. Blakemore went home and we all alone. Alvin was tired and sleepy but could not rest for the reports constantly coming in of the approach of the Yankees. Had a little quiet talk in the afternoon and Nellie and I sang and played hymns with him but Uncle Mack came in the late afternoon and took him home with him. Oh! how I do lament every moment when he is away from us—so little of his society have I enjoyed and he speaks of leaving the latter part of the week. Oh me!

September 6th, 1864

Raining. Busy making Alvin's tobacco bag. He, dear boy, came in to dinner and we had a comfortable chat with him in the afternoon. Sat on the porch at night and Nellie told him of some of her escapades of "Camp Pickens" memory. Had a long talk in Ma's room too—could not bear to go to bed; hated so to leave Alvin. Early has given the Yankees "beans" near Berryville. Nellie's birthday.

September 7th, 1864

. . . Sat on the porch by Alvin and he drew my head to his shoulder and put his arms around me and we had a long sweet talk such as we have never had before. Darling brother! this visit of yours will give me strength to endure much of sorrow and disappointment the coming winter. We had just gone into Grandma's room and were sitting there quietly talking when Dollie ran in almost fainting with excitement to say Mrs. Moffatt and she had come up to tell us the Yankees were coming in town. Alvin bounced and made for the corn field and Mr. S followed suit. Had an hour of intense excitement and then discovered it was a false alarm as usual. Dear me! I wish the authorities would shoot the wretches who make it their business to bring such exciting alarms just for the sake of raising a row. Wonder when Alvin will come back?

September 8th, 1864

Raining. Making biscuits and pies for Alvin to carry with him; he leaves tomorrow. Oh dear! it makes my heart ache to think of it. He came in about ten o'clock and then Uncles Mack and Newton and Mr. Shipe. They stayed at Mr. Lake's last night. Twas a day of confusion and I felt very unwell and to cap the climax Mr. S. and A. were both run off about four o'clock by a new report. Tis too provoking, our pleasure in Alvin's visit has had nothing to mar it but these rumors so exciting and trying. Lying on the bed till after tea and then mending some shirts for Alvin. Poor boy! only one more half day with him!

September 9th, 1864

Bright. Cousin Mack up early to make preparations for leaving. Glad and sorry to see him. Busy making preparations for Alvin. He came home about ten o'clock. Mrs. Moffatt up and Alvin had a great romp with her. Eating peaches, melons and grapes. Had a little conversation with Alvin just before dinner but not near as much as I wished. I have had so little of his society since he came that I've not said half of what I wished to say to him and I shall grieve over it enough. We all sauntered about the yard under the aspens until dinner and immediately after the boys left. Dear Alvin! his last words ring in my ears "Never mind Lou! take good care of yourself and I shall be at home again in December." This shall be my talisman against the distress against his departure. My watchword through the dreary fall. Poor fellow, he lingered as long as he could and made every excuse for turning back to look at us. We went on the house and waved to them as long as they remained in sight and then came down to the empty rooms that had late been musical with his voice and footstep and felt very much like a corpse had but just been carried forth. Had to write Irvie though and it kept me from thinking too much. Three soldiers stayed here tonight—met the boys over the Mountain and Alvin directed them here. Poor Irvie I'm so sorry; very anxious about him since these late battles.

September 10th, 1864

Was upstairs preparing my letter for the mail when a shout from below announced Uncle John's arrival. Glad to see him particularly as he had seen the boys nine miles from here last evening. Seems in good spirits. Got three letters from Irvie—none later than August 15th though and no news. Oh for something since the fall of Atlanta!

September 16th, 1864

Ma and Aunt L. spent the day at Colonel Jacobs'. Cousin James Larue came from Clover Hill to dine here. In the afternoon the children all went with him to the mill and presently I heard Evred screaming and Father bore him into Grandma's room pale and in great agony. His leg was broken. Seeing a large beam of wood resting on a table he endeavored to climb up to it and pulled it over on him—narrowly escaping with his life for the log was heavy enough to have crushed him if it had fallen upon his body. Father went over and brought Dr. Hough to examine it. He thought both bones fractured and when Dr. Dorsey and Uncle Newton came they confirmed the opinion. Poor child. He suffered terribly and I believe my pain was almost as great as his from very sympathy. I was so weak by the time the leg was confined in its bandage that I could scarce sit up. The operation was performed though with much less trouble than I thought it would be. Ma and Aunt L. knew nothing of it all till we sent for them after tea.

September 19th, 1864

Bright and pleasant. Busy till late. Scott over about ten o'clock and sat a couple of hours. Looks thin, poor fellow. Says he's had chills and fever—perhaps this may account for his most singular behavior. He was by turns cynical and sarcastic, then sad and misanthropic and anon teasing and mischievous. His visit has chilled me so. He certainly is "a problem which he who solved dispenses with die guessing." I'm afraid I can never play Oedipus to this riddle. He brought me a piece of music, a new song "The Murmur of the Shells." Says he has something pretty to show me when next he comes. He saw Alvin in Petersburg, says he was writing a letter to me when he left but he had not time to call for it. Nannie Buck came in just before he left but all went before dinner. Scott does not know when he will go.

Heard news this evening of the falling back of our army. Oh! me I feel so very very sad this evening. Uncle John here and a Mr. Taylor stayed all night.

September 20th, 1864

The advance guard of Wickham's brigade passed here on picket this morning. Our army reported on the retreat and the enemy in hot pursuit. Poor broken down soldiers constantly coming for something to eat. Nellie, Laura and I went without our dinners that there might be the more for them. A little before noon there was rapid firing at the river and we could see the enemy very distinctly on Guard Hill. They had a battery there and shelled across this side the river—some of the shells passed quite near us—some talk of our leaving home till it was over but Nellie and I bitterly opposed the move. . . . Firing ceased about three o'clock. Busy baking bread for the soldiers. We thought, of course, Scott had gone but in the late afternoon he came over to bring us a letter from Irvie which had been handed him by Miss Kate Graves and which he had overlooked. With what a mingled feeling of thanksgiving and sorrow we read his announcements of having received a slight wound in the late battle and being now in the hospital. We rejoiced that it was no worse but grieved at having to know of his suffering without having it in our power to relieve him. He writes cheerfully and hopefully—the bone of his wounded limb is untouched and the bullet extracted so I pray God it may be all well with him yet. . . .

Scott left before tea and we tried to persuade him to stay in the mountain tonight but I'm afraid he won't do it. While I write the hostile armies confront each other at the river in a menacing attitude but everything seems unnaturally still—the quiet so dull and dead broken only at intervals by the distant beating of the tattoo or the wail of a bugle. It is the calm preceding the storm. We shall not undress tonight for there's no knowing when we may be aroused to a renewal of strife. How I dread the morning no tongue can tell. Writing to dear Irvie hoping to send it out tomorrow by Scott.

September 21st, 1864

Well the close of this most miserable day is at last here and we breathe again. They commenced fighting at the river by the dawn of day. Our little handful of men retreated and the Yankees with a terrific yell charged them down the hills north of town and under cover of the fog there was such an incessant firing that we thought our poor boys must be murdered by the wholesale. The Rebels retreated through the woods in the rear of town and the Yankees passed directly up the Luray pike only about a regiment remaining in town. Saw a neat capture made by two of Mosby's men right in town. Expected the Yankees would have commenced pillaging and burning first thing upon their entrance but on the contrary they behaved quite decorously.

Boys went out to the scene of conflict. Heard that there were few if any men lost on either side in the fight this morning. Everyone uneasy about

Early for this evening two divisions of cavalry passed through town enroute for Luray and if they cannot in some way be checked they will flank him. I believe though it will all turn out right yet. We had numbers of the Yankees for milk and bread. Some were rude and broke.

[Ends abruptly here]

༄༅༄༅

Uncharacteristically, Lucy laid her diary aside for five months. When she resumed writing in February 1865, she gave a poignant clue as to the cause of this hiatus: "Those sad autumn days my heart was too sad. . . . I had not the spirit to write." Such an affecting statement causes the reader to wonder: what made those autumn days so sad?

To find some answers, I turned to the diary of Lucy's acquaintance Sue Richardson, which was kept faithfully during these months and is accessible in typescript at the Warren Heritage Society in Front Royal, Virginia. Sue mentions Lucy and her family frequently since much visiting took place between the two homes. Perhaps the event that precipitated Lucy's silence was the awesome killing of seven of Mosby's Rangers by their Yankee captors. These killings took place in Front Royal on September 23, just two days after Lucy ceases writing. Sue Richardson's account is as follows: "Seven, all they captured, were brutally shot and hung. Poor Henry Rhodes—hadn't been long in service—was shot in our field, nearly in front of our door. We could see the crowd assembled around him. . . . His poor mother is almost crazy. Mr. Carter and Mr. Overby of Fauquier were hung in the Mountain field on a large walnut tree. . . . It almost kills us to witness it" (69).

Other events of which Sue Richardson gives accounts would have been troubling to Lucy, too. On October 8, the Yankees torched the local mill: "Mill burnt, awful sight and so distressing" (72), affecting the local residents' livelihood. Richardson describes in several October entries the depredations of Yankee soldiers on the homes, possessions, and food supplies of Front Royal citizens. "Cousin Ellen R. sick and living on horsefeed" (76). Apparently, Lucy's family was suffering from similar shortages. Her brother, William R. Buck, recorded in a brief memoir written in 1936: "As the hard times increased with the war, the large family at Bel Air fell into such desperate straits that they were forced to eat a crude feed that had been prepared for the horses by scraping up and grinding the stray grains of corn, rye, etc. and the corn cobs from the mill floor" ("Reminiscences of Bel Air," 3).

November entries in Sue Richardson's diary tell of the sudden death of Cousin Lizzie Buck and of "pillaging at Bel-Air" (81). In December, according to Richardson, Lucy accompanied a friend on a trip to Luray to see the woman's dying father. Lucy herself mentions these events in her first entry after the hiatus, as well as an extended illness she suffered. Both Lucy and Sue Richardson remark on the difficult weather they endured in early 1865, with more snow and colder temperatures than was customary for Virginia. We can speculate, then, that all of these difficulties conspired to silence Lucy; to write about them was to confront them in a way that Lucy "had not the spirit" for.

♔♔♔♔

February 13, 1865

My diary was laid by. Those sad autumn days my heart was too sad. There was too much that   to record I had not the spirit to write. Since then what has not happened of sorrow and   with a feeling of humiliation. I'm a different being from what I was then—the change the worse. When it will end God only knows.[1]

————of toil and apprehension—dreary and dark. Dear Aunt Lizzie died November 8. Henry left the army   .[2] Went to Luray in December. Expecting Irvie home all that month but our hopes were dashed and our anticipation for the winter taken from us. Last visit from the Yankees was just before Christmas when Torbetts whole corps passed on a raid as far as Madison C. H. Amusing reencounter with Lieutenant—now Captain Dahher. Sallie taken sick and the next day I too had to go to bed. The girls had a week of toil during the Christmas season and I unable to help them and so much domestic trouble I felt almost deranged sometimes. Sick for two weeks—chills and fever. Horrid weather all winter—more snow than for many years past and some bitter cold days.

February 19th, 1865

Up early to get the house cleaned up in time for Ma to make an early start. Busy after breakfast—Felt bright. Carrol and Fettie and Bob Buck and Russell Richards here, then Aunt Letitia Buck and Jacquie. Mary Carson and Carey did not come till ten o'clock. Carey brought me two such welcome notes from Mac and Jule. Ma rode behind Father and all started a little after ten. Had a most quiet Sabbath reading, writing and talking. Nellie had a letter from Dick in which he spoke of Alvin's having been ordered to rejoin his regiment. It makes me feel uneasy. N. and I had one of our twilight talks on the stile. Russell still here—had singing tonight till bedtime.

February 20th, 1865

Lovely day. Reading, writing, sewing and as this is my week—housekeeping. Eating walnuts too. Had a note from Ma. Report of a victory by Beauregard over Sherman, wonder if it can be true. A cozy quiet time we had tonight the children being all asleep and Grandma, Laura, Nellie, Clara and I having the fire and candle all to ourselves.

February 21st, 1865

Still fair weather. Laura and Annie spent the day at Uncle Tom's—had a very quiet time of it. Cannonading heard from direction of Winchester. Grand alarm—reported invasion of Yankees—false rumor. No one here for a wonder. Quiet pleasant evening. Report of Beauregard's death—don't credit it.

February 22nd, 1865

Captain Marshall in to dinner. Willie Buck over in the afternoon—political discussion. Frank hurt himself very much with a hot iron. Playing backgammon. Rumor that Charleston and Columbia had fallen. Nothing more than I expected. Dyspeptic.

February 24th, 1865

Bright and pleasant. Writing all morning. Willie Buck came over to give me a lesson in chess. Am afraid I'm too stupid ever to learn the game. After he left enter Uncle Tom with a letter from Cousin ——— ——— and a valentine for Nellie—from Cousin Ed Buck I am sure. Busy sewing making a floral card this evening. Nellie in the parlor playing and singing tonight when a rap at the door was followed by the entrance of Charlie Brown and Wythe Cooke. So glad to see them—two fine young rebels and two very clever ones too. Sat until ten o'clock talking over auld lang syne and singing and playing. Sitting up late tonight laughing and talking in our room.

February 25th, 1865

Up early closing up my housekeeping week. Gray and cloudy. Writing all morning. Raining by noon. Mrs. Robert Turner came in about two o'clock to spend the day. Pleasant little woman. Laura and Orville had gone out to Uncle Newton's this morning and returned at dinner time bringing with them Mollie Richardson and Nannie Buck. Very soon afterward a young soldier Mr. Bruner came in to stay all night. Father voted the children a frolic Saturday night though it was so Allie and Charlie and Wythe were summoned and a right merry time we had of it. The young folks danced a while and then we proceeded to the dining room where "tap-the-rabbit," "fox-and-goose," blindman's buff" and similar dignified games engaged us till after eleven o'clock. Such a wild gay time as we had—hardly knew myself that I could enjoy fun as much as I did. Ate a philopoena with Wythe and mean to ask him for his photograph. Feel quite wearied—we shall only get to bed in time to save ourselves from the charge of Sabbath breaking.

February 27th, 1865

Unsettled. Upstairs reading and writing during the morning. Nannie and Mollie went home. No one here all day. Father went to Mrs. Wheatley's to-night to see Mrs. Kiger—had just gotten back at nine o'clock—says she'll be over tomorrow. Heard a confirmation of this morning's report—Genls. Kelsie and Crooks captured by a party of our cavalry who dashed in to their camp in Cumberland and "gobbled them up."

March 3rd, 1865

Cloudy and showery all forenoon—ceased toward the afternoon. Allie Ashby came up to go to Mr. Hope's with the girls. I did not feel very well and therefore declined going. Was sitting about dusk telling the children stories when a rap at the door was followed by the entrance of Dick Bayley. He told me there was an opposition party at Mr. Overall's and that there would be few at Eliza's assembly so I concluded to go with him. Found none but our party there—all around the table at cards. Willie Jacobs soon came in and after we had had our suppers I stirred them up and we had game after game of romps. Enjoyed ourselves very much till eleven o'clock when we returned home—Dick stays with us tonight.

March 6th, 1865

Lovely day. Cousin E and L left early—Nannie remained with us and Grandma went to Mrs. H's to spend the day. Concluded to have company tonight. Girls all went to Mr. Hope's mill to be *weighed* and to invite Julia and Eliza and Wythe Cooke whom they found there. Sent a note to the "Mountain," one to Oakley and a message to Rose Hill and "Mountain View." Had all our simple preparations made by dusk—a nice fire in the parlor and all—Belle R. and Allie, Willie Buck and Charlie R. came first. They told me of a report in town of Rosser's having been badly defeated and that poor Sam Buck was wounded and had his leg amputated. Feel so sorry to hear it, such a noble boy and gallant soldier as he is. Mrs. Moffatt, Julia and Eliza were next, then Cousin Will Cloud, Dick Bayley, Jacquie and Gussie and last though not least Charlie B and Wythe Cook. A wild time we have had of it and our company did not disperse till two o'clock. Nannie, Belle, Gussie, Allie, Dick and Cousin Will stay with us tonight. Oh me! *so* tired.

March 7th, 1865

Up late but succeeded in getting everything in order before breakfast. Sitting in the parlor chatting and singing. Cousin Will taught me "Aillien Aroon." Gussie and Allie could not be persuaded to remain till after breakfast. Jim came over early after Nannie and Nellie and Belle went with her. Cousin Will and Dick off early too. Laura and I "alone in our glory" feeling stupid and tired. Charlie Brown told us last night that he had heard from the 17th regiment and that Alvin and George Hope had arrived there. There was a mail in last night though of course we got no letters—thinking that Mrs. Roy perhaps might be able to furnish us tidings I put on my cloak and hat and "waded" over. Received a hearty welcome but no news. Benton's last letter

contained no mention of either of the boys. So sorry. Saw a photograph of
the Cols.—looks as if viewed through a magnifying glass—so fat and rosy
has he become. Read a letter from G White—what a delightful scribe he is!
Sat until after twelve gossiping and then waded back home. Dried my feet
and went to bed but could not get my nap. So stupid all day. Tonight reports
of the advance of the Yankees through Rappahannock. Father and I preparing
for their advent tonight by cacheting.

March 9th, 1865

Lovely day. Reading the "Vicar" and sewing. Nellie and I went to investigate
the myrtle bed on the hill side. Eliza and Julia helped us. Rosser's defeat and
Early's stampede at Laceys Spring confirmed. Nothing from Ma—wish we
could *hear*.

March 10th, 1865

Disagreeable morning. Observing the day by fasting. Nellie went over to
prayer meeting in the morning and in the afternoon I went with Russell, who
had come in, and Willie to hear Dr. Hough. A large attendance of soldiers
and everybody else there. One of the most solemn, impressive sermons I ever
listened to—everyone—even the most frivolous seemed to feel it deeply. He
scored our rebellers most soundly—made me feel like forswearing dancing for
the rest of the war. Have heard through Mac Bayley's letter that Henry Buck is
in Phil. in business with Cousin Thos. Fayette Blakemore. Reading tonight.

March 12th, 1865

Most beautiful day. No services in church—after reading during the morning
betook myself to my little sanctum to write to Irvie. A grand alarm of Yankee
Invasion—a great time we had secreting and a great time the boys had
scampering out of town—all for nothing too because the alarm was a false
one. Laura and Nellie went to Mrs. Hope's a little while and when they returned from there Laura went with Evred over to Oakley. Jacquie came in
with Julia and Father went to Belmont. After dinner Jacquie, Nellie, Neville,
Willie and I went on the housetop and sat there talking over old times—then

to the attic room eating walnuts. Laura and Evred home at dusk. Writing tonight. Father not at home till late.

March 13th, 1865

Most delightful morning. Reading, writing and sewing. Dick Bayley in during the morning and had a romp and was off again. Nellie and I made our toilettes and strolled over to Dr. Turner's—spent a pleasant hour and missed tea and Nannie came back with us—found Julia H and Aunt L. Blakemore here. All but Aunt L. left at dusk. We all walked up to Mrs. Hope's with Julia, sat a minute and then walked home. Laura made a black cake and sent it a parting present to Charlie who leaves tomorrow. Ellen wrote a very nice note of thanks in return. Left Aunt L. chatting with the family in Grandma's room and went out on the porch to drink in some of the tranquil loveliness of the night. The day has been one of such beauty and I've felt so light-hearted and happy. While sitting there Willie Buck rode up and very soon after Charlie Brown came in to tell us goodbye. Poor boy! He looks sad. Left at ten o'clock and we were just preparing to retire when there was an alarm of Yankees. Willie mounted his horse and went to town to hear something from them. Came back in a short time saying twas all false. Oh! me these excitements are terrible. Hamp Miller went down to Castleman's Ferry to hear from his wife—left his morning.

March 15th, 1865

Raining. Allie Ashby over. All plaiting straw. Hamp Miller home this evening—could only hear that Ma and Mrs. M. had been for ten days in Shepardstown unable to get out but would be probably home next week. Wish we knew something more direct from them. Allie stayed all night. He and the children had a grand romp tonight.

March 20th, 1865

Warm and pleasant. Cattie Samuels came in very unexpectedly this morning after Sallie Leech left. Glad to see her—very—sat till two o'clock. Nellie, Laura, Orville and I went fishing but were unsuccessful. Miss Tencie and

Annie came over by appointment to walk as far as the river with Sallie. Did not feel like going twas so warm. Had a very delightful trip though, and got home by dusk. Met Mrs. Hamp Miller on the bridge which was the first intimation I had of Ma's having gotten home. Rounded the house and found her on the front porch surrounded with an eager throng. She looks badly—has had a most terrible time and I only wonder she's alive. Her trip has been only partially successful too. I'm mighty glad to have her at home once more. Sitting up till nearly twelve o'clock listening to a recountal of her adventures. Ah me! I feel relieved indeed. Had a note from Jule today.

March 21st, 1865

Quite pleasant. Mrs. Moffatt up early to see Ma. Grandma and Aunt B invited to spend the day at Mrs. Glasscock's—so we had a comparatively quiet time altogether sewing and chatting. Uncle Tom in to dinner. Raining in the afternoon. Three soldiers—returned prisoners came in to stay all night—they were with Charlie Buck at Camp Chase—said he had been exchanged with them—was in Charlottesville and would be on shortly—had a ring which Charlie had made and given them. Reading and writing and playing on the piano. Wrote Cousin Mary Cloud.

March 27th, 1865

Sam Buck came in unexpectedly—has resigned and is going into Mosby's command. He's a nice fellow, so like Alvin, affectionate and kind. Had a game of marbles all of us and a grand romp outdoors then into the house and some music. Sam taught me "Auralea" and "Love's Chiding." We did have such a pleasant time altogether. Ah me! "When shall we all meet again."

March 28th, 1865

Jule and I sat up till very late last night talking and felt rather unwell this morning. Felt a little better after breakfast though. Cousin Tom left early. Sam taught us songs and copied—showed us some complimentary letters from his officers—made a half engagement to go to Luray with us, had a great romp and then left.

The boys went fishing but soon came back. Jule unwell and in bed til noon. While at dinner Mr. and Mrs. Miller came in to spend the evening and not after Mack Irwin! Such a pleasant evening we had! Mack is a great boy and laughed heartily over what I told him on the porch. Made an engagement to spend tomorrow with Mrs. Miller. She left soon after tea and then Jule and Dick, Mack and I and Nellie and Cousin James and the children walked on the river bank till after the stars came out and then Mack and I paused on the porch and talked. Oh! he was so kind and encouraging and humbled me so by his earnest Christian conversation. If I could only be as good as he and Jule! God help me! Felt quiet and sad all evening even after going up to our rooms.

April 5th, 1865

I'm so depressed—feel like we were given up into the hands of our foes indeed. Aunt L. Blakemore was spending the day with us and just before dinner while finishing a letter to Irvie Uncle John came in pale and sad to say Richmond, our own Richmond, had fallen. I felt stunned, sick, wild. But soon the thought came that twas perhaps all for the best and we must bide our time. Our army has fallen back toward Lynchburg. Oh me, me! Light! for this darkness! Light!

April 6th, 1865

Sad all day. Ma went to church this afternoon. Bruner came in very unexpectedly, was seeming so cheerful and bright. He's enroute for Clarke—wrote by him. Cousin Lucie Buck and Emma came in this evening and are with us tonight. Our army is said to be in a starving condition. Oh misery!

April 7th, 1865

Up in my dormitory all morning. Cousin L. and E. left early. Reading "Bride of Lamamoor." The story is such a sad, tragic one that it has depressed my spirit no little. Sitting out on the porch in the moonlight trying the effect of quiet and calm on my excited nerves and thinking oh so wistfully of lang syne when the gate opened and Uncle John rode in. He had heard of a sudden advance of the enemy up the valley and the news accelerated his intended departure. He leaves tomorrow and came to say good-bye—so sorry to see him go and he's loath to leave. Old Aunt Bettie sick.

April 8th, 1865

Willie Buck was over this morning talking bravely with us when Father came in to say Miss Terril and Miss Yate were coming in. They were on their way to Rappahannock to see an invalid brother and had to stop over till tomorrow, when Mr. Harmon promised to take them down in his wagon. Nice girls—very pretty and accomplished—spent quite a pleasant evening. Nannie Buck over. Pickett's division was engaged in the fight that preceded the fall of Richmond. What of our poor boys?

Apirl 10th, 1865

We were quietly sewing this morning when E. Hope came in with a white face to tell us Dick was mortally wounded—the man (Mr. Gannett) who brought him off the field had come with the tidings. It was such a shock— we felt almost heartbroken all day. In the afternoon Father went to Belmont and returned at dusk with Uncle Mack to say that the news more recently received from our poor boy represented him as severely but *not* dangerously wounded, and in the enemy hands. Such a relief to hear this much. Poor fellow if I could only be with and nurse him! We were beaten out of Petersburg but Pickett fought gloriously as he ever does. Many of our poor boys are wounded, many————————we may only pray God to protect them and hope for the best.

Bruner here tonight—has returned from Clarke—brings news that all was well at Bloomfield—makes us cheerful with his news. Feel as if I'd been belabored all day, I'm so stiff and worn out.

April 11th, 1865

Bruner left early. Wrote by him to Uncle John. Dick Bayley in this morning and I think did not relish something Nellie said to him about the absentees from the army for he left very suddenly.

April 12th, 1865

Ma spent the day in town. Came home in the evening with news of Mr. Robert Wells' arrival from prison. Brings such cheerful news from Richmond—says our armies are in fine spirits and oh! ever so many things to dissipate the gloom in our hearts. If we may only be free let trouble come and we'll try to bear them. Old Aunt Bettie died.

April 13th, 1865

Such a day as this has been! A few more would, I believe, kill me. Father came in suddenly pale and grave with the words "Well, I fear the die is cast—Lee has surrendered"—almost torn from his lips.[3] If the heavens had fallen there could have scarcely have been greater consternation and grief in our midst. To remember half the horrible ideas that filled my heart and brain would be impossible—the one thought—subjugation—all staked, all lost. Our dearest hopes dashed—our fondest dreams dispelled—we and our brave ones who had struggled, bled and suffered—slaves and to such a tyrant. God only knows how nearly mad I must have been. Some soldiers came in during the day and confidently denied the report and I felt cheered so much. Ma went to Mr. Hope's and returned with additional confirmation of the dreadful news. Cousins Sue and Emma over and Mr. Berry but I was too near crazy to know much of what they said or did. Oh! me I'm almost tempted to envy poor Aunt Bettie lying cold and still in death in her little cabin tonight. If it had been any but Lee—our peerless Lee! Poor fellow! what a trial to his noble heart. God bless him and comfort him under his trial and give us strength to bear our cross. I'm desperate and wicked tonight.

April 14th, 1865

Took the children down this morning to see poor old Aunt Bettie's remains. Did not go to the funeral. Sam Buck came in—confirmed the news but yet is so naturally cheerful that we involuntarily imbibed some of his brightness. He begged me to go to the Mountain with him. I consented—rather against my own inclination but was glad afterwards—enjoyed the air very much. He's so much like Alvin. Read tonight the correspondence between Lee and Grant relative to the surrender. "Things sad are ever true."

April 15th, 1865

Raining. Young Detheridge came up this morning with news from Dick. He's in Farmville—in the hospital doing well. Dear fellow so glad! He also brings us much cheering news from our army. Johnson is said to have whipped the enemy and oh! I don't know what else. We started home and it rained so hard we were thoroughly drenched. Sam took Laura out to Mountain View—had a bad headache all evening. Have one of my nervous attacks.

[Volume ends abruptly here]

Epilogue

Lucy's diary ended abruptly when she was twenty-three years old, as the reality of the South's defeat took hold. Suzanne Lebsock has noted in *Virginia Women, 1600–1945* that "many diaries, begun in the first flush of the war, simply came to a dead stop" as the war ended (87). Lucy did resume writing, though, and kept a diary regularly until her death. These later diaries have never been published and are now in the possession of Dr. William Pettus Buck.

Lucy began the habit of diary keeping again, after an eight-year lapse, with this entry on New Year's Day, 1873:

> This New Year night of 1873 I resume my Diary which has been neglected since the last Fall of the War. What an age has elapsed since then! I seemed to have lived and suffered a century, and feel that a less noble and worthy being will transcribe a less noble and worthy record of her life than in the old times. Alas! that this should be true! Of yore, my pen _____ were commenced with many a brave resolution for the future, many a bright hope beckoned me on to the coming days. Now, how differently I look upon the advent of each incoming year as the dawn of a very season of trial and sorrow, as but a new season of uncertainty, care and toil. As to work—I've learned to regard that as a true though rough friend, winning one from too much thought of the non-returning Past, and helping me to dull the keen pain of the Present. 'Tis indeed 'The dull narcotic soothing pain.' And as God has thus connected this primal curse into a blessing, may I not trust that He will continue to evolve some good for me out of all the evil that encompasses me? At least He will not give me more to bear than I have strength for.
>
> 'Tis to be hoped that today is no index of its successors—for I have celebrated it by having one of my most terrible, old-fashioned head-aches.

Lucy's diaries for this period are written in many kinds of books—composition books, ledgers, and hardback books with leather covers and printed titles such as that for 1885, which bears the inscription: "Excelsior Daily Journal, 1885."

Lucy never married, nor did her sister Nellie, nor, for that matter, did any of the four surviving Buck daughters. Such a pattern was not uncommon in the post–Civil War era as the loss of southern men was so enormous. In 1897, the Buck family left their beloved home, Bel Air, no longer financially able to maintain the large house. "Such a terrible day as this has been! Wearing to heart, brain, and body," Lucy wrote in her diary on April 6 of that year. The financial reverses resulted from the failure of the business of Lucy's uncle, Marcus Buck of "Belmont." His prosperous vineyard and distillery had produced award-winning wine, but a precipitous decline in the price of wine brought the business to an end in 1875. Lucy's father, William Mason Buck, was one of Marcus Buck's backers, and thus he lost not only Bel Air but also other properties in Front Royal and elsewhere (William Pettus Buck, *Buck Family*, 50). The departure from Bel Air was a sad one, which Lucy described in her diary as a "procession of wagons carrying household goods [which] appeared more as a funeral cortege" (Buck, *Buck Family*, 51).

The Buck family moved into another home, where Mrs. Buck died on January 24, 1904. In recounting her mother's funeral in her journal entry for January 25, 1904, Lucy says, "We left her beside the loved ones gone before and came home, Laura, Nannie, Irving, Willie and I only five out of the thirteen children she had born who were here to follow her to her last rest" (Hale, *On Chester Street*, 98). Her husband, William Mason Buck, had preceded her in death in 1878.

Lucy moved in 1905 into a small cottage on Chester Street in Front Royal, which she aptly named "Cozy Corner." She was just a few months shy of her sixty-third birthday. She and her sister Laura had designed the eight-room home and had it built to their specifications. Both Cozy Corner and Bel Air are still standing in Front Royal today.

Lucy made her final entry on August 19, 1918, the day before she died, a month short of her seventy-sixth birthday. Her final entry reads:

> After a most painful, wearing night, trying vainly for comfort and sleep, I found myself unable to be up and about my duties as usual and it hurt me so to leave Laura not only all her work but mine to do, besides nursing me. She did it all so cheerfully, that it was relieved of much of its trial to me. I suffered a good deal all day, but had a quiet, restful time. No letters, and no one in.

Characteristically, Lucy concludes her entry with an announcement of the lack of news. Lucy Buck was buried in Prospect Hill Cemetery in Front Royal.

Both of Lucy's brothers who served in the Confederate army, Alvin and Irving, survived the Civil War. Irving went on to write a book based on his experiences, entitled *Cleburne and His Command* (1905). Alvin married Henrietta Major of Cedar Grove, Kentucky, in July 1867, and they had nine children, five of whom died in childhood. Irving married Fannie Ricards of Baltimore in January 1871. Younger brothers Carey, Willie, and Evred also married. It is L. N. Buck, son of Evred, who was responsible for the initial transcription of Lucy's diary and its publication in a private edition in 1940.

Appendix

Lucy Buck's Reading Materials

Some accounting of Lucy Buck's wide-ranging reading habits seems useful as a measure of her educational level, her opportunities for learning, and her intellectual interests. As the reader of her diary will note, she had eclectic taste in books. In addition to the Bible, which she read regularly, she mentions no fewer than thirty-five other titles during the four-year period of the diary. Some of these books she read aloud to her father; others she read for her own edification and pleasure. The list ranges from the novels of Sir Walter Scott, an author particularly appealing to the chivalric southerner of this time, to histories and other nonfiction, to the popular women writers of her era: Maria Cummins, Susan Warner, and Mary Virginia Terhune. Some of the books Lucy read were already a century old; others had just been published, suggesting that even in embattled Virginia, it was still possible to obtain new books during the Civil War.

What follows is a listing of the books Lucy Buck mentions, with the appropriate identifying information. The following sources were consulted in identifying these volumes: Online Computer Library Center, Inc.; Research Library Information Network; *The British Library General Catalogue of Printed Books To 1975*; *Confederate Literature: A List of Books and Newspapers, Maps, Music, and Miscellaneous Matter Printed in the South during the Confederacy*, ed. Charles Baxter and James Dearborn (Boston: Boston Athenaeum, 1917); *The American Catalogue of Books, 1861–1866*, ed. James Kelly (New York: Peter Smith, 1938); *The Bibliotheca Americana: A Catalog of American Publications from October, 1852 to January, 1861*, vols. 2, 3, 4, ed. Orville Roorbach (New York: Peter Smith, 1939); *American Bibliography*, vol. 6 (1779–85), vol. 7 (1786–89), ed. Charles E. Evans (Chicago: Columbia Press, 1912).

Titles Mentioned by Lucy Buck in the Text of Her Diary

"Adile"—An error on the part of either the diarist or the first editor. This is most likely *Adele; a Tale*, by Julia Kavanagh (1824–77) (New York, 1853). No listing for *Adile* could be located.

"Alone"—Marion Harland's *Alone*, her first novel, was published in 1854; Harland was the pseudonym of Mary Virginia Terhune, a prolific and famous Virginia writer. Her writing career extended some sixty-eight years, during which "she married, had six children, and wrote twenty-five novels, twenty-five books of household advice, and numerous histories and biographies" (Lebsock, *Virginia Women*, 97).

"the Antiquary"—Sir Walter Scott published *The Antiquary*, a three-volume work, in 1816.

"the Bachelor"—The archives of the Warren Heritage Society in Front Royal contain a list of seventeen volumes identified as the "Buck Collection." Among those is *Reveries of a Bachelor or a Book of the Heart*, by I. K. Marvel (New York, 1851), described on the inventory as "Collection of Essays, somewhat like a diary."

"Bride of Lamamoor"—The fourth Sir Walter Scott title mentioned by Lucy, *The Bride of Lammermoor* (1819) was in volume 2 of the Waverly Novels (*The Antiquary* was in volume 3 and *Woodstock* in volume 12; both titles are also mentioned by Lucy).

"Butler's Analogy"—Joseph Butler, *Butler's Analogy of Religion: Natural and Revealed to the Constitution and Course of Nature* (London, 1736).

"the 'Campaign in Pa.' "—Probably a report issued by Richard Stoddard Ewell (1817–72) entitled *General Ewell's Report of the Pennsylvania Campaign*, later made available in Southern Historical Society Papers (Richmond, 1882), 10:289–307. Ewell served with Longstreet at Gettysburg, which confirms the link Lucy establishes in her comment "the writer was quartered with Gen. Longstreet's staff."

"Charms and Counter-charms"—*Charms and Counter-charms*, a novel by Maria J. McIntosh, published in London in 1849.

"Courtesies of Married Life"—Lucy has misrecorded this title. It should be *The First and the Second Marriages; or, The Courtesies of Wedded Life*, by Mrs. Madeline Leslie (pseudonym) (Boston, 1856). The edition of the book in the Special Collections of the Alderman Library has "Courtesies of Wedded Life" printed in gold on the spine of the red morocco cover. The book is fiction and is about the lives of a clergyman and an attorney living in the same town; among other things, the book treats the subjects of wife abuse and illegitimate children. In her preface, Mrs. Leslie states: "It treats of courtship and marriage, of the relation of husband and wife, of their responsibilities and privileges, of their trials and rewards. It aims to assist them in their reciprocal duties, and in the attainment of the pure and blissful ends of wedlock. It shows how piety enables them to bear with each others' infirmities, how it smooths asperities of temper, assimilates dispositions and tastes, conforms character to the noblest standard, and adorns them with graces surpassing those of the muses." Such a preface suggests awesome expectations for the partners in a marriage; small wonder Lucy and other diarists express hesitations and fears about the institution!

" 'A Day's Ride or a Life's Romance' "—*A Day's Ride* (New York, 1861) is one of some thirty-seven novels written by Charles Lever. (Since this volume of Lucy's diary is lost, it is not possible to determine if she incorrectly recorded the author's surname or if Captain Buck misread her handwriting in transcribing the diary; since Lucy is generally accurate in recording titles and authors, I tend to the latter interpretation.)

"Dollars and Cents"—Written by Anna Warner, whose pseudonym was Amy Lothrop, *Dollars and Cents* was published in two volumes in 1852.

"Dynevor Terrace"—*Dynevor Terrace; or The Clue of Life* was a novel by Charlotte Yonge (1823–1901), published in 1857.

"Franklin's 'Essays' "—Published in 1852, as a one hundredth edition, was *The Life of Benjamin Franklin / Written by Himself: together with his Essays, Humorous, Moral and Literary*.

"First Year of the War"—Edward Pollard, *The First Year of the War* (Richmond, 1862).

"Froissart's Chronicles"—Lucy mentions three books in this passage and indicates her delight at being able to borrow books from friends. *The Ancient Chronicles of Sir John Froissart, of England, France, Spain, Portugal, Scotland, Brittany, and Flanders, and the adjoining countries* was published in London in 1814–16. Froissart lived between 1338 and 1410.

"Grace Truman"—A book called *Grace Truman; or, Love and Principle*, by Mrs. Sallie Rochester Ford (New York, 1857).

"The Greyson Letters"—*The Greyson Letters: Selections from the Correspondence of R. E. H. Greyson* [pseud.] was edited by Henry Rogers and published in Boston in 1858.

"Heir of Radcliffe"—Charlotte Mary Yonge, *The Heir of Redclyffe* (London, c. 1853).

"Henry St. John. Gentleman"—The full title of this text is *Henry St. John, Gentleman, of "Flower of Hundreds," in the county of Prince George, Virginia. A Tale of*

1774–'75. The book was written by John Esten Cooke and published by Harpers in 1859.

"History of the Mexican War"—Probably Nathan Covington Brooks (1809–98), *A Complete History of the Mexican War: Its Causes, Conduct, and Consequences* (Philadelphia, 1849).

"Hyperion"—*Hyperion, A Romance* was written by Henry Wadsworth Longfellow and published in 1839.

"Idyls of the King"—Alfred Tennyson (1809–92) wrote "The Idylls of the King," a long series of connected poems, over a span of years from 1842 to 1885. Thus, only part of the cycle, based on the Arthurian legends, would have been available to Lucy at this time.

"The Lamplighter"—In "sitting up till late . . . reading the Lamplighter," Lucy was joining the thousands of women who read this novel and thereby made it one of the all-time best-sellers of the nineteenth century. Maria S. Cummins, *The Lamplighter* (New York, 1854).

"the life of Patrick Henry"—Several such lives would have been available to Lucy to read aloud to her father, including William Wirt's *Sketches of the Life and Character of Patrick Henry* (New York, 1832) and Samuel Greene Arnold's *The Life of Patrick Henry of Virginia* (New York, 1857).

"Lucretia"—Perhaps *Lucretia and Her Father: A Narrative Founded on Fact*, by a Clergyman of New England, 2d ed. (Hartford, 1828).

"Macaria"—Augusta Jane Evans Wilson, another of the highly popular nineteenth-century women writers (whom Nathaniel Hawthorne dubbed "the maddening scribblers"), published her novel *Macaria* in 1864, interestingly in two editions, one in Richmond and one in New York. Lucy had thus obtained this novel directly after its publication.

"Marmion"—*Marmion: A Tale of Flodden Field*, the second Sir Walter Scott novel mentioned by Lucy, was published in 1808.

"I related 'Opicciola' and 'Rip Van Winkle' "—The oral telling of tales was as important a form of entertainment in the nineteenth century as reading aloud or silently. "Rip Van Winkle," the story of the man who slept a hundred years in the Catskill Mountains, was frequently produced as a play and as an opera in the nineteenth century.

"The Pilgrims of the Rhine"—Edward Bulwer-Lytton, *The Pilgrims of the Rhine*, first published in London, 1834; published in Philadelphia in 1861.

"Queechy"—Susan Warner, *Queechy* (New York, 1852).

"The Raven"—A poem by American author Edgar Allan Poe (1809–49) that was originally published in 1844 and carries the famous refrain "Quoth the Raven 'Nevermore.' "

"Tannhauser"—*Tannhauser; or The Battle of the Bards*, a poem by Neville Temple and Edward Trevor, pseudonyms for Julian Henry Charles Fane and Edward Bulwer-Lytton (Mobile, 1863). The cover title is simply *Tannhauser*. According to *Benet's Reader's Encyclopedia*, Tannhauser was a minor thirteenth-century German lyrical poet who went on the Crusades and who was associated with the knight Tannhauser of popular ballads (986–87). Wagner's adaptation, his 1845 opera *Tannhauser*, involves a singing contest, which is perhaps why Lucy suggests it as reading material.

"the 'Vicar' "—Probably Lucy refers to *The Vicar of Wakefield*, the enormously popular novel by Oliver Goldsmith, a British writer, published originally in 1766.

"Woodstock"—*Woodstock; or, The Cavalier. A Tale of the Year Sixteen hundred and fifty-one*, by Sir Walter Scott, was a three-volume novel published in 1826.

Notes

Introduction

1. Jane Schultz's recent article "Mute Fury: Southern Women's Diaries of Sherman's March to the Sea, 1864–1865" reviews the fears expressed about physical violation in the diaries of thirty-seven Confederate women, although not one of them uses the word *rape*. Noting the social code that taught women to exchange deference for protection, Schultz quotes extensively from diaries to demonstrate the humiliation, the abandonment, and finally the anger that these women felt when men did not uphold their end of the bargain.

2. There is some evidence that Lucy began her diary earlier than December 1861. A reference to an earlier portion is made in a letter from Captain Neville Buck, who first transcribed the diary in the 1930s, to the then owner of the diary, his uncle Willie Buck. "Orville [the son of Alvin Buck, Lucy's brother] has the one which covers the period from the start of the War up to the time these begin. When I finish these I intend to borrow that (he has promised me the loan) so as to complete the work," stated Neville in a letter dated May 18, 1936, and now in the possession of Dr. William Buck of Birmingham, Alabama. However, if such earlier portions once existed, they were never transcribed and are now unknown to the Buck family and presumably lost.

3. This letter and several others by Lucy and members of her family are housed in the Special Collections of Alderman Library at the University of Virginia.

Chapter One. *I Cannot but Feel a Little Sad: December 25, 1861– May 13, 1862*

1. Cooper, in her book *Games from an Edwardian Childhood*, describes "consequences" thus: "Each child has a pencil and paper. They all write a boy's or man's name at the top of their sheet, fold it over, and pass it on. Then they write: 'met . . . (followed by a girl's or woman's name),' and fold it over to pass on. This is followed by where they met, what he said, what she said, what the consequence was, and what the world said, with the papers being folded and passed each time. Finally they are all tossed into a heap. Everyone picks one out and unfolds the story, reading it aloud to much merriment" (22).

2. "My Maryland" was composed by James Ryder Randall in April 1861, while

he was away from his native Maryland in Louisiana. According to Matthew Page Andrews, the pro-Confederacy song became a favorite among Maryland women, two of whom, the Misses Hettie and Jennie Cary, carried the song from Baltimore to the Manassas battlefield, where they sang it for the soldiers in camp in July 1861. It was "widely considered the greatest of American war lyrics" (66–68).

3. I have been unable to identify this painting; "Evangeline" is, of course, the subject of a long and famous poem by Henry Wadsworth Longfellow, published in 1847, which tells a tale of unrequited love during the colonial era in America.

4. For the identification of this title, "Lucretia," and all other titles of books that Lucy Buck mentions, the reader is referred to the Appendix.

5. A "bantling" is a young child.

6. Lucy's frequent mention of the notorious Confederate spy Belle Boyd is one of the intriguing aspects of her diary. Only seventeen when she began her work as a spy, Boyd was from Martinsburg, Virginia (now West Virginia). According to Suzanne Lebsock: "By the fall of 1861 she had moved to her aunt's [the aforementioned Mrs. Stewart] home in Front Royal, where she became a professional spy, a courier for the Confederate intelligence service." She was arrested a total of five times for her activities, "the last time at sea in 1864 as she tried to run the blockade with dispatches intended for England. This time she was banished to Canada, but Belle Boyd once again landed on her feet: she married the Union captain who had arrested her" (*Virginia Women*, 81). Laura Virginia Hale calls her "the most famous woman connected with official activities in the War between the States" (*Belle Boyd*, n.p.). "The Belle Boyd Cottage" serves as part of the Warren Heritage Society today, the historical society of Front Royal.

7. The reference to Esculapius is a bit baffling. *The Oxford Companion to English Literature* lists Aesculapius as the "son of Apollo and Coronis," who, after his death, "was honored as the god of medicine, and was represented holding in his hand a staff, round which is wreathed a serpent, a creature particularly sacred to him" (Harvey, 10). The connection with medicine seems irrelevant; perhaps the connection is with the serpent, as the Confederacy was sometimes thus depicted.

8. The Mason and Slidell Affair was prominently covered in contemporary newspapers. John Slidell served as the Confederacy's ambassador to France, James Mason in the same capacity to Great Britain. "In November, 1861, [they] were enroute to Europe on a British mail ship, the *Trent;* Captain Charles Wilkes of the USS *San Jacinto* stopped the ship off Cuba and removed the two agents; when news reached England, it led to an outburst of condemnation of the United States government." They were freed as a result of diplomatic negotiations the following January (Bowman, 378–79).

9. *Levee* is a term used for a party or reception, sometimes held in the afternoon and often in honor of an individual.

10. "One of the militia companies activated and already headed for the Ferry the day after secession, was the 'Warren Rifles' commanded by Capt. Robert Simp-

son. A graduate of Virginia Military Institute and a reputed teacher, he had added military training to his curriculum at the Front Royal Academy. . . . In 1858, he had recruited among his students a company that was soon well organized, drilled, and equipped" (Hale, *Four Valiant Years*, 9). Among the Warren Rifles recruits was one of Lucy's relatives, Lt. Richard Bayly Buck; letters written to him during the entire war, including those from Lucy, are in Special Collections of the Alderman Library, at the University of Virginia.

11. Philopena is a game "in which a man and a woman who have shared the twin kernels of a nut each try to claim a gift from the other as a forfeit at their next meeting by fulfilling certain conditions (as by being the first to exclaim 'philopena')" (*Webster's Third New International Dictionary*).

12. General Beauregard, whose headquarters were at this time at Manassas, had commanded troops at Fort Sumter and gained the Confederacy its first victory at First Bull Run (Bowman, 314). Very shortly after Lucy penned this entry, Beauregard's headquarters were shifted to Kentucky, and Lucy's friends were thus carried to a distant state (Hale, *Four Valiant Years*, 102–3).

13. Lucy frequently mentions "going to the cars." By this she means the trains, and the purpose of the trip was usually to determine if she and her family had received mail.

14. According to *Hoyle's Games*, "the Game of Cassino is played with an entire pack of cards, generally by four persons, but sometimes by three, and often by two" (118). The goal of the game is to score the most points by capturing or building on other cards.

15. Lucy often notes, especially in the early days of the war, her efforts with her "pupils." These were her younger siblings; there is no evidence to indicate that she accepted pupils from outside the family.

16. The reader will note that Lucy mentions Walter Scott Roy frequently in her diary. Laura Virginia Hale, a Front Royal historian, comments that there may have been a romantic attachment between the two: "Charming, vivacious, and popular, [Lucy] had many beaux but never married, perhaps, it is rumored, because she 'carried a torch' for Walter Scott Roy, who figures much in her diary, not only as Gen. Ashby's audacious scout, but as a welcome visitor to 'Bel Air.' He survived many heroic exploits to return to Front Royal and settle down as a doctor, but he married another girl" (Hale, *On Chester Street*, 97).

17. Fort Donelson in Tennessee surrendered to the Union on February 16, 1862; President Lincoln promoted Grant to major general as a result of this victory (McPherson, 395–402).

18. Jefferson Davis served as provisional president of the Confederacy until his inauguration in Richmond, Virginia, on February 22, 1862. Davis, born in Kentucky, was the son of a farmer; his commitment to the ideals of the Confederacy and to slavery was formed during a military and political career as well as during a decade spent running a Mississippi plantation.

19. The Buck family owned a resort in Capon Springs, West Virginia, which was largely destroyed in the war. The linens that Mr. Buck salvaged from the hotel were later distributed to family and friends; Lucy's diary contains many entries describing these distributions, most of which have been abridged.

20. This was indeed a rumor. General Beauregard lived until 1893.

21. The L. N. Buck edition of Lucy's diary carries this parenthetical explanation for the "place of security": "tied in packages and hung from wire hoops in their skirts" (24).

22. Lucy's news about the *Merrimac* is substantially correct. Having been re-named the *Virginia*, it sank two Federal vessels, the *Cumberland* and the *Congress*, on March 8, 1862. The following day, the more famous battle between the *Merrimac* and the Federal *Monitor* resulted in a draw (McPherson, 375–77).

23. Lucy's reference to Saint Bartholomew's assassins is a historical one. The massacre of Huguenots in France in 1572 was begun on the day of the festival of this saint, August 24 (Harvey, 68).

24. "Porte Crayon" was the nom de plume of Col. David Hunter Strother, a Virginian, who had written for *Harper's Monthly* before the war. Laura Virginia Hale explains why southerners hated him so: "Yet because he cast his lot with the Union and guided the first successful Federal campaign in the Shenandoah Valley, his name was anathema to generations of his fellow Virginians" (*Four Valiant Years,* 120–21).

25. The Battle of Shiloh, or Pittsburg Landing, in Tennessee (April 6-7) was a Confederate defeat, despite the premature telegram sent by Beauregard to Rich-mond announcing victory. Historians count this battle as the first on a major scale in the Civil War: twenty thousand soldiers died, with casualties about evenly split between the North and South (McPherson, 408–14).

26. *The Civil War Almanac* states that on April 18, "at Yorktown, a Confederate attack on Union troops [was] unsuccessful, the latter forces pushing the Southern troops back" (Bowman, 95).

27. Lucy's mention of a "great riot in Baltimore" refers to the events of April 19, 1861. A meeting of secessionists was occurring in Baltimore when the Sixth Mas-sachusetts Regiment arrived in town, en route to Washington. The troops were "attacked by rioters carrying Confederate flags. Nine civilians and four soldiers [were] killed in the melee" (Bowman, 51–52).

28. Lucy's reference to the "Slough of Despond" is a literary one. Christian, the pilgrim who gives his name to John Bunyan's *The Pilgrim's Progress* (1678), must pass through the Slough of Despond on his journey from the City of Destruction to the Celestial City. No doubt Lucy would have read this text as a young girl; its widespread use in Victorian America is illustrated in Louisa May Alcott's use of it in *Little Women* (1868).

29. Lucy is here ridiculing the dialect and the status of the African American by referring to him as a "colored gentleman."

30. *Neuralgia* is a term used more often in the nineteenth century to describe ailments than it is today; it usually indicated a severe pain radiating along the path of certain nerve structures.

31. No decisive battle was fought at Yorktown at this time; the Confederates began a retreat from the area in early May.

32. "Martial law" refers to law imposed during a military occupation and exercised by military authorities.

33. A "quondam visitor" is a former or sometime visitor.

Chapter Two. *"Headquarters" Was Duly Established at Bel Air: May 14, 1862–June 20, 1862*

1. Laura Virginia Hale quotes from a contemporaneous account, published in the *Cincinnati Daily Times*, which describes Union general Kimball's brigades as containing, among others, soldiers from the Fourth Ohio and the Fourteenth Indiana; they marched to Front Royal from New Market, Virginia. The reporter, Mr. Crippen, whom Lucy mentions later in this entry, described Front Royal as "quite rural": "The principal objects of interest are two small churches and the town pump. The streets run all manner of ways. . . . At present, the town is terrifically muddy and awfully gloomy" (*Four Valiant Years*, 133–37).

2. Presumably Lucy means to suggest that Mr. Crippen is of French origin!

3. Destruction to the Buck property during the Yankee encampment was not inconsiderable. William Pettus Buck, in his edition of the diary, includes this note: "The Yankees burned half the rails around the field of wheat of fifty acres and the greater part of the plank fencing of heavy locust posts and oak plank around timothy meadow of the twenty eight acres adjoining town. A portion of the rail fence from a field of thirty-five acres of clover was also destroyed" (Buck, *Sad Earth*, 68).

4. May 23, 1862, was to prove an important day in the history of Front Royal, for it is on that day that the Battle of Front Royal was fought. General Stonewall Jackson, encountering about eight thousand Union troops, wrested control of the town from the Yankees (Bowman, 100). It is said that Belle Boyd, the spy often mentioned by Lucy, played a significant role in this battle by alerting Jackson to the small number of Union forces and encouraging attack (Hale, *Four Valiant Years*, 147).

5. The large number of words that could not be deciphered from the original diary (here indicated by a blank) suggest that Lucy wrote this entry at a feverish pitch.

6. The abbreviation "F F V's" stands for "First Families of Virginia," a term and a status still very much in vogue in Virginia today, 130 years after Lucy's use of it.

7. The sequence of Lucy's writing here—her sorrow at her ill treatment of "that

poor old man," her determination to make it up to him, and then her announcement that she has done so—suggests that a lapse of time must have occurred between paragraphs two and three of this entry.

8. Perhaps Lucy left her journal behind when the Bucks fled Bel Air for safety. A week has elapsed since her previous entry.

9. Lucy is probably referring to the Battle of the Seven Pines, which occurred on May 31, 1862. Its outcome was indecisive, but it did result in the appointment of General Robert E. Lee to the command of the Army of Northern Virginia, to replace General Joseph Johnston, wounded in the battle. Losses of men were about the same for both armies.

Chapter Three. *We Learned to Accommodate Ourselves to Circumstances: June 21, 1862 – December 31, 1862*

1. It is likely that Lucy and her family were taken in by a ruse. Scarcely a month later, it was reported in the Hagerstown, Maryland, newspaper that two Maryland women, dressed as soldiers, had been discovered accompanying Union general Pope's troops. Evidence from other Front Royal diaries suggests that the women were in Front Royal, under disguise, in mid-June 1862 as part of a Union signal corps engaged in collecting and transmitting intelligence. The signal corps was withdrawn suddenly on June 23 (Hale, *Four Valiant Years*, 180–82).

2. Lucy was right to be skeptical of this news. Union general McClellan was not lost in the Seven Days' Campaign, as the battles lasting from June 25–July 1, 1862, are called, nor was Richmond captured by the Yankees.

3. General Beauregard was relieved of his command in June 1862.

4. McPherson elucidates: "July 1862 brought a significant hardening of attitude in both army and executive. John Pope arrived from the West to take command of the newly designated Army of Virginia. . . . One of his first acts in Virginia was a series of general orders authorizing his officers to seize rebel property without compensation, to shoot captured guerillas who had fired on Union troops, to expel from occupied territory any civilians who refused to take the oath of allegiance, and to treat them as spies if they returned" (501).

5. *Webster's Third New International Dictionary* defines *sangaree* as "a tall drink usu. of wine but sometimes of ale, beer, or strong alcoholic liquor that is sweetened, poured into a tumbler of cracked ice, and garnished with nutmeg."

6. Gainesville, Virginia, is located just west of Manassas, and thus it is to the Second Manassas (or Second Bull Run, as the Union would call it, following a Yankee preference for naming battles after a nearby river or stream; see McPherson, 346) that Lucy refers here. The battle was a Confederate victory.

7. Perhaps a day established to give thanks for the recent Confederate victory. Days of thanksgiving and fasting were called for occasionally in the Confederacy, no doubt to create a sense of loyalty and commitment.

8. Lucy may mean a "lovat" jacket; *lovat* is a term for a dusty green color in fabrics, especially in tweeds.

9. The Battle of Sharpsburg (Antietam was the Union name) was indeed one of the bloodiest of the war. Taking place on September 17, 1862, the battle opposed Robert E. Lee against McClellan; it is considered a Union victory. However, Confederate troops were allowed to retreat without pursuit. Casualties "numbered four times the total suffered by American soldiers at the Normandy beaches on June 6, 1944," with six thousand men dead and another seventeen thousand wounded (McPherson, 544). Historians generally believe that this victory paved the way for Lincoln to issue the Emancipation Proclamation.

10. This reference is most likely to the Emancipation Proclamation, which was announced on September 22 and then released on January 1, 1863, although Lucy may have been referring to Lincoln's order, on December 6, to execute thirty-nine American Indians following an uprising in Minnesota.

11. "Lasting kits" are identified in Laura Virginia Hale's personal copy of Lucy Buck's diary as "a kind of shoes." A "last" is a shoe sole, and so perhaps these kits were meant to resole shoes. Warren Heritage Society Archives.

Chapter Four. And Now a New Page Is Spread Before Us: January 1, 1863 – June 8, 1863

1. Such celebrations among African Americans were fairly common at Christmas time, when a rest period of four to six days was often called (Blassingame, 107). The slaves used this time to visit friends and loved ones on nearby plantations and to get married (Sobel, 67). But, on many plantations, there was an onerous side to these festivities, one that is described by escaped slave Harriet Jacobs in a chapter in her autobiography entitled "The Slaves' New Year's Day": "Hiring-day at the south takes place on the 1st of January. . . . [Slaves] gather together their little alls, or more properly speaking, their little nothings, and wait anxiously for the dawning of day. At the appointed hour the grounds are thronged with men, women, and children, waiting, like criminals, to hear their doom pronounced" (Yellin, 15). That "doom" often meant the tragic separation of families.

2. The playing of such games as "blind man's buff" was a popular pastime in the nineteenth century. According to Rosaleen Cooper, the rules are as follows: "One child is blindfolded and then let loose to catch the other children who dance around, tempting him to catch them. When the blind man catches someone he has to say who it is. He feels their hair, their face, their height, and then says 'It's Johnny.' If he's guessed wrong he has to go on trying to catch someone else. . . . [This is] one of the oldest chasing games in the world," having been played in ancient Greece and Rome as well as Ethiopia, China, and Russia. Cooper continues: "At Christmas time in 1664, Samuel Pepys wrote in this diary that he went to bed early, but his wife and her family stayed up until four in the morning playing Blind Man's Buff" (Cooper, 51).

3. Lucy's mention of the "President's message" is most likely a reference to President Jefferson Davis's address to the First Confederate Congress, which had taken place on January 12, 1863; in this address, he expressed his hope that Europe would recognize the Confederacy as an independent nation (Bowman, 127).

4. See chap. 3, n. 7.

5. The "glorious victory at Charleston" is the successful repulse by the South, on April 7, 1863, of the North's naval efforts to recapture Charleston harbor (Bowman, 139).

6. Lucy's information is substantially correct. The Battle of Second Fredericksburg occurred on May 3, 1863, and resulted in a Confederate victory. Both Stonewall Jackson and A. P. Hill were injured the previous day in fighting around Chancellorsville, Jackson accidentally by his own men.

7. It was not a mistake. After having his arm amputated, Jackson died of pneumonia on May 10, 1863. His death was a blow to General Lee, to the South in general, and to the residents of Front Royal who remembered fondly his victory there on May 23, 1862.

8. A reference to American explorer, soldier, and politician John Fremont (1813–90), whose wife was named Jessie.

9. The standoff between defending Confederates and attacking Federals at Vicksburg, Mississippi, lasted more than a month; the town of Vicksburg finally surrendered on July 4, 1863, and did not celebrate "Independence Day" again until World War II.

Chapter Five. *Very, Very Footsore and Weary:*
June 9, 1863–December 31, 1863

1. The flight of the slaves at Bel Air marks the beginning of a new era for Lucy and her family, and the reader will note the regular inclusion henceforth in Lucy's diary entries of her chores and accomplishments in the domestic sphere. She often mentions her fatigue from these new duties. But there is a new alacrity in Lucy's prose, too, resulting perhaps from her increased attention to life around her. On June 19, 1863, Lucy penned a letter to her absent brother, Irvie, in which she talked about the consequences of the departure of the "servants": "Still I shall never regret the last fortnight's experience since it has taught me more useful lessons than would otherwise have been learned in a lifetime" (Warren Heritage Society).

2. A reference to the Emancipation Proclamation, which freed all slaves in Confederate states as of January 1, 1863.

3. The Battle of Second Winchester took place on June 13, 1863, and continued through June 15. It is considered a Southern victory (Bowman, 153).

4. An account of the departure of the Bel Air slaves and the recapture of Horace is included in "Reminiscences of Bel Air," written by Mr. William R. Buck (Lucy's younger brother Willie) in 1936 and part of the Buck file at the Warren Heritage

Society archives: "I remember one day during the war, when I and my younger brothers were the babies in the trundle bed [Willie would have just celebrated his seventh birthday] . . . and investigation disclosed that all the slaves had betaken themselves, in father's wagon and team, to Winchester, and given themselves into the protection of General Milroy. Later in a battle at Winchester, Horace was captured by a soldier from Front Royal, brought back to town, and put in jail. My father, being informed of the matter, went to talk to Horace, who told him the slaves had gone away because one of them had overheard my grandmother tell a neighbor that my father was going to sell his negroes South, a very unlikely tale, for I know my father had no such plan. He told Horace if he would come back and behave himself, he would give him his word never to sell him South. But Horace soon ran away again. My father went to Winchester to see General Milroy about getting back his team and wagon, so sorely needed on the farm, and while there encountered his slaves; little Mary was crying to return home. They later went to Pennsylvania where we sometimes heard from them. Father was given his wagon and two horses, the other two being kept as wages due the slaves" (2).

5. Lucy's comment about writing paper is indicative of the paper shortage experienced during the war. William Pettus Buck, who has the original Lucy Buck diary in his possession, adds this annotation to the June 16, 1863, entry in his edition: "The original diary of Lucy Buck was written on a great assortment of paper in very fine handwriting to allow as much as possible on each page. Some sheets were written on twice in different directions" (198). This latter practice, common in nineteenth-century diaries, is called "cross-hatching."

6. The entries for June 17 and June 22 and several entries following those are duplicated almost word for word in letters Lucy wrote to her brother Irving, which are available in the Warren Heritage Society, Front Royal. This duplication probably indicates that Lucy made her journal entries first and then copied those portions she wished to share with her brother.

7. Lucy probably is referring to the returned slave Horace.

8. Ambrose Powell Hill (1825–65), a Confederate general, was a native Virginian and a graduate of West Point. He had fought in First and Second Manassas, Sharpsburg, and Fredericksburg. Most likely he was passing through Front Royal on his way to fight in the battle of Gettysburg (Bowman, 344).

9. Action at Upperville on June 21 was more in the way of a skirmish or encounter between the troops of General Hooker and General Lee en route to Gettysburg.

10. Lucy's description of the famous battle of Gettysburg, the battle that has come to represent the whole war, remains apt: "a desperate conflict . . . resulting in heavy losses on both sides." Casualties (dead, missing, and wounded) were in excess of fifty thousand men for the North and South combined. The battle lasted three days, July 1-3, so news had reached Lucy fairly quickly. But Lucy's assessment that the battle "was not at all decisive" proved wrong: most historians con-

sider the Northern victory at Gettysburg to have been a crucial turning point in the war.

11. This passage is interesting for its confirmation of the often positive effects of wartime on women's lives: Lucy had passed through many trials in the two years that had elapsed since the start of the war, and the effect of these trials on her nerves and her physique was apparently bracing. She had learned of strengths and talents she possessed that the crises of war had caused her to discover.

12. The draft, enacted by Congress in March 1863, was implemented by the drawing of names, beginning on July 11. The following day, Sunday, in New York City, "hundreds of angry men congregated in bars and vowed to attack the draft offices next morning. They made good their threat, setting off four days of escalating mob violence that terrorized the city and left at least 105 people dead. It was the worst riot in American history" (McPherson, 609–10). Much of the violence was perpetrated by Irish Americans, and much of it was directed against African Americans; an orphanage for black children was burned to the ground.

13. The visit of Robert E. Lee to Bel Air is one of the most compelling passages in Lucy's diary, giving us a glimpse of the famous general in a quiet moment. His wistful remarks to Lucy are suggestive of his frame of mind as he returned to Virginia from his defeat at Gettysburg. Within the month, Lee would tender his resignation to Jefferson Davis; Davis, of course, refused it. Lucy's account of this encounter is calmer than the reader might expect, suggesting that the war, and all associated with it, had become the norm for her and the Buck family.

14. The Battle of Chickamauga took place in Tennessee on September 19-20, 1863. Losses were heavy on both sides; the victory went to the North.

15. *Balmoral* usually refers to a boot or shoe laced up the front; given Lucy's usage of the term here, *balmoral* may refer to a small cap, shaped rather like a tam, another but less common meaning of the word.

Chapter Six. One Day in the Very Heart of Our Army
the Next Abandoned in the Hands of the Yankees:
January 2, 1864–June 6, 1864

1. "Charles Newton Buck, captured in Front Royal, was not exchanged until after the war" (Buck, *Sad Earth*, 248).

2. Although in our video age it may be difficult to imagine a group of adults amusing themselves with parlor games for a full evening, such was the case in the nineteenth century. Lucy and her family and friends played a wide range of games—card games, board games, guessing games, games that centered around romantic themes, and more physical games based on movement or teams. Following is a description of a few of the games played on this evening: "Blindfold" may refer to any of a number of games in which usually only one participant is blindfolded and his or her actions and movements provided the main source of amuse-

ment. Two games played in the nineteenth century carried the name "Fox and Goose." One is the game identified by Cooper as "The Wolf Has Gone to Devonsheer," which is the British name: "The children all stand holding a rope—a skipping rope will do. A grown-up calls out:

> *The wolf has gone to Devonsheer,*
> *He'll be away for seven year.*
> *Sheep, sheep come home.*

The children all scatter for home but the wolf is in hiding and dashes out and catches some of them." According to Cooper, "in Britain and America the villain was often not the wolf but a fox chasing geese" (42). However, "Fox and Geese" was also a popular board game that has been traced back to medieval Scandinavia and is set up on a board with pieces rather like checkers. According to *The Way to Play,* "two unevenly matched forces compete against each other. The smaller force [the fox] usually comprises one or two pieces and has considerable freedom of movement; the larger force [the geese] is made up of numerous pieces but has only restricted maneuverability" (30). "King William" is another game that, according to Cooper, was variously named, depending on location, and was often known as "Roman Soldiers." "The children draw up in two lines facing each other and each line moves forward and back in turn, singing." One line sings a verse demanding bread and wine, "For we are Romans," and the other line denies the request, "For we are English." After several such exchanges the two lines fall upon one another for "a gentle scrimmage" (Cooper, 59–60). "Travellers" is a game of solitaire played with a full deck of cards. We know this game in the twentieth century as "Clock." Cards are laid out in a large circle, with a pile of four representing each of the twelve numbers on the face of a clock. The object is to end the game with all aces in one pile, all kings in another, and so on. "Although the chances of winning this Solitaire are slight, it is fun to play and very fast moving" (Diagram Group, 152).

3. The Battle of the Wilderness took place just west of Chancellorsville, in a dense woods, on May 5-6, 1864. General Longstreet was wounded by a bullet in the shoulder from a Confederate gun; the wound put him out of commission for five months (McPherson, 724–26).

4. Jeb Stuart died on May 12, 1864, from wounds sustained the previous day in the Battle of Yellow Tavern. Lucy calls his death "an irreparable loss," and indeed it was, particularly to the morale of Southern troops at this time.

5. Garibaldi shirts, almost always sewn in red fabric, were inspired by the shirts worn by the Italian revolutionary Garibaldi, whose victories in the summer of 1860 affected women's fashion for half a decade. "His bloused red shirt is always full and buttoned down the front, with a loose sleeve and tight cuff; it is often plain, but in its characteristic form has a tucked bosom and is . . . elaborately decorated with gold or black soutache" (Davenport, 911–12).

6. General Grant's efforts to reach the Confederate capital at Richmond resulted in serious losses at the Battle of Cold Harbor on June 3, 1864.

Chapter Seven. *Wish I Could Hear from Home: June 7, 1864–August 26, 1864*

1. The William Pettus Buck edition carries this annotation, which explains Lucy's preparations for departure: "The home, Bloomfield, belonging to Lucy's Aunt Cattie Larue, sister of William Mason Buck, is located near Berryville, Virginia. Lucy accompanied her mother to Bloomfield en route to Harper's Ferry to obtain provisions for the Bel Air household. A similar trip was made the previous year. Miss Lucy also had the objective of teaching her Cousin Walker, son of John Newton Buck. Uncle John's wife died before the war and their only surviving child, Walker, was living with Aunt Cattie" (259).

Health may have also been a consideration in Lucy's temporary relocation. In a letter dated June 26, 1864, written by Nellie to cousin Richard Bayley Buck, who was serving in the army, Nellie says of Lucy's departure: "We all thought her health required a change, after four years' close confinement at home and it was only after much coaxing we got her off." Nellie describes Lucy as "a dear good kind sister . . . the most truly *unselfish* sister, and friend, I ever saw" (Special Collections, Alderman Library, University of Virginia). Many of the entries in the diary for the next several weeks are characterized by homesickness and a longing to return to Bel Air.

2. Confederate general Jubal Early's incursions in the northern Virginia and Washington areas beginning in late June are made with the intention of an eventual assault on Washington, D.C. Early abandons this plan on July 12 and retreats past Leesburg, Virginia.

3. One of the reasons this was a "memorable day for Bloomfield" is that a baby was born to Cousin Nellie during the night of July 19. Lucy's language is very circumspect in alluding to this childbirth, as was common in nineteenth-century women's diaries in general. Lucy describes a restless night at Bloomfield; the restlessness is partly ascribed to the fear of Yankees but certainly also to the fact that a woman is in labor. Aunt Evelyn, Lucy tells us, comes in "with a candle to get something for Cousin Nellie who she said was *sick*" (emphasis mine), thus demonstrating that even among women relatives the terms *pregnancy* and *labor* are not used. Several references are made in this and ensuing entries to a Mrs. Luke, who was most likely Cousin Nellie's midwife.

4. A "caitiff" is an evil or despicable man.

5. Lucy uses the term "soi disant officer" with its usual derogatory meaning; *soi disant* is a French term meaning "saying oneself." Translated, it carries the connotation of "so-called" or "imitation."

6. *Poltroon* is a synonym for *coward*.

7. Little more than skirmishing takes place between Early and Union general Sheridan in the Winchester area in the waning days of August 1864.

Chapter Eight. Given Up into the Hands of Our Foes:
September 1, 1864–April 15, 1865

1. Lucy calls herself, as she resumes regular writing in her diary, "a different being from what I was then—the change the worse." She suggests that she "felt almost deranged" at times during the preceding winter. Her prose, too, seems to have changed and is characterized in these entries by short, staccato sentences and sentence fragments. She recounts the motions of daily life and alludes less frequently to her emotional state.

There are other telling aspects of these entries. On February 20, she notes, "This is my week—housekeeping," suggesting that the household has now established a regular rotation to substitute for the work previously done by slaves. Though she says on February 13 that all winter she "had not the spirit to write," her entries for February 19, 20, 24, 25, and 26 all allude to dedicating a portion of that day to the task of writing, including two days when she was "writing all morning." Her return to the routine of self-expression must have been comforting and probably indicates a more stable frame of mind.

2. Since this volume of Lucy's diary is lost, it is not possible to determine whether the blanks in this entry occur in the original or represent the inability of the 1940 transcriber, Captain Buck, to decipher Lucy's handwriting. I expect that it is the latter, especially given the topic of the passage. Lucy was clearly writing in a saddened state; she may even have been weeping on the page.

3. As April 9 was the actual day of surrender, Lucy got the devastating news four days after the fact. The formal surrender at Appomattox Courthouse, at which neither Lee nor Grant was present, took place on the day preceding this entry, April 12. Lucy's reaction to the news was apparently a violent one. Her younger brother, Willie, recounted in a memoir written in 1936: "I recall vividly the day when father brought us the news of General Lee's surrender. Mother and my sisters were busy sewing and making over dresses which must last as long as possible, and when father made his announcement, Lucy jumped to her feet, threw down the dresses, and burst into tears" (William R. Buck, "Reminiscences of Bel Air," 4, Warren Heritage Society Archives).

Selected Bibliography

Eighteenth- and Nineteenth-Century Southern Women's Diaries, Letters, and Memoirs

Arpad, Susan, ed. *Sam Curd's Diary: The Diary of a True Woman.* Athens: Ohio University Press, 1984.

Beauchamp, Virginia Walcott, ed. *A Private War: Letters and Diaries of Madge Preston, 1862–1867.* New Brunswick, N.J.: Rutgers University Press, 1987.

Billington, Ray Allen, ed. *The Journal of Charlotte L. Forten.* New York: Norton, 1981.

Brumgardt, John R., ed. *Civil War Nurse: The Diary and Letters of Hannah Ropes.* Knoxville: University of Tennessee Press, 1980.

Buck, L. N., and Mary Wallace Rowe Buck, eds. *Diary of Lucy Rebecca Buck, 1861–1865.* Baltimore: Privately printed, 1940.

Buck, Dr. William Pettus, ed. *Sad Earth, Sweet Heaven: The Diary of Lucy Rebecca Buck.* Birmingham: Cornerstone Publisher, 1973.

Bunkers, Suzanne. *The Diary of Caroline Seabury, 1854–1863.* Madson: University of Wisconsin Press, 1991.

Burr, Virginia Ingraham, ed. *The Secret Eye: The Journal of Ella Gertrude Clanton Thomas, 1848–1889.* Chapel Hill: University of North Carolina Press, 1990.

deButts, Mary Custis Lee, ed. *Growing Up in the 1850's: The Journal of Agnes Lee.* Chapel Hill: University of North Carolina Press, 1984.

Hague, Parthenia Antoinette. *A Blockaded Family: Life in Southern Alabama during the Civil War.* Lincoln: University of Nebraska Press, 1991.

Henderson, Dwight, ed. *The Private Journal of Georgiana Gholson Walker.* Tuscaloosa: Confederate Publishing Co., 1963.

Keckley, Elizabeth. *Behind the Scenes, or Thirty Years a Slave and Four Years in the White House.* New York: Oxford University Press, 1988.

Lander, Ernest McPherson, Jr., and Charles M. McGee Jr., eds. *A Rebel Came Home: The Diary and Letters of Floride Clemson, 1863–1866.* Columbia: University of South Carolina Press, 1988.

Lee, Lucinda. *Journal of a Young Lady of Virginia, 1782.* Published for the Benefit of the Robert E. Lee Memorial Association. Baltimore, 1871.

Pember, Phoebe Yates. *A Southern Woman's Story.* St. Simons Island, Ga.: Mockingbird Press, 1974.

Robertson, Mary D., ed. *Lucy Breckenridge of Grove Hill: The Journal of a Virginia Girl, 1862–1864.* Kent, Ohio: Kent State University Press, 1979.

Romero, Patricia, ed. *A Black Woman's Civil War Memoirs: Susie King Taylor.* New York: Marcus Wiener, 1988.

Schwartz, Gerald, ed. *A Woman Doctor's Civil War: Esther Hill Hawks' Diary.* Columbia: University of South Carolina Press, 1984.

Scott, John A., ed. *Journal of a Residence on a Georgian Plantation in 1833–1839: Frances Anne Kemble.* Athens: University of Georgia Press, 1984.

Smith, Glenn Curtiss, ed. "Diary of a Virginia Schoolmistress." *Madison Quarterly* 9 (March 1949): 25–58.

Spencer, Carrie Esther, Bernard Samuels, and Walter Berry Samuels, eds. *A Civil War Marriage in Virginia: Reminiscences and Letters.* Boyce, Va.: Carr, 1956.

Webb, Allie Bayne Windham, ed. *Mistress of Evergreen Plantation: Rachel O'Connor's Legacy of Letters, 1823–1845.* Albany: SUNY Press, 1983.

Williams, Daisy. *Daisy Williams, 1867–1884.* Edited by Margaret Bannister. Sweet Briar, Va.: Sweet Briar College, 1934.

Woodward, C. Vann, ed. *Mary Chesnut's Civil War.* New Haven: Yale University Press, 1981.

Yellin, Jean Fagan, ed. *Incidents in the Life of a Slave Girl.* Cambridge: Harvard University Press, 1987.

Secondary Sources

Andrews, Matthew Page, ed. *Women of the South in War Times.* Baltimore: Norman Remington, 1920.

Anners, Henry F. *Hoyle's Games.* Philadelphia, 1857.

Ashby, Thomas A., M.D., LL.D. *The Valley Campaigns: Being the Reminiscences of a Non-Combatant While between the Lines in the Shenandoah Valley during the War of the States.* New York: Neale, 1914.

Ayres, Edward L., and John C. Willis, eds. *The Edge of the South: Life in Nineteenth Century Virginia.* Charlottesville: University Press of Virginia, 1991.

Baldwin, Christina. *One to One: Self-Understanding through Journal Writing.* New York: M. Evans and Co., 1977.

Blassingame, John. *The Slave Community: Plantation Life in the Antebellum South.* New York: Oxford University Press, 1978.

Bleser, Carol. *The Hammonds of Redcliffe.* Oxford: Oxford University Press, 1981.
———. *In Joy and In Sorrow: Women, Family, and Marriage in the Victorian South.* Oxford: Oxford University Press, 1991.

Boatner, Mark Mayo, III. *The Civil War Dictionary.* New York: David McKay, 1959.

Bowman, John S. *The Civil War Almanac.* New York: World Almanac Publications, 1983.

Brontë, Charlotte. *Jane Eyre.* New York: Norton, 1971.

Buck, William Pettus. *The Buck Family, Virginia*. Birmingham, Alabama: Privately printed, 1986.

Buck, William R. *Reminiscences of Bel Air*. Front Royal, Va.: Warren Heritage Society Archives, 1936.

Campbell, Helen. *The American Girl's Home Book of Work and Play*. New York, 1883.

Claiborne, John Herbert. *Seventy-Five Years in Old Virginia*. New York: Neale, 1904.

Clinton, Catherine. *The Plantation Mistress: Woman's World in the Old South*. New York: Pantheon, 1982.

Clinton, Catherine, and Nina Silber, eds. *Divided Houses: Gender and the Civil War*. Oxford: Oxford University Press, 1992.

Cooper, Rosaleen. *Games from an Edwardian Childhood*. North Pomfret, Vt.: David and Charles, 1982.

Cott, Nancy. *The Bonds of Womanhood: "Woman's Sphere" in New England, 1780–1835*. New Haven: Yale University Press, 1977.

Davenport, Millia. *The Book of Costume*. vol. 2. New York: Crown, 1948.

Davis, Varina. *Jefferson Davis, Ex President of the Confederate States: A Memoir*. vols. 1, 2. New York, 1890.

Diagram Group. *The Way to Play: The Illustrated Encyclopedia of the Games of the World*. Toronto: Bantam, 1977.

Early, Alice Morse. *Two Centuries of American Costume, 1620–1820*. vols. 1, 2. Rutland, Vt.: Charles E. Tuttle, 1971.

Faust, Drew Gilpin. "Altars of Sacrifice: Confederate Women and the Narratives of War." *Journal of American History* 76 (March 1990): 1200–1228.

Fitzhugh, George. *Sociology for the South*. Richmond, 1854.

Franklin, Penelope. *Private Pages: Diaries of American Women, 1830's–1970's*. New York: Ballantine, 1986.

Friedman, Jean. *The Enclosed Garden: Women and Community in the Evangelical South, 1830–1900*. Chapel Hill: University of North Carolina Press, 1985.

Garrett, Elisabeth Donaghy. *At Home: The American Family, 1750–1870*. New York: Harry N. Abrams, 1990.

Gleason, David King. *Virginia Plantation Homes*. Baton Rouge: Louisiana State University Press, 1989.

Hale, Laura Virginia. *Belle Boyd: Southern Spy of the Shenandoah*. Front Royal, Va.: Warren Rifles Chapter of the United Daughters of the Confederacy, n.d.

———. *A Bicentennial Remembrance: The Revolutionary Years, 1776–1781 in Old Frederick County, Virginia*. Front Royal, Va., 1978.

———. *Four Valiant Years*. Strasburg, Va.: Shenandoah Publishing House, 1968.

———. *On Chester Street*. Stephens City, Va.: Commercial Press, 1985.

Harvey, Sir Paul. *The Oxford Companion to English Literature*. Oxford: Oxford University Press, 1967.

Havard, C. W. H., ed. *Black's Medical Dictionary*. Savage, Md.: Barnes and Noble Books, 1990.

Hensyll, William R. *Stedman's Medical Dictionary*. Baltimore: Williams and Wilkins, 1990.

Johnson, Allen, and Dumas Malone, eds. *Dictionary of American Biography*. New York: Charles Scribner's Sons, 1931.

Johnston, James Hugo. *Race Relations in Virginia and Miscegenation in the South, 1776–1860*. Amherst: University of Massachusetts Press, 1970.

Lebsock, Suzanne. *The Free Women of Petersburg: Status and Culture in a Southern Town, 1784–1860*. New York: Norton, 1984.

———. *Virginia Women, 1600–1945: "A Share of Honour."* Richmond: Virginia State Library, 1987.

Lewis, Jan. *The Pursuit of Happiness: Family and Values in Jefferson's Virginia*. Cambridge: Cambridge University Press, 1983.

Lister, Margot. *Costume: An Illustrated Survey from Ancient Times to the Twentieth Century*. Boston: Plays, 1968.

Loth, Calder, ed. *The Virginia Landmarks Register*. 3d ed. Charlottesville: University Press of Virginia, 1986.

McClellan, Elisabeth. *History of American Costume, 1607–1870*. New York: Tudor, 1937.

MacKethan, Lucinda H. *Daughters of Time: Creating Woman's Voice in Southern Story*. Athens: University of Georgia Press, 1990.

McKitrick, Eric L. *Slavery Defended: The Views of the Old South*. Englewood Cliffs, N.J.: Prentice-Hall, 1963.

McPherson, James M. *The Battle Cry of Freedom: The Civil War Era*. New York: Ballantine, 1989.

Morgan, Edmund S. *Virginians at Home: Family Life in the Eighteenth Century*. Charlottesville: University Press of Virginia, 1952.

Payne, Blanche. *History of Costume: From the Ancient Egyptians to the Twentieth Century*. New York: Harper and Row, 1965.

Perdue, Charles L., Jr., Thomas E. Barden, and Robert K. Phillips, eds. *Weevils in the Wheat: Interviews with Virginia Ex-Slaves*. Charlottesville: University Press of Virginia, 1976.

Robertson, James I. *Civil War Sites in Virginia: A Tour Guide*. Charlottesville: University Press of Virginia, 1982.

Ross, Ishbel. *Rebel Rose*. St. Simons Island, Ga.: Mockingbird Press, 1971.

Schultz, Jane E. "Mute Fury: Southern Women's Diaries of Sherman's March to the Sea, 1864–1865." In *Arms and the Woman: War, Gender, and Literary Representation*, ed. Helen Cooper, Adrienne Munich, and Susan Squier, 59-79. Chapel Hill: University of North Carolina Press, 1989.

Scott, Anne Firor. *The Southern Lady from Pedestal to Politics, 1830–1930*. Chicago: University of Chicago Press, 1970.

Smith, Daniel Blake. *Inside the Great House: Planter Life in Eighteenth Century Chesapeake Society*. Ithaca, N.Y.: Cornell University Press, 1980.

Smith-Rosenberg, Carroll. "The Female World of Love and Ritual." *Signs* 1 (Autumn 1975): 1–29.

Sobel, Mechal. *The World They Made Together: Black and White Values in Eighteenth Century Virginia*. Princeton: Princeton University Press, 1987.

Stowe, Steven M. *Intimacy and Power in the Old South: Ritual in the Lives of the Planters*. Baltimore: Johns Hopkins University Press, 1987.

Strode, Hudson. *Jefferson Davis: Tragic Hero: The Last Twenty-five Years, 1864–1889*. vol. 3. New York: Harcourt, Brace, and World, 1964.

Sutton-Smith, Brian. *The Folkgames of Children*. Austin: University of Texas Press, 1972.

Taylor, William R. *Cavalier and Yankee: The Old South and American National Character*. Cambridge: Harvard University Press, 1979.

Thorne, J. O., ed. *Chamber's Biographical Dictionary*. New York: St. Martin's, 1962.

Tise, Larry E. *Proslavery: A Histoy of the Defense of Slavery in America, 1701–1840*. Athens: University of Georgia Press, 1987.

Vlach, John Michael. *Back of the Big House: The Architecture of Plantation Slavery*. Chapel Hill: University of North Carolina Press, 1993.

Wakelyn, Jon L. *Biographical Dictionary of the Confederacy*. Westport, Connecticut: Greenwood Press, 1977.

Wamsley, James S., with Anne M. Cooper. *Idols, Victims, Pioneers: Virginia's Women from 1607*. Virginia State Chamber of Commerce and the Virginia Commission on the Status of Women, 1976.

Whitney, David C. *The American Presidents*. New York: Prentice-Hall, 1968.

Wiley, Bell Irvin. *Confederate Women*. Westport, Conn.: Greenwood Press, 1975.

Wright, Louis B., ed. *A Voyage to Virginia in 1609*. Charlottesville: University Press of Virginia, 1964.

Wyatt-Brown, Bertram. *Southern Honor: Ethics and Behavior in the Old South*. Oxford: Oxford University Press, 1982.

Index

Southern Voices from the Past
Women's Letters, Diaries, and Writings

Carol Bleser, General Editor

The Diary of Dolly Lunt Burge, 1848–1879
edited by Christine Jacobson Carter

A Heritage of Woe: The Civil War Diary of Grace Brown Elmore, 1861–1868
edited by Marli F. Weiner

Shadows on My Heart: The Civil War Diary of Lucy Rebecca Buck of Virginia
edited by Elizabeth R. Baer

Tokens of Affection: The Letters of a Planter's Daughter in the Old South
edited by Carol Bleser